Lecture Notes in Computer Scien

Edited by G. Goos, J. Hartmanis and J. van Leeuwen

Springer

Berlin
Heidelberg
New York
Barcelona
Hong Kong
London
Milan
Paris
Singapore
Tokyo

Josef Pieprzyk Rei Safavi-Naini
Jennifer Seberry (Eds.)

Information Security and Privacy

4th Australasian Conference, ACISP'99
Wollongong, NSW, Australia, April 7-9, 1999
Proceedings

 Springer

Series Editors

Gerhard Goos, Karlsruhe University, Germany
Juris Hartmanis, Cornell University, NY, USA
Jan van Leeuwen, Utrecht University, The Netherlands

Volume Editors

Josef Pieprzyk
Rei Safavi-Naini
Jennifer Seberry
University of Wollongong
School of Information Technology and Computer Science
Wollongong, NSW 2522, Australia
E-mail: {Josef_Pieprzyk, Rei_Safavi-Naini, Jennifer_Seberry}@uow.edu.au

Cataloging-in-Publication data applied for

Die Deutsche Bibliothek - CIP-Einheitsaufnahme

Information security and privacy : 4th Australasian conference ;
proceedings / ACISP '99, Wollongong, NSW, Australia, April 7 - 9,
1999. Josef Pieprzyk ... (ed.). - Berlin ; Heidelberg ; New York ;
Barcelona ; Hong Kong ; London ; Milan ; Paris ; Singapore ; Tokyo
: Springer, 1999
  (Lecture notes in computer science ; Vol. 1587)
  ISBN 3-540-65756-8

CR Subject Classification (1998): E.3, K.6.5, D.4.6, C.2, E.4, F.2.1-2, K.4.1

ISSN 0302-9743
ISBN 3-540-65756-8 Springer-Verlag Berlin Heidelberg New York

Typesetting: Camera-ready by author
SPIN: 10703993   06/3142 – 5 4 3 2 1 0   Printed on acid-free paper

Preface

The 4th Australasian Conference on Information Security and Privacy was held at the University of Wollongong, Australia. The conference was sponsored by the Centre for Computer Security Research, University of Wollongong, and the Australian Computer Society. The aim of the conference was to bring together people working in different areas of computer, communication, and information security from universities, industry, and government institutions. The conference gave the participants an opportunity to discuss the latest developments in the quickly growing area of information security and privacy.

The program committee accepted 26 papers from 53 submitted. From those accepted, thirteen papers were from Australia, two each from Belgium and China, and one each from Austria, Belarus, France, India, Japan, Korea, Singapore, the USA, and Yugoslavia. Conference sessions covered the following topics: access control and security models, network security, Boolean functions, group communication, cryptanalysis, key management systems, electronic commerce, signature schemes, RSA cryptosystems, and odds and ends.

We would like to thank the members of the program committee who generously spent their time reading and evaluating the papers. We would also like to thank members of the organising committee and, in particular, Chris Charnes, Hossein Ghodosi, Marc Gysin, Tiang-Bing Xia, Cheng-Xin Qu, San Yeow Lee, Yejing Wang, Hua-Xiong Wang, Chih-Hung Li, Willy Susilo, Chintan Shah, Jeffrey Horton, and Ghulam Rasool Chaudhry for their continuous and tireless effort in organising the conference. Finally, we would like to thank the authors of all the submitted papers, especially the accepted ones, and all the participants who made the conference a successful event.

February 1999

Josef Pieprzyk
Rei Safavi-Naini
Jennifer Seberry

FOURTH AUSTRALASIAN CONFERENCE ON INFORMATION SECURITY AND PRIVACY ACISP'99

Sponsored by

Center for Computer Security Research
University of Wollongong, Australia

and

Australian Computer Society

General Chair:

Jennifer Seberry　　　　　　　　　　　　　　　*University of Wollongong*

Program Co-Chairs:

Josef Pieprzyk　　　　　　　　　　　　　　　*University of Wollongong*
Rei Safavi-Naini　　　　　　　　　　　　　　*University of Wollongong*

Program Committee:

Colin Boyd	*Queensland University of Technology, Australia*
Lawrie Brown	*Australian Defence Force Academy, Australia*
Bill Caelli	*Queensland University of Technology, Australia*
Ed Dawson	*Queensland University of Technology, Australia*
Cunsheng Ding	*National University of Singapore, Singapore*
Dieter Gollmann	*Microsoft Research, UK*
Yongfei Han	*Gemplus, Singapore*
Thomas Hardjono	*Bay Networks, US*
Erland Jonsson	*Chalmers University, Sweden*
Svein Knapskog	*University of Trondheim, Norway*
Keith Martin	*Katholieke Universiteit Leuven, Belgium*
Cathy Meadows	*Naval Research Laboratory, US*
Kaisa Nyberg	*Nokia Research Center, Finland*
Choon-Sik Park	*Electronics and Telecommunication Research Institute, Korea*
Dingyi Pei	*Academia Sinica, China*
Steve Roberts	*Witham Pty Ltd, Australia*

Greg Rose	*Qualcomm, Australia*
Ravi Sandhu	*George Mason University, US*
Stafford Tavares	*Queen's University, Canada*
Vijay Varadharajan	*Western Sydney University, Australia*
Yuliang Zheng	*Monash University, Australia*

Referees

N. Asokan	Zhang Jiang	Dingyi Pei
Yun Bai	Erland Jonsson	Josef Pieprzyk
Simon Blackburn	Svein Knapskog	Vincent Rijmen
Colin Boyd	Hu Lei	Steve Roberts
Lawrie Brown	Leszek Maciaszek	Greg Rose
Bill Caelli	Keith Martin	Rei Safavi-Naini
Ed Dawson	Cathy Meadows	Ravi Sandhu
Cunsheng Ding	Bill Millan	Rajan Shankaran
Gary Gaskell	Qi Ming	Stafford Tavares
Janusz Getta	Sang-Jae Moon	Vijay Varadharajan
Dieter Gollmann	Yi Mu	Kapaleeswaran
Marc Gysin	Kenny Nguyen	Viswanathan
Yongfei Han	Kaisa Nyberg	Chuan Wu
Thomas Hardjono	Choon-Sik Park	Yuliang Zheng.

Table of Contents

RSA Cryptosystems

Group Cryptography

Network Security

Electronic Commerce

Access Control

Odds and Ends

Boolean Function Design Using Hill Climbing Methods

William Millan, Andrew Clark and Ed Dawson

Information Security Research Center,
Queensland University of Technology,
GPO Box 2434, Brisbane, Queensland, Australia 4001.
FAX: +61-7-3221 2384
Email: {millan,aclark,dawson}@fit.qut.edu.au

Abstract. This paper outlines a general approach to the iterative incremental improvement of the cryptographic properties of arbitrary Boolean functions. These methods, which are known as hill climbing, offer a fast way to obtain Boolean functions that have properties superior to those of randomly generated functions. They provide a means to improve the attainable compromise between conflicting cryptographic criteria. We give an overview of the different options available, concentrating on reducing the maximum value of the Walsh-Hadamard transform and autocorrelation function. A user selected heuristic allows the methods to be flexible. Thus we obtain Boolean functions that are locally optimal with regard to one or more important cryptographic properties such as nonlinearity and global autocorrelation.

1 Introduction

Cryptography needs ways to find good Boolean functions so that ciphers can resist cryptanalytic attack. The main properties required are high nonlinearity and low autocorrelation, so that linear cryptanalysis [3] and differential cryptanalysis [1] do not succeed faster than exhaustive key search.

In the past the main options for Boolean function design have been random generation and direct construction. Both of these methods have drawbacks. It is difficult to find functions with truly excellent properties via random search, due to the vast size of the search space. Direct constructions can produce functions that are optimum with regard to the designed property, but they may be weak for other cryptographic criteria such as algebraic complexity. Inherent tradeoffs exist between the main cryptographic criteria, and determining the optimum compromise attainable is still an open problem.

A technique called hill climbing was introduced in [6]. The basic idea of hill climbing is to slightly alter a given Boolean function so that a property of interest, such as nonlinearity, is improved. The results of [6] showed clearly that hill climbing was able to considerably improve the nonlinearity of randomly generated Boolean functions. It was shown in [5] that the genetic algorithm was also effective in Boolean function design and then further advances in the genetic algorithm technique were reported in [7]. These papers also showed that applying hill climbing to the result of the genetic algorithm often improved the results. However only the most basic hill climbing approach was considered.

In an effort to provide an effective and flexible design tool, we concentrate in this paper on variations and improvements on the basic hill climbing approach. Firstly, we extend hill climbing to include improvements to the autocorrelation function, then we examine a variety of hill climbing methods that produce Boolean functions which are locally optimal with regard to combinations of user selected criteria. Our techniques are able to improve both nonlinearity and absolute global autocorrelation, either separately or in combination.

This paper is structured as follows. Firstly we review Boolean function properties. In Section 3 we present a simple, complete and direct derivation of the rules for strong hill climbing, an overview of generalised hill climbing options, and a statement of "weak" rules (that improve performance). The experimental results of Section 4 show the advantage of the technique over random generation, and demonstrate that combinations of properties can be improved. Finally, we make comments on some further research directions.

2 Boolean Function Properties

In this section we review some of the important and well known cryptographic properties of Boolean functions. We let $f(x)$ denote the binary truth table of a Boolean function. A Boolean function with n input variables is said to be *balanced* when the Hamming weight is 2^{n-1}. Balance is a primary cryptographic criterion: it ensures that the function cannot be approximated by a constant function.

A useful representation is the *polarity* truth table: $\hat{f}(x) = (-1)^{f(x)}$. When $f(x) = 0$, $\hat{f}(x) = 1$ and when $f(x) = 1$, we have $\hat{f}(x) = -1$. An important observation is that $h(x) = f(x) \oplus g(x) \Longleftrightarrow \hat{h}(x) = \hat{f}(x)\hat{g}(x)$ holds for all Boolean functions. The *Hamming distance* between two Boolean functions is a measure of their mutual correlation. Two functions are considered to be *uncorrelated* when their Hamming distance is equal to 2^{n-1} or equivalently when $\sum_x \hat{f}(x)\hat{g}(x) = 0$.

We denote a *linear* Boolean function, selected by $\omega \in Z_2^n$ as $L_\omega(x) = \omega_1 x_1 \oplus \omega_2 x_2 \oplus \cdots \oplus \omega_n x_n$. A linear function in polarity form is denoted $\hat{L}_\omega(x)$. The set of *affine* functions comprises the set of linear functions and their complements: $A_{\omega,c}(x) = L_\omega(x) \oplus c$. The *nonlinearity* of a Boolean function is the minimum Hamming distance to any affine function. The nonlinearity may be determined from the *Walsh-Hadamard transform* (WHT): $\hat{F}(\omega) = \sum_x \hat{f}(x)\hat{L}_\omega(x)$ by $N_f = \frac{1}{2}(2^n - WH_{max})$, where WH_{max} is the maximum absolute value taken by $\hat{F}(\omega)$. Hence, reducing WH_{max} will increase the nonlinearity.

A result known as Parseval's Theorem states that $\sum_\omega \left(\hat{F}(\omega)\right)^2 = 2^{2n}$. It follows that $2^{\frac{n}{2}} \leq WH_{max}$. For even n, the set of functions that achieve this lower bound are known as *bent* functions [8]. They have the maximum possible nonlinearity, but are never balanced. It is an important open problem to determine the set of balanced functions which maximise nonlinearity.

The *autocorrelation function* (AC) is also important for cryptographic analysis. It is defined as $\hat{r}_f(s) = \sum_x \hat{f}(x)\hat{f}(x \oplus s)$, and we denote the maximum absolute value taken, for $s \neq 0$, as AC_{max}. (When $s = 0$, $\hat{r}(0) = 2^n$ for all functions.) Good cryptographic functions have small AC_{max}. For example the bent functions have $\hat{r}(s) = 0$ for all $s \neq 0$ [4]. The naive calculation of the autocorrelation function is not feasible for moderate n. However, the following well-known theorem shows that the autocorrelation function can be calculated by the inverse Walsh-Hadamard transform applied to the square of the WHT. For all ω it is true that

$$\sum_{s \in Z_2^n} \hat{r}_f(s)(-1)^{s \cdot \omega} = \left(\hat{F}(\omega)\right)^2.$$

A direct proof of this result appears in [2], or it may be obtained by seeing the Walsh-Hadamard transform as a kind of Fast Fourier transform and invoking the convolution theorem.

Upper bounds on the nonlinearity of Boolean functions have been found in [9] which make direct use of the values of the autocorrelation function. In particular, we have $N_f \leq 2^{n-1} - \frac{1}{2}\sqrt{2^n + AC_{max}}$. Some of the methods presented in this paper are intended to decrease AC_{max} directly. Our results have shown that, as expected, the distribution of nonlinearity is also improved in this case.

3 Hill Climbing Methods

The hill climbing approach to Boolean function design was introduced in [6] as a means of improving the nonlinearity of a given Boolean function by making well chosen alterations of one or two places of the truth table. It easy to show that any single truth table change causes $\Delta_{WHT}(\omega) \in \{-2, 2\}$ for all ω. Any two changes cause $\Delta_{WHT}(\omega) \in \{-4, 0, 4\}$. When the two function values satisfy $f(x_1) \neq f(x_2)$ then the Hamming weight will not change. By starting with a balanced function, we can hill climb to a more nonlinear balanced function by the method presented in [6]. That approach did not make an alteration to the truth table unless the nonlinearity is improved by such a change. In this paper we examine the approach of allowing changes so long as the property is not made worse. We may also make this choice seperately for both transform domains.

The distinction between the hill climbing options is based on the idea that we can require strong; weak or no improvement in either or both of WH_{max} and AC_{max}. A strong option requires that the property must be improved at each step. A weak option ensures that the property does not get worse: it may improve or stay the same. When no requirements are placed on a property, it is not considered in assessing whether an input pair may be changed. The nine options are shown in Figure 1. We note that [6] considered the option of strong WHT and no AC. The theory of that option is analysed in Section 3.1. We

WHT   Restrictions

	None	Weak	Strong
None	equivalent to random generation	Slowly improves WHT while AC is ignored.	WHT Hill Climbing. See [6]
Weak	Slowly improves AC while WHT is ignored	Never gets worse for either property Moves along saddles	Improve WHT while AC does not get worse
Strong	AC Hill Climbing See Section 3.2 of this paper	Improve AC while WHT does not get worse	Most restrictive option Stops at saddles

AC Restrictions

Fig. 1. An Overview of Hill Climbing Methods

introduce the complementary option (strong AC and no WHT improvement) in Section 3.2. In Section 3.3 we present the tests required to ensure that the WHT and the AC are not made worse by the choice of input pair to change.

3.1   Improving Nonlinearity

The recent paper [6] has introduced the strong requirements for improvement of the WHT alone, for one and two changes to the truth table. Here we briefly give a more general derivation of the rules for the two change case.

Consider a given Boolean function $f(x)$ in polarity truth table form $\hat{f}(x)$. Now let the truth table output be complemented for two distinct inputs x_1 and x_2. We have $\hat{g}(x_i) = -\hat{f}(x_i)$ for $i \in \{1,2\}$, and $\hat{g}(x) = \hat{f}(x)$ for other x. Now consider the WHT of $g(x)$.

$$\hat{G}(\omega) = \sum_x \hat{g}(x)\hat{L}_\omega(x)$$

$$= \hat{g}(x_1)\hat{L}_\omega(x_1) + \hat{g}(x_2)\hat{L}_\omega(x_2) + \sum_{x \notin \{x_1,x_2\}} \hat{g}(x)\hat{L}_\omega(x)$$

$$= -\left(\hat{f}(x_1)\hat{L}_\omega(x_1) + \hat{f}(x_2)\hat{L}_\omega(x_2)\right) + \sum_{x \notin \{x_1,x_2\}} \hat{f}(x)\hat{L}_\omega(x)$$

We will naturally define the change in the WHT value for all ω as

$$\Delta_{WHT}(\omega) = \hat{G}(\omega) - \hat{F}(\omega).$$

It follows directly that

$$\Delta_{WHT}(\omega) = -2\hat{f}(x_1)\hat{L}_\omega(x_1) - 2\hat{f}(x_2)\hat{L}_\omega(x_2).\qquad(1)$$

This result can be used directly to quickly update the WHT each iteration of a 2-step hill climbing program. It is now a straightforward matter to determine the conditions required for the choice of (x_1, x_2) to complement so that the WHT values change as required. It is clear that two truth table changes ensure $\Delta_{WHT}(\omega) \in \{-4, 0, +4\}$. As in all hill climbing methods, we assume $f(x_1) \neq f(x_2)$ has been fixed, so that the Hamming weight does not change. We have

$$\Delta_{WHT}(\omega) = -4 \iff \text{ both } f(x_i) = L_\omega(x_i) \text{ for } i \in \{1,2\},$$
$$\Delta_{WHT}(\omega) = +4 \iff \text{ both } f(x_i) \neq L_\omega(x_i) \text{ for } i \in \{1,2\},$$
$$\Delta_{WHT}(\omega) \neq -4 \iff \text{ not both } f(x_i) = L_\omega(x_i) \text{ for } i \in \{1,2\} \text{ and}$$
$$\Delta_{WHT}(\omega) \neq +4 \iff \text{ not both } f(x_i) \neq L_\omega(x_i) \text{ for } i \in \{1,2\}.$$

which specifies the tests for all conditions of interest in 2-step hill climbing. When we require definite improvement of the WHT (the strong option: WH_{max} must decrease), take no account of autocorrelation, and wish to maintain the Hamming weight, then we may complement the truth table output for any pair (x_1, x_2) that satisfies all of the following conditions:

(i) $f(x_1) \neq f(x_2)$
(ii) both $f(x_i) = L_\omega(x_i)$ for $i \in \{1,2\}$, for all $\{\omega : \hat{F}(\omega) = WH_{max}\}$
(iii) both $f(x_i) \neq L_\omega(x_i)$ for $i \in \{1,2\}$, for all $\{\omega : \hat{F}(\omega) = -WH_{max}\}$
(iv) not both $f(x_i) \neq L_\omega(x_i)$ for $i \in \{1,2\}$, for all $\{\omega : \hat{F}(\omega) = WH_{max} - 4\}$
(v) not both $f(x_i) = L_\omega(x_i)$ for $i \in \{1,2\}$, for all $\{\omega : \hat{F}(\omega) = -WH_{max} + 4\}$.

These conditions are equivalent to the ones presented in [6]. We now use the same approach to derive the tests required for improvement of the autocorrelation.

3.2 Improving Autocorrelation

Consider changing a Boolean function $f(x)$ by complementing the output for two distinct inputs x_1 and x_2, creating a function $g(x)$ with autocorrelation given by:

$$\hat{r}_g(s) = \sum_x \hat{g}(x)\hat{g}(x \oplus s)$$

$$= 2\hat{g}(x_1)\hat{g}(x_1 \oplus s) + 2\hat{g}(x_2)\hat{g}(x_2 \oplus s) + \sum_{x \notin \{x_1, x_2, x_1 \oplus s, x_2 \oplus s\}} \hat{g}(x)\hat{g}(x \oplus s)$$

$$= -2\hat{f}(x_1)\hat{f}(x_1 \oplus s) - 2\hat{f}(x_2)\hat{f}(x_2 \oplus s) + \sum_{x \notin \{x_1, x_2, x_1 \oplus s, x_2 \oplus s\}} \hat{f}(x)\hat{f}(x \oplus s).$$

For each $s \neq 0$, the change in the value of autocorrelation is

$$\Delta_{AC}(s) = \hat{r}_g(s) - \hat{r}_f(s)$$
$$= -2\hat{f}(x_1)\hat{g}(x_1 \oplus s) - 2\hat{f}(x_2)\hat{g}(x_2 \oplus s) - 2\hat{f}(x_1)\hat{f}(x_1 \oplus s) - 2\hat{f}(x_2)\hat{f}(x_2 \oplus s)$$

We need to examine the particular case when $x_1 \oplus x_2 = s$, since then we have $\hat{g}(x_1 \oplus s) = \hat{g}(x_2) = -\hat{f}(x_2)$ and $\hat{g}(x_2 \oplus s) = \hat{g}(x_1) = -\hat{f}(x_1)$. In this case the formula for autocorrelation changes collapses to

$$\Delta_{AC}(s = x_1 \oplus x_2) = 0. \tag{2}$$

In the remaining general case, we have

$$\Delta_{AC}(s \neq x_1 \oplus x_2) = -4\hat{f}(x_1)\hat{f}(x_1 \oplus s) - 4\hat{f}(x_2)\hat{f}(x_2 \oplus s). \tag{3}$$

Noting that the pair (x_1, x_2) was chosen so that $f(x_1) \neq f(x_2)$, we can determine that

$$\Delta_{AC}(s) = -8 \iff \text{both } f(x_i) = f(x_i \oplus s) \text{ for } i \in \{1, 2\},$$
$$\Delta_{AC}(s) = +8 \iff \text{both } f(x_i) \neq f(x_i \oplus s) \text{ for } i \in \{1, 2\},$$
$$\Delta_{AC}(s) \neq -8 \iff \text{not both } f(x_i) = f(x_i \oplus s) \text{ for } i \in \{1, 2\} \text{ and}$$
$$\Delta_{AC}(s) \neq +8 \iff \text{not both } f(x_i) \neq f(x_i \oplus s) \text{ for } i \in \{1, 2\}.$$

When we require definite improvement of the AC (the strong option: AC_{max} must decrease), take no account of the WHT, and wish to maintain the Hamming weight, then we may complement the truth table output for any pair (x_1, x_2) that satisfies all of the following conditions:

(i) $f(x_1) \neq f(x_2)$
(ii) $x_1 \oplus x_2 \neq s$ and both $f(x_i) = f(x_i \oplus s)$ for $i \in \{1, 2\}$, for all $\{s : \hat{r}(s) = AC_{max}\}$
(iii) $x_1 \oplus x_2 \neq s$ and both $f(x_i) \neq f(x_i \oplus s)$ for $i \in \{1, 2\}$, for all $\{s : \hat{r}(s) = -AC_{max}\}$
(iv) if $x_1 \oplus x_2 \neq s$ then not both $f(x_i) \neq f(x_i \oplus s)$ for $i \in \{1, 2\}$, for all $\{s : \hat{r}(s) = AC_{max} - 8\}$
(v) if $x_1 \oplus x_2 \neq s$ then not both $f(x_i) = f(x_i \oplus s)$ for $i \in \{1, 2\}$, for all $\{s : \hat{r}(s) = -AC_{max} + 8\}$.

3.3   The Weak Improvement Option

Weak requirements are those that guarantee the properties will not be made worse by the truth table alteration. The advantage of this approach is that "saddles" in the property terrain may be traversed, allowing the search space to be more fully explored, and allowing the iterated hill climbing algorithm to locate better local optima. Moving along saddles is prohibited in the strong hill climbing algorithms. More iterations may be performed using weak constraints, not all of which will improve the properties. However, fewer conditions are tested for each candidate pair during each iteration. Our experiments reveal the relative performance of weak and strong hill climbing algorithms.

We may state the weak conditions directly. As usual we require $f(x_1) \neq f(x_2)$. For WH_{max} not to increase we must choose the pair such that:

$$\Delta_{WHT} \neq +4 \text{ for all } \{\omega : \hat{F}(\omega) = WH_{max}\}$$
$$\Delta_{WHT} \neq -4 \text{ for all } \{\omega : \hat{F}(\omega) = -WH_{max}\}.$$

Similarly, for AC_{max} not to increase we check that:

$$\Delta_{AC} \neq +8 \text{ for all } \{s : \hat{r}(s) = AC_{max}\}$$
$$\Delta_{AC} \neq -8 \text{ for all } \{s : \hat{r}(s) = -AC_{max}\}.$$

4 Implementation and Results

To implement these techniques, we simply test all pairs (x_1, x_2) until one is found that satisfies all required conditions for the option chosen. For each pair, we stop testing as soon as one condition is failed. A pair that passes all tests is in the improvement set. (We keep this nomenclature even for the weak cases: we take the improvement set to be the set of pairs which satisfy our option.) We can either find the full improvement set and then select an arbitrary pair, or just use the first valid pair found.

We have examined the five options which include one or both strong options. Each experiment was conducted on one million, eight variable balanced Boolean functions, generated uniformly at random. For each heuristic option, the corresponding hill climbing tests were performed to select a pair of truth table positions to change. The process is iterated until no suitable pairs are found. At that point we have found a Boolean function that cannot be altered in any two places without violating the chosen heuristic option. The properties of interest are the value of nonlinearity (calculated from WH_{max}) and the value of AC_{max}. A cryptographically strong function has high nonlinearity and low AC_{max}. The five heuristic options are: strong for WHT and strong for AC, strong for WHT and weak for AC, strong for WHT and ignore AC, strong for AC and weak for WHT, and strong for AC and ignore WHT. We present our results in four graphs. Each graph depicts the frequency distribution of either AC_{max} or nonlinearity, for the cases where either the WHT rule is strong or the AC rule is strong. Note that the case of both strong appears on all graphs. Also on all graphs we have included the distribution of random balanced functions for reference. In all cases the hill climbing heuristics considered were superior to random generation.

In Figure 2 we show the nonlinearity distribution for the options in which strong rules were used for WHT and no, weak or strong rules were used for AC.

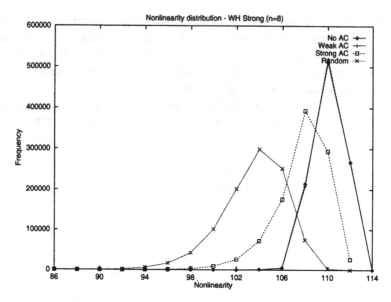

Fig. 2. Nonlinearity distribution for various strong WHT options

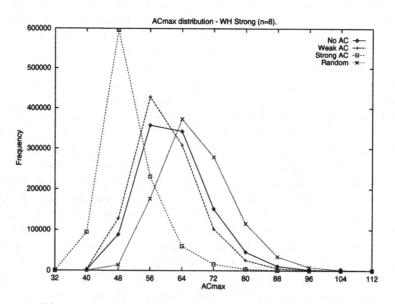

Fig. 3. AC_{max} distribution for various strong WHT options

It is clear that weak AC rules and no AC rules allowed high nonlinearity to be achieved more frequently than when strong AC rules were applied. There was effectively no difference in the nonlinearity performance between the case of no and weak AC rules. In Figure 3 we show the distribution of AC_{max} for the same set of heuristics. Here the advantage of weak rules over no rules is apparent in that lower AC_{max} is obtained. Of course strong rules for AC resulted in even lower values of AC_{max} being obtained. It is interesting to note that even with strong WHT rules and no AC rules, the distribution of AC_{max} is improved over that of random functions. This illustrates the qualitative connection between the maximum values of WHT and AC.

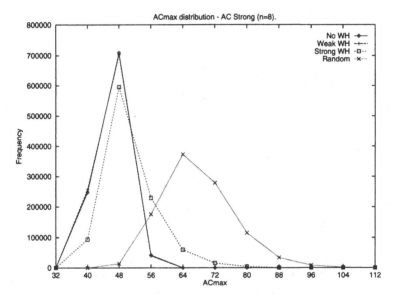

Fig. 4. AC_{max} distribution for various strong AC options

In Figure 4 we show the AC_{max} distribution for the options in which strong rules were used for AC and no, weak or strong rules were used for WHT. It is clear that weak WHT rules and no WHT rules allowed low AC_{max} to be achieved more frequently than when strong WHT rules were applied. There was effectively no difference in the AC_{max} performance between the case of no and weak WHT rules. In Figure 5 we show the distribution of nonlinearity for the same set of heuristics. Here the advantage of weak rules over no rules is again apparent in that high nonlinearity is obtained more frequently. Of course strong rules for WHT resulted in even higher nonlinearity being obtained. It is interesting to note that even with strong AC rules and no WHT rules, the distribution of nonlinearity is improved over that of random functions. This is another illustration of the qualitative connection between the maximum values of WHT and AC. Depending on the emphasis of desired properties, we recommend

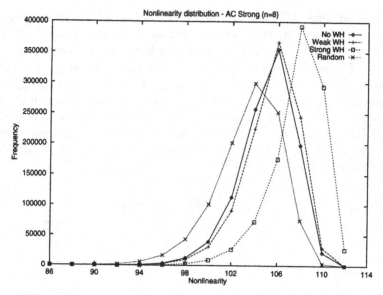

Fig. 5. Nonlinearity distribution for various strong AC options

strong rules for the most desired property, and weak rules for the other. This does not impair the performance with respect to the most important property, but allows better performance with regard to the secondary criterion.

So far we have considered only static heuristics: in which the initially chosen option remains in force throughout all iterations of the hill climbing algorithm. It is possible to use a more flexible approach: *dynamic* heuristics, in which the option chosen is different for successive steps of the iterative hill climbing algorithm. This may be fixed (for example alternating between two particular options) or adaptive (in which some observed property of the current function is used to select the option used in the next step). These approaches may provide better performance than the fixed static heuristics introduced here.

Hill climbing methods are known to improve the performance of genetic algorithms in the search for good cryptographic functions [5]. An interesting avenue for future research is the investigation into the details of how these approaches combine.

References

1. E. Biham and A. Shamir. Differential cryptanalysis of DES-like cryptosystems. In *Advances in Cryptology - Crypto '90, Proceedings*, volume 537 of *Lecture Notes in Computer Science*, pages 2–21. Springer-Verlag, 1991.
2. C. Carlet. Partially-Bent Functions. In *Advances in Cryptology - Crypto '92, Proceedings*, volume 740 of *Lecture Notes in Computer Science*, pages 280–291. Springer-Verlag, 1993.

3. M. Matsui. Linear Cryptanalysis Method for DES Cipher. In *Advances in Cryptology - Eurocrypt '93, Proceedings*, volume 765, pages 386–397. Springer-Verlag, 1994.

4. W. Meier and O. Staffelbach. Nonlinearity Criteria for Cryptographic Functions. In *Advances in Cryptology - Eurocrypt '89, Proceedings*, volume 434, pages 549–562. Springer-Verlag, 1990.

5. W. Millan, A. Clark, and E. Dawson. An Effective Genetic Algorithm for Finding Highly Nonlinear Boolean Functions. In *First International Conference on Information and Communications Security*, volume 1334 of *Lecture Notes in Computer Science*, pages 149–158. Springer-Verlag, 1997.

6. W. Millan, A. Clark, and E. Dawson. Smart Hill Climbing Finds Better Boolean Functions. In *Workshop on Selected Areas in Cryptology 1997, Workshop Record*, pages 50–63, 1997.

7. W. Millan, A. Clark, and E. Dawson. Heuristic Design of Cryptographically Strong Balanced Boolean Functions. In *Advances in Cryptology - Eurocrypt '98, Proceedings*, volume 1403 of *Lecture Notes in Computer Science*, pages 489–499. Springer-Verlag, 1998.

8. O.S. Rothaus. On Bent Functions. *Journal of Combinatorial Theory (A)*, 20:300–305, 1976.

9. X.-M. Zhang and Y. Zheng. Auto-Correlations and New Bounds on the Nonlinearity of Boolean Functions. In *Advances in Cryptology - Eurocrypt '96, Proceedings*, volume 1070, pages 294–306. Springer-Verlag, 1996.

Enumeration of Correlation Immune Boolean Functions

Subhamoy Maitra[1] and Palash Sarkar[2]

[1] Computer and Statistical Service Center, Indian Statistical Institute,
203, B T Road, Calcutta 700 035, INDIA
subho@isical.ac.in
[2] Applied Statistics Unit, Indian Statistical Institute,
203, B T Road, Calcutta 700 035, INDIA
palash@isical.ac.in

Abstract. We introduce new ideas to tackle the enumeration problem for correlation immune functions and provide the best known lower and upper bounds. The lower bound is obtained from sufficient conditions, which are essentially construction procedures for correlation immune functions. We obtain improved necessary conditions and use these to derive better upper bounds. Further, bounds are obtained for the set of functions which satisfy the four conditions of correlation immunity, balancedness, nondegeneracy and nonaffinity. Our work clearly highlights the difficulty of exactly enumerating the set of correlation immune functions.

Keywords : *Correlation Immunity, Enumeration, Boolean Function, Stream Cipher, Nonlinearity, Balancedness, Nondegeneracy, Symmetry.*

1 Introduction

Weakness of Boolean functions against correlation based cryptanalytic attack was introduced by Siegenthaler. He proposed a divide and conquer attack on nonlinear combining functions used in LFSR based stream cipher systems [13]. Towards the resistivity against such divide and conquer attack, Siegenthaler introduced the concept of correlation immunity of Boolean functions in [12]. His idea of correlation immunity was based on information theoretic measures using the concept of mutual information [6]. A characterization of information theoretic notion of correlation immunity, based on Walsh transform, is given in [5]. Construction of correlation immune functions having properties of balancedness, nonlinearity and good algebraic degree have also been considered [12, 11, 10, 1, 7, 3].

Mitchell [8] identified some of the enumeration problems for Boolean functions including correlation immunity. One of the reviewers has kindly pointed out that the enumeration problem for (balanced) correlation immune functions were earlier tackled by Wei Juan Shan in her MSc thesis (1987) and part of her results were published in [15]. Following Mitchell [8], we define several important cryptographic properties of Boolean functions. The definitions are for a scalar valued Boolean function, since in most cases (except balancedness) the enumeration problem for vector valued Boolean function can be trivially reduced to that of the scalar valued one.

Definition 1. *Let* $f(X_n, \ldots, X_1)$ *be a Boolean function.*
C1. Balance. *The function* f *is balanced if the number of ones in its output column is equal to the number of zeros.*
C2. Nonaffinity. *The function* f *is linear/affine if it can be written as* $f(X_n, \ldots, X_1) = \bigoplus_{i=1}^{i=n} a_i X_i \oplus b$, *where* $a_i, b \in \{0, 1\}$. *The function* f *is nonaffine if it is not linear/affine.*
C3. Nondegeneracy. *The function* f *is degenerate if there exists at least one variable* $X_i \in \{X_n \ldots, X_1\}$, *such that,* $f(X_n, \ldots, X_{i+1}, 0, X_{i-1}, \ldots, X_1) = f(X_n, \ldots, X_{i+1}, 1, X_{i-1}, \ldots, X_1)$. *The function* f *is nondegenerate if it is not degenerate.*
C4. Correlation Immunity. *The function* f *is correlation immune if* $Prob(f = X_i) = \frac{1}{2}, \forall i, 1 \leq i \leq n.$
C5. Symmetry. *The function* f *is symmetric if* $f(X_n, \ldots, X_1)$ *is same for all the vectors* $\{X_n, \ldots, X_1\}$ *of same Hamming weight.*

Let $A_n(i_1, \ldots, i_t)$ be the set of n variable Boolean functions which have the properties $Ci_1, \ldots, Ci_t$. The set of all Boolean functions of n variables is denoted by Ω_n, and the set of all correlation immune (CI) Boolean functions of n variables is denoted by A_n, i.e., $A_n = A_n(4)$. It should be noted that by correlation immunity we here mean correlation immunity of order 1. We also denote by $B_n = \Omega_n - A_n$, the set of all n variable non correlation immune (NCI) functions.

Recently counting of CI Boolean functions has received a lot of attention as evident from [14, 9]. *Here we provide the best known lower (Subsection 3.2) and upper (Section 4) bounds on* $|A_n|$. We derive the lower bounds based on sufficient conditions which are essentially detailed construction procedures. The construction provided in Theorem 3 of [14] and Lemma 2 of [9] are special cases of our technique. The upper bound is based on necessary conditions which are refinements of those provided in [9]. Our analysis indicates that it will be difficult to obtain better lower and upper bounds using this kind of construction technique (See Remark 1, 3, 4).

Next we briefly review the work that has already been done on enumeration of CI functions. A lower bound of $2^{2^{n-1}}$ was presented by Mitchell in [8]. The currently known lower bounds for $|A_n|$ are as follows.
(1) $|A_n| \geq 2^{2^{n-1}} + 2^n - 2n + 2^{2^{n-4}} - 2^{n-3}$ by Yang et al, in [14].
(2) $|A_n| \geq |A_{n-1}|^2$ by Park et al in [9]. There $|A_6|$ has been enumerated exactly.
Now, $|A_n|$ being exactly enumerated for some n, the bound in (2) is always better than that given in (1) for all the consecutive values of n. We provide separate improved lower bounds for both (1) and (2) above. Yang and Guo [14] provided

an upper bound $|A_n| \leq \sum_{k=0}^{2^{n-1}} \sum_{r=0}^{k} \binom{2^{n-2}}{r}^2 \binom{2^{n-2}}{k-r}^2$. An improvement $|A_n| \leq \sum_{j=0}^{2^{n-2}} \binom{2^{n-2}}{j}^4$ was obtained by Park et al [9].

We also consider the problem of enumerating $A_n(1,2,3,4)$. It has been observed by Mitchell [8, Page 164] that enumerating $A_n(3,4)$ is a nontrivial task. These were also considered in [14]. The results in [8,14] extensively used the principle of inclusion and exclusion and so the enumeration is not constructive. In [14, Theorem 9] the problem of enumerating $A_n(1,2,3,4)$ is reduced to the problem of enumerating[1] $A_n(1,4)$. Also a lower bound on $|A_n(1,4)|$ does not immediately provide a lower bound on $|A_n(1,2,3,4)|$ using inclusion and exclusion. We argue convincingly that a lower bound on $|A_n(1,4)|$ can be easily used to present a lower bound on $|A_n(1,2,3,4)|$ (see Theorem 8, Section 5). Using constructive methods we provide lower bounds on $|A_n(1,4)|$ in Section 5. We also clarify the Mitchell's conjecture [8] on $A_n(1,2,3,4,5)$. Our techniques and results are significantly different from those of [8,14].

Throughout the paper $\subseteq$ denotes subset and $\subset$ denotes proper subset. Given the truth table of a function f of n input variables, we denote the output column of f in the truth table as f itself, i.e. we also interpret f as a binary string. We write $f = f^u f^l$, where f^u (respectively f^l) is the upper half (respectively lower half) of f. The strings f^r and f^c are respectively the reverse and bitwise complement of f. For $f \in \Omega_n$, we interpret each of the columns (n inputs and 1 output) in the truth table as a string of 0s and 1s of length 2^n. Thus by X_i we mean the string corresponding to the ith column (from the right) in the truth table. Hamming weight or simply the weight (number of 1s in S) of S is denoted as $wt(S)$. The Hamming distance between two strings S_1, S_2 of same length (say λ) is denoted as $D(S_1, S_2)$ and the Walsh Distance is defined as, $wd(S_1, S_2) = \#(S_1 = S_2) - \#(S_1 \neq S_2)$. Note that $wd(S_1, S_2) = \lambda - 2D(S_1, S_2)$. Further, $CIW_n(a) = \{f \in A_n \mid wt(f) = a\}$ and $NCIW_n(a) = \{f \in B_n \mid wt(f) = a\}$. These are required to denote the functions of same weight. We write $C_n(a) = |CIW_n(a)|$ and $N_n(a) = |NCIW_n(a)|$. By $C_n^k(a)$ we mean $(C_n(a))^k$. Note that $CIW_n(2^{n-1}) = A_n(1,4)$. Please refer to the Appendix for most of the proofs in the following sections.

2 Preliminary Results

First we present a few important technical results without proof.

Lemma 1. $Prob(f = X_i) = \frac{1}{2}$ iff $\#(f = 1 \mid X_i = 0) = \#(f = 1 \mid X_i = 1)$. Consequently, $f \in A_n$ iff $D(f, X_i) = 2^{n-1}$ $(wd(f, X_i) = 0)$, $\forall i$, $1 \leq i \leq n$.

Lemma 1 is a simpler version of the Walsh transform characterization of CI functions (see [5]). If f is CI, then considering the leftmost variable of the truth table, we get, $wt(f^u) = wt(f^l)$. Consequently, if $wt(f)$ is odd, then f is NCI.

---

[1] Note that right hand side of Theorem 9, item(iii) [14] should have $A_{m-r,1}(1,4)$ instead of $A_{m-r,1}(4)$.

Proposition 1. *Consider $h_1, h_2 \in \Omega_{n-1}$, with $wt(h_1) = wt(h_2)$ and $f \in \Omega_n$ with $f = h_1 h_2$.*
(1) If both $h_1, h_2 \in A_{n-1}$ then $f \in A_n$. (2) If $h_1 \in A_{n-1}$ and $h_2 \in B_{n-1}$ then $f \in B_n$. (3) If $h_1 = h_2^r$ then $f \in A_n$. (4) If $h_1 \in B_{n-1}$ and $h_1 = h_2$ then $f \in B_n$. (5) If both $h_1, h_2 \in B_{n-1}$, with $h_1 \neq h_2$ and $h_1 \neq h_2^r$, then f may or may not belong to A_n (see Remark 1). (6) If $f \in A_n$ then either both $h_1, h_2 \in A_{n-1}$ or both $h_1, h_2 \in B_{n-1}$.

Remark 1. The main bottleneck in enumerating CI functions is item 5 of Proposition 1, i.e., it is possible to concatenate two NCI functions of same weight and obtain both CI and NCI functions. We provide two such examples.
Let $h_1 = 1000$ and $h_2 = 0100$, where, $h_1, h_2 \in B_2$ and $h_1 \neq h_2$, $h_1 \neq h_2^r$. Let $f \in \Omega_3$, where, $f = h_1 h_2 = 1000\ 0100$. Then $f \in B_3$, i.e., $f \notin A_3$.
Let $h_1 = 10000100$ and $h_2 = 00010010$, where, $h_1, h_2 \in B_3$ and $h_1 \neq h_2$, $h_1 \neq h_2^r$. Let $f \in \Omega_4$, where, $f = h_1 h_2 = 10000100\ 00010010$. Then $f \in A_4$.
For a complete enumeration of CI functions, it is necessary to identify when concatenation of two NCI functions of the same weight gives rise to a CI function. This, in general, is difficult. Here we provide partial solution to the problem.

Lemma 2. *Let $f(X_n, \ldots, X_1)$ be a Boolean function of n variables. Then f is CI iff for any X_i, $1 \leq i \leq n$, $wt(f \& X_i) = wt(f \& X_i^c)$, where $S_1 \& S_2$ is the bitwise AND of S_1 and S_2.*

Lemma 2 is another characterization of CI functions (see also Lemma 5 of [14]). Based on Lemma 2 we can use the principle of inclusion and exclusion to obtain an expression for $|A_n|$. Let $a_i = \{f \in \Omega_n \mid wt(f \& X_i) \neq wt(f \& X_i^c)\}$. and $\bar{a}_i = \Omega_n - a_i$. Let $N(a_i) = |a_i|$ and denote $a_i \cap a_j$ by $a_i a_j$. Then we get the following.

Theorem 1. $A_n = \bar{a}_1 \cap \ldots \cap \bar{a}_n$ and hence $|A_n| = N(\bar{a}_1 \ldots \bar{a}_n) = 2^{2^n} - \binom{n}{1} N(a_1) + \binom{n}{2} N(a_1 a_2) - \ldots + (-1)^n \binom{n}{n} N(a_1 \ldots a_n)$.

Proof: The first statement follows from Lemma 2. The second statement follows from the principle of inclusion and exclusion and noting that for any choice of $i_1, \ldots, i_r$ from $\{1, \ldots, n\}$, $N(a_{i_1} \ldots a_{i_r}) = N(a_1 \ldots a_r)$. □
This expression seems difficult to handle, since it is complicated to evaluate $N(a_1 \ldots a_r)$ for arbitrary r. However, it can be shown $N(a_1) = 2^{2^n} - \binom{2^n}{2^{n-1}}$. The principle of inclusion and exclusion has been extensively used in [8, 14]. So even if Theorem 1 does not provide a practical method of enumeration, the result by itself is quite interesting. We also use generating functions to provide bounds for $C_k(a)$, which is explained in Appendix A1. In [14], it was commented that $|A_n|$ can be represented as $(2^{2^{n-1}})^{c_n}$, with c_n between 1 and 2. Since, $|A_n| > |A_{n-1}|^2$, c_n is strictly increasing, and it is interesting to find out whether this limit is strictly less than 2. Let $(2^{2^{n-1}})^\sigma = \sum_{j=0}^{2^{n-2}} \binom{2^{n-2}}{j}^4$, the upper bound on $|A_n|$ provided in [9]. Then it can be checked that $\lim_{n \to \infty} \sigma = 2$. However, the expression of the form $(2^{2^{n-1}})^{c_n}$ is not very useful for clear

estimation of $|A_n|$. Let $(2^{2^{n-1}})^\sigma = \frac{2^{2^n}}{\tau 2^{f(n)}}$, τ constant, and $f(n)$ a polynomial of n. Then even if $\lim_{n\to\infty} \sigma = 2$, we get, $\lim_{n\to\infty} \left| \frac{A_n}{\Omega_n} \right| = 0$, giving the indication that the number of correlation immune Boolean functions is very few compared to the set of all Boolean functions. ¿From the above discussion it is clear that exact enumeration of $|A_n|$ will be difficult using the techniques discussed in this section and so in the next two sections we concentrate on lower and upper bounds for $|A_n|$.

3 Lower Bounds

In this section we discuss different techniques to attain lower bounds on $|A_n|$.

3.1 Basic Construction

Here we describe a construction technique which improves the lower bound reported in [14]. Mitchell [8] showed that $|A_n|$ has a lower bound of $2^{2^{n-1}}$ by showing that the set of Boolean functions, with the property that inverting the input leaves the output unchanged, is CI. We restate the same as follows.

Lemma 3. $D_n^1 = \{F \in \Omega_n \mid F \text{ palindrome }\} \subset A_n$. Also, $|D_n^1| = 2^{2^{n-1}}$.

Next we show f may be CI even if f is not a palindrome. We define two sets in this direction. $D_n^2 = \{S_1 S_1^r S_2^r S_2 \mid wt(S_1) = wt(S_2), \text{ and } S_1 \neq S_2^r, S_1, S_2 \in \Omega_{n-2}\}$, $D_n^3 = \{SS^c S^c S \mid wt(S) \neq 2^{n-3}, S \in \Omega_{n-2}, S \neq S^r\}$.

Lemma 4. (1) D_n^1, D_n^2, D_n^3 are disjoint proper subsets of A_n, (2) $|D_n^2| = \binom{2^{n-1}}{2^{n-2}} - 2^{2^{n-2}}$ and (3) $|D_n^3| = 2^{2^{n-2}} - \binom{2^{n-2}}{2^{n-3}} - (2^{2^{n-3}} - \binom{2^{n-3}}{2^{n-4}})$.

The following theorem is immediate from Lemma 3 and Lemma 4 which provides a significantly improved lower bound than $(2^{2^{n-1}} + 2^n - 2n + 2^{2^{n-4}} - 2^{n-3})$ given in [14]. The bound in [14] is obtained from several quite complicated subsets of CI functions (see Lemma 4 of [14]). Our construction is much simpler.

Theorem 2. $|A_n| \geq 2^{2^{n-1}} + \binom{2^{n-1}}{2^{n-2}} - \binom{2^{n-2}}{2^{n-3}} - 2^{2^{n-3}} + \binom{2^{n-3}}{2^{n-4}}$.

3.2 Recursive Construction

In this subsection we provide construction methods for correlation immune functions which in turn improve the bound given in [9]. Let us consider the following construction where $F \in \Omega_n$ and $f, g \in \Omega_{n-1}$.
$F(X_1, X_2, \ldots, X_n) = f(X_1, X_2, \ldots, X_{n-1})(1 \oplus X_{n-1})(1 \oplus X_n)$
$\oplus g(X_1, X_2, \ldots, X_{n-1})X_{n-1}(1 \oplus X_n) \oplus g(X_1, X_2, \ldots, X_{n-1})(1 \oplus X_{n-1})X_n$
$\oplus f(X_1, X_2, \ldots, X_{n-1})X_{n-1}X_n$.
$\qquad\qquad\qquad\qquad\qquad\qquad\qquad\qquad\qquad\qquad\qquad\qquad\qquad (1)$
Park et al [9] had shown that if f and g are CI ($f, g \in A_{n-1}$), then F given by (1) above is also CI. From this they obtained the inequality $|A_n| \geq |A_{n-1}|^2, n \geq 3$. We interpret the function F given in (1) as follows.

Proposition 2. *Let $f, g \in \Omega_{n-1}$ and let $F \in \Omega_n$ be a function given by $F = f^u g^l g^u f^l$. Then F is given by (1).*

This interpretation is more intuitive and allows us to generalize the construction procedure. The inequality $\mid A_n \mid \geq \mid A_{n-1} \mid^2$ depends on generation of $F \in A_n$ from $f, g \in A_{n-1}$. Take any 2 functions f and g (not necessarily distinct) from A_{n-1}, and form a function F as given in Proposition 2. Then $F \in A_n$ and the construction process is a bijection, so there are at least $\mid A_{n-1} \mid \times \mid A_{n-1} \mid$ correlation immune functions in A_n. Here we consider generalizations of the construction procedure given in Proposition 2. It has been proved in [9] that the construction in Proposition 2 yields correlation immune functions if both f and g are correlation immune. However, there are other possible ways of constructing $F \in A_n$ from correlation immune functions $f, g \in A_{n-1}$. The following two propositions provide constructions which are similar to Proposition 2.

Proposition 3. *Let $f, g \in A_{n-1}$ and $F = f^u g^u g^l f^l$. Then $F \in A_n$.*

Proof : We show that $wd(F, X_i) = 0$ for all i. For $i \leq n-2$, $wd(F, X_i) = 0$ since f, g are CI. Also, $wd(F, X_j) = 0$, for $j = n-1, n$, holds since $wt(f^u) = wt(f^l)$ and $wt(g^u) = wt(g^l)$. $\qquad\square$

Proposition 4. *Let $f, g \in A_{n-1}$ and $wt(f) = wt(g)$. If $F = fg = f^u f^l g^u g^l$, then $F \in A_n$.*

Different possibilities similar to Propositions 2, 3, 4 are given in List 1.

  List 1 : If $f, g \in A_{n-1}$, then $F \in A_n$ subject to the condition $wt(f) = wt(g)$, except for items 4,6,10 and 12, where $F \in A_n$ without the weight condition. Thus we can choose F from any of the following 12 constructions. However, Proposition 5 shows that all constructions of List 1 do not provide distinct sets.

  1) $f^u f^l g^u g^l$ 2) $f^u f^l g^l g^u$ 3) $f^u g^u f^l g^l$ 4) $f^u g^u g^l f^l$ 5) $f^u g^l f^l g^u$ 6) $f^u g^l g^u f^l$
  7) $f^l f^u g^u g^l$ 8) $f^l f^u g^l g^u$ 9) $f^l g^u f^u g^l$ 10) $f^l g^u g^l f^u$ 11) $f^l g^l f^u g^u$ 12) $f^l g^l g^u f^u$

Proposition 5. *Let f be a correlation immune function and $f = f^u f^l$. Let g be such that $g = g^u g^l = f^l f^u$, i.e. the top and bottom halves of the output string are interchanged. Then g is also correlation immune.*

Definition 2. *(1) $P_n = \{f^u g^u g^l f^l \mid f, g \in A_{n-1}\}$. (2) $Q_n = \{f^u f^l g^u g^l \mid f, g \in A_{n-1},\ wt(f) = wt(g)\}$. (3) $R_n = \{f^u g^u f^l g^l \mid f, g \in A_{n-1},\ wt(f) = wt(g)\}$.*

According to Proposition 5, in the List 1, items 4, 6, 10, 12 represent the same set P_n, items 1, 2, 7, 8 represent the same set Q_n, and items 3, 5, 9, 11 represent the same set R_n.

  Consider $F \in Q_n \cup R_n$. Note that $wt(F) \equiv 0 \bmod 4$. Now, if $F \in P_n$, then $wt(F)$ is either '0 mod 4' or '2 mod 4'. For $F \in P_n$, $wt(F) \equiv 2 \bmod 4$ when exactly one of f, g is of weight '2 mod 4' and another is of weight '0 mod 4'.

  Next we present results towards the enumeration of the sets P_n, Q_n, R_n.

Proposition 6. *$P_n \subset A_n$, $Q_n \subset A_n$, $R_n \subset A_n$ and $(P_n \cup Q_n \cup R_n) \subset A_n$, for $n \geq 4$. Consequently, $\mid A_n \mid \geq \mid P_n \cup Q_n \cup R_n \mid + 2^{2^{n-2}} - \binom{2^{n-2}}{2^{n-3}} - \mid A_{n-2} \mid.$*

In the following we obtain a lower bound on $\mid P_n \cup Q_n \cup R_n \mid$. We can describe $P_n \cup Q_n \cup R_n$ as disjoint union of four sets.
$P_n \cup Q_n \cup R_n = P_n \cup ((Q_n \cap R_n) - P_n) \cup (Q_n - (P_n \cup R_n)) \cup (R_n - (P_n \cup Q_n))$.
Using $P_n \cup Q_n \cup R_n \subset A_n$, for $n \geq 4$, $\mid A_n \mid > \mid P_n \mid + \mid (Q_n \cap R_n) - P_n \mid + \mid Q_n - (P_n \cup R_n) \mid + \mid R_n - (P_n \cup Q_n) \mid$. Now, $\mid P_n \mid = \mid A_{n-1} \mid^2$ (see also [14]). We find lower bounds of the other three sets to further improve the lower bound on $\mid A_n \mid$. First we find functions which belong to $(Q_n \cap R_n) - P_n$. We define the following sets for this purpose.

Definition 3. Let $wt(S_1) = wt(S_2) = wt(S_3) = wt(S_4)$.
(1) $U_n = \{S_1 S_2 S_3 S_4 \mid S_i \in B_{n-2}, 1 \leq i \leq 4$, and $S_1 S_2, S_3 S_4, S_1 S_3, S_2 S_4 \in A_{n-1}$, and $S_1 S_4, S_2 S_3 \in B_{n-1}\}$. (2) $V_n = \{SS^r S^r S \mid S \in B_{n-2}\}$.

Lemma 5. $U_n = (Q_n \cap R_n) - P_n$.

Lemma 6. $V_n \subseteq U_n$. Also, $\mid V_n \mid = \mid B_{n-2} \mid = 2^{2^{n-2}} - \mid A_{n-2} \mid$.

Lemma 7. $V_4 = U_4$ and $V_n \subset U_n$, $n \geq 5$.

The above lemma provides that $U_n - V_n \neq \phi$ for $n \geq 5$. Next we define a few sets to find functions of Q_n which do not belong to $(P_n \cup R_n)$.

Definition 4. Let $wt(S_1) = wt(S_2) = wt(S_3) = wt(S_4)$.
(1) $Q_n^x = \{S_1 S_2 S_3 S_4 \mid S_1, S_2 \in B_{n-2}, S_1 S_2 \in A_{n-1}, S_3, S_4 \in A_{n-2}\}$
$\cup \{S_1 S_2 S_3 S_4 \mid S_3, S_4 \in B_{n-2}, S_3 S_4 \in A_{n-1}, S_1, S_2 \in A_{n-2}\}$
(2) $Q_n^y = \{S_1 S_2 S_3 S_4 \mid S_i \in B_{n-2}, 1 \leq i \leq 4$, and $S_1 S_2, S_3 S_4 \in A_{n-1}$, and $S_1 S_3, S_1 S_4, S_2 S_3, S_2 S_4 \in B_{n-1}\}$. (3) $Q_n^0 = Q_n^x \cup Q_n^y$.
(4) $Q_n^1 = \{S_1 S_1^r S_3 S_4, S_3 S_4 S_1 S_1^r \mid S_1 \in B_{n-2}, S_3, S_4 \in A_{n-2}\}$.

Lemma 8. (1)$Q_n^0 = Q_n - (P_n \cup R_n)$, (2) $Q_4^1 = Q_4^x$, $Q_n^1 \subset Q_n^x$ for $n \geq 5$,
(3) $\mid Q_n^1 \mid = 2 \sum_{r=1}^{2^{n-3}-1} C_{n-2}^2(2r) N_{n-2}(2r)$.

Lemma 9. $Q_n^y \neq \phi$, $n \geq 4$.

Enumeration of Q_4^y is easy, since if we take any two $S_1, S_2 \in B_2$ of same weight with $S_1 \neq S_2$ and $S_1 \neq S_2^r$, we get both $S_1 S_2, S_1 S_2^r \in B_3$. However, the characterization for $n \geq 5$ is complicated. Next we find functions of $R_n - (P_n \cup Q_n)$.

Definition 5. Let $wt(S_1) = wt(S_2) = wt(S_3) = wt(S_4)$.
(1) $R_n^x = \{S_1 S_2 S_3 S_4 \mid S_1, S_3 \in B_{n-2}, S_1 S_3 \in A_{n-1}, S_2, S_4 \in A_{n-2}\}$
$\cup \{S_1 S_2 S_3 S_4 \mid S_2, S_4 \in B_{n-2}, S_2 S_4 \in A_{n-1}, S_1, S_3 \in A_{n-2}\}$
(2) $R_n^y = \{S_1 S_2 S_3 S_4 \mid S_i \in B_{n-2}, 1 \leq i \leq 4$, and $S_1 S_3, S_2 S_4 \in A_{n-1}$, and $S_1 S_2, S_3 S_4, S_2 S_3, S_1 S_4 \in B_{n-1}\}$. (3) $R_n^0 = R_n^x \cup R_n^y$.
(4) $R_n^1 = \{S_1 S_3 S_1^r S_4, S_3 S_1 S_4 S_1^r \mid S_1 \in B_{n-2}, S_3, S_4 \in A_{n-2}\}$.

Remark 2. Lemma 8 and Lemma 9 proved for Q are also true for R. Thus from Lemma 7, Lemma 8, Lemma 9 we get the following theorem.

Theorem 3. *(1)* $P_n \cup Q_n \cup R_n = P_n \cup U_n \cup Q_n^0 \cup R_n^0$ *for* $n \geq 4$.
(2) $P_4 \cup Q_4 \cup R_4 = P_4 \cup V_4 \cup Q_4^1 \cup Q_4^y \cup R_4^1 \cup R_4^y$. *(3) For* $n \geq 5$,
$| A_n | > | P_n \cup Q_n \cup R_n | > | P_n | + | U_n | + | Q_n^1 | + | Q_n^y | + | R_n^1 | + | R_n^y |$.

Proof : It is easy to see that (1) and (3) holds. The proof of (2) holds since $Q_4^x = Q_4^1$ and $R_4^x = R_4^1$, similar to Lemma 7. □

Remark 3. The above theorem suggests that exact enumeration of $P_n \cup Q_n \cup R_n$ for $n > 4$, is difficult using this kind of technique. It is clear from Lemma 7, Lemma 8 and Lemma 9 that the difficulty arises due to the problem of two NCI functions giving rise to a CI function (see Remark 1).

Theorem 4. *For* $n \geq 4$,
$$| A_n | > | A_{n-1} |^2 + 2(2^{2^{n-2}} - | A_{n-2} |) - \binom{2^{n-2}}{2^{n-3}} + 4 \sum_{r=1}^{2^{n-3}-1} C_{n-2}^2(2r) \, N_{n-2}(2r).$$

Lemma 10. *For* $n \geq 4$
$$\sum_{r=1}^{2^{n-3}-1} C_{n-2}^2(2r) \, N_{n-2}(2r) \geq \sum_{r=1}^{2^{n-3}-1} \binom{2^{n-3}}{r}^2 \left(\binom{2^{n-2}}{2r} - \binom{2^{n-3}}{r} \right).$$

Corollary 1. $\sum_{r=1}^{2^{n-3}-1} C_{n-2}^2(2r) \, N_{n-2}(2r) > \dfrac{2^{2^{n-1}}}{2^{\frac{3n}{2}-3}}$

The closed form lower bound in Lemma 10 and Corollary 1 (though a very conservative estimate) clearly indicates that the lower bound of Theorem 4 is a significant improvement over the bound $| A_{n-1} |^2$ obtained in [9].

4 Upper Bound

The upper bound on $| A_n |$ was provided in [14] and it was later improved to $| A_n | \leq \sum_{j=0}^{2^{n-2}} \binom{2^{n-2}}{j}^4$ in [9]. This was obtained by showing that $A_n \subseteq K_n = \bigcup_{|j|=0}^{2^{n-3}} \{f_1 g_2 g_1 f_2 \mid$ where $f = f_1 f_2$, $g = g_1 g_2$, and $f \in Y_{2j}$ and $g \in Y_{-2j}\}$, where, $Y_j = \{f \in \Omega_{n-1} \mid \#(f = X_{n-1}) = \#(f \neq X_{n-1})$ and $\#(f = X_{n-2}) - \#(f \neq X_{n-2}) = 2j\}$, $|j| \leq 2^{n-2}$. The above condition is necessary for a function to be correlation immune. It has been shown in [9] that $F = f^u g^l g^u f^l \in \Omega_n$ is CI, iff $wd(f^u f^l, X_{n-1}) = 0, wd(g^u g^l, X_{n-1}) = 0$ and $wd(f^u f^l, X_i) = -wd(g^u g^l, X_i)$ for $1 \leq i \leq n-2$. However, the following characterization holds,

Theorem 5. $F = f^u g^u g^l f^l \in \Omega_n$, *is CI, iff* $wd(f^u f^l, X_{n-1}) = 0, wd(g^u g^l, X_{n-1}) = 0$ *and for* $1 \leq i \leq n-2$, $wd(f^u f^l, X_i) = -wd(g^u g^l, X_i) \equiv 0 \bmod 4$.

The equivalence to '0 mod 4' in the above theorem was proved for only $i = n - 2$ in [9]. The upper bound in [9] considered only three leftmost variables X_n, X_{n-1}, X_{n-2} in the truth table. One can get better necessary conditions by including variables X_i for $i < n - 2$. However, if we consider the leftmost four variables then the conditions become complicated. So here we take a different approach. We show that there are functions in K_n which are not correlation immune. A lower bound on the number of such functions provide a better upper bound on $| A_n |$. First we require the following two results.

Proposition 7. *Let $F \in \Omega_n$ be of the form $F = F_0F_1F_2F_3F_4F_5F_6F_7$. If k $(0 \le k \le 7)$ of the F_i's are CI functions and the other $8 - k$ F_i's are equal to a NCI function, then F is NCI.*

Proposition 8. *Let $f, g \in \Omega_{n-1}$, with $f = f_1f_2f_3f_4$, and $g = g_1g_2g_3g_4$, where $wt(f_1) = wt(g_2) = a_1$, $wt(f_2) = wt(g_1) = b_1$, $wt(f_3) = wt(g_4) = a_2$, $wt(f_4) = wt(g_3) = b_2$, and $a_1 + b_1 = a_2 + b_2$. Then $F = f_1f_2g_3g_4g_1g_2f_3f_4 \in K_n$.*

The above two Propositions together constitute a sufficient condition for a function f to belong to $K_n - A_n$. A lower bound on the number of such functions provides an improved upper bound on $|A_n|$. So the problem reduces to constructing functions satisfying Proposition 7 and Proposition 8.

Theorem 6. $|A_n| \le \sum_{j=0}^{2^{n-2}} \binom{2^{n-2}}{j}^4 - \sum_{k=0}^{7} \binom{8}{k} \sum_{a=0}^{2^{n-3}} C_{n-3}^k(a) N_{n-3}(a).$

Proof : We consider functions of Ω_{n-3} of same weight. The conditions of Proposition 7, 8 are satisfied if one chooses k functions from $CIW_{n-3}(a)$ and 1 function from $NCIW_{n-3}(a)$, where k is as in Proposition 7. □

Remark 4. We choose only one function from $NCIW_{n-3}(a)$ and repeat it in $8 - k$ places instead of using $8 - k$ possibly different functions from $NCIW_{n-3}(a)$. This is because concatenation of two different NCI functions may generate a CI function (see also Remarks 1, 3).

A more detailed analysis will provide a better upper bound. Depending on the value of k in Proposition 7 several cases arise. For $0 \le k \le 3$, if $a_1 = a_2 = b_1 = b_2$, then $F \in K_n - A_n$. For $k \ge 4$, the situation is more complicated. Let $l_1 = \{f_1, g_2\}$, $l_2 = \{f_2, g_1\}$, $l_3 = \{f_3, g_4\}$, $l_4 = \{f_4, g_3\}$. The k CI functions are to be chosen from the sets l_1, l_2, l_3, l_4. Suppose we choose k_i functions from l_i, with $k_1 + k_2 + k_3 + k_4 = k$. This imposes conditions on a_1, a_2, b_1, b_2 for the resulting F to be in $K_n - A_n$. We omit the complicated analysis here due to lack of space.

5 $A_n(1,2,3,4)$

Here we provide lower bounds for $|A_n(1,2,3,4)|$. In [14] enumeration of $A_n(1,2,3,4)$ was reduced to that of $A_n(1,4)$ using the principle of inclusion and exclusion. Thus the crucial task is to provide a lower bound on $|A_n(1,4)|$. However, a lower bound on $|A_n(1,4)|$ does not immediately provide a lower bound on $|A_n(1,2,3,4)|$ using inclusion and exclusion. Theorem 8 provides an way out here. Moreover, the result shows (using Theorem 7, Theorem 9) the proportion of $|A_n(1,2,3,4)|$ in $|A_n(1,4)|$ is almost equal to 1 for large n. Initially we consider the following sets similar to Subsection 3.1.
(1) $D_n^{1b} = \{F \in \Omega_n \mid wt(F) = 2^{n-1}, F$ is a palindrome $\}$,
(2) $D_n^{2b} = \{S_1 S_1^r S_2^r S_2 \mid wt(S_1) = wt(S_2) = 2^{n-3},$ and $S_1 \ne S_2^r, S_1, S_2 \in \Omega_{n-2}\}$,
and (3) $D_n^{3b} = \{SS^c S^c S \mid wt(S) \ne 2^{n-3}, S \in \Omega_{n-2}, S \ne S^r\}$.

Theorem 7.
$|A_n(1,4)| \ge \binom{2^{n-1}}{2^{n-2}} + 2^{2^{n-2}} + \binom{2^{n-2}}{2^{n-3}}(\binom{2^{n-2}}{2^{n-3}} - 2) - 2^{2^{n-3}} + \binom{2^{n-3}}{2^{n-4}}.$

Theorem 8.
$$| A_n(1,2,3,4) | = | A_n(1,3,4) | - 2 \geq | A_n(1,4) | - n | A_{n-1}(1,4) | - 2.$$

Mitchell [8, Page 164] had commented that enumeration of $A_n(3,4)$ is a nontrivial task. However, similar to Theorem 8, one can show $| A_n(3,4) | \geq | A_n(4) | (1 - \frac{n}{2^{2^{n-2}}})$ and so the enumeration problem for $A_n(3,4)$ is really that of $A_n(4)$. It is also interesting to see that all the functions of $CIW_n(2a)$, where a is odd, are nondegenerate. Now we use the techniques of Subsection 3.2 to provide recursive construction procedures and obtain improved lower bounds for $| A_n(1,4) |$. The technique provides new insights into the difficulty of enumerating such functions. Let us denote $T_n^\alpha = \{ f^u g^u g^l f^l \mid f \in CIW_{n-1}(2a), g \in CIW_{n-1}(2^{n-1} - 2a), 0 \leq a \leq 2^{n-2}, a \neq 2^{n-3} \}$ and $P_n^\alpha = \{ f^u g^u g^l f^l \mid f, g \in A_{n-1}(1,4) \}$.

Proposition 9. *(1)* T_n^α, P_n^α *are mutually disjoint subsets of* $A_n(1,4)$. *(2)* $P_n^\alpha = | A_{n-1}(1,4) |^2$. *(3)* $| T_n^\alpha | = 2 \sum_{i=0}^{2^{n-3}-1} C_{n-1}^2(2i)$, *for* $n \geq 4$.

Proof : Using Proposition 3, $T_n^\alpha, P_n^\alpha \subseteq A_n(4)$. Also it is easy to check that $T_n^\alpha, P_n^\alpha \subseteq A_n(1,4)$ and $T_n^\alpha \cap P_n^\alpha = \phi$.

The proof of (2) is clear from the definition of P_n^α. The proof of (3) is derived from $C_{n-1}(2i) = C_{n-1}(2^{n-1} - 2i)$, since $f \in A_n$ iff $f^c \in A_n$. □

Next we construct a few sets in the same way as in Subsection 3.2.
$V_n^\alpha = \{ SS^r S^r S \mid S \in \Omega_{n-2} - A_{n-2}(1,4), wt(S) = 2^{n-3} \}$,
$Q_n^{1\alpha} = \{ S_1 S_1^r S_3 S_4, S_3 S_4 S_1 S_1^r \mid S_1 \in \Omega_{n-2} - A_{n-2}(1,4), S_3, S_4 \in A_{n-2}(1,4),$
and $wt(S_1) = wt(S_3) = wt(S_4) \}$ and $R_n^{1\alpha} = \{ S_1 S_3 S_1^r S_4, S_3 S_1 S_4 S_1^r$
$\mid S_1 \in \Omega_{n-2} - A_{n-2}(1,4), S_3, S_4 \in A_{n-2}(1,4),$ and $wt(S_1) = wt(S_3) = wt(S_4) \}$.

Proposition 10. *(1)* $T_n^\alpha, P_n^\alpha, V_n^\alpha, Q_n^{1\alpha}, R_n^{1\alpha}$ *are mutually disjoint subsets of*
$A_n(1,4)$. *(2)* $| V_n^\alpha | = \binom{2^{n-2}}{2^{n-3}} - | A_{n-2}(1,4) |$,

(3) $| Q_n^{1\alpha} | = | R_n^{1\alpha} | = 2 | A_{n-2}(1,4) |^2 \left(\binom{2^{n-2}}{2^{n-3}} - | A_{n-2}(1,4) | \right)$.

Theorem 9. *For* $n \geq 4$, $| A_n(1,4) | \geq | A_{n-1}(1,4) |^2 +$
$2 \sum_{i=0}^{2^{n-3}-1} C_{n-1}^2(2i) + \left(\binom{2^{n-2}}{2^{n-3}} - | A_{n-2}(1,4) | \right) \left(1 + 4 | A_{n-2}(1,4) |^2 \right)$.

Proof : The proof follows from Proposition 9 and Proposition 10. □

Mitchell [8, Page 168] remarked that there is no obvious candidate for $A_n(1,2,3,4,5)$. Earlier, a similar conjecture was proposed by Chor et al in [2] that balanced symmetric Boolean functions are all linear and it was disproved in [4] showing there exists n such that $A_n(1,2,4,5) \neq \phi$. We know that all the symmetric functions except the two identity functions 0 and 1 are nondegenerate. Hence, the counterexamples proposed in [4], being balanced, are all nondegenerate. Thus the following theorem answers the question posed by Mitchell [8].

Theorem 10. *There exists* n *such that* $A_n(1,2,3,4,5) \neq \phi$.

Here we reduce the enumeration problem of $A_n(1,2,3,4)$ to that of $A_n(1,4)$ and solve that satisfactorily. A more challenging task in this direction is to enumerate $f \in A_n(1,2,3,4)$ having specified algebraic degree, nonlinearity and order of correlation immunity. Construction problem for such functions have been addressed in [12, 11, 10, 1, 7, 3].

References

1. P. Camion, C. Carlet, P. Charpin, and N. Sendrier. On correlation immune functions. In *Advances in Cryptology - CRYPTO'91*, pages 86–100. Springer-Verlag, 1992.
2. B. Chor, O. Goldreich, J. Hastad, J. Friedman, S. Rudich, and R. Smolensky. The bit extraction problem or t-resilient functions. In *26th IEEE Symposium on Foundations of Computer Science*, pages 396–407, 1985.
3. Eric Filiol and Caroline Fontaine. Highly nonlinear balanced Boolean functions with a good correlation-immunity. In *Advances in Cryptology - EUROCRYPT'98*. Springer-Verlag, 1998.
4. K. Gopalakrisnan, D. G. Hoffman, and D. R. Stinson. A note on a conjecture concerning symmetric resilient functions. *Information Processing Letters*, 47(3):139–143, 1993.
5. Xiao Guo-Zhen and James Massey. A spectral characterization of correlation immune combining functions. *IEEE Transactions on Information Theory*, 34(3):569–571, May 1988.
6. Richard W. Hamming. *Coding And Information Theory*. Prentice Hall Inc., 1980.
7. William Millan, Andrew Clark, and Ed Dawson. Heuristic design of cryptographically strong balanced Boolean functions. In *Advances in Cryptology - EUROCRYPT'98*. Springer-Verlag, 1998.
8. C. J. Mitchell. Enumerating Boolean functions of cryptographic significance. *Journal of Cryptology*, 2(3):155–170, 1990.
9. Park Sung Mo, Lee Sangjin, Sung Soo Hak, and Kim Kwangjo. Improving bounds for the number of correlation immune Boolean functions. *Information Processing Letters*, 61(4):209–212, 1997.
10. J. Seberry, X. M. Zhang, and Y. Zheng. Nonlinearly balanced Boolean functions and their propagation characteristics. In *Advances in Cryptology - CRYPTO'93*, pages 49–60. Springer-Verlag, 1994.
11. J. Seberry, X. M. Zhang, and Y. Zheng. On constructions and nonlinearity of correlation immune Boolean functions. In *Advances in Cryptology - EUROCRYPT'93*, pages 181–199. Springer-Verlag, 1994.
12. T. Siegenthaler. Correlation-immunity of nonlinear combining functions for cryptographic applications. *IEEE Transactions on Information Theory*, IT-30(5):776–780, September 1984.
13. T. Siegenthaler. Decrypting a class of stream ciphers using ciphertext only. *IEEE Transactions on Computer*, C-34(1):81–85, January 1985.
14. Y. X. Yang and B. Guo. Further enumerating Boolean functions of cryptographic significance. *Journal of Cryptology*, 8(3):115–122, 1995.
15. Wei Juan Shan. -. *Journal of Applied Mathematics (in Chinese)*, -, 1991.

Appendix

A1. Generating Function

Let, $g_k(x) = \sum_{a=0}^{2^k} C_k(a)x^a$ and

$$C(x) = \sum_{k \geq 0} g_k(x)y^k = \sum_{k \geq 0} \sum_{a=0}^{2^k} C_k(a)x^a y^k.$$

Also, $h_k(x) = \sum_{a=0}^{2^k} N_k(a)x^a$ and

$$N(x) = \sum_{k \geq 0} h_k(x)y^k = \sum_{k \geq 0} \sum_{a=0}^{2^k} N_k(a)x^a y^k \text{ for NCI functions.}$$

Proposition 11. *(1)* $C_k(a) + N_k(a) = \binom{2^k}{a}$, *(2)* $g_k(x) + h_k(x) = (1+x)^{2^k}$ *and*

(3) $C(x) + N(x) = \sum_{k \geq 0} (1+x)^{2^k} y^k$.

Let $p(x) = \sum_{i \geq 0} p_i x^i$ and $q(x) = \sum_{i \geq 0} q_i x^i$. Define $p(x) \leq q(x)$ if $p_i \leq q_i$ for all $i \geq 0$. Also define $p^{[2]}(x) = \sum_{i \geq 0} (p_i x^i)^2$.

Lemma 11. $h_{n-1}(x) g_{n-1}(x) \leq h_n(x) \leq (1+x)^{2^n} - g_{n-1}^{[2]}(x)$.

Proof : From the Proposition 1 we get, $\sum_{r=0}^{a} N_{n-1}(r) C_{n-1}(a-r) \leq N_n(a) \leq \binom{2^n}{a} - C_{n-1}^2(\frac{a}{2})$. Note that, if a is odd or $\equiv 2 \mod 4$ then $C_{n-1}(\frac{a}{2})$ is zero. The result then follows from the fact that generating function for the convolution of two sequences is the product of the generating functions of the individual sequence. □

A2. Some Proofs of Subsection 3.1
Proof of Lemma 4
Proof : It can be checked that (1) holds. Now we prove (2). We choose an i such that $0 \leq i \leq 2^{n-2}$. So we can choose S_1 in $\binom{2^{n-2}}{i}$ ways. Depending on the choice of S_1, we can choose S_2 in $(\binom{2^{n-2}}{i} - 1)$ ways leaving out S_1^r, since S_1 and S_2^r need to be distinct. Hence, $|D_n^2| = \sum_{i=0}^{2^{n-2}} \binom{2^{n-2}}{i}(\binom{2^{n-2}}{i} - 1) = \sum_{i=0}^{2^{n-2}} \binom{2^{n-2}}{i}^2 - \sum_{i=0}^{2^{n-2}} \binom{2^{n-2}}{i} = \binom{2^{n-1}}{2^{n-2}} - 2^{2^{n-2}}$. The proof of (3) is found by discarding the balanced functions and palindromic functions from Ω_{n-2}. □

A3. Some Proofs of Subsection 3.2
Proof of Proposition 6
Proof : That P_n, Q_n, R_n are proper subsets of A_n will be clear from the remaining part of the proof. Now we prove the last statement. Let $S \in B_{n-2}$, and S is not balanced. It is easy to check that such functions exist for $n \geq 2$. Since, $SS, SS^c \in B_{n-1}$, $SS^c S^c S \notin (P_n \cup Q_n \cup R_n)$. However, it can be checked that $SS^c S^c S$ is a function of the form $X_n \oplus g$, where $g \in \Omega_{n-1}$ and g is balanced. Thus, by Siegenthaler's construction [12, Section VI], $SS^c S^c S \in A_n$.

The last statement holds since there are at least $2^{2^{n-2}} - \binom{2^{n-2}}{2^{n-3}} - |A_{n-2}|$ choices of unbalanced NCI functions S. □

Proof of Lemma 5
Proof : Let $F \in U_n$. Then from Definition 3, $F \in Q_n$, $F \in R_n$, $F \notin P_n$. Thus $U_n \subseteq (Q_n \cap R_n) - P_n$. On the other hand, let $F \in (Q_n \cap R_n) - P_n$. Now F can be written as $S_1 S_2 S_3 S_4$, where $S_1, S_2, S_3, S_4 \in \Omega_{n-2}$. Since $S_1 S_2 \in A_{n-1}$, either both $S_1, S_2 \in A_{n-2}$ or both $S_1, S_2 \in B_{n-2}$ (using Proposition 1). Similarly $S_1 S_3 \in A_{n-1}$ forces either both $S_1, S_3 \in A_{n-2}$ or both $S_1, S_3 \in B_{n-2}$. Since, $S_2 S_3 \in B_{n-1}$, both S_2 and S_3 can't be in A_{n-2}. So, both of them must be in B_{n-2} and hence S_1 is also in B_{n-2}. Similarly it can be shown that S_4 too belongs to B_{n-2}. Thus $F \in U_n$, which implies $(Q_n \cap R_n) - P_n \subseteq U_n$. □

Proof of Lemma 6

Proof : By Lemma 3, if $f = SS^r$, $g = S^rS$ where $S \in B_{n-2}$, then $f, g \in A_{n-1}$. Thus it is easy to see that $V_n \subseteq Q_n$ and also $V_n \subseteq R_n$.

Let $F \in V_n$ and if possible $F \in P_n$. As $F \in P_n$, F is of the form $f^u g^u g^l f^l$ where $f, g \in A_{n-1}$. However, $F \in V_n$, so F is of the form $F = SS^r S^r S$, where $S \in B_{n-2}$. Thus, $f = f^u f^l = SS$. Then by Proposition 1(item 4), $f \notin A_{n-1}$, which is a contradiction. Thus, we get $V_n \cap P_n = \phi$. and hence, $V_n \subseteq (Q_n \cap R_n) - P_n = U_n$. To get $\mid V_n \mid$ note that for S we can choose any function from B_{n-2}. $\square$

Proof of Lemma 7

Proof : First we take $n = 4$. If we try to build $F \in U_4$, we have to start with $S_i \in B_2, 1 \le i \le 4$ of same weight. For S_i, S_j, $i \ne j$, we have, $S_i S_j \in B_3$ unless $S_i = S_j^r$. Hence $S_1 S_2 S_3 S_4$ must be of the form $SS^r S^r S$. So, $V_4 = U_4$.

Consider the case for $n = 5$. Let $S_1 = 10000100$ and $S_2 = 00010010$. Note that, both $S_1, S_2 \in B_3$. So, by item (4) of Proposition 1, $S_1 S_1, S_2 S_2 \in B_4$. However, it can be checked, $S_1 S_2 \in A_4$. So, $S_1 S_2 S_2 S_1 \in U_5$. Also, $S_1 \ne S_2^r$. Thus, $S_1 S_2 S_2 S_1 \notin V_5$. Hence, $V_5 \subset U_5$.

For $n > 5$, say $n = 5 + k$, $k > 0$, take $h_1 = S_1 S_1 \ldots S_1$, (2^k times) and $h_2 = S_2 S_2 \ldots S_2$, (2^k times). Thus, we have, $h_1, h_2 \in B_{3+k}$, $h_1 \ne h_2^r$ and $h_1 h_2 \in A_{4+k}$, which completes the proof. $\square$

Proof of Lemma 8

Proof : Statement (1) can be proved in the same way as Lemma 5 and (2) can be proved similar to Lemma 7. Next we prove (3). Let us consider the form $S_1 S_1^r S_3 S_4$. Since any correlation immune function is of even weight, we only consider the even weight functions of Ω_{n-2}. Also, there is no function in B_{n-2} of weight 0 or 2^{n-2}. Thus we only consider the functions of Ω_{n-2} of weight $2r$, where r varies from 1 to $2^{n-3} - 1$. Now S_3 and S_4 can be any two correlation immune function, and so can be chosen in $C_{n-2}^2(2r)$ ways, whereas S_1 can be chosen in $N_{n-2}(2r)$ ways. Thus we get the choice of $\sum_{r=1}^{2^{n-3}-1} C_{n-2}^2(2r) N_{n-2}(2r)$ functions. Now, the functions of the form $S_1 S_1^r S_3 S_4$ and $S_3 S_4 S_1 S_1^r$ are distinct, since the first one starts with a function from B_{n-2} whereas the second one starts with a function from A_{n-2}. Thus, we get the cardinality of Q_n^1. $\square$

Proof of Lemma 9

Proof : Consider $F = S_1 S_1^r S_2 S_2^r$, where $S_1, S_2 \in B_{n-2}$, $wt(S_1) = wt(S_2)$, and both $S_1 S_2, S_1 S_2^r \in B_{n-1}$. Thus, $F \notin (P_n \cup R_n)$. Also $F \notin Q_n^x$, since all $S_1, S_1^r, S_2, S_2^r \in B_{n-2}$. Now, we have to show the existence of such $S_1, S_2 \in B_{n-2}$. Consider, $wt(S_1) = wt(S_2) = 1$, S_1 is of the form $1000 \ldots 0$ and S_2 is of the form $0100 \ldots 0$. Let $S_1 S_2, S_1 S_2^r$ be functions of input variables $X_1, \ldots, X_{n-1}$. Then $\#(S_1 S_2 = 1 \mid X_{n-2} = 0) = 2$ and $\#(S_1 S_2 = 1 \mid X_{n-2} = 1) = 0$. Thus by Lemma 1, $Prob(S_1 S_2 = X_{n-2}) \ne \frac{1}{2}$. Also, $\#(S_1 S_2^r = 1 \mid X_1 = 0) = 2$ and $\#(S_1 S_2^r = 1 \mid X_1 = 1) = 0$. Thus by Lemma 1, $Prob(S_1 S_2^r = X_1) \ne \frac{1}{2}$. Hence, both $S_1 S_2, S_1 S_2^r \in B_{n-1}$. $\square$

Proof of Theorem 4

Proof : Using Lemma 8, Theorem 3 and Remark 2, $\mid P_n \cup Q_n \cup R_n \mid >$
$\mid A_{n-1} \mid^2 + 2^{2^{n-2}} - \mid A_{n-2} \mid + 4 \sum_{r=1}^{2^{n-3}-1} C_{n-2}^2(2r) N_{n-2}(2r)$. ¿From Proposition 6,
$\mid A_n \mid \geq \mid P_n \cup Q_n \cup R_n \mid + 2^{2^{n-2}} - \binom{2^{n-2}}{2^{n-3}} - \mid A_{n-2} \mid$. □

Proof of Lemma 10

Proof : $C_{n-2}(2r) + N_{n-2}(2r) = \binom{2^{n-2}}{2r}$, a constant for fixed r, $1 \leq r \leq$
$2^{n-3} - 1$. Now, $C_{n-2}^2(2r) N_{n-2}(2r)$ is increasing in $0 \leq C_{n-2}(2r) \leq \frac{2}{3}\binom{2^{n-2}}{2r}$.
Also, $\binom{2^{n-3}}{r} \leq C_{n-2}(2r) \leq \frac{2}{3}\binom{2^{n-2}}{2r}$.
So, $C_{n-2}^2(2r) N_{n-2}(2r) \geq \binom{2^{n-3}}{r}^2 (\binom{2^{n-2}}{2r} - \binom{2^{n-3}}{r})$. Thus,
$\sum_{r=1}^{2^{n-3}-1} C_{n-2}^2(2r) N_{n-2}(2r) \geq \sum_{r=1}^{2^{n-3}-1} \binom{2^{n-3}}{r}^2 (\binom{2^{n-2}}{2r} - \binom{2^{n-3}}{r})$. □

Proof of Corollary 1

Proof : To get the proof, it should be noted that $\binom{2^{n-2}}{2^{n-3}}\binom{2^{n-3}}{2^{n-4}}^2 > 8 \frac{2^{2^{n-1}}}{2^{\frac{3n}{2}}}$,
by using Stirling's approximation $k! = \sqrt{2\pi k} \, (\frac{k}{e})^k$. □

A4. Some Proofs of Section 5

Proof of Theorem 7

Proof : It can be checked that $D_n^{1b}, D_n^{2b}, D_n^{3b}$ are mutually disjoint subsets
of $CIW_n(2^{n-1})$. Now, $\mid D_n^{1b} \mid = \binom{2^{n-1}}{2^{n-2}}$, $\mid D_n^{2b} \mid = \binom{2^{n-2}}{2^{n-3}}(\binom{2^{n-2}}{2^{n-3}} - 1)$, and
$\mid D_n^{3b} \mid = 2^{2^{n-2}} - \binom{2^{n-2}}{2^{n-3}} - (2^{2^{n-3}} - \binom{2^{n-3}}{2^{n-4}})$. □

Proof of Theorem 8

Proof : The equality comes from existence of only two affine functions in
$A_n(1, 3, 4)$. The inequality comes from the fact that there are at most
$n \mid A_{n-1}(1, 4) \mid$ degenerate functions in $A_n(1, 4)$. □

On the Symmetric Property of Homogeneous Boolean Functions

Chengxin Qu, Jennifer Seberry, and Josef Pieprzyk

Centre for Computer Security Research
School of Information Technology and Computer Science
University of Wollongong
Wollongong, NSW 2522, AUSTRALIA
email: cxq01/jennie/josef@cs.uow.edu.au

Abstract. We use combinatorial methods and permutation groups to classify homogeneous boolean functions. The property of symmetry of a boolean function limits the size of the function's class. We exhaustively searched for all boolean functions on V_6. We found two interesting classes of degree 3 homogeneous boolean functions: the first class is degree 3 homogeneous bent boolean functions; and the second is degree 3 homogeneous balanced boolean functions. Both the bent and balanced functions discovered have nice algebraic and combinatorial structures. We note that some structures can be extended to a large boolean space. The application of homogeneous boolean functions for fast implementation on parallel architectures is mooted.

Keywords: S-box Theory, Cryptographically Strong Boolean Faunctions, Symmetric Functions, Homogeneous Functions.

1 Introduction

The S-box theory emerged quite recently as a part of Cryptology. Shannon [1] established its foundations by formulating the principles for secure product cipher design. To get secure encryption algorithms, it is enough to design two elementary blocks: a permutation block (or P-box) and a substitution block (or S-box). P-boxes provide *diffusion* while S-boxes furnish *confusion*. Encryption algorithms, according to Shannon's concepts, are nothing but a sequence of iterations. Each iteration uses a layer of S-boxes controlled by a secret key. Between two consecutive iterations, a single P-box of known structure is used (the P-box is not keyed).

Shannon's product cipher is easy to implement. If we select building blocks at random (so both P-boxes and S-boxes are random), we can still get with a high probability a strong cipher provided we use "a large enough" number of iterations [2]. The real challenge in the S-box theory is how to design S-boxes so we can reduce the number of iterations without loss of security. Boolean functions are universal tools for S-box design and have received considerable attention over the last decade [4, ?]. The cryptographic usefulness of a given boolean function is measured by its cryptographic properties. The collection of these properties includes balance, strict avalanche criterion or SAC, high nonlinearity [10] [9] and higher-degree propagation criteria [3]. If an S-box (or corresponding collection of boolean functions) is implemented as a lookup table, then the length or the form of boolean functions is not important. This is no longer true when the evaluation of the function is done on the fly – this is the case in all MD-type hashing algorithms (MD4, MD5, SHA-1, HAVAL)[15]. It was argued in [13], that symmetric boolean functions can be very efficiently evaluated. Since symmetric boolean functions are composed by a series of homogeneous parts in a boolean space, we study the symmetric properties of boolean functions starting from homogeneous boolean functions.

This work studies homogeneous boolean functions which create subclass of symmetric functions whose terms (in the algebraic normal form) are of the same degree. In particular, we examine symmetric properties of 3-homogeneous bent functions and highly nonlinear balanced ones in V_6.

2 Boolean functions and permutation groups

We first introduce necessary notations. The n-dimension boolean space V_n contains the following 2^n vectors (binary sequences with length n)

$$\alpha_0 = (0, \cdots, 0, 0), \alpha_1 = (0, \cdots, 0, 1), \cdots, \alpha_{2^n-1} = (1, \cdots, 1, 1). \quad (1)$$

Let $\alpha = (a_1, \cdots, a_n)$, $a_i \in GF(2)$, be a vector in V_n. Then a single term of a boolean function on a boolean space V_n is written as $x^\alpha = x_1^{a_1} \cdots x_n^{a_n}$. In general, a boolean function can be represented by its algebraic normal form as

$$f(x) = \bigoplus_{\alpha \in V_n} c_\alpha x^\alpha \qquad c_\alpha = 0 \text{ or } 1. \quad (2)$$

The values of a function form a binary sequence of the length 2^n. For a binary sequence ξ, $wt(\xi)$ denotes its Hamming weight which equals the number of 1s in the sequence. A function, $f(x)$, is called a d-homogeneous if all $\alpha \in V_n$ in the function (2) have the same Hamming weight and equal to d ($wt(\alpha) = d$).

Let S_n denote a permutation group with n entries and e the unit element of S_n. The the order of the group is $n!$. The minimum number of generators of S_n is $n - 1$. For example, the generators can be $(1\ n)$, $(1\ n - 1)$, $\cdots$, $(1\ 2)$. The highest order of the elements of S_n is n. We use the traditional definition of writing $\pi = (i\ j\ \cdots\ k)$ for the permutation

$$\begin{pmatrix} i & j & \cdots & k \\ j & \cdots\cdots & i \end{pmatrix} \quad (3)$$

Definition 1. *Let π be an element of the permutation group S_n. Assume that permutations from S_n are used to permute n variables of a boolean function. So for a permutation $\pi = (ij) \in S_n$, we can write that*

$$\pi\alpha = (ij)(a_1, \cdots, a_i \cdots, a_j, \cdots, a_n) = (a_1, \cdots, a_j \cdots, a_i, \cdots, a_n). \quad (4)$$

We say that a permutation $\pi \in S_n$ acts on a boolean function $f(x)$ if it permutes the function's variables, i.e.

$$\pi f(x) = \pi \bigoplus_{\alpha \in V_n} c_\alpha x^\alpha = \bigoplus_{\pi \alpha \in V_n} c_{\pi \alpha} x^{\pi \alpha} = \bigoplus_{\beta \in V_n} c_\beta x^\beta \qquad (5)$$

where $\pi \alpha = \beta$.

The permutation is a 1-1 transformation for a function $f(x)$. Under the all permutations in S_n, a function $f(x)$ generates a function set $\{\pi f \mid \pi \in S_n\}$. For each boolean function $f(x)$, there exists a minimum subset, denoted by $\mathcal{PG}(f)$, of S_n such that $\{\pi f \mid \pi \in \mathcal{PG}(f)\} = \{\pi f \mid \pi \in S_n\}$.

Lemma 1. *Let π be an element of the permutation group S_n, and $\pi f(x) = g(x)$. Then*

1. *all the functions, $\pi f(x)$ ($\pi \in S_n$), have the same cryptographic properties such as Hamming weight, nonlinearity and SAC* [1];
2. *the set $\{\pi f(x) \mid \pi \in S_n\}$ forms a group if $ef(x) = f(x)$ (e the unit of S_n) is the unite of the set and the group operation "$\circ$" is defined as follows*

$$[\pi_i f(x)] \circ [\pi_j f(x)] = (\pi_i \pi_j) f(x) = \pi_k f(x), \qquad (6)$$

where $\circ$ stands for composition of functions or permutations and all π_i, π_j, $\pi_k \in \mathcal{PG}(f)$. The group is denoted by $PG(f)$.

The group operation "$\circ$" on $PG(f)$ is not the operation in S_n. The equality

$$(\pi_i \pi_j) f(x) = \pi_k f(x) \qquad (7)$$

does not ensure that $\pi_i \pi_j$ is equal to π_k except $\pi_i \pi_j \in \mathcal{PG}(f)$. For example, suppose $\pi_i \pi_j = \pi_k \pi'_k$ and $\pi'_k f(x) = f(x)$. Then we get the above equality and $\pi_i \pi_j \neq \pi_k$ except $\pi'_k = e$.

Proof. Consider the following two parts of the proof.

1. Since the permutation is a linear 1-1 variable transformation, it preserves all the properties of the function $f(x)$.
2. To be a group, the set with the operation $\circ$ must satisfy the following conditions: (i) the unit element must exist; (ii) each element must have the inverse in the set and the left inverse is equal to the right inverse; (iii) the associative rule must hold for the operation; (vi) the set must be closed under the operation.
   The unit element of the set is the function itself $f(x)$. Let $\pi_i f(x)$ be an element of the set. Then the element has its inverse $\pi_j f(x)$, such as $\pi_j = \pi_i^{-1}$, in the set, since

$$[\pi f(x)] \circ [\pi^{-1} f(x)] = [\pi^{-1} f(x)] \circ [\pi f(x)] = f(x). \qquad (8)$$

---

[1] For the cryptographic desirable properties of boolean functions, see paper [4] [10] [12] [11]

According to the definition of group operation,

$$[\pi_i f(x) \circ \pi_j f(x)] \circ \pi_k f(x) = \pi_i f(x) \circ [\pi_j f(x) \circ \pi_k f(x)] \tag{9}$$

is true. Hence the associative rule holds. The set, $\{\pi f(x) \mid \forall \pi \in S_n\}$, contains all different boolean functions generated by permutations in S_n. Therefore, the set is closed. So we have proved that the set, $\{\pi f(x) \mid \pi \in S_n\}$, with composition $\circ$ is a group.

The group $PG(f)$ is a homomorphism to symmetric group S_n. Consider a relation between the groups $PG(f)$ and S_n. There exists subgroups of S_n, say $H(f)$, such that $\pi_i f(x) = f(x)$ for some $\pi_i \in S_n$. For any given boolean function $f(x)$ on V_n, there is at least one subgroup $H(f)$ of S_n which is the subgroup containing the unit element $\{e\}$. By convention, for a given boolean function $f(x)$ we denote $H(f)$ is the biggest subgroup of S_n. Since $PG(f) = PG(f)f(x)$, then

$$S_n = H(f) + \pi_1 H(f) + \pi_2 H(f) + \cdots \qquad \pi_i \in PG(f) \tag{10}$$

where "+" denotes the union of sets. Equation (10) is true, since all the intersection sets, $\pi_i H(f) \cap \pi_j H(f)$, where $\pi_i, \pi_j \in PG(f)$, are empty. Therefore the order of the group $H(f)$ is $|H(f)| = n!/|PG(f)|$.

For a boolean space V_n, there are 2^{2^n} different boolean functions and the size of the permutation group is $n!$. Since $2^{2^n} \gg n!$, it is impossible to discuss all $PG(f)$. However, we can use the permutation group to discuss homogeneous boolean functions in which some of them have nice combinatorial structures. The study of the group $H(f)$ is more important than the group $PG(f)$. For example, the function $f(x) = x_i$ has the group $H(f)$ with order $(n-1)!$ and $f(x) = x_i x_j$ has the group $H(f)$ with order $2(n-2)!$.

Throughout the paper, the boolean function containing all terms of degree d over V_n is denoted by $P_n^{(d)}(x)$. Clearly the group $H(P_n^{(d)}) = S_n$. For the sake of simplicity, we use the natural numbers to encode the terms. For example, 123 stands for $x_1 x_2 x_3$. Thus a function

$$\begin{aligned}
f(x) = \; & x_1 x_2 x_3 \oplus x_1 x_2 x_4 \oplus x_1 x_2 x_5 \oplus x_1 x_2 x_6 \oplus x_1 x_3 x_4 \oplus x_1 x_3 x_5 \oplus \\
& x_1 x_4 x_6 \oplus x_1 x_5 x_6 \oplus x_2 x_3 x_4 \oplus x_2 x_3 x_6 \oplus x_2 x_4 x_5 \oplus x_2 x_5 x_6 \oplus \\
& x_3 x_4 x_5 \oplus x_3 x_4 x_6 \oplus x_3 x_5 x_6 \oplus x_4 x_5 x_6
\end{aligned}$$

can be equivalently represented as

$$f(x) = P_6^{(3)}(x) \oplus x_1 x_3 x_6 \oplus x_1 x_4 x_5 \oplus x_2 x_3 x_5 \oplus x_2 x_4 x_6 \tag{11}$$

or

$$\begin{aligned}
f(x) = \; & 123 \oplus 124 \oplus 125 \oplus 126 \oplus 134 \oplus 135 \oplus 146 \oplus 156 \oplus \\
& 234 \oplus 236 \oplus 245 \oplus 256 \oplus 345 \oplus 346 \oplus 356 \oplus 456. \\
= \; & P_6^{(3)}(x) \oplus 136 \oplus 145 \oplus 235 \oplus 246.
\end{aligned}$$

Combinatorial parameters are useful to discuss homogeneous boolean functions allowing easy determination of in-equivalence. We take each single term as a block so that $x_1x_2x_3$ is the block 123.

We will use the concept of BIBD [17]. BIBD stands for balanced incomplete block design which is a block design within ν varieties and has parameters κ the number of varieties in block, β the number of blocks in the design and $r_1, \cdots, r_\nu$ the numbers of repetitions of varieties respectively. Sometimes we use the parameters $\lambda_1, \lambda_2, \cdots$ to stand for the numbers of repetitions of pairs in the block design. Let ν stand for the space dimension, κ for the order of the function, β for the number of terms in the function and let $r_1, \cdots, r_\nu$ be the numbers of repetitions for variables $x_1, \ldots, x_\nu$ in the function, respectively. Then the structure of a d-homogeneous boolean function can be considered as a BIBD with parameters $\{\nu, \kappa, \beta, r_1, \cdots, r_\nu\}$.

Lemma 2. *Let f be a homogeneous boolean function on V_n. If the element $(ij) \in S_n$ belongs to the group $H(f)$, the repetitions of x_i and x_j must be equal i.e. $r_i = r_j$.*

Proof. By contradiction. Suppose $r_i \neq r_j$, then $(ij)f(x) \neq f(x)$. Then we have $(ij) \notin H(f)$ which is a contradiction.

3 3-homogeneous Boolean Functions

We conducted an exhaustive computer search of all 3-homogeneous function on V_6 and found the complete set of bent[2] and balanced 3-homogeneous boolean functions which exist on V_6. These are used as the basis on which we discuss 3-homogeneous boolean functions.

Definition 2. *Let $f(x)$ be a d-homogeneous boolean function on V_n. Then the homogeneous complement of $f(x)$ is defined by*

$$f_c(x) = P_n^{(d)} \oplus f(x) \tag{12}$$

It is clear that a given homogeneous function $f(x)$ can be equivalently represented by the terms it contains (i.e. the function $f(x)$) or the terms it does not contain (i.e. the function $f_c(x)$). The function $f_c(x)$ preserves all symmetric properties of the function $f(x)$. We use the shorter, $f(x)$ or $f_c(x)$, representation.

3.1 3-homogeneous Bent Functions

We know that the function

$$f(x) = 124 \oplus 125 \oplus 126 \oplus 134 \oplus 135 \oplus 136 \oplus 146 \oplus 156 \oplus$$
$$234 \oplus 235 \oplus 236 \oplus 245 \oplus 256 \oplus 345 \oplus 346 \oplus 456$$
$$= P_6^{(3)}(x) \oplus 123 \oplus 145 \oplus 246 \oplus 356 = P_6^{(3)}(x) \oplus f_c(x)$$

---

[2] For the definition of bent function see the papers, for example, [6], [7], [8].

is bent on V_6, where $f_c(x)$ is the homogeneous complement of $f(x)$,

$$f_c(x) = 123 \oplus 145 \oplus 246 \oplus 356 = P_6^{(3)}(x) \oplus f(x) \qquad (13)$$

The function $f_c(x)$ can be seen as a combinatorial design with parameters as follows,

$$\{v, \kappa, \beta, r_1, r_2, r_3, r_4, r_5, r_6\} = \{6, 3, 4, 2, 2, 2, 2, 2, 2\}. \qquad (14)$$

This is a BIBD$(v, b, k, r, \lambda) =$ BIBD$(4, 6, 3, 2, 1)$ in which the parameters $v = \beta$, $b = \nu$, $k = \kappa$. The group $H(f)$ is generated by the elements $(12)(56)$, $(13)(46)$ and $(24)(35)$. The elements $(12), (13), (14)$ are 3 generators of S_4. If we take the mapping

$$(12) \leftrightarrow (12)(56), \ (13) \leftrightarrow (13)(46), \ (14) \leftrightarrow (24)(35), \qquad (15)$$

we find that $H(f)$ is isomorphic with S_4, i.e. $H(f) \simeq S_4$. Hence the order of $PG(f) = 6!/4! = 30$, which means that there are only 30 bent functions of this kind on V_6. Let $Z_2 = \{e, (16)(34)\}$, $Z_2' = \{e, (16)(25)\}$ and

$$S_3' = \{e, (12)(56), (13)(46), (23)(45), (123)(465), (132)(456)\}.$$

Then the group can be expressed as

$$H(f) = Z_2 \times Z_2' \times S_3'. \qquad (16)$$

There are many ways to represent the groups $H(f)$ and $PG(f)$. The explicit forms of the two groups are as follows.

$$H(f) = \begin{cases} e, & (12)(56), & (13)(46), & (14)(36), \\ (15)(26), & (23)(45), & (24)(35), & (16)(34), \\ (16)(25), & (34)(25), & (25)(1364), & (25)(1463), \\ (34)(1562), & (34)(1265), & (16)(2453), & (16)(2354), \\ (123)(465), & (132)(456), & (124)(365), & (142)(356), \\ (263)(145), & (154)(236), & (135)(264), & (153)(246) \end{cases} \qquad (17)$$

$$PG(f) = \begin{cases} f, & (45)f, & (56)f, & (465)f, \\ (456)f, & (46)f, & (34)f, & (345)f, \\ (34)(56)f, & (3465)f, & (3456)f, & (346)f, \\ (354)f, & (35)f, & (3564)f, & (35)(46)f, \\ (356)f, & (3546)f, & (3654)f, & (365)f, \\ (364)f, & (3645)f, & (36)f, & (36)(45)f, \\ (26)(35)f, & (26)(354)f, & (26)(345)f, & (26)(34)f, \\ (25)(45)f, & (26)f. \end{cases} \qquad (18)$$

For any bent function on V_n, its nonlinearity is

$$N_f = 2^{n-1} - 2^{\frac{n}{2}-1}. \qquad (19)$$

So on V_6, $N_f = 28$.

3.2   3-homogeneous Balanced Functions

We found two classes of balanced functions on V_6. One class contains functions with 14 terms. The other class includes functions with 15 terms. All the boolean functions in the two classes have the nonlinearity $N_f = 24$. Comparing with other balanced boolean functions, it is not lower (for bent $N_f = 28$). There exist more classes of homogeneous balanced boolean functions on the boolean space with $n > 6$. The maximum nonlinearities are 52 on V_7 (maximum for all boolean functions is 56) and 112 on V_8 (for bent function, it is 128).

(A)   A 14-term 3-homogeneous boolean function

$$f(x) = P_6^{(3)} \oplus 126 \oplus 136 \oplus 145 \oplus 234 \oplus 235 \oplus 456 \qquad (20)$$

is balanced and its complement $f_c(x)$ can be characterised by its combinatorial parameters,

$$\{\nu, \kappa, \beta, r_1, r_2, r_3, r_4, r_5, r_6\} = \{6, 3, 6, 3, 3, 3, 3, 3, 3\} \qquad (21)$$

which is also a BIBD$(v, b, k, \lambda_1, \lambda_2)$ = BIBD$(6, 6, 3, 2, 1)$. Under the permutation operations $\{(16), (23), (45)\}$, the function f does not change. Also, the set of permutations

$$\{(124635), (125634), (134625), (135624)\} \qquad (22)$$

leaves the function unchanged. The set

$$\left\{ \begin{array}{llll} e, & (16), & (23), & (45), \\ (16)(23), & (16)(45), & (23)(45), & (16)(23)(45), \\ (124635), & (125634), & (134625), & (135624), \\ (124)(356), & (125)(346), & (134)(256), & (135)(246), \\ (142)(365), & (152)(364), & (153)(264), & (143)(265), \\ (153642), & (143652), & (152643), & (142653) \end{array} \right\} \qquad (23)$$

forms a group $H(f)$. We point out that the group $H(f)$ is not isomorphic to the symmetric group S_4, since S_4 does not contain any element of order 6. The group $H(f)$ is isomorphic to the group

$$A \cap C_1 \cap C_2 \cap C_3 \cap C_4 \qquad (24)$$

where $A = Z_2 \times Z_2 \times Z_2$ is an Abelian group, and C_1, C_2, C_3, C_4 are four cyclic groups of order 6 which are generated by elements

$$(124635), (125634), (134625), (135624),$$

respectively.

The balanced function $f(x)$ can also be expressed as

$$f(x) = P_6^{(3)}(x) \oplus \bigoplus_{h=0}^{5} \pi^h(x_1 x_2 x_6) \qquad (25)$$

where π is an element of order 6 in $H(f)$. Since the order of the group is 24, we have

$$|PG(f)| = \frac{|S_6|}{24} = \frac{6!}{24} = 30, \tag{26}$$

which says that there are 30 3-homogeneous balanced functions with exactly 14 terms only.

(B) A representative of the balanced 3-homogeneous boolean functions with 15 terms

$$f(x) = P_6^{(3)}(x) \oplus x_1x_4x_6 \oplus x_1x_5x_6 \oplus x_2x_3x_5 \oplus x_2x_4x_5 \oplus x_3x_4x_5$$
$$= P_6^{(3)}(x) \oplus 146 \oplus 156 \oplus 235 \oplus 245 \oplus 345.$$

is invariant under the permutation operations $\{e, (16), (23), (16)(23)\}$. Therefore, $H(f) = \{e, (16), (23), (16)(23)\}$ and $PG(f)$ has order 180. Among all 15-term 3-homogeneous boolean functions, there are 4 functions with the same symmetry. We can see the functions

$$\begin{aligned}
f_{c1}(x) &= 146 + 156 + 235 + 245 + 345 \\
f_{c2}(x) &= 146 + 156 + 234 + 245 + 345 \\
f_{c3}(x) &= 145 + 146 + 234 + 235 + 456 \\
f_{c4}(x) &= 145 + 156 + 234 + 235 + 456
\end{aligned} \tag{27}$$

share the same symmetry under the subgroup

$$H(f) = \{e, (16), (23), (16)(23)\}.$$

The four functions also have the relations

$$f_1(x) = (45)f_2 = (12)(36)f_3(x) = (12)(36)(45)f_4(x). \tag{28}$$

The combinatorial parameters of the complementary function of the function are

$$\{\nu, \kappa, \beta, r_1, r_2, r_3, r_4, r_5, r_6\} = \{6, 3, 5, 2, 2, 2, 3, 4, 2\}. \tag{29}$$

4   Discussion

Let V_m and V_n be two boolean spaces. If $m < n$, then V_m is a subspace of V_n, $(V_m \subset V_n)$. If a function is balanced on V_m, the function is balanced on V_n. For $n \leq 5$, there is no 3-homogeneous boolean function which is either balanced or bent. The above discussion can be directly extended to the boolean spaces V_{6n} [14]. 3-homogeneous balanced boolean functions may exist in any boolean space V_n $(n > 5)$. For example,

$$\begin{aligned}
&x_1x_2x_3 \oplus x_1x_2x_4 \oplus x_1x_2x_5 \oplus x_1x_2x_6 \oplus x_1x_2x_7 \oplus x_1x_3x_4 \oplus x_1x_3x_5 \oplus \\
&x_1x_3x_6 \oplus x_1x_3x_7 \oplus x_1x_4x_5 \oplus x_1x_4x_6 \oplus x_1x_4x_7 \oplus x_1x_5x_6 \oplus x_2x_3x_4 \oplus \\
&x_2x_3x_5 \oplus x_2x_3x_6 \oplus x_2x_3x_7 \oplus x_2x_4x_5 \oplus x_2x_4x_6 \oplus x_2x_5x_7 \oplus x_2x_6x_7 \oplus \\
&x_3x_4x_7 \oplus x_3x_5x_7 \oplus x_3x_6x_7 \oplus x_4x_5x_6 \oplus x_4x_5x_7 \oplus x_4x_6x_7 \oplus x_5x_6x_7
\end{aligned}$$

is a balanced on V_7 and

$$x_1x_2x_3 \oplus x_1x_2x_4 \oplus x_1x_2x_5 \oplus x_1x_2x_6 \oplus x_1x_2x_7 \oplus x_1x_2x_8 \oplus x_1x_3x_4 \oplus$$
$$x_1x_3x_5 \oplus x_1x_3x_6 \oplus x_1x_3x_7 \oplus x_1x_3x_8 \oplus x_1x_4x_5 \oplus x_1x_4x_6 \oplus x_1x_4x_7 \oplus$$
$$x_1x_4x_8 \oplus x_1x_5x_7 \oplus x_1x_5x_8 \oplus x_1x_6x_7 \oplus x_1x_6x_8 \oplus x_2x_3x_5 \oplus x_2x_3x_6 \oplus$$
$$x_2x_3x_7 \oplus x_2x_3x_8 \oplus x_2x_4x_5 \oplus x_2x_4x_7 \oplus x_2x_6x_8 \oplus x_2x_7x_8 \oplus x_3x_4x_5 \oplus$$
$$x_3x_4x_7 \oplus x_3x_5x_6 \oplus x_3x_5x_7 \oplus x_3x_5x_8 \oplus x_3x_7x_8 \oplus x_4x_5x_8 \oplus x_4x_6x_8 \oplus$$
$$x_4x_7x_8 \oplus x_5x_6x_7 \oplus x_5x_6x_8 \oplus x_5x_7x_8 \oplus x_6x_7x_8$$

on V_8. So far, we have not found any 3-homogeneous bent functions in V_8 or V_{10}. Since the functions we discuss are homogeneous, every single term in a function has the same properties on the boolean space. Therefore, the repetitions of variables and pairs of variables directly affect the properties of the boolean function. Further study will be undertaken to try to construct boolean functions that satisfy the cryptographic desirable properties through the study of repetitions of variables and pairs.

Acknowledgement

The authors wish to thank Dr Xian-mo Zhang, Dr Chris Charnes and Mr Tianbing Xia for their helpful conversations while we were undertaking this study.

References

1. C. E. Shannon, *Communication theory of secrecy system*, Bell System Technical Journal, 28: 656-715, 1976
2. L. O'Connor, *On the distribution of characteristics in bijective mappings*, Journal of Cryptology, 8: 67-86, 1995.
3. B. Preneel, W. V. Leekwijck, L. V. Linden, R. Govaerts and J. Vandewalle, *Propagation characteristics of boolean functions*, In Advances in Cryptology – EUROCRYPT'90, Lecture Notes in Computer Science, 473, Springer-Verlag, 161-173, 1991.
4. A. F. Webster and S. E. Tavares, *On the design of S-box*, In Advances in Cryptology – CRYPTO'85, Lecture Notes in Computer Science, 219, Springer-Verlag, 523-534, 1986.
5. X. M. Zhang, Y. Zheng, H. Imai, *Differential distribution and other properties of substitution boxes*, Proceedings of JW-ISC'97, Session 1 / Block cipher, 19-29, 1997.
6. O. S. Rothaus, *On "bent" functions*, Journal of Combinatorial Theory (A), Academic Press, Inc., 20:300-305, 1976.
7. J. F. Dillon, *Elementary Hadamard difference set*, PhD Dissertation, University of Maryland, 1976.
8. Kaisa Nyberg, *Construction of bent functions and difference sets*, In Advances in Cryptology – EUROCRYPT'90, Lecture Notes in Computer Science, 473, Springer-Verlag, 151-160, 1991.
9. Josef Pieprzyk, Zhong Li, Jennifer Seberry and Xian Mo Zhang, *Fast-H: A family of fast and strong hashing algorithms*, (preprint) 1997.

10. Carlisle Adams and Stafford Tavares, *The structured design of cryptographically good S-boxes*, Journal of Cryptology, 3:27-41, 1990.

11. Willi Meier and Othmar Staffelbach, *Nonlinearity criteria for cryptographic functions*, Lecture Notes in Computer Science, EUROCRYPT'89, 549-562, 1989.

12. J. Seberry and X.M. Zhang and Y. Zheng, *Highly nonlinear 0-1 balanced functions satisfying strict avalanche criterion*, Advances in Cryptology - AUSCRYPT'92, Lecture Notes in Computer Science, 718, Springer-Verlag, 145-155, 1993.

13. Josef Pieprzyk and Chengxin Qu, *Rotation-symmetric functions and fast hashing*, Information Security and Privacy, ACISP'98, Lecture Notes in Computer Science, 1438, Springer-Verlag, 169-180, 1998.

14. Chengxin Qu, Jennifer Seberry and Josef Pieprzyk, *Homogeneous bent functions*, (preprint), 1998.

15. Alfred J. Menezes, Paul C. Van Oorschot and Scott A. Vanstone, "Handbook of Applied Cryptography", CRC Press, Boca Raton, 1996.

16. Bruce E. Sagan, "The Symmetric Group; Representations, Combinatorial Algorithms, and Symmetric Functions", Wadsworth & Books, Pacific Grove, Calif., 1991.

17. Anne Penfold Street and Deborah J. Street, "Combinatorics of Experimental Design", Oxford Science Publications, Oxford, 1987.

Publicly Verifiable Key Escrow with Limited Time Span

Kapali Viswanathan, Colin Boyd and Ed Dawson

Information Security Research Centre,
Queensland University of Technology,
Brisbane, Australia.
{viswana,boyd,dawson}@fit.qut.edu.au

Abstract. Limiting escrow activity in time has been an important requirement for key escrow systems. Recently two protocols were proposed for limited time span key escrow and contract bidding. We investigate the proposed protocols, bring out certain issues that were neglected in the proposal and amend it in a manner that these issues will be dealt with. Our proposal does not require tamper proofness for security of the system and assumes minimal trust in the trustees of the system to achieve a more robust scheme. The importance of publicly verifiable proofs is highlighted in this paper.

1 Introduction

The fundamental concept behind key escrow proposals is to protect confidentiality of the honest citizen and *revoke* it from the dishonest citizen. While many schemes can be devised to grant or revoke the confidentiality service for selected users (citizens), the judgment whether a citizen is honest or dishonest can only be reached with human involvement. This seems to be one of the weak links in any escrow system. A person in the government might be honest when the government is in control, but when another government takes over (possibly by a coup) the same person may viewed as dishonest. This is applicable for all citizens, even for government officials who might *control* the escrow system. For any escrow system to be complete it should (at least partially) counter this problem.

The main problem related to this phenomenon is decryption (using the escrow mechanism) of ciphertexts that were intercepted in the *past*. The Clipper proposal [13] suffered from this weakness. In the proposal, when the law enforcement agency (LEA) obtains a *single* court order it can decrypt past, present and future communications from/to the target without any form of *restraint*.

Limiting escrow activity in time is essential for escrow systems [9, 7]. Many proposals relied on tamper-proof hardware (or software) to accomplish this requirement. Reliance on tamper-proofness, especially in software, is difficult and will affect scalability of the implementation. Many proposals [4] relied only on certification procedures to accomplish the goal of the protocol. The discussion in this paper is on such schemes.

A similar but contrasting problem is in contract bidding schemes. In these schemes the bidder (citizen) needs protection from an organisation (government). The requirement is that the organisation must not be able to decrypt the ciphertext containing the bid *before* a certain time. This can be viewed as a *future* problem. In the threat model of this problem;

1. if *full control* to decrypt the bid is granted to the *bidder*, he/she may refrain from decrypting the bid (due to unfavourable conditions). This could result in loss for the organisation.
2. if *full control* to decrypt the bid is granted to the *organisation*, it could decrypt the bid well in advance.

In this discussion, we concentrate on the schemes proposed by Burmester *et al* [5] for a private key escrow scheme and a contract bidding scheme, both of which aimed to achieve the time limiting property without relying on tamper-proofness. A multi-party protocol [5] that required the citizen, LEA and *all* trustees to be available during the set-up phase was used. We present a modified scheme that does not require the trustees to be on-line during the registration phase and greatly improves the robustness by using publicly verifiable encryption. This approach will result in a more robust system in which trust on the trustees is minimal.

Section 2 discusses the limited time span escrow solution proposed in [5] and its drawbacks, and section 3 presents amendments to their scheme. Section 4 presents an efficient contract bidding scheme based on verifiable partial key escrow [3, 10]. Section 5 contains the conclusion of this paper.

2 Time controlled key escrow

Burmester *et al* [5] proposed a key escrow system that was claimed to limit the time span of wiretapping. The driving argument in the paper was that *the trustees could be compromised* at some point of time. It was assumed that *at least a minimum number* of the trustees will be honest in *erasing* the old share of the private key after computing the new share from the old share. We point out that the argument that the trustees could be compromised, may result in severe repercussions on the trust model of the system. The actual duties for which the trustees are trusted was not clearly mentioned in their paper. These reasons directly contribute to an attack on the system when a citizen (possibly an influential government officer) conspires with *at least a minimum number* of the trustees, to avoid escrow and still get his/her public key certified. In the l-out-of-l model that was detailed in [5], the minimum number is one.

According to their scheme, citizens can periodically update the private keys and at the same instance the trustees can simultaneously update the respective shares. Also, if at least one of the trustees erases its old share, then it will be difficult to compute the old private key from the existing shares. Only the new private key can be reconstructed. This property is achieved using a homomorphic, one-way function. Let f be an one-way function, s the private key and s_i

be the share for trustee i. When $s = \Pi s_i$, $f(s) = f(\Pi s_i) = \Pi f(s_i)$, f is said to be homomorphic. In [5] squaring in a composite modulus was used to realise f, thus $f(x) = x^2 \bmod n$, where n is a composite number whose factorisation is unknown. Proof of the Diffie-Hellman relationship, $DH(g^{s_1}, g^{s_2}) = g^{s_1 s_2}$, was used in [5] to generate proofs for correctness of the shares generated by the citizens. We use this proof in the off-line mode for our scheme. This can be achieved using the standard hashing approach to generate challenges. A brief description of the key escrow proposal by Burmester *et al.* [5] is presented in appendix A. The following section uses terminologies from the appendix.

2.1 Protocol Failures

The underlying assumption for the development of this scheme was that the trustees could be compromised at some instance of time, but the protocols for the three phases assumed complete trust in the trustees. We argue that these contradictory assumptions in the design of the system are serious flaws. Moreover, it is very difficult to place complete trust in any entity in practice. Secure systems should place minimal trust in necessary parties in a protocol and explicitly mention the assumptions on trust relationships. In this paper, we focus on the type of attacks that allow a citizen to by-pass escrow by conspiring with some of the trustees, and still *use* the system in such a way that the identity of the conspiring trustees cannot be found. There are three potential break-points in the system that could be focuses of such an attack, which are;

1. In the set-up (or registration) phase the LEA *has to unconditionally trust* the trustees to report fraud against the user when they do not receive the discrete logarithm of $\{z_i | i = 1, \cdots, l\}$, the user published in the bulletin board. An attack could allow the user to give a *wrong share* to the trustee and still get his/her public key certified. No mechanism was proposed that would allow any neutral party to detect this fault.
2. In the up-date phase there is no publicly verifiable proof that the trustee will update the shares as prescribed by the protocol. The protocol relied on an implicit trust in the trustee for this update. We note that the only trust on the trustees that was explicitly mentioned in [5] was the deletion of old shares after computing new shares.
3. In the key recovery phase there is no publicly verifiable proof that will guarantee that the trustee will use the correct value of its share $\{s_i | i = 1, \cdots, l\}$. Some of the trustees could use a wrong value of the share that will prevent legal access to the plaintext and be unidentified.

3 Fault Detectable Equitable Key Escrow System

We propose extensions to the scheme proposed by Burmester *et al* [5] that will render a system concording with the primary assumption, namely, *some trustees are compromisable but a threshold of them are assumed to be honest to erase old shares/keys after computing new shares/keys.* No other trust is placed on the trustees. We use publicly verifiable proofs so that any number of neutral entities can check the correctness of operation of the system and detect malicious parties. To achieve this, we use the verifiable encryption scheme proposed by Asokan *et al.* [1]. Due to this mechanism our scheme does not require the existence of secure channels between citizens and trustees as in [5]. This property improves the robustness of the escrow system. Since our proposal is an extension of the scheme proposed by Burmester *et al* [5], our scheme inherits all its security properties.

3.1 Background

In this section the protocols used for publicly verifiable encryption and proof of equality of discrete logarithm will be explained. The protocols will be specified as functions so as to improve clarity in subsequent sections.

1. Publicly Verifiable Encryption: Using publicly verifiable encryption Alice can send a message m encrypted under Bob's public key y_b as C and at the same time prove to a third party Carol that the message encrypted in C is the pre-image of $\mathcal{O}(m)$ without revealing m, where $\mathcal{O}$ is a one-way function. We adopt the verifiable encryption scheme proposed by Asokan *et al* [1]. The merit of this scheme is that the encryption technique is essentially independent of the proof mechanism, which is not the case in the scheme proposed by Stadler to achieve publicly verifiable secret sharing [12]. It is worth noting that the scheme in [1] can be used in [12] to achieve a more generic mechanism for publicly verifiable secret sharing. We present an off-line version of the verifiable encryption scheme in the form of functions, to improve clarity of discussion. The reader is refered to [1] for a complete discussion on this scheme. A brief description and pseudocodes for the functions for the off-line verfiable encryption scheme are presented in appendix B. Subsequent discussions will heavily borrow the terminologies presented in appendix B.

2. Proof of Equality of Discrete Logarithm: Let p be a large prime. When $y = g^x \bmod p$ and $z = m^x \bmod p$, proof of equality of discrete logarithms allows the prover to prove that $\log_g y = \log_m z \bmod p$ without revealing x. There are interactive, zero-knowledge and non-interactive protocols to achieve this proof. We will use a non-interactive version [6] to improve on communication overheads. The function definitions for the generation and verification such proofs are presented in appendix C. Subsequent discussions will borrow terminologies from appendix C.

3.2 System Settings

System settings are essentially similar to that proposed in [5] except for certain additions to the existing parameters. The LEA is trusted to execute the prescribed protocols faithfully. The LEA sets up a public key infrastructure that can be used only for securely communicating with the trustees. The public keys $\{y_i | i = 1, \cdots, l\}$ (corresponding to the private keys $\{x_i | i = 1, \cdots, l\}$) are certified and registered in a public directory. At least a minimum number of the trustees are trusted to change their public-private key pair periodically, publish the new public key and erase the previous private key. This is essential to avoid decryption of the encrypted shares sent to the trustees using their public keys at an arbitrary point of time.

3.3 Set-up Phase

Citizen j generates a large prime number p_j such that $p_j = 2p_{j1}p_{j2}+1$, where p_{j1} and p_{j2} are large primes. Also, $p_{j1} \equiv p_{j2} \equiv 3 \bmod 4$, so that -1 is a quadratic non-residue in the fields $\mathcal{Z}_{p_{j1}}$ and $\mathcal{Z}_{p_{j2}}$. Let $n_j = p_{j1}p_{j2}$. The citizen then chooses $g_j \in \mathcal{Z}_{p_j}$ that is a generator of $\mathcal{Z}_{p_j}$ and its private key $x_j \in_R \mathcal{Z}_{n_j}$. He/she then computes the public key as $y_j = g_j^{x_j}$ mod p_j. The public data will be $\{g_j, y_j, p_j\}$. The private data will be $\{x_j, p_{j1}, p_{j2}\}$. The citizen and the LEA engage in a protocol that has the following steps;

1. Citizen: Computes the shares for the trustees as $x_j = \Pi_{i=1}^l s_i \pmod{p_j - 1}$ and performs verifiable encryption of the shares as, {VerEnc with input (s_i, g, p, y_i) and output$(c_i, D_i, P_{1_i}, \cdots, P_{80_i}) | i = 1, \cdots, l$}. Sends $\{c_i, D_i, P_{1_i}, \cdots, P_{80_i} | i = 1, \cdots, l\}$ to the LEA.
2. LEA: Checks the proofs of verifiable encryption as {CheckVerEnc with input $(c_i, p, g, D_i, P_{1_i}, \cdots, P_{80_i})$ and output$(check_i) | i = 1, \cdots, l$}. If any of the $check_i$ is $FAIL$ then signals error message to the citizen and terminates the protocol.
3. Citizen: Sends $z_{1,\ldots,i} = g^{s_1,\cdots,s_i}$ and the proofs of $z_{1,\ldots,i} = DH(z_{1,\ldots,i-1}, D_i)$ for $i = 2, \cdots, l$ to the LEA.
4. LEA: If proofs for all the Diffie-Hellman relationships are correctly verified, certifies $y_j = z_{1,\ldots,l}$ as the citizen's public key in the system. Forwards the verifiable encryption $\{c_i, D_i, P_{1_i}, \cdots, P_{80_i}\}$ to trustee i, who can decrypt it with the knowledge of x_i as DecryptVerEnc with inputs $(x_i, c_i, P_{1_i}, \cdots, P_{80_i})$ and output(s_i), which is the share of the citizen's secret key. The LEA stores the value of D_i against trustee i's identity along with citizen j's identity.

In the above protocol the LEA need not trust any other entity to check the correctness of the proofs. Moreover, any other neutral entity can verify the correctness of this protocol due to the presence of publicly verifiable proofs.

3.4 Update Protocol

1. Citizen: Computes $x_{j_{new}} = x_j^2 \pmod{p_j - 1}$, computes $y_{j_{new}} = h_j^{x_{j_{new}}}$ mod p_j and proves the relationship $y_{j_{new}} = DH(y_j, y_j)$ to the LEA.
2. LEA: Temporarily stores $y_{j_{new}}$ in local directory along with the citizen's identity.

3. Trustees: Compute $\{s_{i_{new}} = s_i^2 \pmod{p_j - 1} | i = 1, \cdots, l\}$, compute $\{D_{i_{new}} = g_j^{s_{i_{new}}} \bmod p_j | i = 1, \cdots, l\}$ and prove the relationship $\{D_{i_{new}} = DH(D_i, D_i) | i = 1, \cdots, l\}$ to the LEA.

4. LEA: Certifies the new public key of the citizen, replaces the old value of the public key with the new value in the public directory of the citizen, and updates the local directory by replacing the value of D_i with the value of $D_{i_{new}}$.

5. Trustees: Delete and *forget* the old shares.

The modified update protocol enforces the correct and synchronised update of shares when public key is updated. It is noted that this enforcement was absent in [5]. Note that the trustees have to be trusted to perform step 5 correctly, as there are no known techniques that provide such guarantees.

3.5 Key Recovery Phase

The LEA intercepts the ciphertext pair $(A, B) = (g_j^k, My_j^k)$ sent to citizen j, obtains a court order to wiretap the citizen's communication and presents A along with the court order to the LEA. The LEA then engages in a protocol detailed in appendix A.4 with the trustees. If message decryption fails after this protocol, then each trustee proves that it used the correct value of its share using the proof for equality of discrete logarithms described in appendix C. The proof basically proves that $\log_{g_j} D_i = \log_{E_{i-1}} E_i \bmod p_j$, which is to prove that the trustees have used the discrete logarithm of D_i (the share s_i) to compute E_i from E_{i-1}. The LEA and the trustees engage in the following protocol;

1. LEA: Sends A to trustee 1.
2. Trustees: Computes $\{E_i = E_{i-1}^{s_i} \bmod p_j | i = 1, \cdots, l\}$, where $E_0 = A$, and compute proof of equality of discrete log as $\{$LogEq with input $(s_i, g_j, E_{i-1}, D_i, E_i, p_j)$ and output $(d_i, e_i) | i = 1, \cdots, l\}$. Sends $\{E_i, d_i, e_i\}$ to the LEA.
3. LEA: Computes $\{$CheckLogEq with input $(d_i, e_i, g_j, E_{i-1}, D_i, E_i, p_j)$ with output $(check_i) | i = 1, \cdots, l\}$. If $check_i$ is $FAIL$ register fraud against trustee i.
4. LEA: Computes $M = B/E_i \bmod p_j$.

This protocol guarantees message recovery or identification of malfunctioning trustee which ever the case may be.

3.6 Security Analysis

The security of our protocol relies on the security of publicly verifiable encryption [1] and equitable key escrow with limited time span [5].

Proposition 1: Nobody except the corresponding trustee can obtain information about the private key of the user from the verifiably encrypted ciphertexts if the verifiable encryption of Asokan *et al* [1] is secure.

Proposition 2: No citizen can obtain a valid certificate without legal escrow of the private key, even by colluding with a minimum number of trustees.

In order to avoid key escrow and at the same time obtain a valid certificate, the citizen must be able to perform any one of the following:

1. Generate wrong proof that will pass the verification procedure of verifiable encryption, so that a wrong pre-image of the commitment (g^{s_i}) for the encryption can be sent to the authorities. Since the verifiable encryption technique in [1] is assumed to be secure, this will not possible.
2. Generate wrong proof that will pass the verification procedure to prove Diffie-Hellman relationship [5], so that wrong value of shares can be encrypted for the escrow agent. Since the proof in [5] is assumed to be secure, this will not be possible.

Proposition 3: No trustee can use wrong value of the share during key recovery phase and be unidentified, due to publicly verifiable proof of knowledge.

If the trustee uses a different value in the key recovery phase, it must be able to generate wrong proofs for the proof of equality of discrete logarithms to avoid identification. Since the proof of equality of discrete logarithm is assumed to be secure, malicious trustees cannot remain unidentified.

3.7 Computational Requirements

The robustness of our protocol is a result of extra computations. The inclusion of publicly verifiable encryption in the set-up phase is the major source of the computational overhead. Since the set-up protocol is performed only once per user, it is not considerable when the robustness of the protocol is taken into account. The computational requirement for the publicly verifiable encryption is;

Prover: The major computations that the prover has to perform are $2N+1$ hash computations and N exponentiations, where N is the security parameter of the protocol, which is 80 in our protocol. Asokan *et al* [1] suggest that each party can do this using under 2000 modular multiplications.

Verifier: The verifier has to perform $2N + x + 1$ hash computations and N exponentiations, where x is the number of 1's in the challenge c.

The extra computational overhead in the update phase in our scheme as compared to [5], is due to the DH relationship proof that has to be performed once by each trustee and l times by the LEA. In the key recovery phase, if message recovery is successful then computational overhead will be zero.

4 Time controlled auction bidding

We classify contract bidding systems, along with key escrow and electronic voting systems, in the class of systems called compliant (or democratic) systems. These systems, apart from other important properties, have a very delicate trust model and distributed control over data. Entities do not necessarily trust each other or possess complete control over important data, such as information about some plaintext, session key, identity etc,. Shared control over data is a characteristic property of such systems.

In a contract system a bidder wishes to submit and commit to a confidential information known as the bid. Only the bidder can know any information about the bid until a certain time after which the bid must be opened, or publicly known. A simple solution would be to encrypt the bid under the public key of a trusted third party, who will decrypt the bid only after a certain time. But, as stated in the previous section, in practice it is extremely difficult to realise such a trusted party. Another approach would be to *distribute* the capability to open the bid among many entities, of which the bidder could be one. The system can be designed such that decryption of the bid will be trivial when the bidder participates in the bid opening protocol. Also, decryption will be non-trivial but bound in finite time when the bidder does not participate in the bid opening protocol. This finite time can be tuned so that the bid can be decrypted only after the bid opening time.

The scheme proposed in [5] employs double encryption to realise the distributed control to decrypt the bid. It was claimed that the concept of weak encryption was used for this purpose. Two ElGamal cryptosystems are chosen with public keys as $\{g_1, y_1 (= g_1^{x_1} \bmod n)\}$ and $\{g_2, y_2 (= g_2^{x_2} \bmod n)\}$ such that the first cryptosystem provides strong encryption and the second provides weak encryption that could be cryptanalysed using brute force techniques. The bidder verifiably escrows the private key x_1 corresponding to the public key y_1 so that shareholders have its shares and proves that the second cryptosystem is indeed weak. The bidder encrypts the bid m as $(g_1^{r_1}, g_2^{r_2}, m y_1^{r_1} y_2^{r_2})$ with r_1 and r_2 chosen at random from $\mathcal{Z}_n^*$. At the time of opening the tender the bidder reveals x_1 and x_2 to the organisation so as to decrypt the bid. If the bidder does not reveal x_1 and x_2, the organisation obtains x_1 from the shareholders and decrypts the outer encryption to obtain $(g_2^{r_2}, m y_2^{r_2})$. The organisation then has to decrypt this ciphertext using brute force.

4.1 An alternative scheme

We outline an alternative scheme that can use verifiable partial key escrow [3] or publicly verifiable partial key escrow [10] to realise the distributed control to decrypt the bid. The use of escrow technology makes this scheme more streamlined with our paper. The main goal of partial key escrow is;

1. Avoid full escrow of the private key. This considerably reduces trust on the escrow agents.
2. Avoid mass wiretapping.
3. Avoid brute force attack on the unescrowed portion of the private key without the help of the escrow agents. That is to avoid "early key recovery."

Our system consists of the organisation that accepts the bid, the bidder and the shareholders who act as escrow agents. The organisation chooses large primes

p and q such that $p - 1 = 2q$ so that $\mathcal{Z}_p^*$ is a prime order multiplicative group. Henceforth all operation will be modulo p arithmetic unless stated otherwise. The shareholders select two generators $g \in \mathcal{Z}_q$ and $h \in \mathcal{Z}_q^*$ such that $\log_g(h)$ is unknown. This condition is essential for security of the commitment schemes [11, 3]. The committer can commit to $z \in \mathcal{Z}_q$ as $Z = g^z h^v$ for $v \in_R \mathcal{Z}_q$. This is possible because the pair (z, v) is unique for a fixed Z. A suitable threshold cryptosystem is set-up for the shareholders. The bidder registers in the system using the registration procedure, which is;

1. Chooses a private key $s \in_R \mathcal{Z}_q$ such that $s = x + a \bmod q$, where x is a large number and a is a number that has pre-defined bit length l. The value of a is chosen such that it is recovered in 2^l steps. The corresponding public key will be $P = g^s = g^x g^a$.
2. Generates the commitments for x as $X = g^x h^u$ and a bit-by-bit committment for a as $\{A_i = g^{a_i} h^{u_i} | i = 0, \cdots, 2l - 1\}$, where $u, u_0, \cdots, u_{2l-1} \in_R \mathcal{Z}_q$ and a_i is the ith bit of a. The commitments $(X, \{A_i | i = 0, \cdots, 2l - 1\})$ are sent to the shareholders and the organisation.
3. The bidder proves that the commitments define the key. This is done by computing $w = u + \Sigma_{i=0}^{2l-1} u_i 2^i \bmod q$. The value of w is sent to the shareholders and the organisation. This proof can be checked as $Ph^w = X \Pi_{i=0}^{2l-1} A_i^{2^i}$.
4. The bidder proves that the value of a is indeed small by employing the publicly verifiable proof proposed by Mao [10].
5. The bidder escrows the large component x of the private key using any of the verifiable secret sharing schemes.

When all the steps in the registration phase are performed, the bidder encrypts the bid m as $(A, B) = (g^k, mP^k)$. The bidder sends (A, B) to the organisation and proves the correctness of the encryption by employing the verifiable encryption technique detailed in section 3.1.

At the time when the bid is to be opened the bidder reveals the private key s corresponding to the public key P to organisation so that it can decrypt the bid. If the bidder does not reveal the private key, the organisation approaches the shareholders to obtain x. Then it computes $g^a = P/g^x$ and the discrete logarithm of g^a by using appropriate methods (such as Shanks baby-step giant-step [8]) for computing discrete logarithms.

5 Conclusion

We have described certain design flaws in the protocol construction for equitable key escrow for limited time span proposed by Burmester, Desmedt and Seberry [5] that resulted in a type of attack in which the user can avoid escrow by colluding with a minimum number of trustees. We have proposed improvements to the protocol by employing publicly verifiable proof techniques. We also pointed out that such proofs will greatly help in considerably reducing the trust that has to be placed on the trustees. We also presented a design perspective for a contract bidding scheme that uses verifiable partial key escrow and publicly verifiable proof techniques (again to reduce the amount of trust placed on the trustees). Our bidding scheme is a better alternative to the one proposed in [5], as a clearer trust requirements can be specified using publicly verifiable proof techniques.

References

1. N. Asokan, Victor Shoup, and Michael Waidner. Optimistic fair exchange of digital signatures. In *Advances in Cryptology - EUROCRYPT'98*, pages 591–606, 1998.
2. M. Bellare and P. Rogaway. Optimal asymmetric encryption. In *Advances of Cryptology - CRYPTO'94*, pages 92–111, 1994.
3. Mihir Bellare and Shafi Goldwasser. Verifiable partial key escrow. In *Proceedings of the Fourth Annual Conference on Computer and Communications Security, ACM*, 1996.
4. Colin Boyd. Enforcing traceability in software. In *Information and Communication Security - First International Conference, ICICS'97*, pages 398–408. Springer, 1997.
5. Mike Burmester, Yvo Desmedt, and Jennifer Seberry. Equitable key escrow with limited time span. In *Advances in Cryptology - ASIACRYPT'98*, Lecture Notes in Computer Science, pages 380 – 391. Springer-Verlag, 1998.
6. Aymeric de Solages and Jacques Traoré. An efficient fair off-line electronic cash system with extensions to checks and wallets with observers. In *Financial Cryptography '98*, pages 1 – 15, 1998.
7. Jingmin He and Ed Dawson. A new key escrow cryptosystem. In Josef Pieprzyk and Jennifer Seberry, editors, *Information Security and Privacy, ACISP'96*, Lecture Notes in Computer Science, pages 105–114. Springer-Verlag, 1996.
8. D. E. Knuth. *The Art of Computer Programming - Sorting and Searching*, volume 3. Addison-Wesley, Massachusetts, 1973.
9. Arjen K. Lenstra, Peter Winkler, and Yacov Yacobi. A key escrow system with warrant bounds. In *Advances in Cryptology - CRYPTO95*, Lecture Notes in Computer Science, pages 197 – 207, 1995.
10. Wenbo Mao. Publicly verifiable partial key escrow. In Yongfei Han, Tatsuaki Okamoto, and Sihang Qing, editors, *Information and Communications Security*, Lecture Notes in Computer Science, pages 409 – 413. Springer-Verlag, 1997.
11. T. Pedersen. Non-interactive and information theoretic secure verifiable secret sharing. In J. Feigenbaum, editor, *Advances in Cryptology - CRYPTO'91*, Lecture Notes in Computer Science. Springer-Verlag, 1991.
12. Markus Stadler. Publicly verifiable secret sharing. In Ueli Maurer, editor, *Advances in Cryptology - EUROCRYPT'96*, Lecture Notes in Computer Science, pages 190 – 199. Springer-Verlag, 1996.
13. U.S. DEPARTMENT OF COMMERCE / National Institute of Standards and Technology. *Federal Information Processing Standard 185—Escrowed Encryption Standard*, February 1994.

Appendix

A Key Escrow with Limited Time Span

The proposal by Burmester *et al.* is briefly outlined here. For a more complete discussion, we refer to [5].

A.1   System Settings

The user generates a large prime p such that $p - 1$ has two large prime factors p_1 and p_2, such that $p_1 \equiv p_2 \equiv 3 \bmod 4$, so that -1 is a quadratic non-residue in the fields $\mathcal{Z}_{p_1}$ and $\mathcal{Z}_{p_2}$. The user then publishes p and $g \in \mathcal{Z}_p$, such that the order of the element g is $p_1 p_2$.

A.2   Set-up Phase

The user chooses a secure private key $a \in_R \mathcal{Z}^*_{p-1}$ and computes l shares $\{s_i | i = 1, \cdots, l\}$ of a, such that $\Pi s_i = a \pmod{p - 1}$. The user then computes the public key $y_a = g^a \pmod{p}$. The user publishes y_a along with p and g. He/she then engages in a *multi-party* protocol with the law enforcement agency (LEA) and the l trustees in order to obtain a certificate. The multi-party protocol essentially consists of the following steps;

1. The user securely communicates the respective shares to the corresponding trustees and publishes $z_i = g^{s_i}$ for $i = 1, \cdots, l$ in a bulletin board.
2. Each trustee checks if it has received the discrete logarithm of the respective z_i published in the bulletin board. If not the trustee registers a fraud message against the user with the LEA.
3. The user sends $z_{1,2,\cdots,k} = g^{s_1 \cdots s_k}$ for $k = 2, \cdots, l$ to the LEA along with the proofs for $z_{1,2,\cdots,k} = DH(z_{1,2,\cdots,k-1}, z_k)$ for $k = 2, \cdots, l$. It could be noted $z_{1,2,\cdots,l} = y_a$.
4. If no fraud was registered against the user by any of the trustees, the LEA checks the proofs for $z_{1,2,\cdots,k}$ for $k = 2, \cdots, l$ by reading the individual values of z_k from the bulletin board.
5. If the LEA checks the proofs successfully, then it certifies $y_a = z_{1,2,\cdots,l}$ as the users public key in the system.

A.3   Update Phase

The homomorphic property of the squaring operator on the private key is used in this phase. The use r computes the new private key as $a_{new} = a^2$ and trustee i updates the ith share as $s_{i_{new}} = s_i^2$. After computing the new share, at least a threshold of the trustees are it trusted to *erase and forget* the old shares. The user then proves to the LEA that $y_{a_{new}} = g^{a_{new}}$ is the Diffie-Hellman of the old public key y_a, that is $y_{a_{new}} = DH(y_a, y_a)$, to obtain a certificate for the new public key.

A.4   Key Recovery Phase

The users are expected to use the ElGamal cryptosystem to securely communicate using certified public keys. The ciphertext in this system will then be of the form $(g^k, M y_a^k) = (A, B)$ for the public key (y_a, g, p). When the LEA obtains a court order to wire-tap the communication of a user, it intercepts the ciphertexts sent to the user. The ciphertext component A along with the court order are sent to the trustees. The trustees then engage in a multi-party protocol to compute y_a^k from A using their respective shares by computing $C = A^{\prod_{j=1}^l a_i}$, where a_i is the share held by the trustees at that time. When the LEA is given C it can compute the message as, $M = B/C$.

B Function Definitions for Verifiable Encryption

The pseudocode of functions that can be used for verifiable encrption are presented here. These functions can be used to realise an off-line version of the verifiable encryption proposal in [1].

B.1 System Settings

Let $C = \text{Enc}(t, s_1, y)$ be a public key encryption function that encrypts the message s_1 of length k_s under the public key y using the random string t of length k_t bits and $s_1 = \text{Dec}(C, x)$ be the public key decryption function that decrypts the ciphertext C using the private key x corresponding the public key y. The OAE encryption function of Bellare and Rogaway [2], which is based on the RSA problem, is recommended. The one way function is realised by modular exponentiation as $\mathcal{O}(m) = g^m \bmod p$, where $g \in \mathcal{Z}_p^*$ is a generator. A set of hash functions are chosen such that $\mathcal{H}_1 : \{0,1\}^{160} \to \{0,1\}^{k_s+k_t}$, $\mathcal{H}_2 : \{0,1\}^* \to \{0,1\}^{160}$, $\mathcal{H}_3 : \{0,1\}^* \to \{0,1\}^{160}$ and $\mathcal{H}_4 : \{0,1\}^* \to \{0,1\}^{80}$. To verifiably encrypt a message $s_1 \in \mathcal{Z}_p^*$ under the public key y, *the sender / prover* use the functions in the following sub-sections.

B.2 Function VerEnc

1. Select random number r and compute the hash of the value as (t, s_2), which are the higher and lower order bits of the result, respectively. Use t as the randomiser to encrypt s_2 under the public key y. Compute the commitment to the encrypted message as g^{s_2}, where $g \in \mathcal{Z}_p^*$ is the generator of the multiplicative group. Compute the hash value of the ciphertexts and the commitments as h.

2. In a challenge-response mode h is sent to the verifier who chooses a challenge $c \in \{0,1\}$. In our applications we make use of the standard hashing approach to realise an off-line version of the protocol. The user generates many hash values $\{h_j | j = 1, \cdots, n\}$, where n is the security parameter which is 80 in our case. The prover then computes the hash value of all h_j to obtain the challenge c. The prover then uses the bits of c as the challenge.

3. If the jth bit of the challenge c is 0, the prover *opens* the encryption and does not send message information. If the bit is 1 the prover *does not* open the encryption but sends message information that can be decrypted using the private key corresponding to the public key used for encryption.

The algorithm can be described by the function VerEnc as follows:

Function VerEnc with input (s_1, g, p, y)
and output $(c, D, P_1, \cdots, P_{80})$ is
        Compute $D = g^{s_1} \bmod p$;
        For each $j = 1, \cdots, 80$ do
                Select at random: $r_j \in \{0,1\}^{160}$;
                Compute: $(t_j, s_{2_j}) = \mathcal{H}_1(r)$;
                Encrypt : $(A_j, B_j) = (\mathrm{Enc}(t_j, s_{2_j}, y), g^{s_{2_j}} \bmod p)$;
                Compute: $h_j = \mathcal{H}_2(A_j, B_j)$;
      done;
        Compute: $c = \mathcal{H}_4(h_1, \cdots, h_{80})$;
        For each $j = 1, \cdots, 80$ do
                If c_j is 0 then
                /* c_j is the jth bit of c*/
                        Assign: $P_j \leftarrow \{r\}$;
                Else
                        Compute: $s_{3_j} = s_1 + s_{2_j} \bmod p$;
                        Assign: $P_j \leftarrow \{A_j, s_{3_j}\}$;
                EndIf;
      done;
End Function VerEnc;

B.3   Function CheckVerEnc

1. *The verifier* recomputes the hash value h_j in two different ways. If j^{th} bit of c is 0, the encryption can be recomputed with the value of r and hence the value of h_j. If the bit is 1 the verifier recomputes the hash value h_j using the ciphertext and the commitment.

2. *The verifier* then checks if the challenge was generated properly by recomputing the value of c from the values of h_j. If the verifier is able to check this correctly then the proof is accepted.

The algorithm can be described by the function CheckVerEnc as follows:

Function CheckVerEnc with input $(c, p, g, D, P_1, \cdots, P_{80})$
and output $(check)$ is
        For each $j = 1, \cdots, 80$ do
                If c_j is 0 then
                      Assign: $\{r_j\} \leftarrow P_j$;
                      Compute: $(t_j, s_{2_j}) = \mathcal{H}_1(r_j)$;
                      Encrypt : $(A_j, B_j) = (\mathrm{Enc}(t_j, s_{2_j}, y), g^{s_{2_j}} \bmod p)$;
                      Compute: $h_j = \mathcal{H}_2(A_j, B_j)$;
                Else
                      Assign: $\{A_j, s_{3_j}\} \leftarrow P_j$;
                      Compute: $h_j = \mathcal{H}_2(A_j, g^{s_{3_j}}/D)$;
                EndIf;
      done;
        If $c \stackrel{?}{=} \mathcal{H}_4(h_1, \cdots, h_{80})$ then

Assign: $check \leftarrow PASS$;
        Else
                Assign: $check \leftarrow FAIL$;
        EndIf;
End Function CheckVerEnc;

B.4   Function DecryptVerEnc

1. *The receiver* locates the ciphertext with message information by locating the bit position in the challenge c that has a value 1. Note that during decryption j has to be selected at random in order to avoid fraud.
2. *The receiver* can then decrypt the ciphertext using its private key to obtain the message.

The algorithm can be described by the function DecryptVerEnc as follows:

Function DecryptVerEnc with input $(x, c, P_1, \cdots, P_{80})$
and output (s_1) is
        Forever do
                Select at random: $j \in \{1, \cdots, 80\}$
                if c_j is 1 then
                        Assign: $\{A, s_3\} \leftarrow P_j$;
                        Break For loop;
                EndIf;
        done;
        Decrypt: $s_2 = Dec(x, A)$;
        Compute: $s_1 = s_3 - s_2 \bmod p$;
End Function DecryptVerEnc;

C   Function Definitions for Proof of Equality of Discrete Logarithms

The pseudocode to achieve an off-line version for the generation and verification of proofs for equality of discrete logarithms is present in this section. Also, this proof can easily be extended to realise proof for knowledge of discrete logarithm.

C.1   System Settings

Let p be a large prime such that computing discrete logarithms in $\mathcal{Z}_p^*$ is difficult. Let $\mathcal{H}_5 : \{0,1\}^* \rightarrow \{0,1\}^n$ be a cryptographically secure has function with n as the security parameter.

Generation of the Proof: In the following pseudocode note that construction of a valid proof without the knowledge of $\log_g y = \log_m z = x$ is difficult. The algorithm can be described by the function LogEq as follows:

Function LogEq with input (x, g, m, y, z, p)
and output (d, e) is:

        Select at random: $r \in_R \mathcal{Z}_p$;

        Calculate: $d = \mathcal{H}_5(g||m||y||z||g^r||m^r)$;

        Calculate: $e = r - dx \pmod{p-1}$;

End Function LogEq;

Verification of the Proof: The verifier checks the proof using the same hash function with public inputs. The algorithm can be described by the function CheckLogEq as follows:

Function CheckLogEq with input (d, e, g, m, y, z, p)
and output $(check)$ is:

        If $d \overset{?}{=} \mathcal{H}_5(g||m||y||z||g^e y^d||m^e z^d)$ then

          $check \leftarrow PASS$;

        Else

          $check \leftarrow FAIL$;

        EndIf;

End Function CheckLogEq;

Accelerating Key Establishment Protocols for Mobile Communication

Seungwon Lee[1], Seong-Min Hong[2], Hyunsoo Yoon[2], and Yookun Cho[1]

[1] Department of Computer Engineering, Seoul National University(SNU), San 56-1 Shilim-Dong Kwanak-Ku, Seoul, 151-742, KOREA, {leesw,cho}@ssrnet.snu.ac.kr
[2] Department of Computer Science, Korea Advanced Institute of Science and Technology(KAIST), 373-1, Kusong-dong, Yusong-gu, Taejon 305-701, KOREA, {smhong,hyoon}@camars.kaist.ac.kr

Abstract. Mobile communication is more vulnerable to security attacks such as interception and unauthorized access than fixed network communication. To overcome these problems, many protocols have been proposed to provide a secure channel between a mobile station and a base station. However, the public-key based protocols are not fully utilized due to the poor computing power and the small battery capacity of a mobile station.

In this paper, we propose some techniques accelerating public-key based key establishment protocols between a mobile station and a base station. The proposed techniques enable a mobile station to borrow computing power from a base station without revealing its secret information. The proposed schemes accelerate the previous protocols up to five times and reduce the amount of power consumption of a mobile station.

The proposed schemes use SASC (Server-Aided Secret Computation) protocols that are used for smart cards. Our insight is that the unbalanced property in computing power of the mobile communication is similar to that of the smart card system. The acceleration degrees of the proposed schemes are quite different from one another according to the used SASC protocols. In this paper, we analyze the acceleration factors of the proposed schemes and compare them with one another. The analysis shows that one of the approach presents outstanding performance among them.

1 Introduction

Networks of the future will allow and prompt universal access, and mobile communication will make users be able to communicate with others anywhere. However, mobile communication is more vulnerable to security attacks such as interception and unauthorized access than fixed network communication. Therefore, it is vital to make a secure channel between a base station and a mobile station [4, 15].

To make a secure channel, it is required to maintain the confidentiality of a message and provide the mutual authentication between a base station and a mobile station. Many protocols have been proposed to satisfy the above requirements [30, 22, 17, 18, 34, 36, 4, 1, 11, 19]. These protocols are divided into two groups. One group uses public-key cryptosystems and the other group uses secret-key cryptosystems. The mobile communication standards (e.g. GSM [1], DECT [11]) adopt the secret-key based protocols because secret-key cryptosystems are much faster than public-key cryptosystems.

However, the key management of the secret-key based protocol is more complicated and more dangerous than that of the public-key based one. Each mobile station in the secret-key based protocols must keep its secret information, which of all should be stored in AC (Authentication Center). AC becomes the critical component in the system because it should participates in all key establishment protocol executions. Consequently, the communication overhead of AC is increased and one must replicate the AC to reduce the overhead. However, the replication of AC increases the risk of the system. On the other hand, the public-key based protocols only need CA (Certificate Authority) which certifies the public-keys of mobile stations and base stations. CA is less critical than AC because CA only certifies public-keys, whereas AC should manage all secret informations. Furthermore, if there are no more keys to be certified then the CA may even be closed. In addition, only with public-key cryptosystems, we can implement non-repudiation services and easily achieve anonymity.

In spite of the advantages of a public-key cryptosystem, it is not fully utilized because of the poor computing power and the small battery capacity of a mobile station. Consequently, many previous researches for key establishment protocols (i.e., mutual authentication and key agreement protocols) focus on minimizing computational overhead of a mobile station without loss of security.

Beller, Chang, and Yacobi proposed a scheme using both public-key cryptosystems and secret-key cryptosystems for the key establishment protocol[1] [17]. They used MSR (Modular Square Root) algorithm [24] to reduce the computational overhead of a mobile station, and also used Diffie-Hellman key exchange protocol [35] to establish a session key. Carlsen showed that this protocol is vulnerable to a replay attack and immunized it [34]. Mu and Varadharajan showed an attack using the structure of the certificate and proposed the corresponding countermeasure for the attack. But, Beller et. al. seemed to considered the risk in their original proposal. Beller and Yacobi proposed a protocol using ElGamal algorithm [31] in [18]. The protocol reduces the response time of a mobile station by using ElGamal's precomputable property. Boyd and Mathuria showed that the protocol is vulnerable to a man-in-the-middle attack and immunized it [4]. Aziz and Diffie proposed a protocol providing good forward secrecy [2]. Boyd and Mathuria showed that this protocol is also vulnerable to a man-in-the-middle attack and immunized it [4]. We describe these protocols in detail in

---

[1] Tatebayashi, Matsuzaki, and Newman proposed the first key establishment protocol using public-key cryptosystem [30]. After that, Park, Kurosawa, Okamoto, and Tsujii showed that the protocol is not secure and proposed a new key establishment protocol [22]. However, these protocols are End-to-End protocol for providing secure communication channel between mobile stations, and this paper focuses on the link security between a mobile station and a base station.

Section 2.1. Recently, Park proposed another scheme [21] based on Yacobi and Shmuley's general key exchange scheme [37]. However, Martin and Mitchell [16] found an attack and Boyd and Park showed another attack [5].

Although many protocols try to reduce the computational overhead of mobile station, all of them require hundreds of modular multiplications[2]. Consequently, they are not fully utilized because mobile station has a poor computing power and a small battery capacity [17, 4].

In this paper, we propose some techniques accelerating the previous key establishment protocols between a mobile station and a base station. The proposed techniques enable a mobile station to borrow the computing power of a base station to reduce the computational overhead of a mobile station. The proposed techniques accelerate the previous key establishment protocols up to five times and reduce the amount of power consumption of a mobile station.

The proposed techniques use SASC (server-aided secret computation) protocols [23, 12]. SASC protocols enable a smart card to use the computing power of a server (e.g. a card reader or ATM). Our insight is that the relationship between a smart card and a server is similar to that between a mobile station and a base station in mobile communication. The acceleration degrees of the proposed schemes are quite different from one another according to the used SASC protocols. In this paper, we analyze the acceleration factors of the proposed schemes and compare them with one anothers. The analysis shows that one of the approach shows outstanding performance among them.

This paper is organized as follows: Section 2 explains previous key establishment protocols and the existing SASC protocols. Section 3 describes the techniques that accelerate key establishment protocols. We compare the accelerated protocols and the original protocols in Section 4 and conclude in Section 5.

2 Backgrounds

2.1 Key establishment protocols in mobile communication

MSR+DH protocol [34] Beller et al. proposed a key establishment protocol that uses MSR and Diffie-Hellman scheme (from now on, we call it MSR+DH). Afterwards, Carlsen pointed out that the protocol is vulnerable to a message replay attack and improved it using a challenge-response technique [34]. The simplified description for the improved version of MSR+DH protocol is as follows.

1. $B \rightarrow M : B, N_B, PK_B, Cert(B)$
2. $M \rightarrow B : \{x\}_{PK_B}, \{N_B, M, PK_M, Cert(M)\}_x$

---

[2] Beller and Yacobi's scheme reduces the delay through precomputations. However, as the scheme executes the precomputations everytime and it does not reduce the computational overhead itself. We analyze it in detail in Section 4.

B stands for a base station and M is a mobile station in the above description. The arrow shows a message delivery and PK is a public-key. $\{X\}_K$ means that X is encrypted with a key K. A base station sends its public-key with the certificate to a mobile station in step 1. And then, the mobile station verifies the public-key of the base station and encrypts the nonce (N_B) and its public key (PK_M) with the session key (x). The mobile station sends the encrypted message to the base station. After that, both mobile station and base station compute a shared session key using Diffie-Hellman key exchange scheme.

Beller and Yacobi's protocol Beller and Yacobi designed a protocol that uses ElGamal algorithm (from now on, we call it BY), and afterwards, Boyd and Mathuria showed that this protocol is vulnerable to a man-in-the-middle attack and improved it [4]. The abstract description of the improved version of BY protocol is as follows.

1. $B \rightarrow M : B, N_B, PK_B, Cert(B)$
2. $M \rightarrow B : \{x\}_{PK_B}, \{M, PK_M, Cert(M)\}_x, \{h(B, M, N_B, x)\}_{PK_M^{-1}}$
3. $B \rightarrow M : \{N_B\}_x$

BY protocol is similar to MSR+DH protocol except that the mobile station sends its signature ($\{h(B, M, N_B, x)\}_{PK_M^{-1}}$) to the base station in step 2 and the base station sends the encrypted nonce to the mobile station in step 3.

Aziz and Diffie's protocol Aziz and Diffie proposed a key establishment protocol that decides secret-key algorithm in the progress of the protocol and generates a new session key through the session keys generated by a mobile station and a base station [2] (from now on, we call it AD). Afterwards, Boyd and Mathuria showed that this protocol is also vulnerable to a man-in-the-middle attack and improved it [4]. The abstract description of improved version of AD protocol is as follows.

1. $M \rightarrow B : Cert(M), N_M, alg\_list$
2. $B \rightarrow M : Cert(B), N_B, \{x_B\}_{PK_M}, sel\_alg, \{hash(x_B, M, N_M, sel\_alg)\}_{PK_B^{-1}}$
3. $M \rightarrow B : \{x_M\}_{PK_B}, \{hash(x_M, B, N_B)\}_{PK_M^{-1}}$

alg_list stands for the list of secret-key algorithms and sel_alg is the secret-key algorithm selected by a base station. Other symbols mean the same things in the previous descriptions of BY protocol. The established session key between a mobile station and a base station is $x_M \oplus x_B$. x_M stands for the session key generated by the mobile station and x_B is the session key generated by the base station. Although the improved version of AD protocol has the heavy computational overhead at a mobile station side, it provides good forward secrecy [10].

Table 1. Heavy operations at a mobile station side in each protocol assuming that 160-bit exponents are used in ElGamal and DH, and other operands are all 512 bits.

proto -col	operations	type of operation (algorithm)	mod. mul.
MSR +DH	$\{PK_B\}_{PK_M^{-1}}$	generate key(DH)	240
	$\{Cert(B)\}_{PK_{CA}}$	verify certificate(MSR)	1
	$\{x\}_{PK_B}$	encrypt(MSR)	1
IBY	$\{h(B, M, N_B, x)\}_{PK_M^{-1}}$	make signature(ElGamal)	240
	$\{Cert(B)\}_{PK_{CA}}$	verify certificate(MSR)	1
	$\{x\}_{PK_B}$	encrypt(MSR)	1
IAD	$\{\{x\}_{PK_M}\}_{PK_M^{-1}}$	decrypt(RSA)	200
	$\{hash(x_M, B, N_B)\}_{PK_M^{-1}}$	make signature(RSA)	200
	$\{Cert(B)\}_{PK_{CA}}$	verify certificate(MSR)	1
	$\{x\}_{PK_B}$	encrypt(MSR)	1
	$\{\{hash(x_B, \cdots\}_{PK_B^{-1}}\}_{PK_B}$	verify signature(MSR)	1

The computational load of the protocols Table 1 shows the type and the number of heavy operations to be computed at a mobile station side in each of the previous protocols. As we can see in Table 1, the operations using the private-key of the mobile station (i.e., the signature generation and the message decryption) require heavy computations. We assume that RSA decryption and signature generation procedure use Chinese Remainder Theorem to accelerate them [13]. If so, although the number of required modular multiplication is the same as ordinary modular exponentiation, the operand size is one fourth of it.

2.2 Server-aided secret computation

SASC (Server-Aided Secret Computation) protocols enable a client (a smart card) to borrow computing power from a server (e.g., an untrusted auxiliary device like ATM) without revealing its secret information. Matsumoto, Kato, and Imai proposed the first SASC protocol for RSA signature generation [33], and it significantly accelerates the computation. Afterwards, a lot of effective attacks that can threaten SASC protocols have been designed and the corresponding countermeasures also have been proposed [27, 28, 25, 6, 8, 14, 9, 29, 32, 12]. The previous works related with this topic are reviewed in references [23] and [8] in detail.

Server-aided RSA computation In RSA [26], a signer computes two large primes p, q and their product n, and then he chooses a random integer ν which is reciprocal to $\phi(n)(=(p-1)(q-1))$ and finds s which satisfies $s\nu \equiv 1 \mod \phi(n)$. In this setting, the signature S for a message m is $m^s \mod n$, and it can be verified by examining whether $S^\nu \mod n$ is m or not. The objective of SASC protocols is to enable the client to efficiently compute $m^s \mod n$ with the aid of the server.

Splitting-based techniques The first SASC protocol uses decomposition of secret s into several pieces (x_i and a_i, where $s = \sum_{i=0}^{m-1} x_i a_i \bmod \phi(n)$), and reveals some of them(x_i) and conceals the others(a_i) [33]. More advanced ones that are designed afterwards use similar basic decomposition with more refined techniques, and we call them splitting-based techniques. In this paper, we use Beguin and Quisquater's protocol [23] as a representative splitting-based technique, because it is one of the most recent ones and secure against all known attacks. Although a new and strong attack that can totally break the system was proposed by Nguyen and Stern in Asiacrypt'98 [20], it can be easily prevented by slightly changing the parameter selection scheme.

Blinding-based technique Hong, Shin, Lee, and Yoon proposed another approach to server-aided RSA signature generation [12]. The approach is to blind the client's secret s by using a series of random numbers rather than to split it. The other procedures are similar to those of the splitting-based techniques. This scheme is secure against all known passive and active attacks including Nguyen and Stern's attack.

Server-aided DSS computation Beguin and Quisquater designed a server-aided DSS (Digital Signature Standard) computation protocol [3]. The protocol enables a client to fastly compute $a^x \bmod p$ with the aid of a server, where a is a fixed and public integer, p is a fixed and public prime number, and x is a secretly chosen random number. It is a splitting-based technique.

3 Our Approach

3.1 Adaptation of SASC

We simplify the description of SASC protocol to adapt for mobile environment. A mobile station acts as a client, and a base station executes the function of a server. The following description shows the simplified protocols of base station assisted signature generation and decryption. (Those in the parenthesis stand for the decryption procedure.)

Mobile Station   Base Station

---

modified_secrets
$\longrightarrow$
                                        pseudo-signing(/decryption)
pseudo-signed_messages   *with modified_secrets*
(/pseudo-decrypted_messages,
hash_value of the plaintext)
$\longleftarrow$

postcalculation
& verification

In the above description, the amount of data transferred between the mobile station and the base station, such as *modified_secrets* and *pseudo − signed message*, are largely different from one another according to the specific SASC protocol. If splitting-based techniques are used, they are two vectors (i.e., a lot of large numbers). Otherwise, only three integers are transferred in the blinding-based technique, of course, except for a message to be signed(/decrypted) and common modulus. The amount of computation required to be computed at the mobile station side is decided by *postcalculation* and *verification*.

The base station assisted decryption procedure is the same as that of the signature generation in essence. However, we can improve the decryption procedure using the fact that the server is the encrypter, i.e., the base station.

In the *verification* step, the mobile station checks the final result (i.e., the result of *postcalculation* that is computed using *pseudo-decrypted_messages*) of the protocol, and only when the result is correct it proceeds the remain steps of the key establishment protocol. At that time, the mobile station uses the received *hash_value of the plaintext*. (Originally, the mobile station should encrypt the final result with its public-key and compare it with the received ciphertext as in the signature generation. This costs several modular multiplications.) Therefore, in the above decryption, the base station gives the *hash_value of the plaintext*, and the mobile station checks the final result by comparing its hash value to the received hash value. Moreover, this modification reduces the communication overhead as well as several modular multiplications, because the base station does not need to transmit the ciphertext itself.

3.2 Acceleration techniques

MSR+DH acceleration As we can see in Table 1, the only operation that requires intensive computation at a mobile station side is the encryption of the base station's public-key with its private-key after they exchange their public-keys. It can be written as follows :

$$(PK_B)^{PK_M^{-1}} \bmod p, \text{ where } PK_B = g^{PK_B^{-1}} \bmod p.$$

At the sight of the mobile station, PK_B is a variable as it is the base station's public-key, and the exponent (PK_M^{-1}) is a fixed value as it is the private-key of the mobile station itself. Therefore, server-aided RSA computation should be used to speed up the protocol, although g is a fixed integer.

A splitting-based technique and a blinding-based one are all able to be used. However, both techniques should be modified slightly to be applied to Diffie-Hellman scheme. Recent SASC protocols such as Beguin and Quisquater's [23] and Hong et al.'s [12] are designed to use CRT(Chinese Remainder Theorem) to reduce RSA signature generation time, and it is based on the fact that the signer knows the factorization of the modulus n [13]. However, as the modulus p in Diffie-Hellman key exchange protocol is a prime, CRT is not able to be used. Resultantly, it degrades the performance by two times.

We show the procedure that enables a mobile station to borrow the computing power from the base station to execute Diffie-Hellman key exchange. The following scheme is based on Beguin and Quisquater's scheme that is a representative splitting based technique.

1. A mobile station randomly chooses a_is and x_is that satisfies the following equation : $s_1 = \sum_{i=0}^{m-1} a_i x_i \bmod p - 1$. Then, it sends x_is to the base station.

2. The base station computes and returns $(PK_B)^{x_i} \bmod p$ to the mobile station, for $0 \leq i \leq m-1$.

3. The mobile station computes $z \equiv \prod_{i=0}^{m-1} ((PK_B)^{x_i})^{a_i} \bmod p$.

4. The mobile station sends σ which satisfies the following : $\sigma = s_2 \bmod (p-1) + \varrho(p-1)$, where $\varrho \in_R \{0, 1, \cdots, p-2\}$ and $s_2 = s - s_1$.

5. The base station computes and returns $y = (PK_B)^{\sigma} \bmod p$ to the mobile station.

6. The mobile station computes $s = z \times y \bmod p$, and checks if $s^{PK_M} \equiv PK_B \bmod p$, and if not, it stops the succeeding key establishment protocol[3].

Acceleration of improved BY scheme A mobile station should execute two public-key operations and a private-key operation (refer to Table 1). Two public-key operations are a verification of a public-key certificate and an encryption using the base station's public-key. These require only two modular multiplications (one for each), as they all use MSR algorithm.

The operation that requires extensive computation is the signature generation of the mobile station using its private-key. Beller and Yacobi's approach to overcome this problem is to make use of the precomputable property of ElGamal algorithm [18]. Their insight is as follows : When the mobile station generates the signature $\{h(B, M, N_B, x)\}_{PK_B^{-1}}$ to be sent to the base station, $g^r \bmod p$ can be precomputed and stored in advance as it is independent of the message $h(B, M, N_B, x)$ to be signed. Therefore, the mobile station can generate the signature only by three modular multiplications in the call set-up time.

We can accelerate the precomputation ($g^r \bmod p$) by using Beguin and Quisquater's server-aided DSS scheme.

1. The mobile station randomly chooses x_is and b_is which satisfy $r = \sum_{i=0}^{m-1} x_i b_i$, where $0 \leq x_i \leq h$. Then, it sends b_is to the base station.

2. The base station computes $g^{b_i} \bmod p$, for $0 \leq i \leq m-1$. And then, it returns them to the mobile station.

3. The mobile station computes $g^r \equiv \prod_{i=0}^{m-1} (g^{b_i})^{x_i} \bmod p$.

---

[3] For this final result checking, we assume the public exponent PK_B is very small as in the server-aided RSA computation.

Acceleration of improved AD scheme Improved AD protocol makes use of three public-key operations and two private-key operations (refer to Table 1). As public-key operations can be implemented by using MSR encryption and MSR signature verification, they all can be executed by only three modular multiplications in total. The bottleneck of the key establishment protocol is two private-key operations, and therefore SASC techniques should be used twice. We use RSA decryption and signature generation algorithms as the private-key operations.

The first massive computation is the decryption of $\{x_B\}_{PK_M}$ that is received from the base station. We use the blinding-based server-aided RSA computation technique and the simplified decryption procedure in Section 3.1. The second private-key operation is the signature generation for the message $hash($ $x_M, B, N_B)$. It can also be accelerated by using base station assisted RSA signature generation as in Section 3.1. The detail descriptions of these two acceleration schemes are presented in Appendix.

4 Performance Analysis

In this section, we analyze the performance of the acceleration techniques presented in the paper. The basic metric of the performance is the number of modular multiplications required at the mobile station side. We compare the accelerations of the proposed techniques with those of the original key establishment protocols to which they are applied.

The performance comparison is presented in Table 2. We let the size of modulus p and n be 512-bits, and assume that ElGamal algorithm and Diffie-Hellman protocol use 160-bits exponents. We let the public exponent of RSA be short, exactly '3', and assume that RSA decryption algorithm uses CRT.

The security parameters (e.g., h and m in the Beguin and Quisquater's SASC scheme) are selected among the values that are recommended in the original SASC protocol proposals [3, 23, 12]. The security parameters of the splitting-based technique are $<b_R=11, b_{R'}=26, k=3>$. Those of splitting-based techniques are $<h=11, m=29>$ for the RSA and $<b=16, m=40>$ for the ElGamal.

The proposed techniques accelerate the previous key establishment protocols by more than five times at maximum, as we can see Table 2. The factor of acceleration is quite different from one another according to the used SASC protocol. Moreover, the communication overhead of SASC protocol makes the gap be even larger. The overall performance gain is presented in 'F.A.' field of Table 2, including the amount of communication overhead and the expected execution time.

5 Conclusion

RSA signature generation and decryption require full modular exponentiations (i.e., several hundreds of modular multiplications) as Diffie-Hellman key exchange algorithm. Therefore, RSA has not been able to be used as a building

Table 2. Comparison of acceleration techniques assuming that 8-bit μ-processor and 9600bps communication link is used. Communication overhehad is presented in bytes, and computaion time in seconds. '#MM' means the number of modular multiplications, and 'F.A.' means the factor of acceleration.

protocol	used technique	comp.			comm.		time (sec.)	F.A.
		#MM	time	F.A.	byte	time		
MSR+DH	N.A.	242	43.56	1.0	320	0.27	43.8	1.0
MSR+DH	splitting	82	14.76	3.0	3127	2.61	17.4	2.5
MSR+DH	blinding	72	12.96	3.4	704	0.59	13.5	3.2
IBY	N.A.	242	43.56	1.0	384	0.32	43.9	1.0
IBY	splitting	70	12.6	3.5	19968	16.64	29.2	1.5
IAD	N.A.	403	72.54	1.0	512	0.43	73.0	1.0
IAD	splitting	80	14.4	5.0	6190	5.16	19.6	3.7
IAD	blinding	70	12.6	5.8	1472	1.23	13.8	5.3

block for a key establishment protocol in mobile communication. A modular multiplication costs 180ms on a typical 8-bit μ-processor of $6MHz$, and it results that more than 40 seconds are required for key establishment except for communication overhead [17]. Although the computing power of a mobile station has been and is evolving rapidly due to VLSI technology, full modular exponentiations are heavy operations in mobile equipment in the current and near future[4] (partially because of the battery consumption). The proposed acceleration techniques make RSA be able to be considered as a building block of a key establishment protocol in mobile communication. It is a significant contribution as RSA is a very widely spread cryptographic algorithm.

Beller and Yacobi's protocol dramatically reduces the delay for call set-up by using precomputation. However, as the precomputation should be executed on each time, it does not reduce the computation amount itself. It results to be inefficient on continuous execution and at the sight of battery consumption[5]. The proposed scheme reduces the amount of computation required at the mobile station with the aid of base station, and it results to reduce call set-up delay (including continuous execution) and precomputation overhead as presented in Table 2.

References

1. ETSI/TC Recommendation GSM 03.20. Security related network function. *version 3.3.2*, 1991.

---

[4] Although the current PCS(Personal Communication Services) handsets use powerful processors, we can not expect to enjoy enough computing power and battery, as the mobile equipment becomes smaller in size and weight. On the extreme case, one can imagine wearable computer or on-body computing.

[5] Current μ-processors for mobile equipments reduces battery consumption by changing its mode *idle* when there is nothing to do [7]. Therefore, the mode change overhead may be serious according to the usage pattern.

2. A.Aziz and W.Diffie. Privacy and authentication for wireless local area networks. *IEEE Personal Communications*, 1:25–31, 1994.

3. Philippe Beguin and Jean-Jacques Quisquater. Secure acceleration of DSS signatures using insecure server. In *Asiacrypt'94*, pages 249–259, 1994.

4. Colin Boyd and Anish Mathuria. Key establishment protocols for secure mobile communications: A selective survey. In *ACISP'98, Lecture Notes in Computer Science*, volume 1438, pages 344–355, 1998.

5. Colin Boyd and Dong-Gook Park. Public key protocols for wireless communications. In *The 1st International Conference on Information Secuirty and Cryptology(ICISC'98)*, pages 47–57, 1998.

6. B.Pfitzmann and M.Waidner. Attacks on protocols for server-aided RSA computation. In *Eurocrypt'92*, pages 153–162, 1992.

7. Thomas D. Burd and Robert W. Brodersen. Processor design for portable systems. *Journal of VLSI Signal Processing*, 1996.

8. C.H.Lim and P.J.Lee. Security and performance of server-aided RSA computation protocols. In *Crypto'95*, pages 70–83, 1995.

9. C.H.Lim and P.J.Lee. Server(prover/signer)-aided verification of identity proofs and signature. In *Eurocrypt'95*, pages 64–78, 1995.

10. W. Diffie, P.C.V. Oorschot, and M.J. Wiener. Authentication and authenticated key exchanges. In *Designs, Codes and Cryptography*, pages 107–125. Kluwer Academic Publishers, 1992.

11. ETSI. *ETS 300 175-7*, 1992.

12. Seong-Min Hong, Jun-Bum Shin, H.Lee-Kwnag, and Hyunsoo Yoon. A new approach to server-aided secret computation. In *The 1st International Conference on Information Secuirty and Cryptology(ICISC'98)*, pages 33–45, 1998.

13. J.-J.Quisquater and C.Couvreur. Fast decipherment algorithm for RSA public-key cryptosystem. *Electronics Letters*, 18(21):905–907, 1982.

14. J.Burns and C.J.Mitchell. Parameter selection for server-aided RSA computation schemes. *IEEE Trans. on Computers*, 43(2):163–174, 1994.

15. K.Vedder. Security aspects of mobile communications. In *Computer Security and Industrial Cryptography, LNCS 741*, pages 193–210. Springer Verlag, 1993.

16. Keith Martin and Chris Mitchell. Evaluation of authentication protocols for mobile environment value added services. In *Draft, Available on-line as http://isg.rhbnc.ac.uk/cjm/EOAPFM.ZIP*, 1998.

17. M.J.Beller, L.-F.Chang, and Y.Yacobi. Privacy and authentication on a portable communications system. *IEEE Journal on Selected Areas in Communications*, 11:821–829, August 1993.

18. M.J.Beller and Y.Yacobi. Fully-fledged two-way public key authentication and key agreement for low-cost terminals. *Electronics Letters*, 29:999–1001, May 1993.

19. R. Molva, D.Samfat, and G. Tsudik. Authentication of mobile users. *IEEE Network*, pages 26–34, 1994.

20. Phong Nguyen and Jacques Stern. The beguin-quisquater server-aided RSA protocol from crypto'95 is not secure. In *Advances in Cryptology - Asiacrypt'98, LNCS 1514*, pages 372–379. Springer Verlag, 1998.

21. Choonsik Park. On certificate-based security protocols for wireless mobile communication systems. *IEEE Network*, pages 50–55, September/October 1997.

22. Choonsik Park, Kaoru Kurosawa, Tatsuaki Okamoto, and Shigeo Tsujii. On key distribution and authentication in mobile radio networks. In *Advances in Cryptology - Eurocrypt'93*, pages 461–465. Springer Verlag, 1994.

23. P.Beguin and J.J.Quisquater. Fast server-aided RSA signatures secure against active attacks. In *Crypto'95*, pages 57–69, 1995.

24. M.O. Rabin. Digitalized signatures and public-key functions as intractable as factorization. *MIT/LCS/TR-212*, 1979.

25. R.J.Anderson. Attack on server assisted authentication protocols. *Electronics Letters*, 28(15):1473, 1992.

26. R.L.Rivest, A.Shamir, and L.Adleman. A method for obtaining digital signatures and public key cryptosystems. *CACM*, 21:120–126, 1978.

27. S.-M.Yen. Cryptanalysis of secure addition chain for sasc applications. *Electronics Letters*, 31(3):175–176, 1995.

28. S.-M.Yen and C.-S.Laih. More about the active attak on the server-aided secret computation protocol. *Electronics Letters*, 28(24):2250, 1992.

29. S.Kawamura and A.Shimbo. Fast server-aided secret computation protocols for modular exponentiation. *IEEE JSAC*, 11(5):778–784, 1993.

30. Makoto Tatebayashi, Natsume Matsuzaki, and Jr. David B.Newman. Key distribution protocol for digital mobile communication systems. In *Advances in Cryptology - Crypto'89*, pages 324–334. Springer Verlag, 1990.

31. T.ElGamal. A public key cryptosystem and a signature scheme based on discrete logarithms. *IEEE Transactions on Information Theory*, IT-31:469–472, july 1985.

32. T.Matsumoto, H.Imai, C.S.Laih, and S.M.Yen. On verifiable implicit asking protocols for RSA computation. In *Auscrypt92*, pages 296–307, 1993.

33. T.Matsumoto, K.Kato, and H.Imai. Speeding up secret computations with insecure auxiliary devices. In *Crypto'88*, pages 497–506, 1988.

34. U.Carlsen. Optimal privacy and authentication on a portable communications system. *ACM Operating Systems Review*, 28(3):16–23, 1994.

35. W.Diffie and M.E.Hellman. New directions in cryptography. *IEEE Transactions on Computers*, IT-22(6):644–654, June 1976.

36. Y.Mu and V.Varadharajan. On the design of security protocols for mobile communications. In *ACISP'96, Lecture Notes in Computer Science*, pages 134–145, 1996.

37. Y.Yacobi and Z.Shmuley. On key distribution systems. In *Advances in Cryptology - Crypto'89, LNCS 435*, pages 344–355. Springer Verlag, 1989.

Appendix

We show two acceleration schemes for Aziz and Diffie's protocol. The proposed scheme requires some precomputations, however these precomputations are executed only once when the private key d is generated. The client computes t' which satisfies the following equation to conceal the secret d : $t' \equiv \frac{1}{r'_k}(\cdots(\frac{1}{r'_1}(d - r_1) - r_2) - \cdots - r_k) - R \bmod \lambda(N)$. In this equation, '$\frac{1}{r'_i}$' means '$(r'_i)^{-1} \bmod \lambda(N)$', and r_i, r'_i, and R are random numbers which satisfy some conditions. (The detail selection scheme of random numbers is in reference [12].) The clients prepares $u \equiv \prod_{i=1}^{k} \frac{1}{r'_i} \bmod \lambda(N)$. The client computes $w_p \equiv q(q^{-1} \bmod p) \bmod N$ and $w_q \equiv p(p^{-1} \bmod q) \bmod N$. (Note that b_R, $b_{R'}$, and k are security parameters, and they should be selected so as to maximize the performance while keeping the protocol be secure. $b_{R'}$ should be less than $(p-1)/2-1$ and $(q-1)/2-1$ for the security. However, it does not matter because the computation time largely depends on $b_{R'}$.)

The following is the base station assisted decryption of $\{x_B\}_{PK_M}$ that is received from the base station.

1. The mobile station randomly chooses d_1, and then sends n, t, σ_p, and σ_q to the base station, where they satisfy the following equations : $t = t' - u \times d_2 \bmod \lambda(N)$, where $d_2 = d - d_1$, $\sigma_p = d_2 \bmod (p-1) + \varrho_p(p-1)$, $\sigma_q = d_2 \bmod (q-1) + \varrho_q(q-1)$, where $\varrho_p \in_R \{0, \ldots, q-2\}$, and $\varrho_q \in_R \{0, \ldots, p-2\}$.

2. The base station encrypts the message x_B using the mobile station's public-key PK_M. (i.e. $\{x_B\}_{PK_M}$) Then, it computes and returns the following to the mobile station : $(\{x_B\}_{PK_M})^t \bmod n$, $y_p = (\{x_B\}_{PK_M})^{\sigma_p} \bmod n$, and $y_q = (\{x_B\}_{PK_M})^{\sigma_q} \bmod n$. At the same time, it also gives $H = h(x_B)$ to the mobile station.

3. The mobile station makes use of the unblind scheme and CRT to extract x_B from the values received from the base station [12]. If the extracted value x_B satisfies $h(x_B) = H$, the mobile station makes use of x_B in the succeeding key establishment protocol. Otherwise, it stops the protocol.

The following is the acceleration of the second private-key operation, which is the signature generation for the message $hash(x_M, B, N_B)$. Notations are the same as the above scheme.

1. The mobile station sends to the base station $hash(x_M, B, N_B)(= h)$, n, t, σ_p, and σ_q.

2. The base station computes and returns the following : $h^t \bmod n$, $y_p = h^{\sigma_p} \bmod n$, and $y_q = h^{\sigma_q} \bmod n$.

3. The mobile station makes use of the unblind scheme and CRT to generation signature S [12]. If the result S satisfies $\{S\}_{PK_M} = hash(x_M, B, N_B)$, the mobile station makes use of x_M in the succeeding key establishment protocol. Otherwise, it stops the protocol.

Conference Key Agreement from Secret Sharing

Chih-Hung Li and Josef Pieprzyk

Centre for Computer Security Research
School of Information Technology and Computer Science
University of Wollongong
Northfields Avenue
Wollongong 2522
Australia
{cl14, josef}@cs.uow.edu.au

Abstract. The work proposes new conference key agreement protocols based on secret sharing. We discuss roles of the dealer and recovery algorithms in the trust structure which is the necessary condition for any key establishment protocol to achieve the intended security goals. Our conference key agreement protocol tackles the problem of entity authentication in conference key agreement protocols. The entity authentication is replaced by group authentication. To start a new conference all principals have to be active and broadcast their shares. If the conference goes ahead, all principals are sure that all principals are present and alive. The paper is concluded with a discussion about possible modifications and extensions of the protocol.

Keywords: Cryptographic Protocols, Key Establishment Protocols, Key Agreement Protocols, Shamir Secret Sharing.

1 Introduction

Establishment of cryptographic keys is one of the basic cryptographic operations which is always necessary if two or more parties wish to create secure channels for a communication session. Traditionally, cryptographic protocols which deals with multi-party key establishment are called conference key establishment protocols. The part of cryptology which is concerned with key establishment developed its own specific terminology. Principals are all active entities (parties) which can initiate a protocol or be actively involved in it. Key is fresh if has never been used before. Some other terms will be introduced gradually throughout the paper. Key establishment can be achieved by a distribution of a fresh key by a trusted authority (TA) to all principals. This class of protocols is called key distribution protocols. An alternative to key distribution protocols is the class of key agreement protocols. In this class, any principal involved in a protocol contributes to the final form of the secret key.

Needham and Schroeder [10] designed a first key distribution protocol. Two principals who execute the protocol, can obtain a fresh and secret cryptographic key assuming that there is a trusted authority (TA) who has already established secure communication channels between principals and the TA. These channels are necessary to distribute a fresh key (generated by the TA) to the principals. Diffie and Hellman [4] showed how two principals can collaborate to create a common and secret key via insecure channels. The main drawback of their key agreement protocol was the lack of authentication of principals. In result, the protocol is susceptible to the *man-in-the-middle attack*. The Station-to-Station (STS) protocol is a secure version of Diffie-Hellman (DH) protocol and was designed by Diffie, Van Oorschot and M. Wiener [5]. A viable option for conference key establishment is a straightforward application of two-party protocols. As expected, this solution typically introduces heavy communication overhead (see for instance [6, 7, 2]).

The paper is structured as follows. Section 2 presents features of secret sharing which are useful for key establishment protocols. Trust structure necessary to build a secret sharing scheme which constitutes an underlying infrastructure for key establishment protocols, is discussed in Section 3. In Section 4, we highlight the goal of conference key distribution protocols. In Section 5, a new key agreement protocol is described. The last section deliberates on possible extensions and modifications of the protocol.

2 Features of Secret Sharing

Secret sharing was introduced by Shamir [11] and Blakley [1]. Secret sharing includes two algorithms: one for design and distribution of shares (this algorithm is called a dealer) and the other for recovery of the secret (called a recovery algorithm or combiner). The dealer typically generates a fresh secret key and divides it into pieces called shares. Shares are sent via secure channels to principals. At the pooling time when a big enough subset of principals agrees to act, they send their shares to the combiner who recovers the secret key and distributes it among principals. For more precise definitions and description of secret sharing, the reader is referred to [12].

Secret sharing seems to be an ideal vehicle for design of a variety of conference key establishment protocols. The following properties of secret sharing make it especially attractive.

1. The amount of trust assigned to each principal can be mirrored by a proper access structure. If all principals are equally trusted, then a threshold sharing seems to be appropriate.
2. Not all principals have to be active to trigger the conference. This also means that secret sharing used can reflect different requirements as to how big a subset of active principals has to be to call on the conference. Again if the threshold secret sharing is acceptable, then the selection of the threshold enables to manipulate the size of the group who is able to call on the conference.
3. Principal authentication can be replaced by a group authentication. This is a weaker requirement and in general can be less expensive to achieve. This

is the case when principals do not need to know precise composition of the currently active group but they require to be sure that the group is big enough to conduct a valid conference.

Secret sharing exhibits some features which may restrict their applicability for key establishment protocols. Two most serious are:

1. The composition of conference principals must be decided well ahead of the conference. Typically, this is done by the dealer.
2. The dealer must distribute shares to all principals via secure channels.

The first property may not be a real hindrance when the group involved in the conference is known well in advance and its composition is fixed for some time. One can argue that most conferences are of this kind. Moreover, secret sharing developed already methods and techniques to deal with modifications of the group (enrolment and disenrolment [12]). The second feature is unavoidable but can be dealt by conversion of secret sharing into the conditionally secure setting. In other words, once the secret sharing has been set up, it can be used many times.

3 Trust Structure

The existence of trust is the necessary condition for any key establishment protocol to work correctly and to achieve security goals. Needham and Schroeder assumed [10] that there was a TA who generated a fresh key and used prearranged secure channels to distribute it to principals. Diffie, Van Oorschot and Wiener in their STS protocol [5] supposed that any principal running their key agreement protocol had an access to their authenticated public keys. Typically, a TA delivered requested public keys in the form of certificates produced by the TA using its secret key so a principal knowing the public key of TA could check their authenticity.

In secret sharing, the trust structure evolves around the dealer, combiner and secure channels. We now briefly discuss these components of trust.

3.1 Dealer

For key distribution protocols, the dealer plays the role of a TA or a conference chairman who first composes a collection of principals who are eligible to participate in the conference. Next the chairman chooses a proper access structure. The access structure must reflect the hierarchical positions of principals in the group and define clearly the collection of minimal subgroups which can still call on the conference. Once this is done the chairman selects a fresh secret key and divides it into shares. Shares are secretly transported to principals.

For key agreement protocols, there is no trusted authority directly involved in the secret key generation. The model appropriate for this case seems to be secret sharing without a dealer or in other words, every principal plays the role of dealer. A principal designs her own secret sharing with an access structure of her choice uses secret channels to distribute shares to other principals. After all principals have distributed their shares, each principal keeps in her hands her own share plus shares obtained from others. Finally, each principal combines all shares into one hoping that the resulting secret sharing has an access structure acceptable for all.

It is not difficult to notice that this approach can only work if all principals use the same type of secret sharing which allows to merge many secret sharing generated locally into one (without a dealer). A broad class of secret sharing which allows to do this are linear schemes. Even dealing with linear secret sharing does not solve a problem of different access structures selected by individual principals. We however know that if each principal selects a (t, n) Shamir threshold scheme and distributes shares to the same collection of principals, then the resulting scheme is also a threshold scheme. It is easy to check that if each principal selects different threshold but the collection of principal is the same for all, then the threshold of the composed sharing is the largest used by principals.

3.2 Combiner

In secret sharing scheme, we need a combiner who collects the shares from principals and computes the secret key. The key recovered is then distributed to all active principals via secure channels. In key establishment protocols, shares collected by the combiner are not necessary if the combiner is trusted as it can generate a fresh key and distribute it. Note that the purpose of secret sharing is to recover the key while in key establishment protocols any fresh key is good. Certainly, the role of combiner in the context key establishment protocols needs to be redefined. The idea is to get rid of one combiner and replace it by principals who perform the combiner role by themselves. Consider two possible cases.

The case of key distribution protocols. There is a chairman who designs a secret sharing of threshold 2 for a fresh secret. Each principal gets a single share while the chairman holds the secret and one extra share. The extra share is used to trigger the conference by broadcasting it (broadcasting must be authenticated). Each principal, takes her share plus the one broadcast and recovers the secret key. Observe that each principal plays the role of combiner.

Assume that there is no chairman and the trusted dealer does not participate in conferences but sets up a secret sharing with a fresh key. If the secret sharing has the threshold $n + 1$ and the number of all shares is $3n$ (n is the number of all eligible principals) and each principal is assigned 3 shares, then to call on a conference, it is enough if n principals broadcast their shares. Knowing n shares, each principal can recover the secret key using her second share. The third share can be applied to verify the validity of the secret. Clearly, a misbehaving principal can broadcast two or three shares instead of one. If a principal broadcasts two shares, she can recover the secret but cannot verify it. If she announces three shares, she cannot participate in the conference.

The second case is related to key agreement protocols. Assume that a $(n + 1, 2n)$ secret sharing is set up collectively by all n principals so the threshold is

$(n+1)$ and each principal holds 2 shares. Note that to call on a conference, it is enough for principals to broadcast their single shares. After publishing n shares, each principal can applied the second share to recover the secret (the threshold is $(n+1)$).

3.3 Communication Channels

All interactions among principals are done via communication channels. A channel can provide either secrecy or authenticity or both. An enemy who accesses a secrecy channel is unable to understand the message transmitted. Secrecy channels can be implemented using symmetric or asymmetric cryptography. In the case of symmetric cryptography, both the sender and the receiver know the same cryptographic key. In asymmetric (or public key) cryptography, the sender key is public but the receiver's key is secret. Note that the sender must make sure that the key is the authentic public key of the intended receiver.

Authenticity channels do not hide messages but provide check-sums (also called MACs [9]) which can be used to verify their origin. Typically, the receiver can detect whether or not a message comes from the correct source and has not been tampered with during transmission.

Broadcast channels are normally meant be readable by all principals but any modification of the contents of messages will be detected with a high probability by all principals. From now on, if we say that a message is broadcast, we mean that the broadcasting channel is authenticated so any tampering with messages causes principals to reject them. If we say that a message is sent over a secure channel, we assume that the channel provides both secrecy and authenticity.

Key distribution protocols typically apply secure channels implemented using either secret-key or public-key cryptosystems. This was the case for Needham-Schroeder protocols and their successors [10]. Key agreement protocols are normally supported by public-key cryptosystems and broadcasting seems to be a predominant way of message communication ([9]).

4 Goals of Conference Key Establishment Protocols

Conference key establishment protocols are usually designed to achieve a well-defined collection of goals and simultaneously one would expect that they can be run efficiently. The main collection of security goals for key establishment protocols are [9]: (1) key freshness, (2) entity authentication, (3) key confirmation, (4) key authentication, and (5) explicit key authentication.

A key is *fresh* if it has not been generated or used before. *Entity authentication* is a confirmation process which allows one principal to identify correctly the others involved in the protocol. Typically, it allows a principal to check whether other principals are active (alive) at the time when the protocol is being executed. This requirement can be relaxed by defining *group authentication* in which every principal is sure that all principals are alive and present. This allows any principal to identify the group rather than individuals. *Weak group authentication* means that all currently active principals are sure that there is a big enough group of active principals. In most circumstances, a conference is considered to be valid if a quorum of principals is present. The access structure (or the threshold parameter) conveniently determines the size of a big enough group. *Key confirmation* is a property of protocol which allows one principal to make sure that the other parties possess the same common key. *Implicit key authentication* provides an assurance to principals that no one except specific other parties could have gained access to the common key. Implicit key authentication can be also viewed as *key confidentiality*. By *explicit key authentication* we mean that both implicit key authentication and key confirmation hold.

5 A New Conference Key Agreement Protocol

We propose a key agreement which uses overlapping secret sharing schemes to establish a fresh secret key. More precisely, each principal P_i is free to choose her own Shamir secret sharing defined by a polynomial $f_i(z)$. The group, however, works with the combined Shamir scheme based on the polynomial $F(z) = \sum_{i=1}^{n} f_i(z)$. Like in the DH protocol, all principals who want to join a conference can equally contribute to a fresh secret key. The protocol consists of three stages:

1. registration – each principal who wants to join the conference register herself with a trusted registry,
2. initialisation – each principal creates her private secret sharing scheme and distributes shares to all other principals,
3. call for conference – principals broadcast their shares and therefore enable themselves to recover a common secret key.

5.1 Assumptions

The following assumptions are made:

- there are n principals $\{P_1, \ldots, P_n\}$ who want to joint the conference,
- there exists a trusted registry (R) who manages the registration of principals. In particular, the registry keeps a list of public keys of principals,
- public information accessible from the registry is authenticated by the registry. Typically, information is accessible in a form of certificates signed by R,
- secure channels provide both secrecy and authentication and broadcast channels deliver authenticated messages to all principals (messages can be read by all but nobody can modify them without detecting the modification).

Let p and q denote large primes such that q divides $p - 1$. Let G_q be a subgroup of Z_p^* of order q and g be a generator of G_q.

5.2 Registration

Each principal P_i chooses his own private key $x_i \in Z_q^*$ and submits his public key $h_i = g^{x_i} \pmod{p}$ for $i = 1, \ldots, n$ to the registry R. After all principals have completed their registration, the registry R displays a read-only list of public keys together with principals' names. Additionally, R generates a random integer $r \in_R Z_q^*$ on demand and keeps it for a short period of time. Normally, the value is generated whenever a need for conference arises (indicated by principals who wish to call a conference). This value is erased after some time (when the conference has finished). The same value r is never used in two different conferences.

Registration serves three purposes. The first one is that each principal knows other principals who are to join the conference. The second one is that the public keys can be used to implement secure channels between principals. For example, the information provided by registry is enough to encrypt a message using the ElGamal cryptosystem. Assume that $m \in Z_q^*$ and P_i wants to send the message to P_j in encrypted form. First P_i chooses a random integer $v \in Z_q^*$ and computes g^v, h_j^v and $m \times h_j^v$. The pair $(g^v, m \times h_j^v)$ is sent to P_j. The receiver P_j takes the pair and computes $(g^v)^{x_j} = g^{v x_j}$ which later can be used to extract the message $m = m \times h_j^v \times g^{-v x_j}$. The third purpose is to supply principals with fresh (random) elements r which are later used in the protocol.

5.3 Initialisation

This part of protocol is done by each principal independently of each other. The setup phase proceeds as follows:

1. Principal P_i designs a $(n + 1, 2n)$ Shamir threshold scheme, i.e. a scheme with $2n$ shares and with threshold $n + 1$. Let the scheme be defined by a random polynomial $f_i(z)$ of degree at most n. Suppose that

$$f_i(z) = a_{i,0} + a_{i,1} z + \ldots + a_{i,n} z^n$$

where coefficients $a_{i,j} \in Z_q^*$ are chosen at random for $j = 1, \ldots, n$. As usual in Shamir scheme, shares are computed for $2n$ public z co-ordinates. We assume that P_i is assigned a pair of co-ordinates $z_i = (2i - 1, 2i)$.

2. Further P_i prepares pairs of shares $s_{i,j} = f_i(z_j) = (s_{i,j}^{(1)} = f_i(2j - 1), s_{i,j}^{(2)} = f_i(2j))$.

3. Finally, P_i communicates $s_{i,j}^{(2)}$ to the principal P_j; $j = 1, \ldots, n$; $j \neq i$ via a secure channel. In effect, P_i obtains a sequence of n elements $(s_{1,i}^{(2)}, \ldots, s_{n,i}^{(2)})$ and computes her secret share $S_i^{(2)} = \sum_{j=1}^{n} s_{j,i}^{(2)}$ where $S_i^{(2)} = F(2i)$ and the polynomial $F(z) = \sum_{i=1}^{n} f_i(z)$.

Note that during a run of the protocol, the secret $s = F(0) = \sum_{i=1}^{n} a_{i,0}$ is never exposed to principals. From now on $s = F(0)$ will be called a seed to differentiate it from a fresh secret key obtained by all principals involved in the conference.

5.4 Call for Conference

To trigger the conference, principals execute the following steps.

1. The principal P_i contacts the registry and fetches necessary parameters including a random element r and the generator g. If the element r is not on display, P_i asks R for one. P_i also computes $\alpha = g^r$.
2. P_i prepares public shares $\beta_{i,j} = \alpha^{s_{i,j}^{(1)}}$ for $j = 1, \ldots, n$.
3. The principal P_i broadcasts $\beta_{i,j}$ to all principals $j = 1, \ldots, n$. Note that this broadcasting need not be authenticated.
4. After P_i has obtained $\beta_{j,i}$ from other principals, she recovers n public shares

$$\alpha^{S_j^{(1)}} = \alpha^{F(2j-2)} = \alpha^{\sum_{i=1}^{n} s_{i,j}^{(1)}} = \prod_{i=1}^{n} \beta_{i,j}$$

for $j = 1, \ldots, n$.

5. P_i uses n public shares and her secret share, $S_i^{(2)}$ to recover the common secret $S = \alpha^{F(0)} = \alpha^s$. Note that principals still use Lagrange interpolation but for exponents. For details how to compute S, the reader is referred to [3].
6. P_i takes the secret S, her name id_i, and a timestamp TS_i and prepares a string $\varepsilon_i = H(S\|id_i\|TS_i)$ where H is a cryptographically strong, collision-free hash function with a public description. The triplet $(\varepsilon_i, id_i, TS_i)$ is broadcast (note that broadcasting channel is assumed to provide authentication).
7. P_i collects $(\varepsilon_j, id_j, TS_j)$ from other principals, checks their authenticity and verifies them using her own secret S. If the checks hold, P_i is ready for the conference. Otherwise, P_i announces the error and aborts the protocol.

5.5 Security Analysis

The following theorem specifies which security goals are achievable by the protocol.

Theorem 1. *Assume that the protocol is run by a group of honest principals, then the protocol attains the following security goals: (1) key freshness, (2) key confidentiality, (3) group authentication, (4) key confirmation.*

Proof. (1) The registry displays an integer r randomly selected from Z_q^*. Note that the common secret key $S = g^{rs} = \alpha^s$ is fresh as log as r is fresh. The freshness is probabilistic.

(2) Key confidentiality holds as after broadcasting the shares $\alpha^{s_{i,j}^{(1)}}$, all outsiders know n public shares only. As the Shamir scheme is perfect, it means that n shares do not provide any information about the secret when the threshold is $n+1$. Note that key confidentiality is preserved even if the outsider has unlimited computational power (as far as the secret sharing is concerned).

(3) To call on the conference, all principals must be present and alive to broadcast public shares of their private secret sharing schemes – group authentication holds.

(4) After the conference has been called, every principal can check whether other principals are holding the same secret by verifying the triplets $(\varepsilon_j, id_j, TS_j)$ for all $j \neq i$. The key confirmation is satisfied.

What if a subgroup of principals does not follow the protocol ? Let us consider the following possibilities:

1. At the initialisation stage, the subgroup can intentionally lower down the thresholds used in their private secret sharing schemes. This does not effect the work of the protocol as if at least one principal is honest the threshold will be random and equal to $(n+1)$ with the probability $(1-q^{-1})$. If the subgroup increases the threshold of their private scheme, then at the call for conference stage, the principals who are honest will recover inconsistent secrets and will abort the conference with an overwhelming probability. The subgroup of conspirators can establish a conference but without honest principals.

2. At the call for conference stage, the subgroup can broadcast modified shares of their private schemes. This will be detected by honest principals when the secret is verified.

3. A disobedient principal P_i can make public his secret sharing scheme (the polynomial $f_i(z)$). The conference can still be called but without involvement of P_i. This is another way of saying – *call conference whenever you wish*. P_i can still participate in conferences if her share $S_i^{(2)}$ remains secret. If P_i goes further and discloses $S_i^{(2)}$, then the secret key becomes public if the rest of principals follows the protocol. Otherwise if some principals refrain from broadcasting their public shares, the conference will not go ahead.

We claim that the protocol can be used repeatedly to call conferences as the seed s remains secret and to recover the fresh secret key S, the principals need to use secret sharing to compute it.

Recall that the Discrete Logarithm (DL) problem is defined as follows. Given the modulus N, the element g and $h = g^x \bmod N$. What is x ?

We can define a variant (VDL) of the DL problem as follows. Given the modulus N, the elements $g_1, \ldots, g_\ell$ and a sequence of $h_1 = g_1^x, \ldots, h_\ell = g_\ell^x$. What is x ?

Lemma 1. *If the DL is intractable then so is the VDL problem.*

Proof. By contradiction. Assume that there is a probabilistic polynomial-time algorithm A which for any instance of VDL outputs the solution. So if we have an instance of the DL problem determined by the triplet (N, g, h) we can first convert it to an instance of VDL problem by selecting ℓ random values $\gamma_1, \ldots, \gamma_\ell$ and computing $g_1 = g^{\gamma_1}, \ldots, g_\ell = g^{\gamma_\ell}$ and the matching values $h_1 = h^{\gamma_1}, \ldots, h_\ell = h^{\gamma_\ell}$. Now we can input the instance to our algorithm and collect the solution x. It also means that the DL can be solved by our polynomial-time algorithm A. This is the requested contradiction.

Assume that our principals have been running the protocol ℓ times. We define a view $V_i(\ell)$ of principal P_i which specifies the information available to P_i after ℓ successful execution of the protocol. It is easy to verify that

$$V_i(\ell) = \{f_i(z), S_i^{(2)} \rightarrow \text{ (setup stage)}$$
$$\alpha_1 = g^{r_1}, \alpha_1^{S_1^{(1)}}, \ldots, \alpha_1^{S_n^{(1)}}, \alpha_1^s \rightarrow \text{ (1st run)}$$
$$\vdots$$
$$\alpha_\ell = g^{r_\ell}, \alpha_\ell^{S_1^{(1)}}, \ldots, \alpha_\ell^{S_n^{(1)}}, \alpha_\ell^s \rightarrow \text{ (ℓ-th run)}$$
$$+ \text{ public information }\}$$

where $r_1, \ldots, r_\ell$ are random values obtained from R. Note that the strings $\varepsilon_{i,j}$ generated for key confirmation purpose, are omitted from the view. The reason is that the assumption that the hash function is cryptographically strong is not enough to draw any conclusions about the overall security of the protocol. It is expected that hash function must not share any homomorphic property with exponentiation (see [9]).

Theorem 2. *Assume that we consider the protocol without key confirmation. If the principals honestly follow the protocol and run it successfully ℓ times and the applied discrete logarithm instances are intractable, then the seed s remains unknown to principals (and outsiders).*

Proof. (Sketch) An honest principal knows her view $V_i(\ell)$. A principal can derive the seed from secret sharing by trying to compute missing shares. To do this, she must reverse all public shares revealed during a single run of the protocol. This is equivalent to solving instances of DL which are assumed to be intractable. The second way to find the seed s is to ensemble an instance of VDL, which according to Lemma 1 is intractable.

Consider the efficiency of the protocol. The first part in which principals design their private secret sharing schemes is not computationally intensive. The reconstruction of the secret key S and the key verification constitute the main computational overhead. To reconstruct the secret key, principals have to first compute their public shares and later use the Lagrange interpolation to recover the polynomial $\alpha^{F(z)}$ and the secret $S = \alpha^{F(0)}$.

Communication overhead for the protocol consists of two components. The first one involves confidential delivery of the shares $s_{i,j}^{(2)}$ from any single principal to others – this consumes $(n - 1)$ confidential transmissions for every principal. The second component consists of broadcasting shares $\beta_{i,} = \alpha^{s_{i,j}^{(1)}}$. This takes n broadcast transmissions for all principals. Table 1 summarises the communication and computation overhead for the protocol.

Our protocol compares favourably with other key agreement protocols. For example, the protocols by Burmester and Desmedt [2] are designed with a specific network configuration in mind. The most evident weakness of their protocols seems to be the lack of principal authentication. Just and Vaudenay [13] incorporated the authentication of principals into the Burmester-Desmedt protocols but the authentication can be achieved with the neighbouring principals only.

		communication (message sent by each principal)	computation (calculations done by each principal)
registration		1 message sent to registry	1 exponentiation
Setup	preparation		$\approx 2n^2$ multiplications and additions for computations of shares
	distribution	n messages sent to other principals via secure channel	n exponentiations
Call for conference	Share broadcast	n broadcasts	n exponentiations
	Key Calculation		$(n+1)$ exponentiations (Lagrange interpolation)
	Key Confirmation	1 message broadcasts	Hashing of a single message and 1 exponentiation for authentication

Table 1. Communication and computation requirements for the protocol

6 Modifications and Extensions of the Protocol

Consider a modification of the protocol based on $(t+1, 2n)$ secret sharing, i.e. the threshold is $t+1$ and the number of shares is $2n$ ($t < n$) with n principals. To initialise the protocol all n principals are active. This stage is identical to the one used in our protocol. To trigger the conference, it is enough that t principals broadcast their public shares. Let the set of the principals who broadcast the public shares be $\mathcal{A}$. To obtain the common secret key, each principal (including these who have not broadcast their public shares) takes the broadcast public shares and corrects her secret share by removing share contributions received from all principals not in $\mathcal{A}$. In other words, principals are working with a secret sharing defined by $F_{\mathcal{A}}(z) = \sum_{P_i \in \mathcal{A}} f_{P_i}(z)$ where $f_{P_i}(z)$ is the polynomial defining the private secret sharing generated by P_i. The modified protocol has the following remarkable properties.

1. A principal who does not belong to $\mathcal{A}$, can always join the conference later by using the public shares and key confirmation strings ε.

2. A principal not in $\mathcal{A}$ can attend the conference passively, i.e. collect all public information which allow her to obtain the secret key. Later she can read all the information exchanged during the conference without others knowing that she is present.

3. It is possible to add a new principal to the conference (enrolment). It is enough that a newcomer designs her private secret sharing and distributes her shares to other members and other members give her their shares.

4. A principal can be expelled from the group (disenrolment). Assume that the conference group $\mathcal{A}$ decided collectively to remove P_k from the conference. Principals from $\mathcal{A} \setminus P_k$ make public all the shares they have given to P_k at the setup stage. Also they discard all shares obtained from P_k. In effect, the group $\mathcal{A} \setminus P_k$ is working with the secret sharing $F_{\mathcal{A} \setminus P_k} = \sum_{P_i \in \mathcal{A}; P_i \neq P_k} f_{P_i}(z)$. The share of this secret sharing held by P_k is now public. So if $(t-1)$ principals from the group $\mathcal{A} \setminus P_k$ broadcast their shares, all members except P_k can recover the secret. P_k knows her share given to her by the others at the setup stage and $(t-1)$ public shares. This is not enough to recover the secret (the threshold is $t+1$). Other principals know their own secret share, the share owned by P_k and made public, and $(t-1)$ public shares – they can recover the secret key and go ahead with the conference protocol. P_k cannot participate in conference. Observe that the effective threshold drops by one after each expulsion.

The requirements for construction of $(n+1, 2n)$ secret sharing seems to be a bit artificial. The protocol can be converted into the protocol based on (t, n) Shamir scheme with shares divisible into a multiple of 2 subshares and $t = \frac{n+1}{2}$. The construction of Shamir schemes with subshares is given in [8]. In this variant of the protocol, principals handle subshares to initialise and trigger the conference.

Acknowledgement

Authors wish to thank anonymous reviewers for their critical comments.

References

1. G. R. Blakley. Safeguarding cryptographic keys. In *Proc. AFIPS 1979 National Computer Conference*, pages 313–317. AFIPS, 1979.

2. M. Burmester and Y. Desmedt. A secure and efficient conference key distribution system. In A. De Santis, editor, *Advances in Cryptology - EUROCRYPT'94*, pages 275–286. Springer, 1995. Lecture Notes in Computer Science No. 950.

3. C. Charnes, J. Pieprzyk, and R. Safavi-Naini. Conditionally secure secret sharing schemes with disenrolment capability. In *Proceedings of the 2nd ACM Conference on Computer and Comm u nication Security, November 2-4, 1994, Fairfax, Virginia*, pages 89–95, 1994.

4. W. Diffie and M. E. Hellman. New directions in cryptography. *IEEE Trans. Inform. Theory*, IT-22:644–654, November 1976.

5. W. Diffie, P. Van Oorschot, and M. Wiener. Authentication and authenticated key exchanges. *Designs, Codes, and Cryptography*, 2:107–125, 1992.

6. I. Ingemarsson, D. Tang, and C. Wong. A conference key distribution system. *IEEE Trans. Information Theory*, IT-28:714–720, 1982.

7. K. Koyama and K. Ohta. Identity-based conference key distribution systems. In C. Pomerance, editor, *Advances in Cryptology - CRYPTO'87*, pages 175–184. Springer-Verlag, 1988. Lecture Notes in Computer Science No. 293.

8. K. Martin, J. Pieprzyk, R. Safavi-Naini, and H. Wang. Changing thresholds in the absence of secure channels. In *Proceedings of the Fourth Australasian Conference on Information Security and Privacy (ACISP99)*. Springer-Verlag, 1999. see these proceedings.

9. A. Menezes, P. van Oorschot, and S. Vanstone. *Handbook of Applied Cryptography*. CRC Press, Boca Raton, 1997.

10. R. M. Needham and M. D. Schroeder. Using encryption for authentication in large networks of computers. *Communications of the ACM*, 21(12):993–999, December 1978.

11. A. Shamir. How to share a secret. *Communications of the ACM*, 22:612–613, November 1979.

12. D.R. Stinson. An explication of secret sharing schemes. *Designs, Codes and Cryptography*, 2:357–390, 1992.

13. Just, Mike and Vaudenay, Serge (1996). Authenticated multi-party key agreement. *Advances in Cryptology-Asiacrypt '96*, pages 36-49.

On m-Permutation Protection Scheme Against Modification Attack

W. W. Fung[1] and J. W. Gray, III[2]

[1] Department of Computer Science,
Hong Kong University of Science and Technology
Clear Water Bay, Kowloon, Hong Kong
wwfung@cs.ust.hk
[2] RSA Laboratories West,
2955 Campus Drive, Suite 400,
San Mateo, CA 94403-2507, USA
Jgray@rsa.com

Abstract. The EEPROM modification attack was first described by Anderson and Kuhn in [3]. This simple and low-cost attack is very efficient against tamperproof devices carrying a secret key stored in EEPROM. Soon after the attack has been published, we proposed a protection scheme using cascaded m-permutations of hidden wires [8]. This cascaded m-permutation protection scheme uses an $(m \times n)$-bit encoding for an n-bit key and for which the best known attack will take at most $O(n^m)$ probes to compromise the permutations of the hidden wires. However, it is observed that if a particular card (instead of the whole batch of cards) is to be compromised, the complexity can be greatly reduced, and in the best cases, it can even be reduced to linear time complexity. In this paper, we demonstrate how it can be done, and propose a revised m-permutation scheme that would close the loop-hole. It is also proved that the probability of breaking the revised scheme will be $\frac{1}{2^{n-1}}$ for a n-bit key.

1 Introduction

Anderson and Kuhn introduced the EEPROM modification attack in [3]. This is a physical attack in which two microprobing needles are used to set or clear target bits in an effort to infer those bits. In this attack, the location of the key within EEPROM is assumed to be known. This is in fact often the case, since, in practice, a DES key is often stored in the bottom eight bytes of the EEPROM. It is also assumed that EEPROM bits cannot be read directly since equipment to sense the value of an EEPROM bit is substantially more expensive than the microprobing needles.

Anderson and Kuhn's attack makes use of the key parity errors implemented in many applications utilizing DES. Their assumption is that the tamperproof device will not work (e.g., returning an error condition) whenever a key parity error is detected.

Note that in addition to requiring only low-cost equipment, this attack can be carried out with very few probes. In particular, it takes only one or two probes to get each key bit and hence, $2n$ or fewer probes for an n-bit key.

Although Anderson and Kuhn originally described the above attack with respect to a DES key and the associated key-parity bits, the attack can be generalized for an arbitrary key, with or without key-parity bits. In particular, to infer bit i, the attacker runs the device once before setting bit i, and once after setting bit i. If the output changes in any way (e.g., giving a key parity error or simply giving a different output), we know the original value for bit i is zero; if there was no change, the original value was one. Thus, the attack is quite general and can be applied to virtually any key stored in a known EEPROM location. To put our discussion in the most general terms, we use the term *fault* to include any kind of error or output change that can be exploited by an attacker.

In our attempt to devise a scheme to protect the key bits from the modification attack, we proposed a cascaded m−permutation scheme [8] that greatly increases the number of probes needed to carry out an EEPROM modification attack. In this paper, we will discuss the weakness of the cascaded m-permutation scheme for the *individual* card and propose a revised scheme in which the assumption that the attacker cannot see the EEPROM is released. The probability of breaking this scheme is $\frac{1}{2^{n-1}}$ for a n-bit key.

Following the notations in [8], we will use

1. **K** to denote the actual key bit vector. That is, the key value to be used by the card in encrypting, signing, etc.
2. **P** to denote the physical key bit vector. This is the bit pattern stored in the EEPROM.

2   Cascaded m-permutation Protection

2.1   Model

Several assumptions have been made in [8]:

1. the attacker is a class I attacker[1], that is, a "clever outsider with moderately sophisticated equipment".
2. **P** is assumed to be stored in EEPROM and that the attacker cannot read the EEPROM directly.
3. the attacker is not able to see the exact wiring of the device.
4. the attacker can get physical access to one or more of the devices and can operate each one as many times as desired. Other than the hidden wiring, the algorithm is open.

This wiring is considered to be the "batch key", which is known only to the manufacturers and to those who are legitimately programming the device.

In addition, a protection scheme is formally specified by the following entities:

1. n — the length of the actual key $\mathbf{K} = k_0 k_1 \cdots k_{n-1}$

2. p — the length of the physical key $\mathbf{P} = P[0]P[1]\cdots P[p-1]$
3. The function *encode* maps actual keys to physical keys and will be used at the card-programming / card-issuing organization (e.g., the bank) to produce the key patterns to be burned into the chip:

$$encode : \{0,1\}^n \longrightarrow \{0,1\}^p$$

4. The decoding functions and wiring functions will be implemented by the chip manufacturer. For each actual key bit, i, $0 \le i < n$:
   - Define A_i to be the arity (i.e., the number of inputs) of the ith decoding function. (In the expected usage, $A_i \ge 1$.)
   - For $0 \le i < n$, the ith decoding function *decode*$_i$ is the function producing the ith bit of the actual key $\mathbf{K}$ given A_i bits of the physical key $\mathbf{P}$.

$$decode_i : \{0,1\}^{A_i} \longrightarrow \{0,1\}$$

   - For $0 \le i < n$, the ith wiring function determines the offset within $\mathbf{P}$ from where a wire is connected to the ith decoding function:

$$wiring_i : \{1, \cdots, A_i\} \longrightarrow \{0, 1, \cdots, p-1\}$$

For example, $wiring_i(j) = k$ means the jth input bit for the ith decoding function is *wired* from the kth bit of $\mathbf{P}$.

2.2 Permutation

In this approach, the manufacturer chooses (as the batch key) a random permutation of the n-bit key. This permutation is used to form $\mathbf{P}$ at device programming time. To restore the actual key, $\mathbf{K}$, the wiring inverts the permutation. In terms of the above model, this scheme is described as follows.

1. $p = n$
2. $A_i = 1$ for all i
3. $encode = $ permutation function π:

$$\pi : \{0, 1, \cdots, n-1\} \longrightarrow \{0, 1, \cdots, n-1\}$$

4. $wiring_i(1) = \pi^{-1}(i)$
5. $decode_i = $ identity function
   and hence $k_i = P[wiring_i(1)]$

Breaking the Permutation Scheme Even though the attacker does not know the permutation, he can break the permutation scheme in $O(n)$ probes, as follows. First, the attacker applies the original attack and, with $O(n)$ probes, finds the n bits of $\mathbf{P}$.

The attacker starts his attack without knowing the permutation nor the actual key, $\mathbf{K}$. However, he can find the permutation in an additional $O(n)$

probes. In particular, the wiring pattern can be found as follows. As the attacker knows the function of the device (e.g., encryption using DES), he can find the device output (using, e.g., a PC) for the following n (i.e., for DES $n = 56$) actual keys: $0\ldots 01, 0\ldots 10, \cdots, 10\ldots 0$. Let us name these n outputs $\alpha_1, \ldots,$ α_n (with very high probability, these α_i's are distinct).

After computing the α_i, the attacker uses probes to write $0\ldots 01$ to the area storing **P**, operates the device, and compares the encrypted result with all the α_i. Since the protection scheme is simply a permutation, one of the α_i will match. Thus, the first wiring line is identified. Continuing with the remaining $n - 1$ patterns $(0\ldots 10, \cdots, 10\ldots 0)$, all the wiring information can be revealed. And thus, the key **K** is found in $O(n)$ probes.

2.3 Protection Via m Permutations

We showed in [8] that by cascading (i.e. concatenating) m (≥ 2) permutations (i.e. $\mathbf{P} = 1^{st}$ *permuted* $\mathbf{K} \odot \cdots \odot m^{th}$ *permuted* $\mathbf{K}$), it will take the attacker $O(n^m)$ probes to compromise the batch key and **K** :

Theorem 1. *If a protection scheme uses m different permutations cascaded together, a brute-force search will take at most $O(n^m)$ time for the attacker to compromise the batch key and* **K**.

3 Observation

The above theorem only gives an *upper bound* for breaking the whole batch of cards. Usually, we simply need to crack a single card instead of the whole batch of devices. With the above cascaded m-permutation scheme, it is hard to break the whole batch, but it may not be true for the individual card.

One weakness of the cascaded m-permutation scheme is that the number of occurrence of 0s and 1s are preserved, though their locations are permuted. This gives the attacker additional information (the number of 0s and 1s in key **K**) to exploit. Before we proceed to discuss this, the following definitions are introduced:

Definition 1. *A permutation matrix[7] corresponding to a permutation π is a matrix M_π which has the effect of permuting a vector by π when it multiplies the vector. That is, $M_\pi \mathbf{K}$ = permuted* **K**.

M_π will be a $n \times n$ matrix if **K** is of length n, and **K** is considered as a $n \times 1$ column vector. The matrix $M_\pi = (m_{ij})_{n\times n}$ can be derived from π by

$$m_{ij} = \begin{cases} 1 & \text{if } j = \pi(i) \\ 0 & \text{otherwise} \end{cases}$$

(Note that we can also consider **K** as a row vector. In this case, the permuted **K** can be calculated by $\mathbf{K} M_\pi^T$. It is only a matter of choice on notation, and in the following discussion, we will treat **K** as a column vector.)

Using this definition, we can describe the batch key for the cascaded m-permutation as a m-tuples $(M_{\pi_1}, M_{\pi_2}, \cdots, M_{\pi_m})$.

Definition 2. *The* minority ratio *of a key* **K** *of length n is defined as the fraction of occurrence of 0s or 1s in* **K**, *whichever is smaller, to n.*

The following lemma follows naturally from this definition:

Lemma 1. *The* minority ratio, $r \leq \frac{1}{2}$.

Consequently, when an attacker attempts to break a card protected by the above m-permutation scheme, it is observed that the attacker can estimate how much effort is needed if he makes use of the additional information of the occurrence of 0s and 1s via the following theorem:

Theorem 2. *The complexity of breaking an individual card which is protected by the cascaded m-permutation scheme will be discounted multiplicatively by r^m for the brute-force attack, where r is the minority ratio of the n-bit key* **K** *of the card.*

Proof. Let S be $\{0, \cdots, n-1\}$. Define $G_0 = \{i \in S | k_i = 0\}$ and $G_1 = \{i \in S | k_i = 1\}$. Pick

$$G = \begin{cases} G_0 & \text{if } |G_1| > |G_0| \\ G_1 & \text{if } |G_0| \geq |G_1| \end{cases}$$

where $|A|$ denotes the cardinality of set A.

To break an individual card, we need to get $(M_{\pi_1}, M_{\pi_2}, \cdots, M_{\pi_m})$, and $\mathbf{P}$ so that the $\mathbf{K}$ can be derived. Two facts are observed. First, $\mathbf{P}$ can easily be compromised in $O(n)$ time using modification attack. Second, for the individual card, there may exist more than one instance of $(M_{\pi_1}, M_{\pi_2}, \cdots, M_{\pi_m})$ to derive $\mathbf{K}$ correctly together with $\mathbf{P}$. This is obvious because if $r, s \in S - G$, $M_{\pi_i}\mathbf{K} = M'_{\pi_i}\mathbf{K}$ where M'_{π_i} is M_{π_i} with rows r and s interchanged.

As a result, in cracking the batch key, instead of trying all n vectors $000 \cdots 1$, $000 \cdots 10$, $\cdots$, $100 \cdots 0$, we need only to try for cases corresponding to $i \in G$. Hence, the worst case complexity will be reduced multiplicatively by r for each pass of the *for* loop. $\qquad\square$

As a result, the complexity of breaking an individual card depends, to certain extent, on r which in turns depends on the bit pattern of $\mathbf{K}$. In the best case, when r approaches 0 (when $\mathbf{K}$ has only a few 0s (or 1s) while the majority of the bits are 1s (or 0s)), the complexity will fall to a near-linear complexity for this special case.

In the worst case, as r is bounded by $\frac{1}{2}$, we have the following corollary:

Corollary 1. *The complexity of breaking an individual card which is protected by the cascaded m-permutation scheme is bounded by $(\frac{n}{2})^m$ for the brute-force attack.*

4 Revised scheme

To cover the holes that we described in the last section, we propose in this section a scheme in which

1. the bit occurrence of 0s and 1s in $\mathbf{K}$ will be unknown to the attacker;
2. we do not care if the EEPROM can be read directly somehow.

The motivation for this scheme is that instead of storing the permuted $\mathbf{K}$ as $\mathbf{P}$, we store permuted versions of $\mathbf{K}$ *xor*'ed with two independently chosen n-bit words $\mathbf{K}_{D_i}$ which will be dumped after use.

The basic set-up is the same as the cascaded m-permutation scheme but with the following amendments:

1. m must be odd
2. $\mathbf{P}$ is no longer $M_{\pi_1}\mathbf{K} \odot \cdots \odot M_{\pi_m}\mathbf{K}$; instead, it will be $\mathbf{P} = \mathbf{P}_1 \odot \mathbf{P}_2 \odot \cdots \odot \mathbf{P}_m$ where

$$\mathbf{P}_1 = M_{\pi_1}(\mathbf{K} \oplus M_{\pi_2}\mathbf{K}_{D_2} \oplus M_{\pi_3}\mathbf{K}_{D_3})$$
$$\mathbf{P}_2 = M_{\pi_2}(\mathbf{K} \oplus M_{\pi_3}\mathbf{K}_{D_3} \oplus M_{\pi_4}\mathbf{K}_{D_4})$$
$$\vdots$$
$$\mathbf{P}_i = M_{\pi_i}(\mathbf{K} \oplus M_{\pi_{(i+1 \bmod m)}}\mathbf{K}_{D_{(i+1 \bmod m)}} \oplus M_{\pi_{(i+2 \bmod m)}}\mathbf{K}_{D_{(i+2 \bmod m)}})$$
$$\vdots$$
$$\mathbf{P}_m = M_{\pi_m}(\mathbf{K} \oplus M_{\pi_1}\mathbf{K}_{D_1} \oplus M_{\pi_2}\mathbf{K}_{D_2})$$

and, to help resolve the value of $\mathbf{K}$, we store another m n-bit words $(\mathbf{P}_{D_1}, \mathbf{P}_{D_2}, \cdots, \mathbf{P}_{D_m})$ in EEPROM:

$$\mathbf{P}_{D_1} = \mathbf{K} \oplus \mathbf{K}_{D_1}$$
$$\mathbf{P}_{D_2} = \mathbf{K} \oplus \mathbf{K}_{D_2}$$
$$\vdots$$
$$\mathbf{P}_{D_m} = \mathbf{K} \oplus \mathbf{K}_{D_m}$$

Note that $\mathbf{K}_{D_i}$'s will be dumped after use. Their values can only be deduced when both $\mathbf{K}$ and the corresponding $\mathbf{P}_{D_i}$'s are known.

3. One candidate of decoding function is to get $\mathbf{K}$ by the following decoding function:

$$\bigoplus_{i=1}^{m} M_{\pi_i}^{-1}\mathbf{P}_i$$

where the hidden wiring implements the $M_{\pi_i}^{-1}$'s.

Property 1. If $\mathbf{P}_i$'s are set up as above, then

$$\bigoplus_{i=1}^{m} M_{\pi_i}^{-1}\mathbf{P}_i = \begin{cases} \mathbf{K} & \text{if } m \text{ is odd} \\ 0 & \text{if } m \text{ is even} \end{cases}$$

As a result, if m is odd, the above decoding function will always return the correct value of $\mathbf{K}$ if the card has not been tampered.

However, it is not an ideal decoding function as the attacker can compromise the ith permutation details, via technique described in section 2.2, by comparing encrypted result of vector with only one bit on, i.e., by setting the $\mathbf{P}_i$ to $000\cdots1$, $000\cdots10$, $\cdots$, $100\cdots0$ one by one while setting other $\mathbf{P}_j$'s $(j \neq i)$ to $000\cdots0$ and compare the result with the encrypted pattern of $000\cdots1$, $000\cdots10$, $\cdots$, $100\cdots0$ respectively.

A method is needed to ensures that the above system of equations are satisfied. That is, we need to find an expression for $\mathbf{K}$ that is not expensive (in terms of complexity in building the circuit) to calculate, and at the same time, avoid the above attack. Our approach is to find an initial guess of $\mathbf{K}$ first, and then substitute it into the above system of equations:

1. $\mathbf{K}$ is initially set as $\bigoplus_{i=1}^{m} M_{\pi_i}^{-1}\mathbf{P}_i$
2. rearrange the above system of equations for $\mathbf{P}_i$'s; we have then, for all i,

$$\mathbf{K} = M_{\pi_i}^{-1}\mathbf{P}_i \oplus M_{\pi_{(i+1 \bmod m)}}\mathbf{K}_{D_{(i+1 \bmod m)}} \oplus M_{\pi_{(i+2 \bmod m)}}\mathbf{K}_{D_{(i+2 \bmod m)}}$$

$$= M_{\pi_i}^{-1}\mathbf{P}_i \oplus$$

$$M_{\pi_{(i+1 \bmod m)}}(\mathbf{P}_{D_{(i+1 \bmod m)}} \oplus (\bigoplus_{i=1}^{m} M_{\pi_i}^{-1}\mathbf{P}_i)) \oplus$$

$$M_{\pi_{(i+2 \bmod m)}}(\mathbf{P}_{D_{(i+2 \bmod m)}} \oplus (\bigoplus_{i=1}^{m} M_{\pi_i}^{-1}\mathbf{P}_i))$$

If $\mathbf{P}_i$'s has not been tampered with, the correct $\mathbf{K}$ will be returned if we logically AND, or logically OR all these m $\mathbf{K}$'s. Hence, $\mathbf{K}$ can be calculated via the following steps:

1. Calculate $\mathbf{K}_{\text{and}}$ by:

$$\mathbf{K}_{\text{and}} = \bigwedge_{i=1}^{m} \left\{ M_{\pi_i}^{-1}\mathbf{P}_i \oplus M_{\pi_{(i+1 \bmod m)}}(\mathbf{P}_{D_{(i+1 \bmod m)}} \oplus (\bigoplus_{i=1}^{m} M_{\pi_i}^{-1}\mathbf{P}_i)) \oplus \right.$$
$$\left. M_{\pi_{(i+2 \bmod m)}}(\mathbf{P}_{D_{(i+2 \bmod m)}} \oplus (\bigoplus_{i=1}^{m} M_{\pi_i}^{-1}\mathbf{P}_i)) \right\}$$

2. Calculate $\mathbf{K}_{\text{or}}$ by:

$$\mathbf{K}_{\text{or}} = \bigvee_{i=1}^{m} \left\{ M_{\pi_i}^{-1}\mathbf{P}_i \oplus M_{\pi_{(i+1 \bmod m)}}(\mathbf{P}_{D_{(i+1 \bmod m)}} \oplus (\bigoplus_{i=1}^{m} M_{\pi_i}^{-1}\mathbf{P}_i)) \oplus \right.$$
$$\left. M_{\pi_{(i+2 \bmod m)}}(\mathbf{P}_{D_{(i+2 \bmod m)}} \oplus (\bigoplus_{i=1}^{m} M_{\pi_i}^{-1}\mathbf{P}_i)) \right\}$$

3. If $\mathbf{K}_{\text{and}} = \mathbf{K}$ and $\mathbf{K}_{\text{or}} = \mathbf{K}$, then return $\mathbf{K}$; else return an error message.

With these steps, it is of high probability that an error message will be returned if the attacker applies an attack by setting one P_i to $00 \cdots 1$ while setting the other P_j's $(j \neq i)$ to $00 \cdots 0$.

5 Analysis

First, the following property on binomial coefficients C_i^n of $(1 + x)^n$ is noted:

Property 2. $\sum_0^{\lfloor \frac{n}{2} \rfloor} C_{2i}^n = \sum_0^{\lfloor \frac{n+1}{2} \rfloor - 1} C_{2i+1}^n = 2^{n-1}$

That is, the sum of coefficients of even-powered terms is equal to the sum of coefficients of odd-powered terms.

Proof. This follows directly from the fact that $C_k^n = C_k^{n-1} + C_{k-1}^{n-1}$. □

With this property, we further note that in *most* of the cases, the attacker has a probability of $\frac{1}{2^{n-1}}$ to guess for the correct n-bit key. This security is based on the following properties.

Property 3. If π is an unknown permutation, X and Y are random variables of n-bit binary words in which $X = M_\pi Y$, then

$$P(Y = y | X = x) = P(X = x | Y = y) = \frac{1}{C_{nr}^n}$$

where r is the minority factor of y (and x) as defined in section 3.

Proof. To apply an unknown permutation π on x (or y) with minority ratio r, there will be C_{nr}^n possible distinct combination of bit pattern for y (or x) and hence the result. □

Property 4. If π_i's are unknown permutations, X_{D_i}'s are independently chosen random variables of n-bit binary words, and X and Y are random variables of n-bit binary words satisfying

$$Y = M_{\pi_1}(X \oplus M_{\pi_2} X_{D_2} \oplus M_{\pi_3} X_{D_1}),$$

then

$$P(X = x | Y = y) = P(X = x)$$

Proof. Let $R = M_{\pi_2} X_{D_2} \oplus M_{\pi_3} X_{D_1}$, $Y' = X \oplus R$. Then $Y = M_{\pi_1} Y'$. By Bayes' theorem,

$$P(X = x | Y' = y') = \frac{P(X = x \wedge Y' = y')}{P(Y' = y')}$$

As

$$
\begin{aligned}
P(X = x \wedge Y' = y') &= P(X = x \wedge R = y' \oplus x) \\
&= P(X = x)P(R = y' \oplus x) \qquad \text{due to independence} \\
&= P(X = x)\alpha, \qquad \text{say}
\end{aligned}
$$

and

$$P(Y' = y') = \sum_x P(X = x \wedge Y' = y')$$

$$= \sum_x P(X = x)\alpha = \alpha \sum_x P(X = x) = \alpha$$

we have

$$P(X = x|Y' = y') = \frac{P(X = x)\alpha}{\alpha} = P(X = x)$$

Hence,

$$P(X = x|Y = y) = \frac{P(X = x \wedge Y = y)}{P(Y = y)}$$

$$= \frac{P(X = x \wedge Y' = y')}{P(Y' = y')} \qquad \text{as } \pi_1 \text{ is 1-1 and onto}$$

$$= P(X = x|Y' = y') = P(X = x)$$

□

Property 5. If π_1 and π_2 are two unknown permutations, W_1 and W_2 are two n-bit words (with n_1 and n_2 1s respectively), then the probability of guessing $W = M_{\pi_1} W_1 \oplus M_{\pi_2} W_2$ is given by

$$\frac{1}{\sum_{i=0}^{\frac{u-l}{2}} C_{l+2i}^n}$$

where

$$l = |n_1 - n_2|$$

$$u = \begin{cases} n_1 + n_2 & \text{if } n_1 + n_2 \le n \\ 2n - (n_1 + n_2) & \text{if } n_1 + n_2 > n \end{cases}$$

Given $m \ge 3$, for any m n-bit words $W_1, W_2, \cdots, W_m$ (with $n_1, n_2, \cdots,$ and n_m 1s respectively), if there exist

1. two words W_i and W_j, $i \ne j$ such that the resulting $W' = M_{\pi_i} W_i \oplus M_{\pi_j} W_j$ has possibly $l, l+2, \cdots,$ and u 1s; and
2. a third word W_k, $k \ne i, k \ne j$, such that $l \le n_k \le u$ and $n_i + n_j + n_k \ge n$,

then the probability of guessing $W = \bigoplus_{i=1}^m M_{\pi_i} W_i$ is $\frac{1}{2^{n-1}}$.

Proof. In this proof, we first imagine all the 1s of W_i's sink down to the bottom of the column vectors while the 0s float at the top, and then try to figure out the total number of possible bit patterns of the resulting vector when the 1s of one vector start to float gradually to the top.

For $m = 2$ case: if $W = M_{\pi_1} W_1 \oplus M_{\pi_2} W_2$, then W has at least $|n_1 - n_2|$ 1s when the 1s of the *shorter* vector *cancels* out part of the 1s of the *longer* vector (as $1 \oplus 1 = 0$). W will have at most $n_1 + n_2$ 1s when the 1s from W_1 and W_2 stack up within the n-bit boundary. If $n_1 + n_2$ is greater than n, some of the $n_1 + n_2$ 1s will be forced to coincide with each other (which has the effect of losing 1s as $1 \oplus 1 = 0$), and the resulting number of 1s in W will be $n - (n_1 + n_2 - n) = 2n - (n_1 + n_2)$.

Hence, W is expected to have at least l 1s and at most u 1s. It is also noted that the oddity of l and u are the same, and so $u - l$ is even. When the shorter vector starts to float upwards to the top, the number of 1s will be incremented by 2 each time . Therefore, the possible number of 1s in W can only be $l, l+2, \cdots, u$, and so the possible number of bit patterns for W will be $\sum_{i=0}^{\frac{u-l}{2}} C_{l+2i}^n$ and hence the probability of guessing the correct bit pattern is $1/(\sum_{i=0}^{\frac{u-l}{2}} C_{l+2i}^n)$

For $m \geq 3$ case: if $W' = M_{\pi_i} W_i \oplus M_{\pi_j} W_j$ has possibly $l, l+2, \cdots,$ and u 1s and W_k has n_k 1s where $l \leq n_k \leq u$ and $n_i + n_j + n_k \geq n$, then depending whether n_k is odd or even, $W'' = W' \oplus M_{\pi_k} W_k$ will possibly have $1, 3, \cdots, 2(\lfloor \frac{n+1}{2} \rfloor - 1) + 1$ 1s if $n_k + l$ is odd; while it will possibly have $0, 2, \cdots, 2(\lfloor \frac{n}{2} \rfloor)$ 1s if $n_k + l$ is even. Therefore, there will be $\sum_0^{\lfloor \frac{n}{2} \rfloor} C_{2i}^n = \sum_0^{\lfloor \frac{n+1}{2} \rfloor - 1} C_{2i+1}^n = 2^{n-1}$ different bit patterns for W'' and hence the probability of guessing its value is $\frac{1}{2^{n-1}}$. By adding more terms to W'' will not increase the possible bit patterns; it simply provides alternative *routes* to get to a particular bit pattern. □

In virtue of the above properties, the knowledge of $\mathbf{P}_i$'s as described by the revised scheme doesn't leak any information of $\mathbf{K}$. As these $\mathbf{P}_i$'s are independent to each other, the probability of guessing $\mathbf{K}$ will be $\frac{1}{2^{n-1}}$ if there are at least 3 $\mathbf{P}_i$'s satisfying the above properties, and the security is approximate to guessing an unknown key of $n - 1$ bit long.

The extra $\mathbf{P}_{D_i}$ stored in the EEPROM will not help much to the attacker as it is basically an one-time pad setup and its existence is unconditionally secure.

As the security of the scheme is affected by the number of 1s in $\mathbf{P}_i$'s, it would be wise to abandon candidate $\mathbf{P}_i$'s with very small number of 1s or very large number of 1s. For example, if $\mathbf{P}_i = 111 \cdots 1$, it contributes no protection at all, as any permutation applied to this value will remain the same.

6   Discussion

In this paper, we proposed a revised scheme that would close the loopholes (due to information leaked by the number of occurrence of 0s and 1s) by storing m (e.g. $m = 3$) $\mathbf{P}_i$'s each of which is formed by first *xor*'ing $\mathbf{K}$ with two permuted versions of independent chosen n-bit words $\mathbf{K}_{D_{(i+1 \bmod m)}}$ and $\mathbf{K}_{D_{(i+2 \bmod m)}}$, and then permuting the result. With this setup, two goals are achieved: (1) the bit occurrence of 0s and 1s are hidden, as each $\mathbf{P}_i$ is now more than a permuted version of $\mathbf{K}$, and (2) the attacker has only a probability of $\frac{1}{2^{n-1}}$ to guess for the n-bit key $\mathbf{K}$. In addition, the restriction that EEPROM cannot be read directly has been released. But then, as the whole security relies on the difficulty in solving for the batch key, this method would fail for attackers who can access to equipment that can reverse-engineer the whole card and be able to see the wiring configuration (that is, see the M_{π_i}'s).

Acknowledgments

We would like to thank Dr. M.J. Golin for his helpful comments and numerous remarks on this work.

References

1. D.G. Abraham, G.M. Dolan, G.P. Double, and J.V. Stevens, "Transaction Security System", in *IBM Systems Journal*, volume 30, number 2, (1991), p.206–229.
2. R. Anderson and M. Kuhn, "Tamper Resistance – a Cautionary Note" in *Proceedings of the Second USENIX Workshop on Electronic Commerce (1996)*, p.1–11.
3. R. Anderson and M. Kuhn, "Low Cost Attacks on Tamper Resistant Devices", in *Security Protocols : 5th International Workshop*, (1997), p.125–136.
4. F. Bao, R.H. Deng, Y. Han, A. Jeng, A.D. Narasimhalu, and T. Ngair, "Breaking Public Key Cryptosystems on Tamper Resistant Devices in the Presence of Transient Faults", in *Security Protocols : International Workshop '97*
5. D. Boneh, R.A. DeMillo, and R.J. Lipton, "On the Importance of Checking Cryptographic Protocols for Faults", in *Advances in Cryptology - EUROCRYPT '97*, p.37–51.
6. E. Biham and A. Shamir, "Differential Fault Analysis of Secret Key Cryptosystems", in *Advances in Cryptology - CRYPTO '97*, p.513–25
7. T.H. Cormen, C.E. Leiserson and R.L. Rivest, "Introduction to Algorithms", *MIT Press*, 1990.
8. W.W. Fung and J.W. Gray, "Protection Against EEPROM Modification Attacks", in *Information Security and Privacy: Third Australasian Conference, ACISP'98*, 1998, p.250–260.
9. M.R. Garey and D.S. Johnson, "Computers and Intractability", *W.H. Freeman & Co.*, 1979.
10. C.E. Shannon, "Communication Theory of Secrecy System", in *Computer Security Journal* Vol.6, No.2, 1990, p.7–66.

Inversion Attack and Branching

Jovan Dj. Golić[1], Andrew Clark[2], and Ed Dawson[2]

[1] School of Electrical Engineering, University of Belgrade
Bulevar Revolucije 73, 11001 Belgrade, Yugoslavia
Email: golic@galeb.etf.bg.ac.yu
[2] Information Security Research Centre, Queensland University of Technology
GPO Box 2434, Brisbane Q 4001, Australia
Email: {aclark,dawson}@fit.qut.edu.au

Abstract. The generalized inversion attack on nonlinear filter generators is developed and analyzed by the theory of critical branching processes. Unlike the inversion attack which requires that the filter function be linear in the first or the last input variable, this attack can be applied for any filter function. Both theory and systematic experiments conducted show that its time complexity remains close to 2^M, M being the input memory size, while the additional memory space required is relatively small for most the filter functions.

1 Introduction

Nonlinear filter generators are popular building blocks in shift register based keystream generators for stream cipher applications, because they enable one to achieve the cryptographic security with a relatively small number of shift registers, see [7], [6]. A binary nonlinear filter generator consists of a single binary linear feedback shift register (LFSR), with a typically primitive feedback polynomial, and a nonlinear boolean function whose inputs are taken from some shift register stages to produce the output. A nonlinear filter generator should be designed so as to resist all known cryptanalytic attacks applicable. The objective of the cryptanalytic attacks considered is to determine the unknown, secret key controlled LFSR initial state from a sufficiently long segment of the known keystream sequence. A set of design criteria to achieve a long period, a high linear complexity, and good statistical properties of the keystream sequence as well as the resistance to the fast correlation attack [5], to the conditional correlation attack [1], and to the inversion attack [3] is recommended in [3].

Let r be the LFSR length, let n denote the number of nondegenerate input variables of the filter function f, let $\gamma = (\gamma_i)_{i=1}^n$ denote the tapping sequence specifying the inputs to f, and let $M = \gamma_n - \gamma_1$ denote the input memory size of the nonlinear filter generator regarded as a finite input memory combiner with one input and one output [3].

The inversion attack [3] applies as such to the case when the filter function is linear in the first or the last input variable, and runs forwards or backwards accordingly. This case is important as the only known case when the output sequence of a nonlinear filter generator as a combiner with one input and one output is purely random for every possible choice of the tapping sequence γ given that the input sequence is purely random. It is even conjectured in [3] that other such cases may not exist at all. The attack consists in guessing the unknown M bits of the initial memory state, which is a part of the unknown LFSR initial state, then in the (unique) inversion of the first $r-M$ bits of the known keystream sequence into the corresponding $r - M$ bits of the LFSR sequence, and, finally, in checking the output sequence produced from the LFSR sequence obtained by the linear recursion from the determined r bits on additional $M + c$ bits of the keystream sequence (where c is a small positive integer). Its computational complexity is at worst 2^M, or 2^{M-1} on average.

To render the inversion attack infeasible, γ should be such that M is large and preferably close to its maximum possible value $r - 1$. In addition, to prevent reducing the effective input memory size by a uniform decimation technique [3], the greatest common divisor of $(\gamma_i - \gamma_1)_{i=1}^n$ should be equal to one.

Another way of preventing the inversion attack is to choose f that is linear in neither the first nor the last input variable. Of course, if M is large, then it is not possible to check by the exhaustive analysis of the associated augmented function ($M + 1$ successive bits as a function of $2M + 1$ input ones) whether the output is purely random given that the input is such. Nevertheless, if the design criteria related to positive difference sets and correlation immunity are respected, then it is not practically possible to find a statistical weakness in the output even if it exists. However, a more general, so-called generalized inversion attack is also suggested in [3] which may work for any filter function. It goes along similar lines as the inversion attack with the only difference that the first $r-M$ keystream bits are not necessarily uniquely inverted into the corresponding $r - M$ input bits of the LFSR sequence.

Instead, a binary tree structure of maximum depth $r - M$ is formed to store all possible solutions for the $r - M$ input bits, for every guessed initial memory state. It is also suggested in [3] that the theory of branching processes may be used to analyze the size of the resulting trees. While it is certainly true that the correct (very likely, unique) LFSR sequence must be found by this attack, it remains to analyze its complexity, especially if $r - M$ is large. The main question to be answered is whether the resulting trees are then so large that the complexity gets close to 2^r, which would render the attack ineffective. This is exactly the main objective of this paper. We will show both by the theory of branching processes and experimentally that the complexity of the generalized inversion attack is, perhaps surprisingly, also very close to 2^M regardless of the choice of the filter function. Consequently, the choice of f cannot prevent the inversion attack in its generalized form.

The inversion attack [3] is briefly reviewed in Section 2, the generalized inversion attack is described and further developed in Section 3 and analyzed by the theory of critical branching processes (outlined in the Appendix) in Section 4, experimental results are presented and discussed in Section 5, and the conclusions are given in Section 6.

2 Inversion Attack

Let $x = (x(t))_{t=-r}^{\infty}$ be a binary maximum-length sequence of period $2^r - 1$ $((x(t))_{t=-r}^{-1}$ is the LFSR initial state), let $f(z_1, \ldots, z_n)$ be a boolean function of n, $n \leq r$, nondegenerate input variables, and let $\gamma = (\gamma_i)_{i=1}^{n}$ be an increasing sequence of nonnegative integers such that $\gamma_1 = 0$ and $\gamma_n \leq r - 1$. Then the output sequence $y = (y(t))_{t=0}^{\infty}$ of the nonlinear filter generator is defined by

$$y(t) = f(x(t - \gamma_1), \ldots, x(t - \gamma_n)), \quad t \geq 0. \tag{1}$$

If we assume that the input sequence is purely random, that is, a sequence of balanced (uniformly distributed) and independent bits (binary random variables) and that the filter function is balanced (has balanced output given a balanced input), then the output sequence is not necessarily such. It is shown in [3] that the output sequence is purely random for every tapping sequence if $f(z_1, \ldots, z_n) = z_1 + g(z_2, \ldots, z_n)$ or $f(z_1, \ldots, z_n) = g(z_1, \ldots, z_{n-1}) + z_n$.

The objective of the inversion attack is to reconstruct the LFSR initial state from a segment of the keystream sequence, given the LFSR feedback polynomial of degree r, the filter function f, and the tapping sequence γ. The attack runs forwards or backwards depending on whether f is linear in the first or the last input variable, respectively. In the former case, put (1) into the form

$$x(t) = y(t) + g(x(t - \gamma_2), \ldots, x(t - \gamma_n)), \quad t \geq 0, \tag{2}$$

which means that the nonlinear filter generator as a combiner with one input and one output is invertible if the initial memory state is known. The forward inversion attack then goes as follows.

1. Assume (not previously checked) M bits $(x(t))_{t=-M}^{-1}$ of the unknown initial memory state.
2. By using (2), generate a segment $(x(t))_{t=0}^{r-M-1}$ of the input sequence from a known segment $(y(t))_{t=0}^{r-M-1}$ of the keystream sequence.
3. By using the LFSR linear recursion, generate a sequence $(x(t))_{t=r-M}^{N-1}$ from the first r bits $(x(t))_{t=-M}^{r-M-1}$.
4. By using (1), compute $(\hat{y}(t))_{t=r-M}^{N-1}$ from $(x(t))_{t=r-2M}^{N-1}$ and compare with the observed $(y(t))_{t=r-M}^{N-1}$. If they are the same, then accept the assumed initial memory state and stop. Otherwise, go to step 1.

It takes 2^{M-1} trials on average to find a correct initial memory state. One may as well examine all 2^M initial memory states. In that case, the algorithm yields all the LFSR sequences that produce the given keystream sequence of length N. The found candidate initial states could then be examined on a longer sequence as well, which may reduce their number. If the determined LFSR sequence is not unique, then any such sequence is a satisfactory solution (equivalent LFSR initial states yielding the same keystream sequence), but for most filter functions this situation is very unlikely.

3   Generalized Inversion Attack

The generalized inversion attack as suggested in [3] applies to an arbitrary filter function f which need not be linear in the first or the last input variable. Without essential loss of generality, f is assumed to be balanced. For such a function, there exists a nonzero fraction p_+ of values of the input variables $(z_2, \ldots, z_n)$ where f is equal to zero or one (equally likely) regardless of z_1 and, similarly, a nonzero fraction p_- of values of the input variables $(z_1, \ldots, z_{n-1})$ where f is equal to zero or one (equally likely) regardless of z_n. In this case, one should find the minimum of p_+ and p_- and then accordingly apply the generalized inversion attack in the forward or backward direction. In the generalized inversion attack, the objective is to find all possible, not necessarily unique, input sequences of length $r - M$ consistent with a given segment of the keystream sequence of the same length, for each assumed initial memory state, whereas the rest is the same as in the inversion attack. The (generalized) inversion attack thus exploits the dependence between the input and the output sequence to the maximum possible extent.

3.1   Forward and Backward Attacks

In the forward generalized inversion attack, given the current output bit $y(t)$ and a guessed current memory state $(x(i))_{i=t-M}^{t-1}$ (the preceding M input bits), the basic equation (1) may have a unique solution for $x(t)$, may have no solution for $x(t)$, or may have two solutions for $x(t)$ (both zero and one). Given a segment of $r - M$ successive output bits, proceeding forwards one bit at a time, one can thus obtain and store all possible solutions for an input sequence in a binary tree structure of maximum depth $r - M$. Each node in the tree represents an internal memory state of M successive input bits. Similarly, in the backward inversion attack, one proceeds backwards one bit at a time, each time finding from equation (1) all possible solutions for $x(t - M)$ given the current output bit $y(t)$ and a guessed current memory state $(x(i))_{i=t-M+1}^{t}$ (the next M input bits). Accordingly, without loss of generality, from now on we will deal only with the forward generalized inversion attack.

Let, for simplicity, $p = p_+$. In the probabilistic model where the LFSR initial state is chosen uniformly at random, any $M + 1$, $M \leq r - 1$, successive input bits (defining the inputs to f) are balanced and independent. Without essential difference, the given keystream sequence can be considered either as fixed or as purely random and independent of the LFSR sequence. In this model, for any $t \geq 0$, the number of possible solutions for the current input bit $x(t)$ is a nonnegative integer random variable Z with the probability distribution, independent of t,

$$\Pr\{Z = 0\} = \frac{p}{2}, \quad \Pr\{Z = 1\} = 1 - p, \quad \Pr\{Z = 2\} = \frac{p}{2}. \tag{3}$$

Its expected value and variance are given by

$$\mu = 1, \quad \sigma^2 = p. \tag{4}$$

3.2 Basic Attack

It is interesting to examine the case $p = 1$, when f does not effectively depend on the first input variable z_1, in more detail. Then M is bigger than the effective memory size, and guessing M successive input bits is the same as guessing all the input bits to f as well as some additional input bits if $\gamma_2 - \gamma_1 > 1$. Accordingly, the attack can then be reduced to the so-called *basic generalized inversion attack*, in which one guesses $M + 1$ successive input bits $(x(i))_{i=t-M}^{t}$ and then checks whether the corresponding output bit determined by f is the same as the observed $y(t)$ or not. If not, then there is no solution for the next input bit $x(t+1)$ and the guess is discarded as incorrect. If yes, then there are two possible solutions for $x(t+1)$ and the search is continued in the same manner for both of them. In the probabilistic model as above, the number of solutions for $x(t+1)$ is a random variable Z defined by (3) for $p = 1$. It takes only two values, 0 and 2, each with probability $1/2$, and has the expected value and variance both equal to 1, see (4).

Initially, exactly one half of the guesses are discarded, so that the total effective number of initial guesses is in fact 2^M, which is the same as before. Of course, the corresponding 2^{M+1} trees, half of which are empty, store all the solutions for the input sequences of length $r - M$ given the known output sequence of the same length which are the same as above, but the trees are different. Each node contains $M + 1$ rather than M successive input bits and the trees have maximum depth $r - M - 1$ rather than $r - M$, but the nodes at the first and the last level have to be checked if they are consistent with the first and the last output bit, respectively. The main difference from the generalized inversion attack described above is that the nodes at each level have to be generated before they are tested for consistency with the corresponding output bit. The trees can be grouped in 2^M pairs each corresponding to the same initial memory state and each pair can be aggregated into a single tree, the same as above, in an obvious way by discarding all the nodes without branches leaving out. So, the basic generalized inversion attack is less efficient, as should be expected, since it does not make use of p_+ being smaller than 1. The basic attack can also run in the backward direction as well.

3.3 Binary Trees

In the forward generalized inversion attack, for each assumed initial memory state $(x(t))_{t=-M}^{-1}$, the obtained binary tree, representing all the solutions for the next $r - M$ bits $(x(t))_{t=0}^{r-M-1}$ consistent with the known $r - M$ output bits $(y(t))_{t=0}^{r-M-1}$, is, of course, unique given $(y(t))_{t=0}^{r-M-1}$. For each $1 \leq n \leq r - M$, let Z_n denote the number of nodes at level n, that is, the number input segments $(x(t))_{t=0}^{n-1}$ of length n that are consistent with the output segment $(y(t))_{t=0}^{n-1}$. The initial level $n = 0$ contains only one node representing an initial memory state $(x(t))_{t=-M}^{-1}$, whereas each node in the tree represents an internal memory state of M successive input bits. In practice, one can also store only one level at a time, but then each node at level n should represent an input segment of variable size n, $1 \leq n \leq r - M$, rather than of constant size M. Another possibility would be to store only one bit per node, but then the whole tree must be kept, and for each node, the internal state needed for the construction process is recovered by backtracking through the preceding $M - 1$ levels.

Let $Y_n = \sum_{l=1}^{n} Z_l$ denote the total number of nodes in the tree up to level n, without counting the initial node. Then the (normalized) time and space complexities of the tree construction process are given as $\sum Y_{r-M}/(r - M)$ and $\max\{Y_{r-M}\}$, where the sum and the maximum are both over all 2^M initial memory states. If one stores input segments of variable size rather than internal memory states, then the space complexity (in bits) for a single tree is $\max\{l\, Z_l : 1 \leq l \leq r - M\}$ rather than $M\, Y_{r-M}$. The total number of the obtained solutions for input segments $(x(t))_{t=-M}^{r-M-1}$ of length r that are consistent with the given output segment is given as $\sum Z_{r-M}$ where the sum is over all 2^M initial memory states. Note that for the basic generalized inversion attack, the figures are slightly different. Namely, the space complexity is $\max\{Y_{r-M-1}\}$, the time complexity is $\sum(1 + Y_{r-M-1})/(r - M)$, and the total number of solutions is $\sum Z_{r-M}/2$ (the nodes at level $r - M$ are not effectively produced), where the sums and the maximum are over all 2^{M+1} initial guesses.

Consequently, the main problem to be addressed is how large these values can grow as $r - M$ increases.

4 Probabilistic Analysis via Branching Processes

4.1 Probabilistic Models

The basic probabilistic model to be considered is one in which $(x(t))_{t=-M}^{-1}$ is uniformly distributed and $(y(t))_{t=0}^{r-M-1}$ is a random variable indepedently generated from a uniformly distributed LFSR initial state. Note that $(y(t))_{t=0}^{r-M-1}$ need not be uniformly distributed and in fact is not likely to be such if $p > 0$. In particular, some output segments may not be possible at all. In the related, but different model where the output segment is uniformly distributed, the expected values of both Z_n and Y_n/n are equal to 1 for each $1 \leq n \leq r - M$. So, in this model, the expected total number of consistent solutions for $(x(t))_{t=-M}^{r-M-1}$ (to be checked in the final stage of the generalized inversion attack) as well as the expected time complexity of the tree construction are both exactly 2^M, which is the same as in the inversion attack.

Not only can the expected values be different in the realistic, basic model, but also it is conceivable that Z_{r-M} and/or $Y_{r-M}/(r - M)$ can be big depending on a particular output segment. In the inversion attack, where $p = 0$, this is not possible, because the variance of Z_n is zero for every guessed initial memory state. More generally, if the output segment is uniformly distributed and $p > 0$, then the number of solutions is exactly 2^M for each output segment, but the variance of Z_n need not be equal to zero for every guessed initial memory state. Consequently, the problem here is to estimate the expected values and the variances as well as the probability distributions of both Z_n and Y_n/n in the basic probabilistic model.

The variances and the probability distributions of Z_n and Y_n/n in general depend on a particular filter function and on a chosen tapping sequence as well. They could be estimated empirically in various cases of interest, as is demonstrated in the next section. However, a reasonably good approximation providing insight into the size of the random tree spanned can be obtained by the theory of critical branching processes outlined in the Appendix. One may consider the random tree produced by the random initial memory state and the random or a fixed output segment. In both the cases, the associated branching process is one with the branching probability distribution defined by (3). It is a *critical Galton-Watson process* with the expected value 1 and the variance p of the branching random variable Z_1.

The random tree produced by the associated branching process is not the same as the random one obtained by the tree construction process. The reason for this is that in the branching process the branching probability distribution for a given node is independent of the nodes at the same or the preceding levels (the history), whereas in the tree construction process there is a dependence between the nodes as a result of successive inputs to the filter function having some bits in common. Note that the dependence is not influenced by the LFSR recursion, since only r successive bits of the LFSR sequence are examined. This dependence is relatively weak if the tapping sequence defines a positive difference set and is stronger if it is equidistant, that is, if $\gamma = (\delta i)_{i=0}^{n-1}$ where δ is a positive integer. As a consequence, the probability distributions of both the variables Z_n and Y_n/n are somewhat different. However, the difference is expected to be relatively small for both their expected values and variances, as they are only affected by relatively weak pairwise and triplewise dependences between different levels in the random tree generated by the tree construction process.

4.2 Expected Values and Variances

In view of Theorem 1 from the Appendix, we then get that for the associated branching process, $E(Z_n) = 1$, $\text{Var}(Z_n) = pn$, and $\Pr\{Z_n > 0\} = 1 - f^{(n)}(0)$ where $f^{(n)}(s)$ is the self-composition (10) of the generating function, $f(s) = p/2 + (1-p)s + ps^2/2$, of the branching probability distribution (3). This probability can be evaluated numerically. For any n, $\Pr\{Z_n > 0\} \le 1 - p/2$ and for large n, $\Pr\{Z_n > 0\} \approx 2/(pn)$, provided $p > 0$. If p is very small, than this probability is close to 1, unless n is very large. Accordingly, the expected fraction of the guessed initial memory states giving rise to at least one input segment of length n that is consistent with the given output segment of length n is $1 - f^{(n)}(0)$. On the other hand, Theorem 2 from the Appendix gives that $E(Y_n/n) = 1$ and $\text{Var}(Y_n/n) = pn/3$. In view of the Chebyshev inequality $\Pr\{|Y_n/n - E(Y_n/n)| \ge \varepsilon\} \le \text{Var}(Y_n/n)/\varepsilon^2$, we then get that Y_n/n is with high probability $O(\sqrt{n})$ and the multiplicative constant is not big. Note that in the case of interest $n = r - M$.

It is interesting to see how large Z_n and Y_n/n can grow when conditioned on the event that there exists at least one input segment of length n that is consistent with the output segment. At least one such initial memory state exists, corresponding to the original LFSR sequence producing the given output sequence. Theorem 3 from the Appendix shows that for $p > 0$ and large n, $E(Z_n|Z_n > 0) \approx pn/2$ and $\text{Var}(Z_n|Z_n > 0) \approx p^2n^2/4$. This means that the number of solutions is with high probability linear in n, provided at least one such solution exists. As for Y_n/n, the note from the Appendix shows that for $p > 0$ and large n, $E(Y_n/n|Z_n > 0) = O(pn)$ and $\text{Var}(Y_n/n|Z_n > 0) = O(p^2n^2)$, so that Y_n/n is then with high probability $O(pn)$. Consequently, the resulting tree is then bigger than on average, but still relatively small even if $n = r - M$ is big.

4.3 Correction Factor

One may take the estimates given above as good approximations for the random tree generated by the tree construction process. Recall that in the basic probabilistic model, one first chooses a random uniformly distributed LFSR initial state, then generates the corresponding output segment of length $r - M$, and, finally, independently chooses a uniformly distributed initial memory state and constructs the corresponding tree. So, for each achievable output segment of length $r - M$, one in fact constructs 2^M trees corresponding to all possible initial memory states. The above estimates would have been good approximations if all 2^{r-M} output segments were achievable. Since this is not the case, a correction has to be made. Namely, the random variables Z_n and Y_n/n have to be conditioned on the *achievability* event that there exists at least one initial memory state, among 2^M of them, with at least one input segment of length n consistent with the output segment. The conditioning event is the same as the one that the output segment is achievable or, in terms of the theory of branching processes, that among 2^M independently generated trees there exists at least one of depth n. It is easily seen that the expected fraction of achievable output segments of length n is then

$$q_n = 1 - f^{(n)}(0)^{2^M} \sim 1 - \left(1 - \frac{2}{pn}\right)^{2^M}. \tag{5}$$

Thus, the theory of branching processes helps one analyze how many output segments of a given length are expected to occur at the output of a nonlinear filter generator which reflects its statistical properties. Consequently, for any $n \geq 1$, the random variable Z_n in the original branching process is a mixture of the zero random variable, with probability $1 - q_n$, and the random variable Z_n conditioned on the achievability event, with probability q_n. Both $E(Z_n)$ and $\Pr\{Z_n > 0\}$ then increase by the multiplicative factor q_n^{-1}, whereas $\text{Var}(Z_n)$ approximately increases by the same factor. The random variable Y_n/n is more difficult to analyze, but it is clear that one may expect that the trees produced from achievable output segments by the basic probabilistic model are bigger in size about q_n^{-1} times up to level n than the ones produced by arbitrary, not necessarily achievable output segments. In particular, for $n = r - M$, the correction factor q_{r-M}^{-1} becomes significant if $2^M(1 - f^{(r-M)}(0)) \leq 1$.

4.4   Time and Space Complexities

As noted before, the time and space complexities of the tree construction process are given as $T = \sum Y_{r-M}/(r-M)$ and $S = \max\{Y_{r-M}\}$, where the sum and the maximum are both over all 2^M initial memory states. The analysis conducted above based on the theory of critical branching processes shows that the expected time complexity is about $q_{r-M}^{-1} 2^M$ and that with high probability, under the reasonable independence assumption,

$$T \leq q_{r-M}^{-1} 2^M + 2^{M/2}(r-M)^{1/2}\sqrt{3pq_{r-M}^{-1}}. \tag{6}$$

Note that the correction factor q_{r-M}^{-1} depends on $r-M$, M, and p, and for $p > 0$ and large $r-M$ satisfies $q_{r-M}^{-1} \leq p(r-M)/2$. The total number of obtained input segments of length r consistent with the given output segment of length $r-M$ is $K = \sum Z_{r-M}$ and has about the same expected value as T and the variance three times bigger. As a result, it satisfies a relation analogous to (6).

However, the space complexity increases only linearly with M. This is a consequence of the exponential probability distribution (17) given in Theorem 3 in the Appendix. Namely, the expected number of levels in all 2^M trees of depth n with the number of nodes not smaller than nc is for large n very close to

$$2^M \cdot \sum_{l=1}^{n} \frac{2}{\sigma^2 l} e^{-2cn/(\sigma^2 l)} < 2^M \cdot \frac{2}{\sigma^2} e^{-2c/\sigma^2} \sum_{l=1}^{n} \frac{1}{l} \tag{7}$$

where $\sum_{l=1}^{n} \approx 0.577 + \ln n$, 0.577 approximating the Euler constant. On the condition that this number is not bigger than a given constant, it follows that c increases linearly with M. Hence, with high probability

$$S \leq \frac{r-M}{1-f^{(r-M)}(0)} + O\left(M(r-M)^{3/2}\sqrt{p(1-f^{(r-M)}(0))^{-1}}\right) \tag{8}$$

which for $p > 0$ and large $r-M$ reduces to

$$S \leq \frac{p}{2}(r-M) + O\left(Mp(r-M)^2\right) \tag{9}$$

where the multiplicative constant is relatively small (the first additive term is included to encompass the case when $p = 0$). Here, the bigger correction factor $(1 - f^{(r-M)}(0))^{-1}$ is used instead of q_{r-M}^{-1}, because S is determined by the tree of the maximum size which very likely has full depth $r-M$, and at least one such tree is produced (the correct initial memory state).

It is clear that, unlike the time and space complexities, the fraction of achievable output segments of any given length as well as the total number of input segmens consistent with a given output segment are both indepedent of whether the attack is applied in its forward ($p = p_+$), backward ($p = p_-$), or basic ($p = 1$) form. So, (5) is only an approximation. It is reasonable to expect that the approximation corresponding to the minimum of p_+ and p_- is better, especially if this minimum is relatively small.

5 Experimental Results

In this section, we present results obtained by systematic experimental analysis of various nonlinear filter generators. The shift register length chosen is $r = 100$ which is sufficiently big to study the effect of a large tree depth $r - M$. The primitive feedback polynomial chosen is $1 + x^2 + x^7 + x^8 + x^{100}$. We study the filter functions, f, with $n = 5$ and $n = 10$ input variables, and for each f selected, two tap settings, γ, are considered, one adjacent and the other corresponding to a full positive difference set, for $n = 5$, and to a random set, for $n = 10$ (since the memory size, M, would have been too large if we had chosen a full positive difference set for $n = 10$). The experimental results for each of the four cases are shown in Tables 1-4, respectively. In each case, we have randomly chosen 3 filter functions f with different probabilities $(p_+, p_-) = (0, 0.5)$, $(0.125, 0.875)$, and $(0.5, 0.5)$, and for each of them we have run the forward and backward generalized inversion attack as well as the forward basic generalized inversion attack attack for 50 randomly chosen LFSR initial states.

The results shown are the average number of solutions for consistent input segments of length r per each initial memory state guessed (that is, $K/2^M$ for the forward and backward attacks and $K/2^{M+1}$ for the basic one), the average time complexity of the tree construction process per each initial memory state guessed (that is, $T/2^M$ for the forward and backward attacks and $T/2^{M+1}$ for the basic one), the space complexity S, and the fraction of trees reaching the full depth $r - M$ for all the attacks. Note that in the basic attacks the level $r - M - 1$ is not empty after checking for consistency if and only if the level $r - M$ is not empty before checking for consistency. All the results are averaged over 50 randomly chosen LFSR initial states.

p_+	p_-	#Solutions	Time	Space	Prob	Attack
0.000	0.500	1.000	1.000	96.0	1.000	Forward
		1.000	1.000	1294.9	0.062	Backward
		0.500	1.000	190.0	0.500	Basic Fwd
0.125	0.875	25.156	8.635	2585.6	0.464	Forward
		25.156	8.434	6852.5	0.160	Backward
		12.578	8.461	4655.8	0.256	Basic Fwd
0.500	0.500	92.946	19.974	9550.0	0.185	Forward
		92.946	20.511	7984.8	0.305	Backward
		46.473	19.206	17142.7	0.123	Basic Fwd

Table 1. $(r, n, M) = (100, 5, 4)$, $\gamma = \{0, 1, 2, 3, 4\}$.

Table 5 contains the probability for a tree to reach the full depth, to be compared with the 'Prob' column of Tables 1-4, the fraction of achievable output segments of required lengths, and the corresponding correction factor for the number of solutions and for the time complexity. All of them are computed according to the theory of critical branching processes. Each found consistent

p_+	p_-	#Solutions	Time	Space	Prob	Attack
0.000	0.500	1.000	1.000	85.0	1.000	Forward
		1.000	1.000	107017.1	0.002	Backward
		0.500	1.000	168.0	0.500	Basic Fwd
0.125	0.875	4.544	1.989	4147.3	0.254	Forward
		4.544	1.885	841161.8	0.000	Backward
		2.272	1.959	7367.3	0.129	Basic Fwd
0.500	0.500	2.088	1.335	17551.8	0.025	Forward
		2.088	1.277	76110.2	0.003	Backward
		1.044	1.326	30788.8	0.013	Basic Fwd

Table 2. $(r,n,M) = (100,5,15)$, $\gamma = \{0, 1, 3, 7, 15\}$.

p_+	p_-	#Solutions	Time	Space	Prob	Attack
0.000	0.500	1.000	1.000	91.0	1.000	Forward
		1.000	1.000	3808.6	0.040	Backward
		0.500	1.000	180.0	0.500	Basic Fwd
0.125	0.875	2.198	1.384	1189.4	0.211	Forward
		2.198	1.421	7115.0	0.029	Backward
		1.099	1.375	2248.6	0.108	Basic Fwd
0.500	0.500	2.534	1.481	3821.1	0.058	Forward
		2.534	1.459	3596.4	0.067	Backward
		1.267	1.469	7218.4	0.031	Basic Fwd

Table 3. $(r,n,M) = (100,10,9)$, $\gamma = \{0, 1, 2, 3, 4, 5, 6, 7, 8, 9\}$.

p_+	p_-	#Solutions	Time	Space	Prob	Attack
0.000	0.500	1.000	1.000	85.0	1.000	Forward
		1.000	1.000	11232.8	0.028	Backward
		0.500	1.000	168.0	0.500	Basic Fwd
0.125	0.875	1.094	1.035	2891.5	0.148	Forward
		1.094	1.038	23706.4	0.011	Backward
		0.547	1.034	5310.7	0.075	Basic Fwd
0.500	0.500	1.278	1.120	10627.5	0.025	Forward
		1.278	1.103	8975.3	0.033	Backward
		0.639	1.119	20008.2	0.013	Basic Fwd

Table 4. $(r,n,M) = (100,10,15)$, $\gamma = \{0, 2, 3, 6, 7, 9, 10, 11, 14, 15\}$.

input segment of length r was then tested on an additional segment of the keystream sequence (the final stage of the inversion attack). For each examined nonlinear filter generator and every chosen LFSR initial state, it turns out that exactly one input sequence is consistent with the given keystream sequence, as should be expected since the number of input variables n is relatively small compared to r.

(r,n,M)	p				
	0.000	0.125	0.500	0.875	1.000
	$1 - f^{(r-M)}(0)$				
$(100,5,4)$	1.000	0.140	0.039	0.022	0.020
$(100,5,15)$	1.000	0.156	0.043	0.025	0.022
$(100,10,9)$	1.000	0.147	0.041	0.023	0.021
$(100,10,15)$	1.000	0.156	0.043	0.025	0.022
	q_{r-M}				
$(100,5,4)$	1.000	0.911	0.468	0.303	0.271
$(100,5,15)$	1.000	1.000	1.000	1.000	1.000
$(100,10,9)$	1.000	1.000	1.000	1.000	1.000
$(100,10,15)$	1.000	1.000	1.000	1.000	1.000
	q_{r-M}^{-1}				
$(100,5,4)$	1.000	1.098	2.136	3.300	3.695
$(100,5,15)$	1.000	1.000	1.000	1.000	1.000
$(100,10,9)$	1.000	1.000	1.000	1.000	1.000
$(100,10,15)$	1.000	1.000	1.000	1.000	1.000

Table 5. Full depth probabilities.

The experimental results shown generally agree very well with the theory of critical branching processes. In fact, by comparing Tables 2 and 4, where the memory sizes are the same, but the numbers of input variables are different, one may conclude that the dependence induced by overlapping successive inputs to the filter function (Table 4) tends to reduce the size of the constructed trees. The tables show that the space complexity required is smaller if the attack is run in the direction corresponding to the minimum of p_+ and p_-, as predicted by the theory, but, interestingly, the time complexities are mutually close for both the directions. The time complexities are exactly the same if p_+ or p_- is equal to zero. As the total number of solutions is the same in each case for all the attacks, the normalized number of solutions is halved for the basic attacks. However, no general conclusion can be drawn as to whether the number of solutions and the time complexity are determined by the minimum or the maximum of p_+ and p_-, see the '#Solutions' and 'Time' columns of Tables 1 and 2. The trees produced by the basic generalized inversion attack are roughly twice as big (the 'Time' and 'Space' columns) as those produced by the generalized inversion attack in the same direction (for simplicity, only the basic attack in the forward direction is displayed).

To demonstrate the accordance with the theory, consider Tables 1 and 2, for example. The number of solutions (per initial memory state guessed, column '#Solutions') is bigger in Table 1 than in Table 2, because the number of possible initial memory states is much smaller, so that the variance becomes significant, see (6), and because the correction factor is bigger than 1 for Table 1, unlike the other tables, see Table 5. The same holds for the time complexity (column 'Time'), except that the figures are smaller since the variance is smaller, see (6). The fact that the space complexity (column 'Space') is bigger in Table 2 than in Table 1 is also consistent with the theory, because the product $M(r - M)^2$ is then bigger, see (8) and (9).

6 Conclusions

The theory of critical branching processes is applied to analyze the time and space complexities of the generalized inversion attack on nonlinear filter generators. Both theory and systematic experimental results obtained show that, perhaps surprisingly, almost regardless of the choice of the filter function, the attack has time complexity close to 2^M, M being the input memory size, and requires relatively small additional storage. Consequently, the choice of the filter function that is linear in neither the first nor the last input variable is likely to spoil the output statistics, but does not prevent the inversion attack in its generalized form. The inversion attack is infeasible if M is sufficiently large, provided that the tapping sequence is such that M cannot be reduced by the uniform decimation technique. The attack can also be applied to nonlinear filter generators with multiple outputs, where the theory of subcritical branching processes is expected to be useful.

Appendix

Critical Branching Processes

Only the basic type of branching processes called the Galton-Watson processes will be considered, see [4], [2]. Such a branching process is a Markov chain $\{Z_n\}_{n=0}^{\infty}$ on the nonnegative integers whose transition function is defined in terms of a given probability distribution $\{p_k\}_{k=0}^{\infty}$. The initial random variable Z_0 takes value 1 with probability 1, and for any $n \geq 1$, the random variable Z_n conditioned on $Z_{n-1} = i$ is the sum of i independent identically distributed random variables with the probability distribution $\{p_k\}_{k=0}^{\infty}$ (if $i = 0$, then $Z_n = 1$). The process can be regarded as a random (finite or infinite) tree with Z_n being the number of nodes at level $n \geq 0$, where the number of branches leaving any node in the tree is equal to k with probability p_k, independently of other nodes at the same or previous levels. The generating function characterizing the probability distribution of Z_n can be expressed as the self-composition of the generating function $f(s) = \sum_{k=0}^{\infty} p_k s^k$ of $\{p_k\}_{k=0}^{\infty}$, which is the probability distribution of Z_1. Precisely, if $f^{(n)}(s)$, $0 \leq s \leq 1$, denotes the generating function of the probability distribution of Z_n and if $f^{(0)} = s$, then for every $n \geq 1$,

$$f^{(n)}(s) = f(f^{(n-1)}(s)). \tag{10}$$

The basic characteristic of a branching process is the expected number of branches leaving any node, that is,

$$\mu = E(Z_1) = \sum_{k=0}^{\infty} k \, p_k. \tag{11}$$

A branching process is called subcritical, critical, or supercritical if $\mu < 1$, $\mu = 1$, or $\mu > 1$, respectively. The extinction probability defined as the probability of a tree being finite is 1 for subcritical and (perhaps unexpectedly) critical processes and smaller than 1 for supercritical processes. We are here only interested in critical processes, whose main properties are given by the following theorem, see [2], [4]. Let $\sigma^2 = \mathrm{Var}(Z_1)$ be the variance of Z_1.

Theorem 1. *In the critical case, $\mu = 1$, if $\sigma^2 > 0$ ($p_1 < 1$) and $\sigma^2 < \infty$, then for any $n \geq 1$,*

$$E(Z_n) = 1 \tag{12}$$

$$\mathrm{Var}(Z_n) = \sigma^2 n \tag{13}$$

$$\Pr\{Z_n > 0\} = 1 - f^{(n)}(0) \sim \frac{2}{\sigma^2 n}. \tag{14}$$

Equation (14) implies that the extinction probability, $\lim_{n \to \infty} \Pr\{Z_n > 0\}$, is equal to 1, while the rate of convergence is relatively slow. The variance grows linearly with n although the expected value remains equal to 1.

It is also interesting to study the total number of nodes in a random tree up to level n, not counting the initial node, that is, the random variable $Y_n = \sum_{l=1}^{n} Z_l$, for any $n \geq 1$. Its generating function satisfies a recursion which reduces to a functional equation with a unique solution if $n \to \infty$, see [4]. Its expected value follows trivially, while its variance can be determined after a certain manipulation.

Theorem 2. *In the critical case, $\mu = 1$, if $\sigma^2 > 0$, then for any $n \geq 1$,*

$$E(Y_n) = n \tag{15}$$

$$\mathrm{Var}(Y_n) = \frac{\sigma^2}{6} n(n+1)(2n+1) \sim \frac{\sigma^2}{3} n^3. \tag{16}$$

Note that, although the extinction probability is 1, the expected value grows linearly with n and the variance increases as n^3 which is by a multiplicative factor n faster than what would hold if the random variables Z_l were independent.

Another interesting random variables to be considered are Z_n and Y_n conditioned on the event $\{Z_n > 0\}$. They are the number of nodes at level n and the total number of nodes up to level n, not counting the initial one, in a random tree reaching level n. The probability distribution of $Z_n|\{Z_n > 0\}$ is simply obtained by dividing the probability distribution of Z_n by $\Pr\{Z_n > 0\}$, see Theorem 1. The limit distribution of $Z_n/n|\{Z_n > 0\}$ in the critical case has been characterized by Yaglom, see [4], [2]. By computing the expected value [2] and variance, we can then formulate the following theorem.

Theorem 3. *In the critical case, $\mu = 1$, if $0 < \sigma^2 < \infty$, then*

$$\lim_{n \to \infty} \Pr\left\{ \frac{Z_n}{n} > z | Z_n > 0 \right\} = e^{-2z/\sigma^2}, \quad z \geq 0, \tag{17}$$

$$E(Z_n|Z_n > 0) = \frac{1}{1 - f^{(n)}(0)} \sim \frac{\sigma^2}{2} n \tag{18}$$

$$\mathrm{Var}(Z_n|Z_n > 0) = \frac{1}{1 - f^{(n)}(0)} \left(\sigma^2 n - \frac{f^{(n)}(0)}{1 - f^{(n)}(0)} \right) \sim \frac{\sigma^4}{4} n^2. \tag{19}$$

The probability distribution of the conditioned random variable $Y_n|\{Z_n > 0\}$ is not treated in the standard books on branching processes like [4] and [2]. Nevertheless, the previous theorems and the results regarding the conditioned random variable $Z_n|\{Z_{n+k} > 0\}$ presented in [2] lead us to conclude that in the critical case, $E(Y_n|Z_n > 0) = O(n(1 - f^{(n)}(0))^{-1}) = O(\sigma^2 n^2)$ and $\mathrm{Var}(Y_n|Z_n > 0) = O(\sigma^2 n^3 (1 - f^{(n)}(0))^{-1}) = O(\sigma^2 n^4)$.

References

1. R. J. Anderson, "Searching for the optimum correlation attack," Fast Software Encryption – Leuven '94, *Lecture Notes in Computer Science*, vol. 1008, B. Preneel ed., Springer-Verlag, pp. 137-143, 1995.
2. K. B. Athreya and P. E. Ney, *Branching Processes*. Springer-Verlag, Berlin, 1972.
3. J. Dj. Golić, "On the security of nonlinear filter generators," Fast Software Encryption – Cambridge '96, *Lecture Notes in Computer Science*, vol. 1039, D. Gollmann ed., Springer-Verlag, pp. 173-188, 1996.
4. T. H. Harris, *The Theory of Branching Processes*. Springer-Verlag, Berlin, 1963.
5. W. Meier and O. Staffelbach, "Fast correlation attacks on certain stream ciphers," *Journal of Cryptology*, vol. 1(3), pp. 159-176, 1989.
6. A. Menezes, P. van Oorschot, and S. Vanstone, *Handbook of Applied Cryptography*. New York: CRC Press, 1997.
7. R. A. Rueppel, *Analysis and Design of Stream Ciphers*. Berlin: Springer-Verlag, 1986.

Fail-Stop Threshold Signature Schemes Based on Elliptic Curves*

Willy Susilo, Rei Safavi-Naini, and Josef Pieprzyk

Centre for Computer Security Research
School of IT and CS
University of Wollongong
Wollongong 2522, AUSTRALIA
{s05, rei, josef}@uow.edu.au

Abstract. Fail-stop signatures provide security for a sender against a forger with unlimited computational power. In this paper we present a fail-stop signature scheme based on discrete logarithm problem for elliptic curves and then show that the signing process can be distributed among a group of senders to obtain a threshold signature scheme. The threshold signature scheme has a cheater detection property and allows the combiner to detect a sender who is submitting false shares. We will show that our fail-stop signature scheme works in the two commonly used models of signature schemes, with or without a trusted authority.

1 Introduction

Digital signature schemes are the most important cryptographic primitive for providing authentication in an electronic world. Digital signatures, introduced in the pioneering paper of Diffie and Hellman [7], allow a signer with a secret key to sign messages such that anyone with access to the corresponding public key be able to verify authenticity of the message. A digital signature scheme uses an instance of a hard mathematical problem as the basis of its claimed security. This means that the security is in computational sense and an enemy with unlimited resources can always forge the signature by solving underlying instance of the problem. To ensure security, parameters of the instances are chosen such that solving the instance of the problem would be beyond the computational means of the prospective attacker. A classical digital signature scheme has the disadvantage that there is no mechanism in the signature scheme to protect the signer against possible forgeries; that is if a signed message passes the verification test then it is assumed to be generated by the owner of the secret key. This effectively means that an all powerful enemy can always succeed in forging signatures.

To protect against this attack, fail-stop signatures (FSS) are proposed [27, 19,13]. In a fail-stop signature, in the case of forgery, the presumed signer is

---

* This work is in part supported by Australian Research Council Grant Number A49703076

able to prove that a forgery has happened. This is done by showing that the underlying intractability assumption of the system is broken. The system will be stopped at this stage- hence the name fail-stop. In this way, a polynomially bounded signer is protected against a forger with an unlimited computational power. A fail-stop signature scheme is a one-time digital signature that can be used for signing a single message for a specified secret and public key. However there are ways of extending the scheme to work for multiple messages [5, 26, 16, 1]. Fail-stop signature schemes can be made much more efficient if there is a single recipient [15, 17]. This is a common requirement in applications such as electronic payment where the bank is the sole recipient.

In a fail-stop signature scheme the sender and the receivers are all polynomially bounded, whereas the enemy has an unlimited computing power [26, 25, 18].

1.1 Previous Works

As noted in [3, 20, 25], fail-stop signature schemes exist if computing discrete logarithms or factoring large integers is hard. The first general construction of fail-stop signature [27], uses a one-time signature scheme (similar to [11]) and requires messages to be signed bit by bit. This construction is not efficient.

In [14] an efficient construction for a fail-stop signature for a single recipient model, that is the bank in an on-line payment system, is proposed. The main drawback of this system is that it does not allow public verification. Signature generation is a 3-round protocol between the signer and the recipient and so is expensive in terms of communication.

In [26], an efficient fail-stop signature scheme based on discrete logarithm, with public verification, is presented. The underlying intractability assumption for the scheme is that the discrete logarithm problem is difficult. In the case of dispute, the presumed signer can solve the instance of discrete logarithm problem, and prove that the underlying assumption does not hold.

In [25], fail-stop signature schemes using 'bundling homomorphism' are proposed. This is a generalisation of [26] but has a more complicated key exchange phase. The proof of forgery is done by the presumed signer by presenting two different signatures, the forged one and the one generated by the valid signer, and the proof-test is by showing that the two signatures collide under the 'bundling homomorphism'. A special case of this construction uses difficulty of factoring as the underlying assumption of the system.

The existence condition for fail-stop signature schemes is recently relaxed [3, 20, 25] and it is shown that a fail-stop signature scheme only exists if one-way permutations exist.

1.2 Our Contributions

In this paper, we propose a fail-stop signature scheme based on discrete logarithm problem over elliptic curves. For more information on elliptic curve, we refer the reader to [12]. The construction is essentially the same as the one given in [26] but it has the added key efficiency advantage of elliptic curve cryptosystems. We describe our scheme in a model where a centre that is trusted by all the recipients is present. This is similar to the model given in [26,6]. However we show that the role of the centre can be played by any of the recipients, hence resulting in a system with a single recipient. We show that the scheme can be transformed into a (t, n) threshold signature scheme where signature generation requires collaboration of t senders [23,2].

The proposed scheme allows detection of cheaters during the share submission phase and so protects against a sender submitting junk instead of valid shares in an attempt to disrupt the system operation.

The paper is organised as follows. In the next section, we present the basic concepts and definitions of fail-stop signature schemes and introduce the notations that are used throughout the rest of the paper. In section 3, we present our fail-stop signature scheme and in section 4, we extend it to a fail-stop threshold signature scheme. Section 5 concludes the paper.

2   Preliminaries

We briefly review the definition and requirements of fail-stop signatures and refer the reader to [19,18] for a more complete account.

A fail-stop signature scheme, similar to an ordinary digital signature scheme, consists of two procedures for generation and verification of signatures:

1. *Sign*: algorithm for signing messages,
2. *Verify*: algorithm for verifying signatures.

It also includes two more algorithms:

3. *Prove*: algorithm for proving a forgery,
4. *Proof-test*: algorithm for testing the proof of forgery.

A secure fail-stop signature scheme must satisfy the following properties [25, 18].

1. If the signer signs a message, the recipient can verify the signature.
2. A polynomially bounded forger cannot create forged signatures that successfully pass the verification test.
3. When a forger with an unlimited computational power succeeds in forging a signature that passes the verification test, the presumed signer can construct a proof of forgery and convince a third party that a forgery has occurred.
4. A polynomially bounded signer cannot create a signature that he can later prove to be a forgery.

To achieve the above properties, for each public key, there must exist many matching secret keys such that different secret keys create different signatures on the same message. The real signer knows only one of the secret keys, and can construct one of the many possible signatures on a given message. However an enemy with unlimited computing power, although can generate all the signatures but cannot determine which one will be used by the signer. Thus, it would be possible for the signer to provide a proof of forgery by generating a second signature on the message with a forged signature, and use the two signatures to break the underlying assumption of the scheme, hence proving the forgery.

To show security of a fail-stop signature [26, 18], it suffices to prove the following properties.

1. There exists a probabilistic polynomial time algorithm *proof* that takes a pair of secret and public key, a message and a forged signature for that message, and outputs a proof of forgery.
2. An enemy with unlimited computing power who knows the public key of the signer and his/her signature on a message, cannot find the secret key of the signer. Thus, he/she would not be able to construct signer's signature on a new message.
3. A polynomially bounded signer cannot construct a valid signature on a message, and later prove that it is a forgery.

These properties show that fail-stop signatures are unconditionally secure for the signer (first two requirements), and computationally secure for the recipient (third requirement).

Fail-stop signatures schemes are studied in two different model, where the main difference between the models is the existence of a centre (or a dealer) which is trusted by the recipients. The fail-stop signature schemes with a trusted centre, for example [26, 6], allow public verification and use a two-party protocol between the signer and the centre to generate the required keys.

This is to ensure that the signer cannot later deny his own signature and provide a proof of forgery for it. Fail-stop signature schemes without trusted centre, for example [25], are obtained by allowing every recipient to act as a centre. This results in a more efficient key exchange at the expense of loosing public verifiability property for the signature.

Elliptic Curves

Elliptic curve cryptosystems have attracted much attention in recent years because of the relatively small size of keys they require. An elliptic curve over $GF(p)$ is the set of points (x, y) with $x, y \in GF(p)$ satisfying the equation

$$y^2 = x^3 + ax + b$$

together with a special element denoted $\mathcal{O}$ and called the point at infinity. Addition operation on the points of an elliptic curve can be defined that makes it into an abelian group. For more precise definition of addition operation, we refer the reader to [12].

Let $E_p(a, b)$ denotes an elliptic curve of the form

$$y^2 = x^3 + ax + b \bmod p$$

where p is a prime number, $x^3 + ax + b = 0 \bmod p$ does not have multiple roots, and $4a^3 + 27b^2 \neq 0 \bmod p$.

$\#E_p(a, b)$ denotes the order of $E_p(a, b)$ and can be calculated in polynomial time using algorithms such as Schoof's algorithm [22, 8, 10], and combination of Schoof's algorithm with Shanks' baby-step giant-step algorithm [12].

Definition 1. *[12] An elliptic curve discrete logarithm problem (ECDL) is defined as follows. Let $\alpha \in E_p(a, b)$ be a point of order q, and let $\beta = d\alpha$. Given α and β, determine the unique integer d, where $0 \leq d \leq q$.*

ECDL is intractable [12] if the curve is well-chosen. In particular it is an easy problem for supersingular and anomalous curves.

3 A Fail Stop Signature Scheme based on Elliptic Curves

3.1 Model

Our model is similar to [6]. In this model, there is a centre, $\mathcal{D}$ who is trusted by the recipients (and not necessarily by the sender), who sets up the system, but is not involved in signature generation or verification. There is a sender, $\mathcal{S}$, who has a secret key. A recipient can verify a signature by using the sender's public key. In the case of dispute, the sender can prove that he can solve ECDL problem.

3.2 Scheme

System Setup

1. $\mathcal{D}$ chooses an elliptic curve such that $q = \#E_p(a, b)$ is also prime.
2. $\mathcal{D}$ randomly chooses a point $\alpha \in E_p(a, b)$, and a number $d \in GF(q)$. He calculates $\beta = d\alpha$ over $E_p(a, b)$ and discards d. Finally he publishes $(E_p(a, b), q, \alpha, \beta)$.

A simple algorithm to find such a curve is to randomly select a curve, find its order, discard the curve if the order is non-prime and repeat the process. It is conjectured that this type of curve can be obtained in $O(1/\log p)$ [9].

Sender's Key Generation

1. $\mathcal{S}$ checks to see if α and β belong to $E_p(a, b)$. If not, reject the public parameters.
2. If the public parameters are accepted, $\mathcal{S}$ chooses a 4-tuple, (k_1, k_2, k_3, k_4), $k_i \in GF(q), 1 \leq i \leq 4$, as his secret key.
3. $\mathcal{S}$ computes
$$\alpha_1 = k_3\alpha + k_1\beta \text{ over } E_p(a, b)$$
$$\alpha_2 = k_4\alpha + k_2\beta \text{ over } E_p(a, b)$$
and publishes (α_1, α_2) as his public key.

Message Signing

To generate the signature for a message $M \in GF(q)$, $\mathcal{S}$ computes

$$s_1 = k_1 M + k_2 \bmod q$$

$$s_2 = k_3 M + k_4 \bmod q$$

and publishes (s_1, s_2) as his signature on M.

Verification

A recipient can verify validity of a signature by testing testing the following equality.

$$s_2\alpha + s_1\beta \stackrel{?}{=} M\alpha_1 + \alpha_2 \text{ over } E_p(a, b)$$

Proof of forgery

In the case of forgery, where a forged signature, namely (s_1', s_2') passes the verification test, the presumed signer $\mathcal{S}$ can provide a proof of forgery by executing several steps:

1. Construct his own signature, (s_1, s_2), on M.
2. Compute $d = \frac{s_2' - s_2}{s_1 - s_1'} \bmod q$, and use this value as the proof of forgery.

Theorem 1. *If there is a forged signature that passes the verification test, the sender is able to solve ECDL problem.*

Proof. Suppose there exists a forged signature, (s_1', s_2'), on a single message M, that passes the verification test. The presumed sender produces his own signature, (s_1, s_2), which also passes the verification test. In this case, the following two equations hold:

$$s_2\alpha + s_1\beta = M\alpha_1 + \alpha_2 \text{ over } E_p(a, b)$$

and

$$s_2'\alpha + s_1'\beta = M\alpha_1 + \alpha_2 \text{ over } E_p(a, b)$$

Thus,

$$s_2\alpha + s_1\beta = s_2'\alpha + s_1'\beta \text{ over } E_p(a, b)$$
$$s_2\alpha - s_2'\alpha = s_1'\beta - s_1\beta \text{ over } E_p(a, b)$$
$$(s_2 - s_2')\alpha = (s_1' - s_1)\beta \text{ over } E_p(a, b)$$
$$= (s_1' - s_1)d\alpha \text{ over } E_p(a, b) \qquad (1)$$
$$(s_2 - s_2') = (s_1' - s_1)d \bmod q \qquad (2)$$
$$d = \frac{s_2 - s_2'}{s_1' - s_1} \bmod q \qquad (3)$$

The correctness of deriving equation 2 from 1 is ensured by the following lemmas.

Lemma 1. *[12, 24, 10] Any elliptic curve $E_p(a, b)$, where $q = \#E_p(a, b)$ is also prime, forms a cyclic group, which is isomorphic to $GF(q)$. Thus, any point other than the point at infinity is a generator of $E_p(a, b)$.*

Lemma 2. *If there is an equation of the form,*

$$c\gamma = a\gamma + b\gamma$$

over a curve $E_p(a, b)$ where $a, b, c \in GF(q)$ and $\gamma \in E_p(a, b)$, and $q = \#E_p(a, b)$ is prime, then we have

$$c = a + b \bmod q$$

3.3 Security Considerations

Lemma 3. *There are q^2 equally likely secret keys that match with the sender's public key.*

Theorem 2. *An enemy with unlimited computational power, knowing the public key of S and the signature on a message M, can calculate q possible secret keys that could have been used for signing the message.*

Theorem 3. *The signer can prove a forgery with probability $= \frac{q-1}{q}$.*

Corollary 1. *An enemy with unlimited computational power cannot compute the signer's signature on a new message.*

Theorem 4. *A computationally bounded signer cannot make signatures which he can later prove to be forgeries.*

Theorem 2, 3, 4 show that the proposed scheme satisfies all the requirements of fail-stop signatures mentioned in section 2.

Note that the secret key is a one-time key. If two different messages are signed using the same secret key, the secret key can be uniquely determined.

3.4 Signing Multiple Messages

In order to sign multiple messages, the approaches from [26] can be followed. However, this results growth exponentially in the number of keys. A recently proposed method of converting a one-time fail-stop signature to sign multiple messages by using accumulator ([1]). This method can be used in our scheme to enable signing multiple long messages, by choosing an accumulator a^{RSA} (as in [1]).

3.5 Second Model of Fail Stop Signatures

The fail-stop signature proposed above can be used in the second model of FSS signatures, that is without a trusted party [25], by allowing a recipient to play the role of the trusted party and hold the value d, secret from the sender. In this case the system set-up phase in section 3.2 will be performed by the recipient.

4 Fail-Stop Threshold Signature with Cheater Detection

4.1 Preliminaries

In a conventional (t, n) threshold signature scheme, there are n senders in which t of them must collaborate to generate a valid signature [23, 2].

In a fail-stop threshold signature, signature generation is similar to a conventional threshold signature, but in the case of a forged signature, senders are able to provide a proof of forgery. In the following we describe a fail-stop threshold signature scheme which is based on the FSS scheme given above. It has been equipped with cheater detection property to protect against participants sending false shares.

4.2 Model

Our model follows the construction as in [26, 6]. There is a group of n senders, $\mathcal{G} = S_1, S_2, \cdots, S_n$, a group coordinator $\mathcal{R}$, and a combiner $\mathcal{C}$, who is only trusted in combining partial signatures, and a centre $\mathcal{D}$ that is trusted by all the recipients. Neither $\mathcal{D}$ nor $\mathcal{R}$ are involved in signature generation. In case of dispute, senders can provide a proof of forgery by solving the ECDL problem.

As in the previous section, this model can be modified without having a centre $\mathcal{D}$, without changing any other setting and steps. Thus, it follows the model introduced in [25].

4.3 Signature Scheme

Initialisation

Initialisation consists of two steps,

1. System Setup
2. Group Coordinator's Setup

System Setup

1. $\mathcal{D}$ chooses an elliptic curve $E_p(a, b)$ such that $q = \#E_p(a, b)$ is also prime.
2. $\mathcal{D}$ randomly chooses a point $\alpha \in E_p(a, b)$, and a number $d \in GF(q)$. He calculates $\beta = d\alpha$ over $E_p(a, b)$ and discards d. Finally, he publishes $(E_p(a, b), q, \alpha, \beta)$.

Group Coordinator's Setup

$\mathcal{R}$ does the following.

1. Verify whether (α, β) is correctly located in $E_p(a, b)$. If not reject the public parameters.

2. Randomly choose 4 non-zero elements of $GF(q)$, k_1, k_2, k_3, k_4, $k_i \in GF(q)$, and compute

$$\alpha_1 = k_3\alpha + k_1 \beta \ over \ E_p(a, b)$$

$$\alpha_2 = k_4\alpha + k_2 \beta \ over \ E_p(a, b)$$

Publish (α_1, α_2).

3. Randomly choose n non-zero elements of $GF(q)$, $I_1, I_2, \cdots, I_n$, and publish them as identities of $S_1, \cdots S_n$.

4. Randomly choose $4(t-1)$ elements of $GF(q)$, $a_{1,1}, a_{1,2}, a_{1,3}, a_{1,4}, \cdots, a_{t-1,1}$, $a_{t-1,2}, a_{t-1,3}, a_{t-1,4}$, and calculate

$$e_{l,i} = k_i + \sum_{j=1}^{t-1} a_{j,i} I_l^j \ mod \ q \quad 1 \leq l \leq n, \ 1 \leq i \leq 4$$

5. Randomly choose $4n$ non-zero elements of $GF(q)$, $b_{1,1}, b_{1,2}, b_{1,3}, b_{1,4}, \cdots, b_{n,1}$, $b_{n,2}, b_{n,3}, b_{n,4}$, and another value $\lambda \in GF(q)$. Calculate

$$f_{i,j} = e_{i,j} + \lambda b_{i,j} \ mod \ q \quad 1 \leq i \leq n, \ 1 \leq j \leq 4$$

and secretly send $(e_{i,j}, b_{i,j})$, $1 \leq j \leq 4$, to S_i, $1 \leq i \leq n$.

6. Secretly send λ and $f_{i,j}$, $1 \leq i \leq n$, $1 \leq j \leq 4$, to $\mathcal{C}$.

Share Pooling

Without losing generality, assume that t participants in $\mathcal{G}$, denote by $S_1, \cdots, S_t$, agree to sign a non-zero message $M \in GF(q)$. Each participant S_i calculates his partial signature as follows

$$\rho_i = \prod_{k=1, k \neq i}^{k=t} \left(\frac{-I_k}{I_i - I_k} \right)$$

$$\mathcal{V}_{i,j} = e_{i,j} \rho_i, \quad j = 1, 2, 3, 4$$

Then he computes

$$\sigma_{i,1} = \mathcal{V}_{i,1} M + \mathcal{V}_{i,2} \ mod \ q$$

$$\sigma_{i,2} = \mathcal{V}_{i,3} M + \mathcal{V}_{i,4} \ mod \ q$$

$$\kappa_{i,1} = (b_{i,1} M + b_{i,2}) \rho_i \ mod \ q$$

$$\kappa_{i,2} = (b_{i,3} M + b_{i,4}) \rho_i \ mod \ q$$

and sends $(\rho_i, \sigma_{i,1}, \sigma_{i,2}, \kappa_{i,1}, \kappa_{i,2}, M)$ to the combiner $\mathcal{C}$.

Share Verification by the Combiner

On receiving a share from S_i, $\mathcal{C}$ can verify the share by checking whether

$$f_{i,1}\rho_i M + f_{i,2}\rho_i \stackrel{?}{=} \sigma_{i,1} + \lambda\kappa_{i,1} \bmod q$$

and

$$f_{i,3}\rho_i M + f_{i,4}\rho_i \stackrel{?}{=} \sigma_{i,2} + \lambda\kappa_{i,2} \bmod q$$

If the above equations do not hold the partial signature is rejected, otherwise it is accepted.

Message signing

After $\mathcal{C}$ accepts the shares from S_i, where $1 \le i \le t$, she can construct the signature by calculating

$$s_1 = \sum_{i=1}^{t} \sigma_{i,1} \bmod q$$

$$s_2 = \sum_{i=1}^{t} \sigma_{i,2} \bmod q$$

and publishes (s_1, s_2) as a threshold signature on message M.

Signature Verification

The group's signature (s_1, s_2) can be verified by checking

$$s_2\alpha + s_1\beta \stackrel{?}{=} M\alpha_1 + \alpha_2 \text{ over } E_p(a, b)$$

Proof of Forgery

In case of dispute, when a forged signature (s_1', s_2') passes the verification test, any t participants in $\mathcal{G}$ can execute the above scheme to generate their own signature on the same message, namely (s_1, s_2). Since both (s_1, s_2) and (s_1', s_2') pass signature verification, the participants are able to solve ECDL by calculating

$$d = \frac{s_2 - s_2'}{s_1' - s_1} \bmod q$$

and use this value as a proof of forgery.

4.4   Fail-stop Multisignature Scheme

A multisignature scheme [4, 21] can be viewed as an (n, n) threshold scheme and hence by appropriate choice of parameters, the proposed threshold scheme can be easily turned into a multisignature scheme.

5 Conclusions

Fail-stop signatures have the desirable property that forgery can be proved and hence the signer is protected against an all powerful forger. In this paper, we propose a fail-stop signature scheme based on elliptic curves. The scheme is essentially the same as the one proposed [26], but replaces the original verification process on the cyclic group generated by a generator of $GF(p)$ with the cyclic group generated by a point on a suitably chosen elliptic curve. The main advantage of it being lowering the size of the prime. We used the scheme to construct a fail-stop threshold signature scheme, where collaboration of t participants in a group is needed to sign a message. Our scheme has cheater detection property and hence provide against senders trying to disrupt the scheme by sending junk instead of valid partial signatures.

References

1. Niko Bari'c and Birgit Pfitzmann. Collision-Free Accumulators and Fail-Stop Signature Schemes without Trees. *Eurocrypt '97, Lecture Notes in Computer Science 1233*, pages 480-494, 1997.
2. G. Blakley. Safeguarding Cryptographic Keys. *Proceedings of AFIPS 1979 National Computer Conference*, 48:313-317, 1979.
3. Gerrit Bleumer, Birgit Pfitzmann, and Michael Waidner. A Remark on a Signature Scheme where Forgery can be Proved. *Eurocrypt '90, Lecture Notes in Computer Science 437*, pages 441-445, 1991.
4. C. Boyd. Digital Multisignatures. Cryptography and Coding, ed. H. Beker and F. Piper, Clarendon Press, Oxford, pages 241-246, 1989.
5. David Chaum, Eugène van Heijst, and Birgit Pfitzmann. Cryptographically Strong Undeniable Signatures, Unconditionally Secure for the Signer. *Interner Bericht, Fakultät für Informatik*, Universität Karlsruhe, 1/91, 1990.
6. Ivan B. Damgård, Torben P. Pedersen, and Birgit Pfitzmann. On the Existence of Statistically Hiding Bit Commitment Schemes and Fail-Stop Signatures. *Journal of Cryptology*, 10/3:163-194, 1997.
7. Whitfield Diffie and Martin Hellman. New Directions in Cryptography. *IEEE IT*, 22:644-654, 1976.
8. Tetsuya Izu, Jun Kogure, Masayuku Noro, and Kazuhiro Yokoyama. Efficient Implementation of Schoof's Algorithm. *Asiacrypt '98, Lecture Notes in Computer Science 1519*, pages 66-79, 1998.
9. Neal Koblitz. *A Course in Number Theory and Cryptography*. Springer-Verlag, Berlin, 1994.
10. Neal Koblitz. *Algebraic Aspects of Cryptography*. Springer-Verlag, Berlin, 1997.
11. Leslie Lamport. Constructing Digital Signatures from a One-Way Function. *PSRI International CSL-98*, 1979.
12. Alfred J. Menezes. *Elliptic Curve Public Key Cryptosystems*. Kluwer Academic Publishers, 1993.
13. Torben Pryds Pedersen and Birgit Pfitzmann. Fail-Stop Signatures. *SIAM Journal on Computing*, 26/2:291-330, 1997.
14. Birgit Pfitzmann. Fail-stop Signatures: Principles and Applications. *Proc. Compsec '91, 8th world conference on computer security, audit and control*, pages 125-134, 1991.

15. Birgit Pfitzmann. Sorting Out Signature Schemes, and some Theory of Secure Reactive Systems. *Hildesheimer Informatik-Berichte, Institute für Informatik*, 1993.
16. Birgit Pfitzmann. Fail-Stop Signatures Without Trees. *Hildesheimer Informatik-Berichte, Institut für Informatik*, 16/94, 1994.
17. Birgit Pfitzmann. Sorting Out Signature Schemes. *CWI Quarterly*, 8/2:147-172, 1995.
18. Birgit Pfitzmann. *Digital Signature Schemes – General Framework and Fail-Stop Signatures*. Lecture Notes in Computer Science 1100, Springer-Verlag, 1996.
19. Birgit Pfitzmann and Michael Waidner. Formal Aspects of Fail-stop Signatures. *Interner Bericht, Fakultät für Informatik*, 22/90, 1990.
20. Birgit Pfitzmann and Michael Waidner. Fail-stop Signatures and their Application. *SECURICOM 91, 9th Worldwide Congress on Computer and Communications Security and Protection*, pages 145-160, 1991.
21. Josef Pieprzyk, Jennifer Seberry, Chris Charnes and Rei Safavi-Naini. *Crypto and Applications II*. The CRC Handbook of Algorithms and Theory of Computation, ed. Mikhail J Atallah, to appear.
22. René Schoof. Counting Points on Elliptic Curves Over Finite Fields. *Journal de Théeorie des Nombres, Bordeaux*, 7:219-254, 1995.
23. A. Shamir. How to Share a Secret. *Communications of the ACM*, 22:612-613, November 1979.
24. Douglas R. Stinson. *Cryptography: Theory and Practice*. CRC Press, Boca Raton, New York, 1995.
25. Eugène van Heijst, Torben Pedersen, and Birgit Pfitzmann. New Constructions of Fail-Stop Signatures and Lower Bounds. *Crypto '92, Lecture Notes in Computer Science 740*, pages 15-30, 1993.
26. E. van Heyst and T.P. Pedersen. How to Make Efficient Fail-Stop Signatures. *Eurocrypt '92*, pages 337-346, 1992.
27. Michael Waidner and Birgit Pfitzmann. The Dining Cryptographers in the Disco: Unconditional Sender and Recipient Untraceability with Computationally Secure Serviceability. *Eurocrypt '89, Lecture Notes in Computer Science 434*, 1990.

APPENDIX

Proof of Lemma 2:

Proof. According to lemma 1, every point on $E_p(a, b)$, including γ, is a generator of the group and has order q, where $q = \#E_p(a, b)$. The lemma follows from the basic property of the cyclic group generated by γ.

Proof of Lemma 3:

Proof. Knowing a public key (α_1, α_2), gives the following two equations: (over $E_p(a, b)$)

$$\alpha_1 = k_3\alpha + k_1\beta$$
$$\alpha_2 = k_4\alpha + k_2\beta$$

Since $\beta = d\alpha$, we have:

$$\alpha_1 = k_3\alpha + k_1 d\alpha$$

$$\alpha_2 = k_4\alpha + k_2 d\alpha$$

or

$$\alpha_1 = (k_3 + k_1 d)\alpha$$

$$\alpha_2 = (k_4 + k_2 d)\alpha$$

Solving the ECDL problem we have:

$$k_3 + k_1 d = c_1 \ mod \ q$$

$$k_4 + k_2 d = c_2 \ mod \ q$$

where $c_1, c_2 \in GF(q)$. Equivalently,

$$\begin{pmatrix} d\ 0\ 1\ 0 \\ 0\ d\ 0\ 1 \end{pmatrix} \begin{pmatrix} k_1 \\ k_2 \\ k_3 \\ k_4 \end{pmatrix} = \begin{pmatrix} c_1 \\ c_2 \end{pmatrix} \ mod \ q \tag{4}$$

This is a set of 2 linear equations in 4 unknowns where the rank of the coefficient matrix is equal to 2. Hence there are q^2 solutions corresponding to assigning arbitrary values ($mod \ q$) to k_3 and k_4 (q^2 possibilities), and calculating the values of k_1 and k_2.

Proof of Theorem 2:

Proof. Knowing the public key,

$$\alpha_1 = k_3\alpha + k_1\beta$$

$$\alpha_2 = k_4\alpha + k_2\beta$$

and the signature on M, namely

$$s_1 = k_1 M + k_2 \ mod \ q$$

$$s_2 = k_3 M + k_4 \ mod \ q$$

the enemy with unlimited power can solve the ECDL problem and rewrite these equations as follows

$$c_1 = k_3 + dk_1 \ mod \ q$$
$$c_2 = k_4 + dk_2 \ mod \ q$$
$$s_1' = k_1 M + k_2 \ mod \ q$$
$$s_2' = k_3 M + k_4 \ mod \ q$$

where $c_1, c_2 \in GF(q)$ and (s'_1, s'_2) is an acceptable signature on x. Next, he can rewrite these equations as follows

$$
\begin{pmatrix}
d & 0 & 1 & 0 \\
0 & d & 0 & 1 \\
M & 1 & 0 & 0 \\
0 & 0 & M & 1
\end{pmatrix}
\begin{pmatrix}
k_1 \\
k_2 \\
k_3 \\
k_4
\end{pmatrix}
=
\begin{pmatrix}
c_1 \\
c_2 \\
s'_1 \\
s'_2
\end{pmatrix}
\; mod \; q
$$

It is easy to see that this matrix has rank 3 (This is true because $dr_3 - r_2 - Mr_1 + r_4 = 0$, where r_i is the ith row of the matrix, and noting that the submatrix consisting of the first 3 columns has 3 independent rows), and so there are exactly q solutions to this equation.

Proof of Theorem 3:

Proof. Given a forged signature that passes the verification test, the presumed signer can generate a different signature which passes the verification test with probability $\frac{q-1}{q}$, where q is the number of possible signatures on a message (this can be seen from the Theorem 2).

Proof of Corollary 1:

Proof. The proof can be deduced from Theorem 2.

Proof of Theorem 4:

Proof. To be able to deny a signature, the signer must find another secret key that matches with his public key. This requires that he finds (k'_1, k'_2, k'_3, k'_4) that satisfy

$$
\alpha_1 = k'_3 \alpha + k'_1 \beta \quad over \; E_p(a, b)
$$

$$
\alpha_2 = k'_4 \alpha + k'_2 \beta \quad over \; E_p(a, b)
$$

for the published value (α_1, α_2), which because of the hardness of ECDL problem, is hard.

Divertible Zero-Knowledge Proof of Polynomial Relations and Blind Group Signature

Khanh Quoc Nguyen, Yi Mu and Vijay Varadharajan

School of Computing and Information Technology,
University of Western Sydney, Nepean
PO Box 10, Kingswood, NSW 2747, Australia
Email: kenny,yimu,vijay@cit.nepean.uws.edu.au

Abstract. A divertible protocol is a protocol between three parties in which one party is able to divert another party's proof of some facts to prove some other facts to the other party. This paper presents a divertible protocol to prove multi-variant polynomial relations. Its direct application to blind group signature is also shown.

1 Introduction

1.1 Divertible Proofs

A divertible proof is a protocol between three parties in which one party is able to divert another party's proof of some facts to prove some other facts to the other party. These three parties are usually referred to as the intermediate, the prover and the verifier. The notion of divertible protocol was first introduced by Desmedt, Goutier and Bengio in [8]. It plays a significant role in cryptographic research both negatively and positively. The first well-known application of divertible protocols is the so-called Mafia fraud. In this scenario, Vera could possibly identify herself as Alice to Bob by simply acting as the intermediate between Alice (the prover) and Bob (the verifier). This problem was identified in [8]. However, divertible protocols also have positive applications. The first is to prevent subliminal channel. The concept of subliminal channel was introduced by Simmons[14]. Basically, a subliminal channel allows two parties to exchange secret information in the full view of another party by hiding the information in some "innocent-looking" communication. However the third party is not able to detect the existence of the exchange. Using divertible protocols, the third party could prevent the subliminal channel by diverting the communication between the other two parties so that they can still receive the legitimate communication but would not be able to receive their secret information. Blind signature is another practical application of divertible protocols. A blind signature is defined as a protocol between a signer and a verifier such that as a result of the protocol execution, the receiver gets a signature from the signer while the signer obtains no substantial information about the signature. Blind signature was initially proposed for the purpose of electronic cash by Chaum[3]. Ohta and Okamoto[12] were the first to suggest how divertible protocols are can be used to construct blind signatures.

1.2 Group Signature

A group signature scheme is a protocol that allows any member of a group to sign on the behalf of the group while it is infeasible for anyone who is not a group member to sign on the behalf of the group. Signatures are verified using a single group public key. It is also infeasible to identify the signer for a given signature or to determine whether two signatures are signed by the same group member. In group signature schemes, there exists a group manager who can identify the member who issues the signature for any given signature. Group signature was first proposed by Chaum[4]. Several improvements and extensions have been proposed in[6, 1]. In all these proposals, the size of a signature is linearly dependent on the size of the group. Recently, Camenisch and Stadler proposed the first two fixed size group signature schemes[2]. Their signatures are based on non-interactive proofs of the possession of a valid membership certificate.

1.3 Our Contribution

In this paper, we present a divertible zero-knowledge proof of polynomial relations. We then show how to construct a blind version of one of Camenish-Stadler group signatures using our divertible protocol. Even though zero-knowledge proof of polynomial relations are already given in [10, 7], making them to be divertible is not an easy task. Unlike normal divertible protocols where the commitments of facts seen by both the prover and the verifier can be the same, a divertible proof of polynomial relations requires the commitments of the facts seen by the prover and the verifier to be different. In fact, they have to be witness-indistinguishable. This is required to achieve signature unlinkability in the corresponding blind group signatures.

The rest of this paper is organized as follows: Section 2 presents divertible proofs of knowledge of secrets, proofs of addition and multiplication relations. They are used as building blocks in the general construction of a divertible proof of polynomial relations, which is presented in Section 3. Finally, section 4 shows how a blind Camenish-Stadler group signature is constructed using the divertible proof of polynomial relations.

2 Preliminaries

Let Alice be the prover, Vera be the intermediate and Bob be the verifier. Also let g and h be members of the multiplicative group of order n over a finite field $[0, .., p-1]$, where p is a prime number such that $\log_g(h)$ is not known to both Alice and Vera. For simplicity, all computations in this section are computed modulo p, unless explicitly mentioned.

We now give the realization of a commitment scheme, a basic protocol, an addition protocol and a multiplication protocol. The basic protocol is a divertible proof of knowledge of secret. The addition protocol is a divertible proof of the addition relation and the multiplication protocol is a divertible proof of the multiplication relation between secrets concealed in the involved commitments. These three protocols are used in the realization of our divertible proof of polynomial relation.

2.1 A Commitment Scheme

A commitment of a value x in Z_n is constructed as $s = g^x h^r$, where r is a random number. It reveals no information about the secret x while it is infeasible for the sender to open the commitment without the knowledge of $log_g(h)$ (Lemma 1). The commitment is opened by revealing x, r. This commitment scheme is well-known and was first introduced in[13].

Lemma 1. *Assuming that $log_g(h)$ is not known, it is infeasible to know more than one 2-tuple (x, r) such that $g^x h^r = s$ for any constant s.*

Proof. To prove the lemma, we show that the knowledge of any two different 2-tuples (x_1, r_1) and (x_2, r_2) that satisfy $g^{x_1} h^{r_1} = g^{x_2} h^{r_2} = s$, is equivalent to the knowledge of $log_g(h)$.

Given $log_g(h)$, we choose a 2-tuple (x_1, r_1) at random and form $x_2 = x_1 + log_g(h)$ and $r_2 = r_1 - 1$. Then the two 2-tuples (x_1, r_1) and (x_2, r_2) are clearly different, satisfying:

$$g^{x_2} h^{r_2} = g^{x_1} g^{log_g(h)} h^{r_1 - 1} = g^{x_1} h h^{r_1 - 1} = g^{x_1} h^{r_1}$$

On the other hand, given any two different 2-tuples (x_1, r_1) and (x_2, r_2), satisfying $g^{x_1} h^{r_1} = g^{x_2} h^{r_2}$, we have:

$$1 = \frac{(g^{x_1} h^{r_1})}{(g^{x_2} h^{r_2})} = g^{x_1 - x_2} h^{r_1 - r_2}$$

This implies $log_g(h) = -(x_1 - x_2)(r_1 - r_2)^{-1} \mod n$. Here $(r_1 - r_2) \neq 0$ because the 2-tuples (x_1, r_1) and (x_2, r_2) are different. Therefore the lemma follows.

2.2 Basic protocol

Setting: Alice has a commitment $s = g^x h^r$. Vera has a commitment σ for which she knows ρ such that $\sigma = sh^\rho$. Here Vera knows neither the value of x nor the value of r.

Objective: The basic protocol is a zero-knowledge protocol in which Vera diverts Alice's proof of secrets for the commitment s to prove to Bob the knowledge of secrets for the commitment σ.

Basic Protocol: The protocol is described in figure 1.

Alice	Vera	Bob
$(x, r, s = g^x h^r)$	$(\rho, \sigma = sh^\rho)$	(σ)

Alice:
$$u, v \in_R Z_n$$
$$w = g^u h^v$$

$\xrightarrow{\quad w \quad}$

Vera:
$$\kappa, \lambda, \mu \in_R Z_n$$
$$\omega = w^\kappa g^\lambda h^\mu$$

$\xrightarrow{\quad \omega \quad}$

Bob:
$$\gamma \in_R Z_n$$

$\xleftarrow{\quad \gamma \quad}$

Vera:
$$c = \frac{\gamma}{\kappa}$$

$\xleftarrow{\quad c \quad}$

Alice:
$$a = u - cx \bmod n$$
$$b = v - cr \bmod n$$

$\xrightarrow{\quad a,b \quad}$

Vera:
$$w \stackrel{?}{=} s^c g^a h^b$$
$$\alpha = a\kappa + \lambda$$
$$\beta = b\kappa - \gamma\rho + \mu$$

$\xrightarrow{\quad \alpha,\beta \quad}$

Bob:
$$g^\alpha h^\beta \sigma^\gamma \stackrel{?}{=} \omega$$

$$V_{Alice} = \{x, r, s, w, c, a, b\} \qquad V_{Bob} = \{\sigma, \omega, \gamma, \alpha, \beta\}$$

Figure 1: Divertible Proof of Knowledge

Lemma 2. (Completeness) *If Alice and Vera follow the protocol, Bob always accepts the proof.*

Proof. As $\sigma = sh^\rho$, $\gamma = c\kappa$ and $s = g^x h^r$, we have $g^\alpha h^\beta \sigma^\gamma = g^{a\kappa+\lambda} h^{b\kappa-\gamma\rho+\mu}$
$s^\gamma h^{\gamma\rho} = g^{\kappa(u-cx)+\lambda} h^{\kappa(v-cr)+\mu} g^{xc\kappa} h^{rc\kappa} = (g^u h^v)^\kappa g^\lambda h^\mu = w^\kappa g^\lambda h^\mu = \omega$

Lemma 3. (Soundness) *The basic protocol convinces Bob of the knowledge of secret concealed in the commitment σ with an overwhelming probability.*

Proof. First observe that in order to convince Bob, Vera must be able to respond correctly to at least one challenge γ. On the other hand, if Vera can answer two different challenges γ_1, γ_2 correctly, then we have $g^{\alpha_1} h^{\beta_1} \sigma^{\gamma_1} = g^{\alpha_2} h^{\beta_2} \sigma^{\gamma_2} = \omega$, where α_i, β_i is Vera's response for challenge γ_i ($i = 1, 2$). This implies $1 = g^{\alpha_1-\alpha_2} h^{\beta_1-\beta_2} \sigma^{\gamma_1-\gamma_2}$. As $\gamma_1 \neq \gamma_2$, we have $\sigma = (g^{\alpha_1-\alpha_2} h^{\beta_1-\beta_2})^{(\gamma_1-\gamma_2)}$, i.e., Vera is able to prove the secrets of commitment ω. Thus the scenario, where Vera convinces Bob of the knowledge of secret of ω while having no access to the secret of ω, only occurs when Vera is able to respond correctly to one challenge; this happens to be the same challenge γ from Bob. As γ is chosen at random by Bob, this happens with $1/n$ probability. Hence, the basic protocol convinces Bob the knowledge of secrets of commitment σ with an overwhelming probability of $(1 - 1/n)$.

Lemma 4. (Witness-Indistinguishable) *For any instance of the protocol run, Alice's view (V_{Alice}) and Bob's view (V_{Bob}) of the protocol is statistically independent.*

Proof. To show that V_{Alice} and V_{Bob} of the same instance of the protocol is statistically independent, we show that there exists a legitimate instance S of the protocl for any $V_{Alice} = \{x_1, r_1, s_1, w_1, c_1, a_1, b_1\}$ and $V_{Bob} = \{\sigma_2, \omega_2, \gamma_2, \alpha_2, \beta_2\}$. Here V_{Alice} and V_{Bob} do not necessarily come from the same instance of the protocol.

To prove that S is legitimate, we show that there exists $\rho, \kappa, \lambda, \mu$ that satisfy

$$\sigma_2 = s_1 h^\rho \tag{1}$$

$$\omega_2 = w_1^\kappa g^\lambda h^\mu \tag{2}$$

$$\gamma_2 = c_1 \kappa \tag{3}$$

$$\alpha_2 = a_1 \kappa + \lambda \tag{4}$$

$$\beta_2 = b_1 \kappa - \gamma_2 \rho + \mu \tag{5}$$

As $\sigma_2, s_1, \gamma_2, c_1$ are known, there exists unique ρ, κ that satisfy (1) and (3). Moreover as $\alpha_2 = a_1\kappa + \lambda$, there exists an unique legitimate λ satisfying (4). Similarly, there also exists a unique legitimate μ that satisfies (5). Hence there exists a unique tuple $\{\rho, \kappa, \lambda, \mu\}$ that satisfies (1), (3), (4) and (5). Now we show that this tuple also satisfies (2).

Because V_{Alice} and V_{Bob} are legitimate, we have $w_1 = s_1^{c_1} g^{a_1} h^{b_1}$ and $\omega_2 = g^{\alpha_2} h^{\beta_2} \sigma_2^{\gamma_2}$. Thus $\omega_2 = g^{\alpha_2} h^{\beta_2} \sigma_2^{\gamma_2} = g^{a_1\kappa+\lambda} h^{b_1\kappa - \gamma_2\rho+\mu} s^{c_1\kappa} h^{\rho\gamma_2} = (g^{a_1} h^{b_1} s^{c_1})^\kappa g^\lambda h^\mu = w^\kappa g^\lambda h^\mu$, i.e, $\{\rho, \kappa, \lambda, \mu\}$ satisfies (2).

2.3 Addition

Setting: Alice has three commitments $s_i = g^{x_i} h^{r_i}$ ($i = 1, 2, 3$) that satisfy $x_3 = ax_1 + bx_2 \bmod n$. Vera has three commitments σ_i ($i = 1, 2, 3$) for which she knows ρ_i ($i = 1, 2, 3$) such that $\sigma_i = s_i h^{\rho_i}$. Here Vera knows neither the value of x_i nor the value of r_i ($i = 1, 2, 3$).

Action: Addition protocol is a zero-knowledge protocol in which Vera diverts Alice's proof of addition relation $x_3 = ax_1 + bx_2 \bmod n$ of the secrets x_1, x_2, x_3 concealed in s_1, s_2, s_3 to prove to Bob the relation $x_3 = ax_1 + bx_2 \bmod n$ of the secrets x_1, x_2, x_3 concealed in the commitments $\sigma_1, \sigma_2, \sigma_3$. Here a, b are some public constants. This protocol only demonstrates the addition relation. *It does not prove the knowledge of the concealed secrets.*

Addition Protocol

Alice	Vera	Bob
$(x_i, r_i, s_i = g^{x_i} h^{r_i})$	$(\rho_i, \sigma_i = s h^{\rho_i})$	$(\sigma_1, \sigma_2, \sigma_3)$
for $(i = 1, 2, 3)$	$(i = 1, 2, 3)$	

$r = r_3 - a r_1 - b r_2 \bmod n$

$$\xrightarrow{\quad r \quad}$$

$$\rho = r + \rho_3 - a\rho_1 - b\rho_2$$

$$\xrightarrow{\quad \rho \quad}$$

$$\sigma_3 \overset{?}{=} \sigma_1^a \sigma_2^b h^\rho$$

Figure 2 Divertible Proof of Addition Relation

Lemma 5. (Completeness) *If Alice and Vera follow the protocol, Bob always accepts the proof.*

Proof. We have $\sigma_1^a \sigma_2^b h^\rho = g^{ax_1 + bx_2} h^{ar_1 + br_2 + a\rho_1 + b\rho_2 + \rho}$ because of $\sigma_i = sh^{\rho_i} = g^{x_i} h^{r_i + \rho_i}$ $(i = 1, 2, 3)$.

Also $\rho = r + \rho_3 - a\rho_1 - b\rho_2 = r_3 - ar_1 - br_2 - a\rho_1 - b\rho_2$ and $x_3 = ax_1 + bx_2$, hence we have $g^{ax_1 + bx_2} h^{ar_1 + br_2 + a\rho_1 + b\rho_2 + \rho} = g^{x_3} h^{r_3} = \sigma_3$.

Lemma 6. (Soundness) *If $\sigma_3 \overset{?}{=} \sigma_1 \sigma_2 h^\rho$ holds, Bob is convinced with an overwhelming probability that the addition relation between secrets holds.*

Proof. The addition protocol does not prove the knowledge of secrets; it only proves the addition relation. Assume that σ_i is a commitment computed as $g^{x_i} h^{r_i}$ $(i = 1, 2, 3)$. Then according to Lemma 1, $\sigma_3 = \sigma_1 \sigma_2 h^\rho$ holds only when two 2-tuples (x_3, r_3) and $(x_1 + x_2, r_1 + r_2 + \rho)$ are identical. Thus $\sigma_3 = \sigma_1 \sigma_2 h^\rho$ demonstrates the addition relation $x_3 = x_1 + x_2$, where x_i is the secret concealed in the commitment σ_i.

Lemma 7. (Witness-Indistinguishable) *For any instance of the protocol run, Alice's view and Bob's view of the protocol are statistically independent.*

Proof. Given an Alice's view and a Bob's view, it is straightforward to prove the existence of a legitimate instance of the addition protocol using a technique similar to the one given in the proof part of Lemma 4. Here the views do not necessarily come from the same instance. Thus addition protocol is witness-indistinguishable.

2.4 Multiplication Protocol

Setting: Alice has three commitments $s_i = g^{x_i} h^{r_i}$ $(i = 1, 2, 3)$ that satisfy $x_3 = x_1 x_2 \bmod n$. Vera has three commitments σ_i $(i = 1, 2, 3)$ for which she knows ρ_i $(i = 1, 2, 3)$ such that $\sigma_i = s_i h^{\rho_i}$. Here Vera knows neither the value of x_i nor r_i $(i = 1, 2, 3)$.

Action: Multiplication protocol is a zero-knowledge protocol in which Vera diverts Alice's proof of multiplication relation $x_3 = x_1 x_2 \bmod n$ of the secrets x_1, x_2, x_3 concealed in s_1, s_2, s_3 to prove to Bob the multiplication $x_3 = x_1 x_2 \bmod n$ of the secrets x_1, x_2, x_3 concealed in the commitments $\sigma_1, \sigma_2, \sigma_3$.

Alice	Vera	Bob
$(x_i, r_i, s_i = g^{x_i} h^{r_i})$	$(\rho_i, \sigma_i = s_i h^{\rho_i})$	$(\sigma_1, \sigma_2, \sigma_3)$
for $(i = 1, 2, 3)$	$(i = 1, 2, 3)$	

$$u, v_1, v_2 \in_R Z_n$$
$$w_1 = g^u h^{v_1}$$
$$w_2 = s_2^u h^{v_2}$$

$\xrightarrow{\quad w_1, w_2 \quad}$

$$\kappa, \lambda, \mu_1, \mu_2 \in_R Z_q$$
$$\omega_1 = w_1^\kappa g^\lambda h^{\mu_1}$$
$$\omega_2 = w_2^\kappa \sigma_2^\lambda h^{\mu_2}$$

$\xrightarrow{\quad \omega_1, \omega_2 \quad}$

$$\gamma \in_R Z_n$$

$\xleftarrow{\quad \gamma \quad}$

$$c = \frac{\gamma}{\kappa}$$

$\xleftarrow{\quad c \quad}$

$$a = u - cx_1 \bmod n$$
$$b_1 = v_1 - cr_1 \bmod n$$
$$b_2 = v_2 - cr_3 \bmod n$$

$\xrightarrow{\quad a, b_1, b_2 \quad}$

$$\alpha = a\kappa + \lambda$$
$$\beta_1 = b_1 \kappa - \gamma \rho_1 + \mu_1$$
$$\beta_2 = b_2 \kappa - \gamma \rho_3 - \alpha \rho_2 + \mu_2$$

$\xrightarrow{\quad \alpha, \beta_1, \beta_2 \quad}$

$$g^\alpha h^{\beta_1} \sigma_1^\gamma \stackrel{?}{=} \omega_1$$
$$\sigma_2^\alpha h^{\beta_2} \sigma_3^\gamma \stackrel{?}{=} \omega_2$$

Figure 3 Divertible Proof of Multiplication Relation

Lemma 8. (Completeness) *If Alice and Vera follow the protocol, Bob always accepts the proof.*

Proof. To prove the completeness, we show that $g^\alpha h^{\beta_1} \sigma_1^\gamma = \omega_1$ and $\sigma_2^\alpha h^{\beta_2} \sigma_3^\gamma = \omega_2$ hold. Since $c = \frac{\gamma}{\kappa}$, $\gamma = c\kappa$. Then we have

$$g^\alpha h^{\beta_1} \sigma_1^\gamma = g^{a\kappa + \lambda} h^{b_1 \kappa - \gamma \rho_1 + \mu_1} (s_1 h^{\rho_1})^\gamma = g^{a\kappa + \lambda} h^{b_1 \kappa + \mu_1} s_1^\gamma$$
$$= g^{\kappa(u - cx_1) + \lambda} h^{\kappa(v_1 - cr_1) + \mu_1} g^{c\kappa x_1} h^{c\kappa r_1} = g^{\kappa u + \lambda} h^{\kappa v_1 + \mu_1} = \omega_1.$$

Similarly it is straightforward to verify that $\sigma_2^\alpha h^{\beta_2} \sigma_3^\gamma = \omega_2$ holds.

Lemma 9. (Soundness) *If $g^\alpha h^{\beta_1} \sigma_1^\gamma = \omega_1$ and $\sigma_2^\alpha h^{\beta_2} \sigma_3^\gamma = \omega_2$ hold, Bob is convinced with an overwhelming probability that the multiplication relation between secrets holds.*

Proof. The multiplication protocol consists of two instances of the basic protocol that run in parallel. The first instance convinces Bob of the knowledge of secret for the commitment σ_1 with respect to the base $[g, h]$ and the second instance convinces the knowledge of secret for the commitment σ_3 with respect to the base $[\sigma_2, h]$. According to the proof of Lemma 3, they hold with an overwhelming probability. Moreover, in these two instances, Vera sends the same α in both instances to prove the knowledge of the discrete logarithm part of the base g, σ_2 in the representation of σ_1, σ_3 to the base $[g, h]$ and $[\sigma_2, h]$ respectively. This indicates that the exponent of the base g in the representation of σ_1 to the base $[g, h]$ equals to that of the base σ_2 in the representation of σ_3 to the base $[\sigma_2, h]$. This shows that the exponent of the base g in the representation of σ_3 to the base $[g, h]$ is the product of the exponents of the base g in the representations of σ_1 and σ_2 to the base $[g, h]$ which proves the multiplication relation between secrets.

Lemma 10. (Witness-Indistinguishable) *For any instance of the protocol run, Alice's view and Bob's view of the protocol are statistically independent.*

Proof. Given any Alice's view and Bob's view, it is straightforward to prove that there exists a legitimate instance of the multiplication protocol using a technique similar to the one given in the proof part of Lemma 4. Thus the protocol is witness-indistinguishable.

3 Divertible Zero-Knowledge Proof of Polynomial Relation

Divertible zero-knowledge proof of polynomial relation is a protocol in which Vera is able to divert Alice's proof of polynomial relation to Bob. After any instance of the protocol, Alice's view and Bob's view of the protocol are statistically independent.

More specifically, let $f(X_1, .., X_k)$ be the given multi-variable polynomial. The relation to be demonstrated, is the knowledge of a k-tuple $(x_1, .., x_k)$ satisfying $f(x_1, .., x_t) \equiv 0 \bmod n$. The divertible protocol works as follows:

THE GENERAL PROTOCOL

STEP 1:
  First Alice creates an arithmetic circuit corresponding to the polynomial according to the following BNF:

$$f = c \bmod n | X_i \bmod n | f + f \bmod n | f * f \bmod n$$

Clearly, the circuit only consists of addition and multiplication gates. Then Alice makes t commitments $s_1, .., s_t$ such that s_i conceals the value of x_i. Also Alice makes m commitments $s_{t+1}, .., s_{t+m}$, each concealing the output of some gate in the circuit. Here m is the number of gates in the circuit and there is only one commitment concealing the secret of any particular gate. Without the loss of generality, let us assume that s_{t+m} is the commitment of the final gate, i.e., $s_{t+m} = g^{f(x_1,...,x_n)} h^{r_{t+m}} = h^{r_{t+m}}$

STEP 2:

Alice then sends $t + m$ commitments $s_1, .., s_{t+m}$ to Vera, who in turn chooses $t + m$ random numbers ρ_i and forms $\sigma_i = s_i h^{\rho_i}$ $(i = 1, .., t+m)$. Vera then sends all the values of σ_i to Bob $(i = 1, .., t+m)$.

STEP 3:

Alice, Vera and Bob run t instances of the basic protocol to convince Bob the knowledge of secrets concealed in the t commitment $s_1, .., s_t$.

STEP 4:

For each gate, let s_i, s_j be Alice's commitments concealing the inputs of the gate and s_k be Alice's commitment concealing the output of the gate. Similarly let σ_i, σ_j and σ_k be Vera's commitments concealing the two inputs and output of the gate. Vera together with Alice and Bob run the multiplication(addition) protocol to convince Bob of the multiplication(addition) relation between secrets concealed in σ_i, σ_j and σ_k.

STEP 5:

Alice opens the commitments s_{t+m}, showing r_{t+m}. Vera, in turn, gives Bob the value $r = r_{t+m} + \rho_{t+m}$. Bob accepts the proof if and only if all proofs in steps 3 and 4 hold and $\sigma_{t+m} = h^r$.

This model has been used in[7] for normal (i.e., non-divertible) polynomial relation. It is straightforward to realize the model's completeness and soundness. Interested readers are referred to [7].

3.1 Divertible Zero-Knowledge Protocol to Confirm $ax^5 + b \equiv 0 \bmod n$

As an example, we show a divertible zero-knowledge protocol to confirm the knowledge of x such that $ax^5 + b \equiv 0 \bmod n$.

The protocol works as follows:

1. First Alice sends to Vera 4 commitments $\mathtt{commit}(x^i) = g^{(x^i)} h^{r_i}$ $(i = 1, 2, 4, 5)$ which are calculated by Alice.
2. Vera sends to Bob 4 commitments: $\mathtt{commit}'(x^i) = \mathtt{commit}(x^i) h^{\rho_i}$, where ρ_i $(i = 1, 2, 4, 5)$ are numbers known only to Vera.
3. Alice, Vera and Bob then run three multiplication protocols where Alice is the prover, Vera is the intermediate and Bob is the verifier, to prove the following relations:

1: $x_2 = x_1^2$
2: $x_4 = x_2^2$
3: $x_5 = x_4 x_1$

where x_i is the secret committed in $\texttt{commit}(x^i)$ and $\texttt{commit}'(x^i)$.

4. Alice, Vera and Bob run an addition protocol to prove the relation $ax_5 + b = 0 \bmod n$ for Alice's commitment $\texttt{commit}(x^5)$ and Vera's commitment $\texttt{commit}'(x^5)$. Here the committed secret is x_5, and the two other committed values are 1 and 0. These two numbers are public information. It is straightforward to see that our addition protocol also works in this case.

Once the process is completed, Bob is convinced of the knowledge of x such that $ax^5 + b = 0 \bmod n$.

4 Blind Group Signature

A group signature allows members of a group to sign on behalf of the group. Signatures are verified using a single group public key. There also exists a group manager who could detect the misbehaviour of the group members.

In [2], Camenisch and Stadler proposed two fixed size group signature schemes in that the size of signatures and the private keys are independent of the size of the group. In this section, we show how to blind the more efficient proposal of these two schemes.

In that scheme, a group signature consists of two non-interactive proofs; the first proves the knowledge of a valid certificate and the second proves that the group manager can identify the member who issues the signatures. A membership certificate is in the form of (x, y) that satisfies $ax^\alpha + by^\beta = c \bmod n$, where $a, b, c, \alpha, \beta, n$ are public information and n is a large RSA modulus chosen by the group manager. A proof of knowledge that the group manager can "open" the signature is a proof of knowledge of (r, s) such that $A = g^r h^s$ and $B = g_X^r$ where A, B are components of the signature and $s = ax^\alpha$, where g_X is the manager's public key.

To obtain a blind Camenisch-Stadler group signature, we only have to convert the non-interactive proofs in a signature to be divertible[12]. Hence the signature generation procedure is now a set of two divertible protocols in which the signer plays the role of the prover and the receiver plays the roles of both the intermediate and the verifier. The first is to prove the knowledge of (x, y) that satisfies the polynomial relation $ax^\alpha + by^\beta = c \bmod n$. This can be easily realized using our divertible proof of polynomial relation. The second proof is to prove the relation $A' = g^\rho A$ and $B' = Bg_X^\rho$, where ρ is secretly generated by the receiver, and $A = g^r h^{ax^\alpha}$ and $B = g_X^r$ are commitments generated by the signer and seen by the receiver. The divertible proof of this relation consists of the two instances of the basic protocol in parallel to prove the knowledge of (r', s) of $A' = g^{r'} h^s$ and $B' = g_X^{r'}$, where $A' = Ag^{r'-r}$ and $B' = Bg_X^{r'-r}$; $r - r'$ is chosen secretly by the user and A, B are the normal signature components computed by the signer. To ensure that the value of s is indeed ax^α, the commitment of ax^α of the first proof must be identical to A.

All the proofs *must* use the same challenge γ, which is computed as $\gamma = h(m\|\texttt{inf})$, where h is a secure one-way hash function, m is the message, $\|$ denotes the concatenation and $\texttt{inf}$ is the concatenation of all the commitments *seen by Bob* in the whole process. This technique is well-known and is proven to be secure in previous work [9, 11]. The blind signature on the message m then consists of all the information used by Bob to verify the relation $ax^\alpha + by^\beta = c \bmod n$.

The completeness of this blind signature scheme is clear. This is because a signature generation procedure is a set of divertible protocols. It results in two non-interactive proofs, which forms a legitimate signature. On the other hand, our divertible proof of polynomial relation is sound. The technique of running two instances of a proof of knowledge of the discrete logarithm to prove the equality of the two discrete logarithms is well-known and secure [5]. In fact, it is also used in the original signature scheme. Hence our blind signature is sound. Finally, as the divertible protocols ensure that the receiver's view of the overall procotol and the signer's view of the protocol are witness-indistinguishable, the signer can not link any signature to any signature generating instance, i.e., the blindness property holds.

References

1. J. Camenisch, "Efficient and Generalized Group Signatures", Advances in Cryptology - EUROCRYPT'97 Proceedings, Springer-Verlag 1997, pp. 465-479.
2. J. Camenisch and M. Stadler, *Efficient Group Signatures for Large Groups*, Advances of Cryptology: Proceedings of Crypto'97, Springer-Verlag, 1997, pp. 465-479.
3. D. Chaum, "Blind Signatures for Untraceable Payments", Advances in Cryptology: Proceedings of Crypto 82, Plenum Press, 1983, pp. 199-203.
4. D. Chaum, E. van Heijst, "Group Signatures", Advances in Cryptology - EUROCRYPT'91 Proceedings. Springer-Verlag, 1991, pp. 257-265.
5. D. Chaum and T. Pedersen. "Wallet databases with observers", Advances in Cryptology - CRYPTO'92, Springer-Verlag, 1993, pp. 89-105.
6. L. Chen and T.P. Petersen, "New Group Signature Schemes", Advances in Cryptology - EUROCRYPT'94 Proceedings, Springer-Verlag 1995, pp. 171-181.
7. R. Cramer and I. Damgard, " Zero-Knowledge Proofs for Finite Field Arithmetic or: Can Zero-Knowledge be for Free?", Advances of Cryptology - Proceedings of Crypto'98, to appear.
8. Y. Desmedt, C. Goutier and S. Bengio, "Special Uses and Abuses of the Fiat-Shamir Passport Protocol", Advances in Cryptology - CRYPTO'87 Proceedings, Springer-Verlag, 1988, pp. 21-39.
9. A. Fiat and A. Shamir, "How to Prove Yourself: Practical Solutions to Identification and Signature Problems", Advances in Cryptology - CRYPTO'86 Proceedings, Springer-Verlag, 1987, pp. 186-194.
10. E. Fujisaki and T.Okamoto, *Statistical Zero-Knowledge Protocols to Prove Modular Polynomial Relations*, Advances of Cryptology - Proceedings of Crypto'97, Springer-Verlag 1997, pp. 16-30.
11. T. Okamoto, "Provably Secure and Practical Identification Schemes and Corresponding Signature Schemes", Advances in Cryptology -CRYPTO'92 Proceedings, Springer-Verlag, 1993, pp.54-65.

12. T. Okamoto and K. Ohta, "Disposable Zero-Knowledge Authentication and Their Applications to Untraceable Electronic Cash", Advances in Cryptology - CRYPTO'89 Proceedings, Springer-Verlag, 1990, pp. 134-149.
13. T.P. Pedersen, "Non-Interactive and Information-Theoretic Secure Verifiable Secret Sharing", Advances in Cryptology- CRYPTO'91 Proceedings, Springer-Verlag, 1992, pp. 129–140.
14. G.J. Simmons, "The Prisoner's Problem and the Subliminal Channel", Advances in Cryptology: Proceedings of Crypto 83, Pleum Press, 1984, pp. 51-67.

Repudiation of Cheating and Non-repudiation of Zhang's Proxy Signature Schemes

Hossein Ghodosi
Josef Pieprzyk

Centre for Computer Security Research
School of Information Technology and Computer Science
University of Wollongong
NSW 2522 AUSTRALIA
e-mail: hossein/josef@uow.edu.au

Abstract. The paper discusses the correctness of Lee, Hwang and Wang's comments on on Zhang's proxy signature schemes. In particular, it is shown that the cheating attack proposed by Lee, Hwang and Wang can be detected by the owner of the signature scheme. It is argued that considering the context in which proxy signatures are used, the attack is not a security problem. The work is concluded by a discussion about the non-repudiation controversy incorrectly observed by Lee, Hwang and Wang.

Keywords: Cryptography, Digital Signatures, Proxy Signatures, ElGamal signatures.

1 Introduction

One of the greatest achievements of modern cryptography is the invention of digital signatures. Digital signatures should be in a sense similar to hand-written ones. That is, recipient must be able to verify the signature. A hand-written signature is verified by comparing it to other, authentic signatures. In contrast to hand-written signatures which are independent of messages, digital signatures must somehow reflect both the message and the signer. That is, digital signatures have to create some sort of encapsulation of the document such that any interference with either its contents or the signature will be detected with a very high probability. In order to achieve this requirement, digital signatures can be generated by a signer who holds a secret information which reflects somehow her identity. To verify digital signatures, the receiver of a document applies a publicly known algorithm.

Several digital signature schemes have been proposed in the literature. In this paper we consider an ElGamal [1] type digital signature scheme. The scheme is due to Nyberg-Rueppel [2] and is used in [3], [4] and [5]. The system parameters are as follows:

- a large prime p,

- a prime factor q of $p - 1$,
- an element $g \in \mathbb{Z}^*_p$ of order q,
- a signer holds his/her secret key $x \in \mathbb{Z}_q$ and publishes the corresponding public key $y = g^x \pmod{p}$

We assume that $m = h(M)$, where M is the original message with an arbitrary length and $h(\cdot)$ is a public cryptographically strong hash function. If the signer wants to sign m, $0 \le m < p$ then he selects a random $k \in \mathbb{Z}_q$ and computes,

$$r = mg^k \pmod{p}$$
$$s = rx + k \pmod{q}$$

The pair (r, s) is the signature of the message m. To verify the validity of a signature, one can check,

$$m \stackrel{?}{=} g^{-s} y^r r \pmod{p}.$$

If equation holds then the signature is accepted, otherwise the signature is rejected.

1.1 Proxy Signature

Typically, the owner of the signature scheme may wish to delegate the power of signing to a proxy who will be able to sign messages on behalf of the owner. The following properties are expected to hold for the delegation.

1. The receiver of the signature should be able to verify the proxy signature in similar way to the verification of the owner signature.
2. The proxy signature must be distinguishable from the signature generated by the owner.
3. The signature must be non-repudiable, that is, neither the owner nor the proxy must be able to sign in place of the other party. In other words they cannot deny their signatures.

Proxy signatures were proposed to facilitate this kind of delegation (for more details, see [6] and [3]). In [4, 3] Zhang proposed proxy signature schemes that satisfy the requirements mentioned above. In [5] Lee, Hwang and Wang analyse two proxy signature schemes proposed in [4] and [3]. They claim that Zhang's proxy signature schemes are subject to a cheating attack that enables the proxy signer to get the original signer to sign any message chosen by the proxy. They also argue that Zhang's second scheme is not non-repudiable. That is, the original signer can obtain the proxy signer secret and thus can sign any message in place of the proxy signer.

In this paper we show that the cheating attack proposed by Lee, Hwang and Wang can be detected by the original signer. Moreover, we will show that the non-repudiation controversy given in [5] is due to some misconceptions of the authors. The organisation of the paper is as follows. First we give a brief review of two Zhang's proxy signature schemes. In Section 3 we consider Lee-Hwang-Wang's arguments on Zhang's schemes. Finally, in Section 4 we will show why Lee-Hwang-Wang's arguments are not correct.

2 Zhang's Proxy Signature Schemes

Consider a large prime p, a prime factor q of $p-1$ and an element $g \in \mathbb{Z}_p^*$ of order q. Assume that Alice, who is keeping a secret key $x \in \mathbb{Z}_q$ and has published the corresponding public key $y = g^x \pmod{p}$, wants to delegate signing capability to Bob. The first scheme is constructed as follows.

1. Alice selects a random number $\bar{k}$ and computes $\bar{r} = g^{\bar{k}} \pmod{p}$, and sends $\bar{r}$ to Bob.
2. Bob randomly chooses $\alpha \in \mathbb{Z}_q$ and computes $r = g^\alpha \bar{r} \pmod{p}$, and then communicates r to Alice.
3. Alice computes $\bar{s} = rx + \bar{k} \pmod{q}$ and forwards $\bar{s}$ to Bob.
4. Bob computes $s = \bar{s} + \alpha \pmod{q}$ and accepts s as a valid proxy signature key, if the following equation holds:

$$g^s = y^r r \pmod{p}.$$

Hence, Bob can apply the previously mentioned ElGamal type digital signature scheme to sign any given message using his secret key s. The verification algorithm, however, uses the public key $y' = y^r r \pmod{p}$.

In [3] Zhang proposed another variant of the proxy signature scheme. This scheme requires the following exchange of messages between Alice and Bob.

– Alice selects a random number $\bar{k}$ and computes $\bar{r} = g^{\bar{k}} \pmod{p}$, and sends $\bar{r}$ to Bob.
– Bob randomly chooses $\beta \in \mathbb{Z}_q$ and computes $r = \bar{r}^\beta \pmod{p}$, and $r' = r\beta^{-1} \pmod{q}$, then communicates r' to Alice.
– Alice computes $\bar{s} = r'x + \bar{k} \pmod{q}$ and forwards $\bar{s}$ to Bob.
– Bob computes $s = \bar{s}\beta \pmod{q}$ and accepts s as a valid proxy signature key, if the following equation holds:

$$g^s = y^r r \pmod{p}.$$

The generation of proxy signature and its verification is similar to previous scheme.

3 Lee-Hwang-Wang's Remarks on Zhang's Schemes

3.1 Cheating Attack

Lee, Hwang and Wang [5] argued that a dishonest proxy signer, Bob, could cheat Alice and get her signature on any message of his choice. Their attack works as following.

$$
\begin{array}{ll}
\text{Alice} \xrightarrow{\quad \bar{r}=g^{\bar{k}} \pmod{p} \quad} \text{Bob} \\[4pt]
\text{Alice} \xleftarrow{\quad r=m\bar{r} \pmod{p} \quad} \text{Bob} \\[4pt]
\text{Alice} \xrightarrow{\quad \bar{s}=rx+\bar{k} \pmod{q} \quad} \text{Bob}
\end{array}
$$

Instead of choosing a random α and computing g^α, Bob calculates $r = m\bar{r}$, where m is a message of his choice. Hence, at the end of the protocol, Bob gets Alice's signature $(r, \bar{s})$ on message m.

3.2 Non-repudiation Controversy

In [5] Lee, Hwang and Wang also claimed that Zhang's second scheme was not non-repudiable. Their argument is that, after the proxy signer (Bob) generates his signature (r, S_{Bob}) on a message, the original signer (Alice) can get the value r to calculate,

$$\beta = rr'^{-1} \pmod{q},$$

since she knows r' from the key delegation protocol. Hence, Alice obtains Bob's secret key as,

$$s = \bar{s}\beta \pmod{q},$$

and therefore can sign any message in place of Bob.

4 Our Observations

In this section we analyse the above mentioned remarks on Zhang's proxy signature schemes and show why they are not correct.

4.1 Comments on Cheating in a Proxy Signature

In a sense, the Lee-Hwang-Wang cheating attack works. However, a cheating attack is successful only if it is not detectable. Here we show that the original signer (Alice) can prove that the proxy signer (Bob) has been cheating in the key delegation protocol. We have to stress that all messages exchanged between two parties during the key delegation protocol have to be authenticated, otherwise anybody could impersonate Bob and get a proxy key from Alice. To be fair to Lee, Hwang and Wang, we can argue in their favour by saying that:

1. the existence of a trusted third party necessary to solve a dispute between the owner (Alice) and proxy (Bob), is a rather strong assumption,
2. by the time Alice notices that her alleged signature has been generated on her behalf, it may be too late: the damage may already be done.

The first argument is not really working as by the principle of proxy delegation the proxy, Bob, is delegated to sign any message on behalf of Alice, even a message which has been explicitly forbidden by Alice. If Bob disobeys Alice's orders, he will be a subject to a disciplinary action or to court proceedings both of which involve a trusted third party. So the existence of a trusted third party is already embedded into the proxy signature scheme.

The second argument does not stick either. If Bob is malicious and tries to inflict the maximum possible damage to Alice, he would rather adhere strictly to the delegation protocol. So later he may be able to sign any messages on her behalf. If Bob cheats in the delegated protocol, then he can get Alice's signature for a single message of his choice. We will show later the cheating will be detected by Alice anyway. Moreover, Alice can prove to a trusted third party that Bob was cheating. This is similar to the case when Bob has signed a message which was explicitly forbidden by Alice.

4.2 Cheating Detection

In case of suspected cheating, Alice can detect it by running the following steps.

1. Alice looks through the transcripts of key delegation protocols to identify the signature of message m in question.
2. If Alice has been cheated in the second step of the key delegation protocol, she can detect the cheating by finding,

$$r \stackrel{?}{=} m\bar{r} \pmod{p},$$

where $\bar{r}$ was generated by herself in the first step and r was authenticated by Bob in the second step (in addition, Alice knows $\bar{k}$ such that $\bar{r} = g^{\bar{k}}$).
3. In order to prove that Bob is a cheater, Alice asks Bob (as a proxy signer) to sign a given message. If Bob is able to sign the message then Alice must accept the authorship of the signature, otherwise Bob is a cheater.

To show the correctness of our arguments, we note that:

- If Bob selects a message, m, of his choice then he cannot find a corresponding α such that $g^\alpha = m \pmod{p}$ provided the selected instance of discrete logarithm is hard.
- Since Bob does not know α, he cannot find $s = \bar{s} + \alpha \pmod{q}$ and therefore cannot sign the message as a proxy signer.

That is to say that Alice can easily prove that m is not a genuine message she has signed. This means that Bob is a cheater. In conclusion, the weakness indicated by Lee-Hwang and Wang is not a security problem.

4.3 Non-repudiation Considerations

In this section, we show that the claim in [5] in which Zhang's second proxy signature scheme is not non-repudiable is incorrect. The message exchanged in the protocol is as follows:

$$\text{Alice} \xrightarrow{\bar{r}=g^{\bar{k}} \pmod{p}} \text{Bob}$$
$$\text{Alice} \xleftarrow{r'=\bar{r}^\beta \beta^{-1} \pmod{p}} \text{Bob}$$
$$\text{Alice} \xrightarrow{\bar{s}=r'x+\bar{k} \pmod{q}} \text{Bob}$$

Bob computes,

$$s = \bar{s}\beta \pmod{q}$$

and accepts s as a valid proxy key, if the following equation holds:

$$g^s = y^r r \pmod{p}.$$

Bob's public key is $y' = g^s \pmod{p}$.

Our observation is that:

- If Bob cheats in the key delegation phase then he is not able to sign any message (the same arguments as for the scheme one) and hence Lee-Hwang-Wang's proof of not non-repudiability of Zhang scheme is not applicable in this case.
- If Bob does not cheat in the key delegation phase then he can sign any message. However, the attack mentioned in [5] does not work. In fact, the authors of [5] were not aware that in ElGamal type signature the signer selects a fresh random number for each signature and therefore r is different from that used in key delegation protocol. That is, Alice cannot compute Bob's secret key in the way discussed by Lee, Hwang and Wang. In other words, the claim that Zhang's second proxy signature scheme is not non-repudiable is incorrect.

Acknowledgements

The authors would like to thank an anonymous referee for their critical comments. The first author also would like to thank the University of Tehran for financial support of his study.

References

1. T. ElGamal, "A Public Key Cryptosystem and a Signature Scheme Based on Discrete Logarithms," *IEEE Trans. on Inform. Theory*, vol. IT-31, pp. 469–472, July 1985.
2. K. Nyberg and R. Rueppel, "A New Signature Scheme Based on the DSA Giving Message Recovery," in *Proceedings of 1st ACM Conference on Computer and Communications Security*, 1993.
3. K. Zhang, "Threshold Proxy Signature Scheme," *1997 Information Security Workshop, Japan*, pp. 191–197, 1997.
4. K. Zhang, *Nonrepudiable Proxy Signature Scheme*. Manuscript, 1997.
5. N. Lee, T. Hwang, and C. Wang, "On Zhang's Nonrepudiable Proxy Signature Scheme," in *Proceedings of ACISP '98 –Australasian Conference on Information Security and Privacy* (C. Boyd and E. Dawson, eds.), vol. 1438 of *Lecture Notes in Computer Science*, pp. 415–422, Springer-Verlag (Berlin), 1998.
6. M. Mambo, K. Usuda, and E. Okamoto, "Proxy Signatures: Delegation of the Power to Sign Messages," *IEICE Trans. Fundamentals*, vol. E79-A, pp. 1338–1354, Sept. 1996. also, "Proxy Signatures for Delegating Signing Operation" In *Proc. 3rd ACM Conference on Computer and Communications Security*, 1996.

On the Security of an RSA Based Encryption Scheme

Siguna Müller[*]

University of Klagenfurt, Department of Mathematics,
A-9020 Klagenfurt, Austria
siguna.mueller@uni-klu.ac.at

Abstract. In [21] some simple modifications of the RSA, respectively Dickson/LUC, cryptosystems have been presented which are practical and provably as secure in difficulty as factorizing their modulus. Similar to Rabin's provable secure cryptosystem, these schemes are vulnerable to chosen ciphertext attacks. We are going to provide a method for immunizing the RSA based system against adaptive chosen ciphertext attacks and simultaneously provide information authentication capability. By means of probabilistic encoding, the scheme achieves semantic security and plaintext awareness in the standard (i.e. non random oracle) model under the assumption of a collision-resistant hash function and the factorization intractability of the receiver's modulus.

1 Introduction

1.1 Chosen ciphertext security

A considerable amount of research has been done in recent years, both from the theoretical and practical point of view, in the pursuit of the construction of public key cryptosystems secure against chosen ciphertext attacks. In such an attack, the adversary obtains the decryption equipment and is allowed to sequentially query it as a black box (an input-output oracle). Informally, the system is said to be secure under a chosen ciphertext attack, if the attacker cannot decrypt a new message. Typically, one distinguishes between a weak form of this attack, known as a lunch-time attack, and the strongest possible form, known as an adaptive chosen ciphertext attack. In a lunch-time attack, the adversary queries the decryption oracle some number of times, after which he obtains the ciphertext that he wishes to cryptanalyze, and is not allowed to query the decryption oracle further. (The name visualizes the situation where the supervisor is out of the office, e.g. for lunch, and the attacker is using the opportunity to play with the equipment over the break but he has no meaningful ciphertext in his possession.) In an adaptive attack, the adversary has access to the decryption equipment even after receiving the object ciphertext to be cryptanalyzed. The attacker is allowed to continue to query the deciphering algorithm with any ciphertext, except the exact object ciphertext.

[*] Research supported by the Österreichischen Fonds zur Förderung der wissenschaftlichen Forschung, FWF-Project no. P 13088-MAT.

1.2   Previous results

Among the several types of attacks to cryptosystems, the most severe certainly is the chosen ciphertext attack, since the attacker may choose different ciphertexts himself and can use the knowledge obtained in the query and answer process to extract the plaintext of an object ciphertext.

For many years, no public key system was shown to be secure under a chosen ciphertext attack. Rabin pioneered the research of constructing provably secure public key cryptosystems by designing a scheme with the property that extracting the complete plaintext of an object ciphertext is computationally equivalent to factoring large numbers. Blum and Goldwasser [5] invented the first efficient probabilistic public key system that hides all partial information.

A common drawback with these and related cryptosystems is that, although secure against chosen plaintext attacks, they are easily compromised by chosen ciphertext attacks. Thus, the question of how to design, respectively, prove security against such attacks was open for a while.

Theoretical Chosen Ciphertext Secure Systems.

The notion of chosen ciphertext security against lunch-time attacks was first defined and implemented in [23]. The first provably secure scheme against adaptive chosen ciphertext attacks was first presented in [12]. The security of their schemes relies on the notion called *non-malleability*. Informally, it requires that it is infeasible, given a ciphertext, to create a different ciphertext such that their plaintexts are related in a known manner. Unfortunately these suggestions are impractical as they rely on general and expensive constructions for non-interactive zero-knowledge proofs. Also, the resulting ciphertexts are in general much longer than the original plaintexts. These disadvantages make the cryptosystems difficult to realize in practice.

Practical Chosen Ciphertext Secure Systems.

Practical approaches to constructing such systems were first initiated by Damgård [10] and further extended by Zheng and Seberry [35], [36] who also proved Damgård's scheme to be insecure against adaptively chosen ciphertext attacks. The fundamental ideas of Zheng and Seberry are a general method for securing cryptographic schemes against active attacks. Their methods are based on *sole-samplable* (encoding-) functions. Basically, this means that there is no other way to generate a legitimate ciphertext than to choose the message first, and then to encrypt this message by means of the encoding function. Their immunization process consists of appending to each ciphertext a tag that is correlated to the message to be enciphered. This value serves as a second, independent information (cf. also [10]) that is the basis for a validity-check routine which will output the decrypted message only when this check condition is satisfied. Additionally, they present a method for adding authentication capability to their cryptosystems. Although being secure against chosen ciphertext attacks, Lim and Lee [18] have pointed out that some of Zheng's and Seberry's cryptosystems might just fail under known plaintext attacks, a weakness that is overcome by the ZS Diffie-Hellman digital signature based scheme, and the improved schemes [37], where the security tag depends both on the message to be deciphered and on the sender's secret key. Lim and Lee suggest an immunization method where the validity-check is based on the ciphertext and not on the recovered plaintext. Similarly to Zheng's and Seberry's systems, their argument is based on the idea that an attacker cannot produce legitimate ciphertexts without knowing the plaintext. However, their proposed scheme has been broken in [13].

A desirable property of any cryptoscheme is a proof that breaking it is as difficult as solving a computational problem that is widely believed to be difficult, such as integer factorization or the discrete logarithm problem. Consequently, the *provable security* obtained by relying on such complexity theoretic assumption, is to be understood in the sense, that an attack on the scheme implies an attack on the underlying primitive it employs.

In this regard, although the schemes mentioned in the previous paragraph are conjectured to be secure against chosen ciphertext attacks, one of their disadvantages is, that no proofs based on known intractability assumptions are presented.

Motivated by the problem of demonstrating provable security in terms of an underlying intractability assumption, Bellare and Rogaway [1], [2], [3] presented practical and provably secure schemes in the *random oracle model*. They suggest first designing cryptographic protocols in an *ideal system*, and then replacing oracle access by the computation of an "appropriately chosen" function. Based on the assumption of "ideal" hash functions, they present two semantically secure encryption schemes by utilizing the RSA, respectively the Diffie-Hellman, primitive.

Another provable secure scheme has recently been proposed by Okamoto and Uchiyama [24]. Their scheme is shown to be as secure as the intractability of factoring $n = p^2 q$. Similar to Rabin's scheme, the provable security makes their system vulnerable to active attacks. In order to obtain security against chosen ciphertext attacks they suggest a modification based on the random oracle model.

Tsiounis and Yung [31] presented an ElGamal based instantiation of an encryption scheme that is non-malleable under adaptive chosen ciphertext attacks. They basically also rely on the random oracle model but minimize the importance of the model in that it only serves as an unpredictable beacon.

However, some problems with the random oracle model have recently been described by Canetty, Goldreich, and Halevi [9]. They prove that there are encryption and signature schemes which are secure in the random oracle model, but have no secure implementation (replacement of the random oracle by any easy to evaluate function) in the "real world" (where a random oracle does not exist).

A natural goal thus is designing a chosen ciphertext secure system which is practical and proven *secure under standard intractability assumptions* and which does not rely on the random oracle model. The first scheme of this kind has recently been established by Cramer and Shoup [8], [30]. Their proof of security relies only on the hardness of the Diffie-Hellman decision problem and the collision intractability of a hash function.

The new scheme. In this paper we are dealing with a very simple modification of RSA, in particular, with the factorization-equivalent RSA method [21] (cf. also [32]). Recall that plain RSA is malleable (cf. [30]). Moreover, both RSA, and even certain protocols based on the randomized RSA modification PKCS #1, are insecure against chosen ciphertext attacks (cf. [4], [11], [30]). By contrast, our approach represents an authentication-enhanced immunization method against active attacks. Our resulting scheme is both practical and provably as secure as factorizing its modulus. We use probabilistic encryption to utilize randomness to obtain plaintext awareness and provable semantic security against adaptively chosen ciphertext attacks. Other than the previous security enhanced RSA instantiations [1], [2], [3], we do not rely on the random oracle model. Our method also differs from the previous schemes in that it is based on the more general factorization-, as opposed to the more specific RSA, primitive.

2 The factorization-equivalent RSA modification

As indicated above, most of the existing provable secure encryption schemes rely on the random oracle model. However, as mentioned, there does exist an adaptive chosen ciphertext secure ElGamal modification [8] that does not rely on random oracles. Since this scheme is based on the intractability of the *Diffie-Hellman decision problem*, it is clearly of great interest to establish a secure system outside the random oracle model, which is provable secure under the *factorization intractability* of $n = pq$. Even after exhaustive research, the factorization problem is still considered to be very hard. In spite of spectacular progress of recent years in developing fast factorization algorithms (cf. [17], [25]), an appropriately chosen, sufficiently large modulus $n = pq$ still cannot be factorized by current techniques.

Although it has been shown that the semantic security of ElGamal encryption is actually equivalent to the Diffie-Hellman decision problem (cf. [31]), it remains an open question, if the corresponding result in terms of original RSA and the factorization problem is true. That is, while it is well-known that the RSA public-key cryptosystem [27] can be broken if its modulus $n = pq$ can be factored, it is not known if the opposite is true (cf. [6]). This problem has led to the development of a variety of PKCSs (cf. [16], [19], [21], [28], [29], [32], [33], [34]) whose security is equivalent to the difficulty of factoring the modulus n, i.e., for which knowledge of the factorization of the modulus is necessary in order to retrieve plaintext from ciphertext without the use of the decryption key.

A common problem of all these provable secure schemes is their vulnerability to chosen ciphertext attacks which is based on the general underlying method for establishing this security.

Since RSA is certainly one of the most widely used cryptosystems, the goal of this paper is to immunize the simple RSA modification [21] against adaptively chosen ciphertext attacks.

2.1 Description of the factorization-equivalent RSA modification

The crucial point for this scheme consists of choosing e and d according to a certain principle which had also been the basic idea in [32]. Observe that choices for e are known for which RSA is provably not equivalent to factorization (cf. [6], [7]).

Key Generation. Let p and q be sufficiently large primes with $p \equiv q \equiv 3$ (mod 4), put $k = \frac{(p-1)(q-1)}{4}$ and let e and d be odd integers that are chosen according to $ed \equiv \frac{k+1}{2}$ (mod k). Set $Q \equiv qq^* - pp^*$ (mod n), where $n = pq$ and $q^* \equiv q^{-1}$ (mod p) and $p^* \equiv p^{-1}$ (mod q).

The *public key*, is (n, e) and the *private key* is (p, q, d, Q).

Encryption. Given a message $a \in \mathbf{Z}_n^*$, the encryption algorithm runs similarly to the original RSA scheme by calculating $c \equiv a^{2e}$ (mod n). Additionally, it is necessary to evaluate $B_1 \equiv a$ (mod 2) with $B_1 \in \{0, 1\}$ and $B_2 = \left(\frac{a}{n}\right)$.

The *ciphertext* is
$$[c, B_1, B_2].$$

For this scheme, the choice of e and d implies that $a^{2ed} \equiv \pm a$ (mod p) and $a^{2ed} \equiv \pm a$ (mod q). Consequently, there will be four different possible decrypted messages modulo n. The information values B_1 and B_2 will be used to let the receiver retrieve the message that was originally sent.

Decryption. On receiving $[c, B_1, B_2]$ the designer firstly calculates

$$\begin{cases} K \equiv c^d \quad (\text{mod } n) & if \;\; B_2 = 1, \\ K \equiv \frac{c^d}{Q} \quad (\text{mod } n) & if \;\; B_2 = -1, \end{cases}$$

where $0 < K < n$. Finally, the correct message is $a \equiv K$ or $n - K$ (mod n) whichever satisfies $a \equiv B_1$ (mod 2).

2.2 Security analysis

It has been shown in [21] that decrypting the above RSA modification and factorizing the modulus are computationally equivalent. However, by the same token, the proof also enables factoring the modulus under a chosen ciphertext attack.

Proposition 1. *If E and D denote the modified RSA en- and decryption algorithms of section 2.1, then for any $a \in \mathbf{Z}_n^*$ with $\left(\frac{a}{n}\right) = -1$ one obtains a non-trivial factor of n by the determination of $\gcd(D(E(a)) - a, n)$, where in the decryption procedure B_2 is assigned the value 1 instead of -1. More specifically, if $B_2 = 1$ and $\left(\frac{a}{n}\right) = -1$, then $D(E(a)) \equiv E(D(a)) \equiv \pm a$ (mod p) and $D(E(a)) \equiv E(D(a)) \equiv \pm a$ (mod q), but not simultaneously modulo n.*

Proof. The first statement appears as Lemma 3.2 in [21]. Clearly, by properties of the power polynomial, $D(E(a)) \equiv E(D(a)) \equiv a^{2ed}$ (mod n) and the second statement again follows from [21]. □

3   The proposed immunization method

We present a simple method for securing the modified RSA cryptoscheme [21] against adaptive chosen ciphertext attacks. In view of Proposition 1 it becomes obvious that the attack will cause a total break of the system if instead of the (correctly) decrypted message a, the value $\pm b$ (mod n) with $b \equiv a$ (mod p) and $b \equiv -a$ (mod q) will be returned. Certainly, without knowing the correct values $\left(\frac{a}{n}\right)$ and a (mod 2) of the original message a, there is no way for the receiver, to distinguish between the correct and the wrong value, a and b, respectively. Since the decryption process is not injective, the decrypter will not simply obtain the original message a, but rather four possible solutions. As a result, the encrypter needs to provide the information values B_1 and B_2 indicating which of these ambiguously decoded messages is the correct one. Upon transmitting another information bit for B_2 than the one which would help to identify the correct message a, the sender can obviously manipulate the decoder to decrypt the wrong message b, which will immediately enable him to factorize n.

A principal goal thus consists of preventing the above total forgery of the system that is caused by forging the value B_2. The main idea for the immunization method will be to append to each ciphertext another information value that is correlated to the sender's secret key and the message to be enciphered. This additional information will be used in the decryption scheme to locate any forged ciphertext. Moreover, this internal validity test will detect any non-legitimate and any non-authentic ciphertexts, and will also ensure plaintext awareness.

Setup of the scheme.

Let user A's modulus be denoted by $n_A = p_A q_A$, where the primes p_A, q_A are equivalent 3   (mod 4). As before, each user A possesses a secret deciphering key and a public enciphering key, which we will denote as e_A and d_A, respectively, where $e = e_A$ and $d = d_A$ are chosen as in section 2.1. Additionally, let $s_A \equiv t_A^{-1}$ (mod $\phi(n_A)$) for $2 \nmid t_A$ be another secret key which the user A will need for signing, and let t_A be made publicly known.

We will assume throughout, that n_A is chosen in a way which makes it computationally infeasible to find the factorization of n_A.

Assume that h is a cryptographic hash function that maps strings of arbitrary finite length into strings of fixed length. Given h and an input x, computing $h(x)$ must be easy. A *one-way hash function* must provide both *preimage resistance* and *second preimage resistance*, i.e., it must be computationally infeasible to find, respectively, any input which hashes to any pre-specified output, and any second input which has the same output as any specified input. A *collision resistant hash function* is a one-way hash function that provides the additional property of *collision resistance*, i.e., it must be computationally infeasible to find two distinct inputs that hash to the same result.

In the following, h will always denote a collision resistant hash function.

If $n = pq, p \equiv q \equiv 3$ (mod 4) for primes p and q, and if $b \in \mathbf{Z}_n^*$ is a publicly known value (e.g. e_A or e_B), then it is known that Rabin's signature function (cf. [26]) $f : \mathbf{Z}_n^* \mapsto \mathbf{Z}_n^*$, $x \mapsto x(x+b)$ (mod n) is provably as difficult to invert, as it is to find the factors of n. For the remainder of the paper let f be the Rabin function for $n = n_A$. The reason for employing this function will become more obvious later on when establishing the proof of semantic security of the scheme.

In the following, let $x\|y$ denote concatenation of two strings x and y, and let $n_{min} = \min\{n_A, n_B\}$, where n_A is the receiver's, and n_B is the sender's modulus, respectively.

We now extend the RSA scheme of [21] to provide enhanced security. A message $m \in \{1, ..., n_{min}\}$ can be sent secretly from B to A in the following way.

Enciphering Algorithm (user B):

1. Select randomly $r \in \{1, ..., n_{min}\}$ such that for $r' \equiv r^{s_B} \pmod{n_B}$, $m' \equiv rm^{s_B} \pmod{n_B}$,
$$r' < n_{min}, \ m' < n_{min}, 2|r'. \tag{1}$$

2. Compute $c_1 \equiv (m')^{2e_A} \pmod{n_A}$.
3. Compute $c_2 = h(m^{e_A} \pmod{n_A}) \| f(r'))$.
4. Let $c_3 \equiv (r')^{2e_A} \pmod{n_A}$.
5. Set $B_1 \equiv m' \pmod 2$, $B_2 = \left(\frac{m'}{n_A}\right)$, $b_2 = \left(\frac{r'}{n_A}\right)$, where $B_1 \in \{0, 1\}$.
6. Send $C = [c_1, c_2, c_3, B_1, B_2, b_2]$ to user A.

Deciphering Algorithm (user A):

1. Compute $c_1^{d_A} \pmod{n_A}$ and get the unique value M' by means of B_1 and B_2 as in section 2.1 (cf. [21]).
2. Compute $c_3^{d_A} \pmod{n_A}$ and get the unique *even* value R' by means of b_2.
3. Compute $R = (R')^{t_B} \pmod{n_B}$, $M \equiv \left(\frac{M'}{R}\right)^{t_B} \pmod{n_B}$.
4. – if $M > n_{min}$ or $M' > n_{min}$ output NULL,
   – if $R' > n_{min}$ or $2 \nmid R'$ output NULL,
   – if $R > n_{min}$ output NULL,
   – otherwise, check that
$$h\left(M^{e_A} \pmod{n_A}\right) \| f(R')) = c_2. \tag{2}$$

If OK, output $m \equiv M \pmod{n_A}$, else output NULL.

Remark 1. We generally use the notation $a \equiv b \pmod N$ to denote the principal remainder a, that is the unique integer $a \in \{0, ..., N-1\}$ that is congruent to b modulo N.

4 Unambiguous decryption of the proposed scheme

4.1 Authenticity and unique decoding

Observe that in the basic authenticated RSA 'sign then encrypt' system the sender's modulus n_B always has to be smaller than the receiver's modulus n_A in order to guarantee unique decoding. Here, since r' and m' are defined modulo

n_B, property (1) ensures that decryption will always be uniquely possible when working with both n_A and n_B. Namely, if $n_B < n_A$, the uniqueness obviously is guaranteed, while for $n_A < n_B$, both the factors r' and m' have to be less than n_A which allows unique en- and decryption modulo n_A.

Essentially, the blinding of the message m by m^{s_B} (mod n_B) frustrates any attempt of creating a 'useful' message without knowing B's secret key s_B.

4.2 Unambiguity of the decoding algorithm

We now verify that the decryption of an encryption of a message yields the message. For simplicity, we give two definitions.

Definition 1. *Let us define a tuple $C = [c_1, c_2, c_3, B_1, B_2, b_2]$ to be a valid ciphertext, if the decryption oracle does not output 'NULL'. Any c_i of a valid ciphertext will be referred to as a 'valid c_i'.*

Definition 2. *Let m' be a fixed integer. A legitimate choice of B_1, respectively B_2, with respect to m' is understood to be the unique value $B_1 \in \{0, 1\}$, respectively B_2, that is obtained by $B_1 \equiv m'$ (mod 2), respectively $B_2 = \left(\frac{m'}{n_A}\right)$. A legitimate choice of b_2, is defined similarly. Additionally, let the non-legitimate choice of B_1 be $\overline{B_1} \equiv B_1 + 1$ (mod 2), where $\overline{B_1} \in \{0, 1\}$ and B_1 is the legitimate choice with respect to m'. Let analogously $\overline{B_2}$ and $\overline{b_2}$ be defined in the obvious manner.*

Observe, that by hypothesis (1), r' is even, so that the analogous information r' (mod 2) $=: b_1$ is already fixed to 0 and does not have to be explicitly given as part of the ciphertext.

We will assume throughout that $b_2, B_2 \neq 0$.

In the following, we show that no adversary can apply Proposition 1 so as to fool the deciphering algorithm into outputting one of the three 'wrong' messages.

Lemma 1. *Let C be a given valid ciphertext. Suppose an adversary wants to modify C so as to obtain another valid ciphertext. Then any non-legitimate choice $\overline{b_2}$ will cause the decryption oracle to reject, provided factorization of n_A is hard and the adversary does not find a collision in h.*

Proof. If $\overline{b_2}$ is $-b_2$, where b_2 is the legitimate choice with respect to r', then $c_3^{d_A}$ (mod n_A) will, instead of r' (mod n_A) evaluate to $\pm \overline{r'}$ (mod n_A), where $\overline{r'} \equiv r'$ (mod p_A), $\overline{r'} \equiv -r'$ (mod q_A). By the collision-freeness of h, the value R' obtained from $\pm \overline{r'}$ (mod n_A) will be rejected by the test for the valid c_2. The only way to pass the validity test is to calculate a modified c_2 as the hash-value with respect to $\pm \overline{r'}$ (mod n_A). To achieve this, however, since h is collision-resistant, the adversary has to know $\pm \overline{r'}$ (mod n_A). But knowing this value would immediately enable the adversary to factorize n_A, which is impossible. $\qquad \square$

Consider now the unambiguity of decoding a valid c_3. Recall that the underlying en- and deciphering procedure $r' \mapsto (r')^{2e_A d_A} \pmod{n_A}$ yields $\pm r' \pmod{p_A}$, $\pm r' \pmod{q_A}$, which gives rise to four different possible values modulo n_A in the deciphering process. Unambiguous decoding relies only on the auxiliary value b_2 since b_1 equals zero by construction. As b_2 can only be the legitimate value by Lemma 1, no attacker is able to fool the deciphering oracle into outputting the 'wrong' values for $r' \pmod{n_A}$. We thus obtain the following.

Corollary 1. *If C is a valid ciphertext with entries defined above, then $c_3 \equiv (r')^{2e_A} \pmod{n_A}$ will always unambiguously be decrypted into $r' \pmod{n_A}$.*

Similarly as in Lemma 1 the following can be shown.

Lemma 2. *Let C be a valid ciphertext. Suppose an adversary wants to modify C so as to obtain another valid ciphertext. Then any non-legitimate choice $\overline{B_2}$ will cause the decryption oracle to reject, provided factorization of n_A is hard and the adversary does not find a collision in h.*

Lemma 3. *Assume that an adversary does not find a collision in h. Then, given a valid ciphertext C, an adversary can only modify B_1 into the non-legitimate choice $\overline{B_1}$ to obtain another valid ciphertext, if he knows the corresponding message and the random value.*

Proof. By Corollary 1, r' ($< n_{min}$) and thus, $r \equiv (r')^{t_B} \pmod{n_B}$ will unambiguously be calculated in the deciphering process. By the non-legitimate choice $\overline{B_1}$ the first step of the decryption procedure will evaluate to $-m' \pmod{n_A}$ instead of $m' \pmod{n_A}$. Therefore, $\overline{m} \equiv \left(\frac{-m' \pmod{n_A}}{r}\right)^{t_B} \pmod{n_B}$ will instead of $\left(\frac{m'}{r}\right)^{t_B} \pmod{n_B}$ be the input for the validity check (2). Because of the collision-freeness of h, the test will certainly reject for the valid c_2. Consequently, c_2 would need to be adapted so that the test does not reject. Again, by the collision-freeness of h, the only way to do so, is to evaluate c_2 from $M = \overline{m}$ and $R = r$ in (2). $\square$

Corollary 2. *Let C be a valid ciphertext with respect to the unknown message m relative to r. Then $c_1 \equiv (m')^{2e_A} \pmod{n_A}$ will always unambiguously be decrypted into $m' \pmod{n_A}$.*

In summarizing, we have.

Theorem 1. *For the above cryptosystem it is always true that decryption of an encryption of an unknown message yields the message.*

5 Security analysis of the proposed scheme

5.1 The notions

Semantic security. Informally, a cryptosystem is semantically secure (cf. [14]), if whatever can be computed by an attacker about the plaintext given an object ciphertext, can also be computed without the object ciphertext. Semantic security ensures that no partial information on the plaintext is leaked from an object ciphertext to probabilistic polynomial time bounded attackers. We further distinguish between semantic security against (a) *chosen plaintext* attacks and semantic security against (b) *adaptive chosen ciphertext* attacks.

Formally, the setup is like this. Let the adversary be given $A's$ public encryption key and also access to (a), the enciphering algorithm, respectively, (b) the deciphering algorithm.

In the case of (b), the adversary makes arbitrary queries to the decryption oracle, decrypting ciphertexts of his choice. (In case (a) the adversary never has access to the decryption oracle.)

Next, the adversary chooses two messages, m_0, m_1, and sends these to the encryption oracle, which chooses a bit $b \in \{0, 1\}$ at random, and encrypts m_b. The corresponding ciphertext C is given to the adversary. The adversary does not see the bit b. Now the challenge to the adversary consists of determining for which of the two messages C is the ciphertext.

After receiving the object ciphertext C from the encryption oracle, the adversary continues to query the corresponding oracle (for (a) respectively (b)), subject only to the restriction that in case (b) the query must be different to the exact object ciphertext C.

Finally, the adversary outputs $b' \in \{0, 1\}$ which is his guess of the value b.

The scheme is semantically secure (with respect to (a) respectively (b)) if the probability that $b' = b$ is at most $1/2 + \epsilon$ where ϵ is negligibly small.

Remark 2. Observe that by deterministic encryption (e.g. plain RSA) the same message m_b encrypted at different times will always give the same cryptogram which would be recognized by the adversary. Therefore, a basic requirement for semantic security is that the cryptosystem is probabilistic.

Plaintext awareness. The idea is that an adversary "knows" the decryption of the message which he encrypts in the sense that he cannot produce a ciphertext C without being able to compute the plaintext m for which C is the ciphertext. Plaintext awareness implies non-malleability, since it prevents any adversary from modifying a given ciphertext so as to induce a desired change in the plaintext. For a formal definition of plaintext awareness we refer to [2], [3].

5.2 The main results

We now proceed to show the semantic security and plaintext awareness of the modified RSA scheme described above.

Theorem 2. *The above cryptosystem is semantically secure against adaptive chosen plaintext attacks assuming that the factorization of $n_A = p_A q_A$ is hard.*

Proof. Suppose that C_1 and C_2 are two valid ciphertexts. Under the factorization intractability of n_A and the introduction of the random value r, no probabilistic polynomial time algorithm can distinguish between C_1 and C_2. Namely, if the factorization of $n_A = p_A q_A$ is hard, then extracting the whole values m' from c_1, respectively r' from c_3, is practically impossible. It thus follows from Näslund's recent results (cf. [22], [15]), that all individual bits of c_1 and c_3 are secure. Now even if h leaks some partial information, by the same argument, all individual bits of m and r' are secure, since all the bits induced by the RSA, respectively the Rabin function, m^{e_A} (mod n_A), respectively $f(r')$, are secure. $\quad\square$

Lemma 4. *With notation as above, if C is a valid ciphertext, then any change to c_2 conducted without knowing the corresponding message and the random value, will cause the decryption oracle to reject, provided the adversary does not find a collision in h.*

Proof. The assertion follows from the collision resistance of h. In detail, given any modified $\overline{c_2}$ the hash value in the left hand side of (2) will not be equal to this $\overline{c_2}$ and the test will reject.

We will show that the adversary needs to have knowledge of the message and the blinding factor relative to this message, if he wants to construct a valid ciphertext.

The test (2) will only be passed, if a modified c_2, $\overline{c_2}$, is evaluated as the image of the hash-function h. In other words, the adversary can firstly choose a z and set $c_1^{d_A}$ (mod n_A) $= z$. Secondly, the adversary can choose w and set $c_3^{d_A}$ (mod n_A) $= w$. Now he can compute a modified c_2 as the hash-value relative to z and w as

$$h\left(\left(\frac{z}{w^{t_B} \ (\text{mod } n_B)}\right)^{e_A} \ (\text{mod } n_A) \ || \ f(w)\right)$$

and can construct a valid ciphertext from $c_1 \equiv z^{2e_A}$ (mod n_A) and $c_3 \equiv w^{2e_A}$ (mod n_A). Since, by construction, the validity check will pass, the decryption oracle will return the message $\frac{z}{w^{t_B} \ (\text{mod } n_B)}$ (mod n_A) which certainly can be computed by the adversary. In other words, whenever an adversary can construct a valid ciphertext, he also knows the corresponding message. $\quad\square$

Similarly, by the collision-resistance of h, we obtain.

Lemma 5. *If C is a ciphertext, then any modified value of c_3, $\overline{c_3}$, (respectively, any modified $\overline{c_1}$) obtained without knowledge of the message and the corresponding random value, will cause the decryption oracle to reject, provided the adversary does not find a collision in h.*

It follows from the proof of Lemma 4 for c_2, and similarly, for c_1 and c_3 that being able to produce a valid ciphertext implies the knowledge of the message. We thus have shown.

Theorem 3. *If h is collision-resistant, then the above cryptosystem is plaintext aware.*

Theorem 4. *The above cryptosystem is non-malleable and semantically secure against adaptive chosen ciphertext attacks assuming that (1) the hash function h is collision resistant and (2) the factorization of $n_A = p_A q_A$ is hard.*

Proof. Both assertions are consequences of the established plaintext-awareness. The first statement follows, since no adversary can produce a valid ciphertext without knowing the corresponding plaintext. Also the second statement follows immediately, since querying the deciphering algorithm with any legitimate ciphertext C yields no new information, because the plaintext to this ciphertext already has to be known. Thus, any adaptively chosen ciphertext attacker can completely be simulated by a chosen plaintext attacker when creating any legitimate ciphertext. Therefore the chosen ciphertext security follows from the above proved chosen plaintext security. □

6 Summary

Designing provable strong cryptoschemes is one of the most fundamental tasks in cryptography. Certainly, the one-time-pad provides the theoretically strongest possible form of security. However, due to the practical difficulties of this and other theoretical secure cryptosystems, many researchers have adapted the notion of security by relying on some standard complexity-theoretic assumption. In this paper we rely on the assumption of the factorization intractability of properly chosen large numbers.

Since RSA is undoubtedly the most popular one among all the factorization based encryption schemes, we have proposed some method of strengthening RSA against active attacks. By means of probabilistic encoding and by introducing an internal validity check routine in the deciphering algorithm the proposed scheme is shown to have the property that the adversary can create ciphertexts only of strings for which he "knows" the corresponding plaintexts. Consequently, our scheme is not only semantically secure but also non-malleable and secure against chosen ciphertext attacks. Although provable security typically results in longer cryptograms and slower en- and deciphering algorithms, our scheme remains practical. In detail, the message length is about twice that of original RSA, plus the length of some hash output. Plain en- and decryption require three exponentiations, respectively. The intertwined signing algorithm requires two additional exponentiations in both the en- and deciphering algorithms. Additionally, in both the en- and deciphering process, the evaluation of some cryptographic hash function is needed. Contrary to the previous RSA enhancements we only rely on the factorization primitive and the existence of a collision resistant hash function.

7 Acknowledgments

I am grateful to Winfried B. Müller for many fruitful discussions and for his insightful suggestions and remarks. I would also like to thank the anonymous referees for their helpful comments.

References

1. M. Bellare, P. Rogaway: Random oracles are practical: A paradigm for designing efficient protocols. Extended abstract in *Proc. First Annual Conference on Computer and Communications Security, ACM*, 1993; full paper available at http://www.cs.ucdavis.edu/~rogaway/papers/.
2. M. Bellare, P. Rogaway: Optimal asymmetric encryption – How to encrypt with RSA. Extended abstract in *Advances in Cryptology - Eurocrypt 94, LNCS* 950, A. De Santis (ed.), pp. 92–111, 1995.
3. M. Bellare, P. Rogaway: Minimizing the use of random oracles in authenticated encryption schemes. Shortened version in the *Proceedings of ICICS'97, LNCS* 1334, Y. Han, T. Okamoto, S. Qing (eds.), pp. 1–16, 1997; full version promised to be available at http://www.cs.ucdavis.edu/~rogaway/papers/.
4. D. Bleichenbacher: Chosen Ciphertext Attacks Against Protocols Based on the RSA Encryption Standard PKCS #1. *Advances in Cryptology - Crypto'98, LNCS* 1462, H. Krawczyk (ed.), pp. 1–12, 1998.
5. M. Blum, S. Goldwasser: An Efficient Probabilistic Public-Key Encryption Scheme Which Hides All Partial Information, *Advances of Cryptology - Crypto '84, LNCS* 196, G.R. Blakely, D. Chaum (eds.), pp. 289–299, 1985.
6. D. Boneh, R. Venkatesan: Breaking RSA May Not Be Equivalent to Factoring, *Advances of Cryptology - Eurocrypt '98, LNCS* 1403, K. Nyberg (ed.), pp. 59–71, 1998.
7. D. Coppersmith, M. Franklin, J. Patarin, M. Reiter: Low-Exponent RSA with Related Messages. *Advances of Cryptology - Eurocrypt' 96, LNCS* 1070, U. Maurer (ed.), pp. 1–9, 1996.
8. R. Cramer, V. Shoup: A Practical Public Key Cryptosystem Provable Secure against Adaptive Chosen Ciphertext Attack, *Advances of Cryptology - Crypto '98, LNCS* 1462, H. Krawczyk (ed.), pp. 13–25, 1998.
9. R. Canetti, O. Goldreich, S. Halevi: The random oracle model, revisited. In: *30 th Annual ACM Symposium on Theory of Computing*, 1998.
10. I. Damgård: Towards practical public key cryptosystems secure against chosen ciphertext attacks. *Advances in Cryptology - Crypto'91, LNCS* 576, J. Feigenbaum (ed.), pp. 445–456, 1992.
11. D. W. Davida: Chosen Signature Cryptanalysis of the RSA (MIT) Public Key Cryptosystem. TR-CS-82-2, University of Wisconsin-Milwaukee, 1982.
12. D. Dolev, C. Dwork, M. Naor: Non-malleable cryptography. In *23rd Annual ACM Symposium on Theory of Computing*, pp. 542–552, 1991.
13. Y. Frankel, M. Yung: Cryptanalysis of immunized LL public key systems. *Advances in Cryptology - Crypto'95, LNCS* 963, Don Coppersmith (ed.), pp. 287–296, 1995.
14. S. Goldwasser, S. Micali: Probabilistic Encryption. *Journal of Computer and System Sciences* 28, pp. 270–299, April 1984.
15. J. Håstad, M. Näslund: The Security of Individual RSA Bits. To appear in the *Proceedings of FOCS '98*, IEEE.
16. K. Kurosawa, T. Ito, M. Takeuchi: Public key cryptosystem using a reciprocal number with the same intractability as factoring a large number. *Cryptologia*, no 12, pp. 225–233, 1988.
17. A. K. Lenstra, H. W. Lenstra Jr.: The Development of the Number Field Sieve. Springer-Verlag, Berlin, 1993.
18. C. H. Lim, P. J. Lee: Another method for attaining security against adaptively chosen ciphertext attacks. *Advances in Cryptology - Crypto'93, LNCS* 773, D. R. Stinson (ed.), pp. 420–434, 1994.

19. J. H. Loxton, D. D. Khoo, G. J. Bird, J. Seberry: A Cubic RSA Code Equivalent to Factorization. *Journal of Cryptology*, no 5, pp. 139–150, 1992.

20. A. J. Menezes, P. C. van Oorschot, A. A. Vanstone: *Handbook of Applied Cryptography*. CRC Press, Boca Raton, New York, London, Tokyo, 1997.

21. S. Müller, W. B. Müller: The Security of Public Key Cryptosystems Based on Integer Factorization. *Information Security and Privacy – ACISP'98, LNCS* 1438, C. Boyd, E. Dawson (eds.), pp. 7–23, 1998.

22. M. Näslund: Bit Extraction, Hard-Core Predicates, and the Bit Security of RSA. Doctoral Dissertation, Royal Institute of Technology, Stockholm, Sweden, 1998; http://www.nada.kth.se:80/~matsn/.

23. M. Naor, M. Yung: Public-key cryptosystems provably secure against chosen ciphertext attacks. In *22nd Annual ACM Symposium on Theory of Computing*, pp. 427–437, 1990.

24. T. Okamoto, S. Uchiyama: A New Public-Key Cryptosystem as Secure as Factoring. *Advances of Cryptology - Eurocrypt'98, LNCS* 1403, K. Nyberg (ed.), pp. 308–318, 1998.

25. C. Pomerance: The number field sieve. *Proceedings of Symposia in Applied Mathematics*, Vol. 48, pp. 465–480, 1994.

26. M. O. Rabin: Digitalized signatures and public-key functions as intractable as factorization. MIT/LCS/TR-212, MIT Laboratory for Computer Science, 1979.

27. R. L. Rivest, A. Shamir, L. Adleman: A method for obtaining digital signatures and public-key cryptosystems. *Comm. ACM*, no 21, pp. 120–126, 1978.

28. R. Scheidler: A Public-Key Cryptosystem Using Purely Periodic Fields. *J. Cryptology*, no 11, pp. 109–124, 1998.

29. R. Scheidler, H. C. Williams: A Public-Key Cryptosystem Utilizing Cyclotomic Fields. *Designs, Codes and Cryptography*, no 6, pp. 117–131, 1995.

30. V. Shoup: Why Chosen Ciphertext Security Matters. Research Report RZ 3076, IBM Research Division Zürich, 1998; http://www.cs.wisc.edu/~shoup/papers/.

31. Y. Tsiounis, M. Yung: On the security of ElGamal-based encryption. To appear in the 1998 International Workshop on Practice and Theory in Public Key Cryptography (PKC '98); http://www.ccs.neu.edu/home/yiannis/pubs.html.

32. H. C. Williams: A modification of the RSA Public-Key Encryption Procedure. *IEEE Trans. Inf. Theory*, Vol. IT-26, no 6, pp. 726–729, 1980.

33. H. C. Williams: Some Public-Key Crypto-Functions as Intractable as Factorization. *Cryptologia*, no 9, pp. 223–237, 1985.

34. H. C. Williams: An M^3 public-Key Encryption Scheme. *Advances in Cryptology - Crypto'85, LNCS* 218, H.C. Williams (ed.), pp. 358–368, 1986.

35. Y. Zheng, J. Seberry: Practical approaches to attaining security against adaptively chosen ciphertext attacks. *Advances in Cryptology - Crypto'92, LNCS* 740, E.F. Brickell (ed.), pp. 292–304, 1993.

36. Y. Zheng, J. Seberry: Immunizing public key cryptosystems against chosen ciphertext attacks. The Special Issue on Secure Communications, *IEEE Journal on Selected Areas in Communications*, Vol. 11, No. 5, pp. 715–724, June 1993.

37. Y. Zheng: Improved public key cryptosystems secure against chosen ciphertext attacks, Preprint No.94-1, Department of Computer Science, University of Wollongong, 24 January 1994; http://www.pscit.monash.edu.au/~yuliang/pubs/.

Generalised Cycling Attacks on RSA and Strong RSA Primes [*]

Marc Gysin and Jennifer Seberry

Centre for Computer Security Research
School of Information Technology and Computer Science
The University of Wollongong
Wollongong, NSW 2522
Australia
[marc,jennie]@cs.uow.edu.au

Abstract. Given an RSA modulus n, a ciphertext c and the encryption exponent e, one can construct the sequence

$$x_0 = c \bmod n, \quad x_{i+1} = x_i^e \bmod n, \quad i = 0, 1, \ldots$$

until $gcd(x_{i+1} - x_0, n) \neq 1$ or $i > B$, B a given boundary. If $i \leq B$, there are two cases. Case 1: $gcd(x_{i+1} - x_0, n) = n$. In this case $x_i = m$ and the secret message m can be recovered. Case 2: $1 \neq gcd(x_{i+1} - x_0, n) \neq n$. In this case, the RSA modulus n can be factorised. If $i \leq B$, then Case 2 is much more likely to occur than Case 1. This attack is called a *cycling attack*. We introduce some new *generalised cycling attacks*. These attacks work *without* the knowledge of e and c. Therefore, these attacks can be used as factorisation algorithms. We also translate these attacks to elliptic curves. For this case we call these attacks *EC generalised cycling attacks*. Finally, we review criteria that a strong RSA prime must satisfy.

1 Preliminaries

The reader is assumed to be familiar with the RSA cryptosystem, [RivShaAdl78]. A brief introduction to Lucas sequences and elliptic curves is given in the appendix. Throughout this paper we will use the following notations. If $x_0, x_1, x_2, \ldots$ is a sequence of elements, then $\{X\}$ will denote the whole sequence. If the elements are taken modulo a certain number, say p, and the sequence is periodic, then we will denote its period by $\pi_{\{X\},p}$. We write $a \mid b$ for a divides b. $(a|n)$ denotes the Legendre or Jacobi symbol if n is prime or composite, respectively.

1.1 The Carmichael and Omega Function

We will make use of the Carmichael and Omega functions $\lambda(\cdot)$ and $\Omega(\cdot, \cdot)$, respectively. $\lambda(\cdot)$ is defined as follows (see, for example, [Riesel85]):

---

[*] Supported by ARC Large Grants A9803826, A49703117

$$\lambda(2) = 1, \ \lambda(4) = 2, \ \lambda(8) = 2,$$

and for $k > 3$

$$\lambda(2^k) = 2\lambda(2^{k-1}).$$

For prime $p \geq 3$ and $k > 1$ we have

$$\lambda(p) = p - 1, \ \lambda(p^k) = p\lambda(p^{k-1}).$$

Finally, for $n = p_1^{e_1} \cdot \ldots \cdot p_k^{e_k}$, p_i prime, $e_i \geq 1$:

$$\lambda(n) = lcm(\lambda(p_1^{e_1}), \ldots, \lambda(p_k^{e_k})).$$

The Carmichael function $\lambda(\cdot)$ and the well known Euler totient function $\phi(\cdot)$ are intimately connected. If, for example, $U(Z_n)$ denotes the multiplicative group of units in Z_n, then we can describe the following via these two functions:

- the order of the group $|U(Z_n)|$ is equal to $\phi(n)$;
- the maximum order of an element $z \in U(Z_n)$ is $\lambda(n)$;
- as a consequence of the above two statements: $U(Z_n)$ is cyclic if and only if $\lambda(n) = \phi(n)$.

The Omega function $\Omega(\cdot, \cdot)$ is defined as follows:

$$\Omega(2, D) = \begin{cases} 1 & D \text{ is even} \\ 3 & D \text{ is odd} \end{cases}$$

and for $k > 1$

$$\Omega(2^k, D) = 2\Omega(2^{k-1}, D).$$

For prime $p \geq 3$ and $k > 1$ we have

$$\Omega(p, D) = p - (D|p), \ (D|p) \neq 0$$
$$\Omega(p, D) = 2, \ (D|p) = 0,$$
$$\Omega(p^k, D) = p\Omega(p^{k-1}, D)$$

Finally, for $n = p_1^{e_1} \cdot \ldots \cdot p_k^{e_k}$, p_i prime, $e_i \geq 1$:

$$\Omega(n, D) = lcm(\Omega(p_1^{e_1}, D), \ldots, \Omega(p_k^{e_k}, D)).$$

2 Generalised Cycling Attacks on RSA Moduli $n = pq$

2.1 Introduction: The Function $Enc(\cdot, \cdot)$

In this section we show that all the attacks involve the same function, subsequently called the $Enc(\cdot, \cdot)$ function. $Enc(\cdot, \cdot)$ means a generalised RSA or Rabin encryption function. In this paper we define $Enc(\cdot, \cdot)$ for three different mathematical settings, namely:

- the multiplicative group of $U(Z_n)$ or $U(Z_p)$;
- Lucas sequences $V(P, 1) \bmod p$ or $V(P, 1) \bmod n$;
- the additive group of points on an elliptic curve $E(F_p)$ or $E(Z_n)$.

Other mathematical settings are possible. Let m be an element of the corresponding mathematical setting $\mathcal{M}$ and let $x \in Z$. Then the function $Enc(\cdot, \cdot)$: $\mathcal{M} \times Z \rightarrow \mathcal{M}$ is defined as follows.

$$Enc(m, x) = \begin{cases} m^x & \text{for integers modulo a prime or composite} \\ V_x(m, 1) & \text{for Lucas sequences modulo a prime or composite} \\ x \cdot m & \text{for elliptic curves over } F_p \text{ or } Z_n \end{cases}$$

Note that m must be an element of the corresponding mathematical setting $\mathcal{M}$. In particular, for the last case (elliptic curve), m must be a point on the elliptic curve. From the definition of $Enc(\cdot, \cdot)$, we have $Enc(Enc(m, x_1), x_2) = Enc(Enc(m, x_2), x_1) = Enc(m, x_1 x_2)$. Let now, for prime p and $D = P^2 - 4$

$$\Psi(p) = \begin{cases} \lambda(p) & \text{for integers } \bmod p \\ \Omega(p, D) & \text{for Lucas sequences } \bmod p \\ p + 1 + t_1 & \text{for elliptic curves over } F_p \end{cases}$$

and for RSA modulus $n = pq$ and $D = P^2 - 4$

$$\Psi(pq) = \begin{cases} \lambda(pq) & \text{for integers } \bmod n \\ \Omega(pq, D) & \text{for Lucas sequences } \bmod n \\ (p + 1 + t_1)(q + 1 + t_2) & \text{for elliptic curves over } Z_n \end{cases}$$

where $(p + 1 + t_1)$ and $(q + 1 + t_2)$ are the orders of the additive groups of the elliptic curves over F_p and F_q, respectively. Observe that now $Enc(m, x) \equiv m \bmod p$ for $x \equiv 1 \bmod \Psi(p)$ and $Enc(m, x) \equiv m \bmod n$ for $x \equiv 1 \bmod \Psi(n)$ [1]. For the cycling attacks one now hopes that either $F(\Psi(p))$ or $F(\Psi(q))$ for this mathematical setting is smooth (smooth is defined below), that is, $F(\Psi(p))$ or $F(\Psi(q))$ has only small factors. $F(\cdot)$ is a function which depends on the particular attack chosen. For each of the three mathematical settings, there are now two possible cycling attacks.

Attack 1: $x_0 = Enc(seed, e^0)$, $x_{i+1} = Enc(x_i, e) = Enc(seed, e^{i+1})$, $i = 0, 1, \ldots$

Attack 2: $x_0 = Enc(seed, \tilde{V}_0(\tilde{P}, 1))$, $x_{i+1} = Enc(seed, \tilde{V}_{i+1}(\tilde{P}, 1))$, $i = 0, 1, \ldots$

where $\tilde{V}(\tilde{P}, 1)$ is a Lucas sequence.

---

[1] The reader may have noted that $\Psi(\cdot)$ does not necessarily coincide with the order/period of the corresponding mathematical setting. However, the following statement is always true: the maximum order/period of an element of the corresponding mathematical setting divides $\Psi(\cdot)$. Also to be more precise, the function $\Psi(\cdot)$ has one, two or three arguments depending on whether one is working with integers modulo a prime or composite, Lucas sequences or elliptic curves, respectively. This is omitted for the sake of simplicity.

The cycling attacks described under Attack 1 will have a complexity whose upper bound is given by $min(\lambda(\Psi(p)), \lambda(\Psi(q)))$ whereas the upper bound of the complexity of the cycling attacks described under Attack 2 will be $min(\Omega(\Psi(p), \tilde{P}^2 - 4), \Omega(\Psi(q), \tilde{P}^2 - 4))$. More precisely, the running times of attacks belonging to Attack 1 will divide $O(min(\lambda(\Psi(p)), \lambda(\Psi(q))))$ whereas the running times of attacks belonging to Attack 2 will divide $O(min(\Omega(\Psi(p), \tilde{P}^2 - 4), \Omega(\Psi(q), \tilde{P}^2 - 4)))$.

In the subsequent sections, we describe cycling attacks mod n. All the sequences $\{X\}$ have a possible empty aperiodic part and a periodic part (or cycle) of length $\pi_{\{X\},n}$. To understand the behaviour of $\{X\} = x_i$ mod n, we must first study $\{X\}$ mod p and calculate the period $\pi_{\{X\},p}$, that is, the length of the periodic part of $\{X\}$ mod p. The aperiodic part, if it exists, is usually very small ($O(\log p)$ elements). All the attacks have the following calculations in common:

Algorithm Cycling Attack:

Input: n, starting values $seed, start_0, \ldots$;
* parameters $par_0, par_1, \ldots$, a boundary B*
Output: "success",p,q; or "fail"

---

set $x_0 = Enc(seed, \cdot)$ mod n;
set $start = |\log n|$;
repeat
* set $x_{i+1} = Enc(x_i, \cdot)$ mod n;*
until $i \geq start$;
repeat
* set $x_{i+1} = Enc(x_i, \cdot)$ mod n;*
* set $test = gcd(x_{i+1} - x_{start}, n)$;*
until $test \neq 1$ or $i > B$;
If $test \neq 1$ and $test \neq n$ then Output("success",test,n:test); else Output("fail");

Instead of starting with *seed*, a random number, it is a good idea to let $seed = Enc(seed, 2)$. Since all the group orders/periods considered in this paper are even, x_0 may now have half of the original order, or the sequence associated with x_0 may now have half of the original period. This would increase the efficiency of the algorithm by 100%. The only purpose of the first repeat–loop is to skip a possible aperiodic part of the sequence $\{X\}$. (This repeat loop can be omitted if it is known that $\{X\}$ can not have an aperiodic part.) That is, x_{start} should now be in the periodic part of $\{X\}$. In the second repeat–loop we are trying to factorise n. (As in many factorisation algorithms we could accumulate a product of x_i's mod n and test for the *gcd* in, say, every 100th step to speed up the performance.) There are now three possible cases:

– The period $\pi_{\{X\},p}$ or $\pi_{\{X\},q}$ is less or equal than the boundary B: and $\pi_{\{X\},p} \neq \pi_{\{X\},q}$: In this case, $1 < test < n$ and the algorithm succeeds.
– The periods $\pi_{\{X\},p}$ and $\pi_{\{X\},q}$ are less or equal than the boundary B; and $\pi_{\{X\},p} = \pi_{\{X\},q}$: This case occurs with very low probability. In this case

test $= n$ and the algorithm fails. We can simply retry the algorithm with some other *seed* and/or parameters.

- The periods $\pi_{\{X\},p}$ and $\pi_{\{X\},q}$ are greater than the boundary B: In this case *test* $= 1$ and the algorithm fails.

All the attacks subsequently described have in common that the next element x_{i+1} in the sequence can be calculated from the current element x_i in $O(1)$ steps. We need one theorem for further discussions. A proof of this theorem is given in the technical report, [GysSeb98].

Theorem 1. *Let $\{X\}$ and $\{Y\}$ be two sequences. Let $\{X\} = x_i = seed^i$ and $\{Y\} = y_i = V_i(P, 1)$, let $n > 0$, $gcd(seed, n) = 1$. Then*

(i) the period $\pi_{\{X\},n}$ of $\{X\}$ mod n satisfies: $\pi_{\{X\},n} \mid \lambda(n)$;
(ii) the period $\pi_{\{Y\},n}$ of $\{Y\}$ mod n satisfies: $\pi_{\{Y\},n} \mid \Omega(n, P^2 - 4)$.

2.2 $Enc(\cdot, \cdot)$: Integers mod n

Attack 1 Let

$$x_0 = seed \bmod p, \quad x_{i+1} = x_i^e \bmod p$$

where $seed, e \geq 2$. We examine the period of x_i mod p. We first note that $x_i = seed^{e^i} \bmod p$. We consider $e^i \bmod p - 1$. [2] If $p - 1 = e^t \ell$ and $gcd(e, \ell) = 1$, then

- the above sequence will have a maximum aperiodic part of length t;
- for the period $\pi_{\{X\},p}$ we have $\pi_{\{X\},p} \mid \lambda(\ell)$.

The algorithm has a high chance of success if either $\lambda(\lambda(p))$ or $\lambda(\lambda(q))$ is either small or smooth.

Prevention of the attack:
To prevent this attack the designer of a public–key cryptosystem or CSPRBG of the RSA or Rabin type must choose p and q such that $\lambda(\lambda(p))$ and $\lambda(\lambda(q))$ are not small and not smooth. In particular, a strong prime p designed to withstand this attack must have the following properties:

- $p - 1$ must have a large factor, say t;
- $t - 1$ must have a large factor.

Similar statements can be made about the other prime q.

---

[2] More precisely, we have to consider e^i modulo the order of *seed* mod p. Since the order of *seed* mod p divides $p - 1$ and $\lambda(x) \mid \lambda(y)$ and $\Omega(x, D) \mid \Omega(y, D)$ for $x \mid y$ and we only state $\pi_{\{X\},p}$ divides some number, everything works out nicely at the end. The aperiodic part might be less than the maximum number stated because the order of *seed* mod p divides $p - 1$ and is not necessarily equal to $p - 1$. Similar considerations need to be made for all the other algorithms but they are omitted for the sake of simplicity.

Attack 2 Let

$$x_0 = seed^{V_0} \bmod p, \quad x_1 = seed^{V_1} \bmod p, \quad x_{i+1} = seed^{V_{i+1}} \bmod p$$

where $seed \geq 2$ and $V(P, 1)$ is a Lucas sequence. We examine the period of $x_i \bmod p$. We consider $V(P, 1) \bmod p - 1$ and note that $\pi_{V(P,1),p-1} \mid \Omega(p - 1, P^2 - 4)$. There is no aperiodic part. The algorithm has a high chance of success if either $\Omega(\lambda(p), P^2 - 4) = \Omega(p - 1, P^2 - 4)$ or $\Omega(\lambda(q), P^2 - 4) = \Omega(q - 1, P^2 - 4)$ is either small or smooth.

Remark:
In the repeat loop $x_{i+1} = x_i^P \cdot x_{i-1}^{-1} = seed^{PV_i(P,1) - V_{i-1}(P,1)} = seed^{V_{i+1}(P,1)}$. Therefore, one does not need to keep track of the individuals values of $V(P, 1)$ since these are calculated implicitly.

Prevention of the attack:
To prevent this attack the designer of a public–key cryptosystem or CSPRBG of the RSA or Rabin type must choose p and q such that $\Omega(\lambda(p), D)$ and $\Omega(\lambda(q), D)$ are not small and not smooth for any values of D. In particular, a strong prime p designed to withstand this attack must have the following properties:

- $p - 1$ must have a large factor, say t;
- $t - 1$ *and* $t + 1$ must have a large factor.

Similar statements can be made about the other prime q.

2.3 $Enc(\cdot, \cdot)$: Lucas Sequences

Attack 1 Let

$$x_0 = V_1(P, 1) \bmod p, \quad x_{i+1} = V_{e^{i+1}}(P, 1) \bmod p$$

where $e \geq 2$. We examine the period of $x_i \bmod p$. If $\left(P^2 - 4|p\right) = 1$, then we have to examine $e^j \bmod p - 1$, if $\left(P^2 - 4|p\right) = -1$, then we have to examine $e^j \bmod p + 1$. The case $\left(P^2 - 4|p\right) = 0$ occurs with neglible probability. The case $\left(P^2 - 4|p\right) = 1$ has the same complexity as the attack in Section 2.2 (since in this case $\lambda(\Omega(p, P^2 - 4)) = \lambda(\lambda(p))$). Therefore, we assume $\left(P^2 - 4|p\right) = -1$. If, now, $p + 1 = e^t \ell$ and $gcd(e, \ell) = 1$, then

- the above sequence will have a maximum aperiodic part of length t;
- for the period $\pi_{\{x\},p}$ we have $\pi_{\{x\},p} \mid \lambda(\ell)$.

The algorithm has a high chance of success if either $\lambda(\Omega(p, P^2 - 4))$ or $\lambda(\Omega(q, P^2 - 4))$ is either small or smooth.

Remarks:
(i) We need to explain how to calculate $V_{e^{i+1}}(P, 1) \bmod p$ from $V_{e^i}(P, 1) \bmod p$. We let

$$M = \begin{bmatrix} 0 & 1 \\ -1 & P \end{bmatrix},$$

then V_j can easily be derived from M^j (see also appendix). (ii) For $e = 2$ the calculations in the repeat–loops can be simplified to $x_{i+1} = x_i^2 - 2 \bmod n$. This is because $x_{i+1} = V_2(x_i, 1) = x_i^2 - 2 \bmod n$.

Prevention of the attack:
To prevent this attack the designer of a public–key cryptosystem or CSPRBG of the RSA or Rabin type must choose p and q such that $\lambda(\Omega(p, D))$ and $\lambda(\Omega(q, D))$ are not small and not smooth for any values of D. In particular, a strong prime p designed to withstand this attack must have the following properties:

- $p - 1$ and $p + 1$ must have a large factor, say t and w;
- $t - 1$ and $w - 1$ must have a large factor.

Similar statements can be made about the other prime q.

Attack 2 Let $V(P, 1)$ and $\tilde{V}(\tilde{P}, 1)$ be two Lucas sequences. Let

$$x_0 = V_{\tilde{V}_0(\tilde{P},1)}(P, 1) \bmod p, \quad x_{i+1} = V_{\tilde{V}_{i+1}(\tilde{P},1)}(P, 1) \bmod p$$

We examine the period of $x_i \bmod p$. Since $V(P, 1) \bmod p$ has a period which divides $\Omega(p, P^2 - 4)$, $x_i \bmod p$ has a period which divides $\Omega(\Omega(p, P^2 - 4), \tilde{P}^2 - 4)$. There is no aperiodic part. Note that $\Omega(p, P^2 - 4) = p - 1$, if $(P^2 - 4|p) = 1$ and $\Omega(p, P^2 - 4) = p + 1$, if $(P^2 - 4|p) = -1$. The case $(P^2 - 4|p) = 0$ occurs with neglible probability. We only examine the case $(P^2 - 4|p) = -1$ and, if $p + 1$ has a large factor, say t, $\left(\tilde{P}^2 - 4|t\right) = -1$ since all the other cases are implicitly covered by the above attacks.

Remarks:
(i) Again we need to describe how one can calculate $V_{\tilde{V}_{i+1}(\tilde{P},1)}(P, 1)$ from $V_{\tilde{V}_i(\tilde{P},1)}(P, 1)$ in $O(1)$ steps. The idea is similar to the above. Let M be as above and let M_i be a sequence of 2×2 matrixes. In particular,

$$M_0 = M^{\tilde{V}_0(\tilde{P},1)} = M^2, \quad M_1 = M^{\tilde{V}_1(\tilde{P},1)} = M^{\tilde{P}}$$

and then

$$M_{i+1} = M_i^{\tilde{P}} \times M_{i-1}^{-1} = M^{\tilde{P}\tilde{V}_i(\tilde{P},1) - \tilde{V}_{i-1}(\tilde{P},1)} = M^{\tilde{V}_{i+1}(\tilde{P},1)}.$$

Therefore, there is no need to keep track of the individual values of $\tilde{V}(\tilde{P}, 1)$ since these are calculated implicitly. (ii) A simple implementation of this algorithm turns out to be about two to three times slower than a simple implementation of the algorithm in Section 2.2, due to the many matrix–operations involved. However, this algorithm is the most general one, in the sense that it induces the strongest requirement on a strong prime p or q (see also below). In particular, a strong prime p or q designed to withstand this attack withstands all previous attacks.

The algorithm has a high chance of success if either $\Omega(\Omega(p, P^2 - 4), \tilde{P}^2 - 4)$ or $\Omega(\Omega(q, P^2 - 4), \tilde{P}^2 - 4)$ is either small or smooth.

Prevention of the attack:
To prevent this attack the designer of a public–key cryptosystem or CSPRBG of the RSA or Rabin type must choose p and q such that $\Omega(\Omega(p, D), \tilde{D})$ and $\Omega(\Omega(q, D), \tilde{D})$ are not small and not smooth for any values of D and $\tilde{D}$. In particular, a strong prime p designed to withstand this attack must have the following properties:

- $p - 1$ and $p + 1$ must have a large factor, say t and w;
- $t - 1$, $w - 1$ and $t + 1$, $w + 1$ must have a large factor.

Similar statements can be made about the other prime q.

2.4 $Enc(\cdot, \cdot)$: Elliptic Curves

Two more attacks involving elliptic curves are elaborated in the following sections. These are slightly different to the generalised cycling attacks, since there might be a failure of the inversion step during the addition of points on the elliptic curve (which is the most welcome since then we can factorise n). However, the general idea is exactly the same except that the mathematical setting involved is the additive group of points on an elliptic curve. The elliptic curves are the most promising because of the large variety of group orders they offer. That is, if below one elliptic curve "does not work" there is a chance that another one "does work and will be successful".

Attack 1 Let $x_0 = P = (x, y)$ be a point on an elliptic curve over F_p, let $e \geq 2$. We then form the sequence of points $\{X\}$, where $x_{i+1} = e \cdot x_i$. (That is, $x_{i+1} = x_i + x_i + \ldots + x_i$, where '+' is performed e times and '+' corresponds to the addition of two points on the elliptic curve over F_p.) Let $o = \#E(F_p)$ denote the number of points on this particular elliptic curve. (We do not make any further considerations about the group structure of $E(F_p)$. This does not falsify our analyses - however upper bounds given could be slightly improved by considering such group structures.) If $o = e^t \ell$ and $gcd(e, \ell) = 1$, then

- the above sequence will have a maximum aperiodic part of length t;
- for the period $\pi_{\{X\}, p}$ we have $\pi_{\{X\}, p} \mid \lambda(\ell)$.

The algorithm:
The algorithm takes a point $P = (x, y)$ and the parameter a as an input. These determine the elliptic curve $y^2 = x^3 + ax + b \bmod n$ uniquely. The function $xcoord(P)$ returns the x–coordinate of the point P. There are now two possible outcomes that lead to the factorisation of n: (i) $x_{i+1} = x_{start} \bmod p$, or, $x_{i+1} = x_{start} \bmod q$ but not both (in fact, $xcoord(x_{i+1}) = xcoord(x_{start}) \bmod p$, or, $xcoord(x_{i+1}) = xcoord(x_{start}) \bmod q$ but not both is sufficient and may occurs earlier). (ii) The inversion step for the partial addition of two points on $E(Z_n)$

fails. This is indicated by the variable $invfail$ in the algorithm. If this occurs, then the variable $test$ will be set accordingly, that is, $test$ now holds p or q.

An algorithm for factorising $n = pq$ can now be sketched as follows:

Input: n, $P = (x,y)$, a, e, B; Output: "success",p,q; or "fail"

---

set $b = y^2 - x^3 - ax \mod n$;
set $start = |\log_e n|$;
set $x_0 = P$;
repeat
    set $x_{i+1} = e \times x_i$;
until $i \geq start$;
repeat
    set $x_{i+1} = e \times x_i$; (This sets also $invfail$ and $test$ *)*
    if not $invfail$ then set $test = gcd(xcoord(x_{i+1}) - xcoord(x_{start}), n)$;
until $test \neq 1$ or $invfail$ or $i > B$;
If $test \neq 1$ and $test \neq n$ then Output("success",test,n:test); else Output("fail");

Remarks:
(i) Instead of testing $gcd(xcoord(x_{i+1}) - xcoord(x_{start}), n)$, we could test $gcd(ycoord(x_{i+1}) - ycoord(x_{start}), n)$ or both. (ii) Doubling the x–coordinate of a point is independent of the y–coordinate. Therefore, for $e = 2$, the algorithm can be simplified as follows: choose $a, b, x_0 \in Z_n$ such that $x_0^3 + ax_0 + b$ is a square. In the repeat–loops we set:

$$x_{i+1} = \frac{x_i^4 - 2ax_i^2 + a^2 - 8x_i b}{4x_i^3 + 4ax_i + 4b} \mod n.$$

This equation is obtained from the doubling of point equation and the elliptic curve equation and some simple transformations.

Prevention of the attack:
Since the orders o of various elliptic curves are in between $p+1-t$ and $p+1+t$, where $t^2 = 4p$, it is impossible to design a strong prime to withstand *all* of these specific attacks. The best advice is to choose a large prime p. "Large" depends on security requirements and on the amount of computing cycles that can be performed in a given time unit. This will be discussed in another paper.

Attack 2 Let $P = (x,y)$ be a point on an elliptic curve over F_p. Let $V(\tilde{P}, 1)$ be a Lucas sequence. We then form the sequence of points $\{X\}$, where $x_0 = V_0(\tilde{P}, 1) \cdot P$, $x_{i+1} = V_{i+1}(\tilde{P}, 1) \cdot P$. Let $o = \#E(F_p)$ denote the number of points on this particular elliptic curve. For the period $\pi_{\{X\},p}$ we now have $\pi_{\{X\},p} \mid \Omega(o, \tilde{P}^2 - 4)$. There is no aperiodic part.

The algorithm:

The algorithm takes a point $P = (x, y)$ and the parameter a as an input. These determine the elliptic curve $y^2 = x^3 + ax + b \bmod n$ uniquely. The function $xcoord(P)$ returns the x–coordinate of the point P. As above there are now two possible outcomes that lead to the factorisation of n. The second possibility (failure of the inversion step) is again indicated in the variable $invfail$ and $test$ below. Given $\tilde{P}$, the algorithm calculates the sequence $\{X\}$ where $x_i = V_i(\tilde{P}, 1) \cdot P$. Note that $V_i(\tilde{P}, 1)$ does not need to be calculated explicitly. If $x_{i-1} = V_{i-1}(\tilde{P}, 1) \cdot P$ and $x_i = V_i(\tilde{P}, 1) \cdot P$ then $x_{i+1} = \tilde{P} \cdot x_i - x_{i-1} = V_{i+1}(\tilde{P}, 1) \cdot P$. An algorithm for factorising $n = pq$ can now be sketched as follows:

Input: n, $P = (x, y)$, a, $\tilde{P}$, B; Output: "success",p,q; or "fail"

----

set $b = y^2 - x^3 - ax \bmod n$;
set $x_0 = 2 \times P$;
set $x_1 = \tilde{P} \times P$;
set $start = 0$;
repeat
    set $x_{i+1} = \tilde{P} \times x_i - x_{i-1}$; (* This sets also invfail and test *)
    if not $invfail$ then set $test = gcd(xcoord(x_{i+1}) - xcoord(x_{start}), n)$;
until $test \neq 1$ or $invfail$ or $i > B$;
If $test \neq 1$ and $test \neq n$ then Output("success",test,n:test); else Output("fail");

Prevention of the attack:

The comments for the prevention of this attack are now similar to those of the previous subsection.

3   Comparison with Pollard's ρ Method

Observe the similarity of the algorithm in Sections 2.2 and 2.3, for $e = 2$ and some instances of Pollard's ρ method, [Pollard75]. If we compare these three methods for factorising an RSA modulus $n = pq$ we have:

$$x_0 = seed, \ x_{i+1} = x_i^2 + c \bmod n, \ c \neq 0, -2, \text{Pollard's } \rho \text{ method}$$
$$x_0 = seed, \ x_{i+1} = x_i^2 \bmod n, \qquad\qquad \text{algorithm in 2.2}$$
$$x_0 = seed, \ x_{i+1} = x_i^2 - 2 \bmod n, \qquad\quad\ \text{algorithm in 2.3}$$

Note that Pollard's ρ method requires $c \neq 0, -2$ while the other two algorithms use exactly these values of c. A contradiction? Not according to the authors. The idea behind Pollard's ρ method is to construct a cyclic sequence with some *random* properties. It can be shown that due to these random properties, factorisation of n is obtained after $O(\sqrt{p})$ or $O(\sqrt{q})$ steps (whichever is smaller). The algorithms in Section 2.2 and 2.3 try to exploit some anticipated *structure* of p and/or q in order to achieve factorisation – a different scenario.

4   Conclusion and Future Research

Strong RSA Primes A strong RSA prime until now was a prime p where (1):

- $p - 1$ has a large factor, say t;
- $p + 1$ has a large factor;
- $t - 1$ has a large factor.

Applying our generalised cycling attacks described above, we obtain the following symmetric conditions. A strong RSA prime is a prime p where (2):

- $p - 1$ and $p + 1$ both have a large factor, say t and w;
- $t - 1$ and $t + 1$ both have a large factor;
- $w - 1$ and $w + 1$ both have a large factor.

There is no reason to prefer (1) to (2) (see also below). The attacks that give rise to (2) have the same order of complexity as the attacks that imply (1). However, it is certainly debatable to drop all of these conditions, that is, (1) and (2) (or only insist on $p - 1$ and $p + 1$ having a large factor). This is because (1) and (2) offer no protection against the elliptic curve method, [Lenstra87] and the EC generalised cycling attacks presented in this paper. Moreover, primes that satisfy (1) and/or (2) might be too "sparse" and/or "not random enough" – a disastrous scenario from an information security point of view.

At this moment the attacks described in this paper are of theoretical value only. We do not anticipate that the attacks pose a practical threat to RSA if the primes are chosen large enough. In future research we will (i) quantify primes of a given size that are susceptible to generalised cycling attacks and therefore throw more light on the above discussion; (ii) examine and discuss the EC generalised cycling attacks and variants thereof.

Maurer's Theorem 6, [Maurer95], Does not Apply Maurer's Theorem 6 in [Maurer95] does not apply to the attacks presented here. [Maurer95], Page 148 states that "Iterated t–fold encryption in an RSA cryptosystem reveals the plaintext x if and only if $x^{e^u} \equiv x(\bmod\ m)$ for some $u \leq t$, i.e., if and only if $e^u \equiv 1(\bmod\ ord_m(x))$ for some $u \leq t$" (remark: m in [Maurer95] is the RSA modulus, that is, n in our paper). Page 149 concludes "Theorem 6 illustrates that, in order to prevent decipherability by iterated encryption, the condition, suggested by Rivest [78] and other, that $p' - 1$ (where p' is the largest factor of $p - 1$) must also have a very large prime factor p'', is unnecessary." The scenario considered in [Maurer95] corresponds to Case 1 in the abstract of our paper. Case 2 (cycling attacks and EC generalised cycling attacks) is *not* considered. Hence, Theorem 6 covers only Case 1 and does not apply to our attacks.

References

[AlyMue96] H. Aly and W.B. Mueller, Cryptosystems based on Dickson polynomials, *PRAGOCRYPT'96 preproceedings*, 493–503, 1996.

[AndVau96] R. Anderson and S. Vaudenay, Minding your p's and q's, *ASIACRYPT'96*, Springer LNCS 1163, 26–35, 1996.

[BBS86] L. Blum, M. Blum and M. Shub, A simple unpredictable pseudorandom number generator, *SIAM Journal on Computing*, 15, 364–383, 1986.

[BleBosLen95] D. Bleichenbacher, W. Bosma, A.K. Lenstra, Some remarks on Lucas-based cryptosystems, *CRYPTO'95*, Springer LNCS 963, 386–396, 1995.

[CCY95] C.Y. Chen, C.C. Chang, W.P. Yang, A $\lambda(p-1)$ method of factoring RSA's modulus, *Cryptography Policy and Algorithms Conference, CPAC'95 preproceedings, Brisbane 1995*, 225–231, 1995.

[GysSeb98] M. Gysin and J. Seberry, Generalised cycling attacks on RSA, technical report, TR 1998/1, 1998.

[Huber91] K. Huber, Some considerations concerning the selections of RSA moduli, *EUROCRYPT'91*, Springer LNCS 547, 294–301, 1991.

[Koblitz87] N. Koblitz, Elliptic curve cryptosystems, *Mathematics of Computation*, Vol 48, 177, 203–209, 1987.

[KMOV92] K. Koyama, U. Maurer, T. Okamoto and S.A. Vanstone, New public–key schemes based on elliptic curves over the ring Z_n, *CRYPTO'91*, Springer LNCS 576, 252–266, 1992.

[Lenstra87] H.W. Lenstra, Factoring integers with elliptic curves, *Annals of Mathematics* 126, 649–673, 1987.

[Lucas1878] F.E.A. Lucas, Théorie des fonctions numériques simplement périodiques, *American Journal of Mathematics*, 1, 184–240/289–321, 1878.

[Maurer95] U.M. Maurer, Fast generation of prime numbers and secure public–key cryptographic parameters, *Journal of Cryptology*, Vol. 8, 3, 123–155, 1995.

[MeyMue96] B. Meier and V. Mueller, A public–key cryptosystem based on elliptic curves over Z/nZ equivalent to factoring, *EUROCRYPT'96*, Springer LNCS 1070, 49–59, 1996.

[Menezes93] A.J. Menezes, *Elliptic Curve Public Key Cryptosystems*, Kluwer Academic Publishers, Massachusetts, USA, 1993.

[MenOorVan97] A.J. Menezes, P.C. van Oorschot, S.A. Vanstone, *Handbook of Applied Cryptography*, CRC Press, Boca Raton, USA, 1997.

[Pollard74] J.M. Pollard, Theorems on factorisations and primality testing, *Proceedings of the Cambridge Philosophical Society*, 76, 521–528, 1974.

[Pollard75] J.M. Pollard, A Monte Carlo method for factorisation, *Nordisk Tidskrift för Informationsbehandling (BIT)*, 15, 331–334, 1975.

[Rabin79] M.O. Rabin, Digitalized signatures and public–key functions as intractable as factorization, MIT/LCS/TR-212, MIT Laboratory for Computer Science, 1979.

[Riesel85] H. Riesel, *Prime Numbers and Computer Methods for Factorization*, Progress in Mathematics, Vol 57, Birkhaeuser, Boston, 1985.

[RivShaAdl78] R. Rivest, A. Shamir and L. Adleman, A method for obtaining digital signatures and public–key cryptosystems, *Communications of the ACM*, 21, 2, 120–126, 1978.

[SmiSkin94] P. Smith and C. Skinner, A public–key cryptosystem and a digital signature algorithm based on the Lucas function, *ASIACRYPT'94*, pre-proceedings, 298–306, Wollongong, 1994.

[Stinson95] D.R. Stinson, *Cryptography Theory and Practice*, CRC Press, Boca Raton, USA, 1995.

[Vajda89] S.Vajda, *Fibonacci & Lucas Numbers and the Golden Section: Theory and Applications*, Halsted Press, John Wiley and Sons, New York, 1989.

[Williams82] H.C. Williams, A $p+1$ method of factoring, *Mathematics of Computation*, 39, 225–234, 1982.

A Appendix

A.1 Lucas Sequences

Let $P \geq 3$, $V_0 = 2$, $V_1 = P$ and for $n \geq 2$, $V_n = PV_{n-1} - QV_{n-2}$. This sequence is called a Lucas sequence. (Often instead of only writing V_n we write $V_n(P, Q)$. The whole sequence $\{V\}$ will be denoted by $V(P, Q)$.) The following properties (amongst many others) are elementary and well known:

1. If α and β are distinct roots of the polynomial $x^2 - Px + Q = 0$, then $V_n = \alpha^n + \beta^n$.
2. $V_n(V_k(P, Q), Q^k) = V_{nk}(P, Q)$. In particular, if $Q = 1$, then $V_n(V_k(P, 1), 1) = V_{nk}(P, 1) = V_k(V_n(P, Q), 1)$. This property forms the basis for many RSA and ElGamal type cryptosystems.

Note that if $Q = 0$ then $V_n = P^n$ for $n \geq 1$. In other words, Lucas sequences can be looked at as generalised exponentiation. This property and the above mentioned property (2.) is the basis for many RSA and ElGamal type cryptosystems, cryptographically secure pseudo–random bit generators (CSPRBG), and factorisation algorithms based on Lucas sequences.

Let us now try to calculate the period $\pi_{V(P,1),p}$ of $V(P, 1) \bmod p$, p prime. Let $D = P^2 - 4Q = P^2 - 4$, $D \neq 0$ and assume D is square–free. From above we have

$$\alpha = \frac{P + \sqrt{D}}{2}, \quad \beta = \frac{P - \sqrt{D}}{2}$$

and using Fermat's theorem in the quadratic field $Z_p[\sqrt{D}]$

$$\alpha^p \equiv (\frac{P + \sqrt{D}}{2})^p \equiv \frac{1}{2^p}(P^p + \sqrt{D}^p) \equiv \frac{1}{2}(P + \sqrt{D}^p) \bmod p.$$

Since

$$\sqrt{D}^p \equiv (D^{\frac{1}{2}})^p \equiv D^{\frac{p-1}{2}} D^{\frac{1}{2}} \equiv (D|p) \sqrt{D} \bmod p,$$

we obtain

$$\alpha^p \equiv \begin{cases} \alpha \bmod p \ (D|p) = 1 \\ \beta \bmod p \ (D|p) = -1 \end{cases}$$

and similarly for β

$$\beta^p \equiv \begin{cases} \beta \bmod p \ (D|p) = 1 \\ \alpha \bmod p \ (D|p) = -1 \end{cases}$$

It can be shown that,

$$Z_p[\sqrt{D}] \simeq \begin{cases} GF(p) \ (D|p) = 1 \\ GF(p^2) \ (D|p) = -1 \end{cases}$$

This property allows us to calculate $V_{p-1}, V_p, V_{p+1}, V_{p+2} \bmod p$ for the two cases $(D|p) = 1$ and $(D|p) = -1$. The values are shown in Table 1. Note that $V_p(P, 1) \equiv P \bmod p$. This property can be used for probablistic primality tests based on Lucas sequences.

	V_{p-1}	V_p	V_{p+1}	V_{p+2}
$(D\|p) = 1$	2	P	V_2	V_3
$(D\|p) = -1$	V_2	P	2	P

Table 1. Some values of $V(P,1) \bmod p$.

Since $V_0 = 2$, $V_1 = P$ and the sequence is fully determined by its last two elements we now have for $(D|p) = 1$, $V(P,1) \bmod p$ repeats itself after at most $p-1$ steps; and for $(D|p) = -1$, $V(P,1) \bmod p$ repeats itself after at most $p+1$ steps. More precisely, $\pi_{V(P,1),p} \mid p - (D|p)$.

$V(P,1) \bmod p$ is symmetric. More precisely, $V_i \equiv V_{\pi_{V(P,1),p}-i} \bmod p$. This can be seen as follows. $V_{i-1} = PV_i - V_{i+1}$. Therefore, $V_{\pi_{V(P,1),p}-1} \equiv PV_{\pi_{V(P,1),p}} - V_{\pi_{V(P,1),p}+1} \equiv PV_0 - V_1 \equiv P \equiv V_1 \bmod p$ as claimed. The proof that $V_i \equiv V_{\pi_{V(P,1),p}-i} \bmod p$ follows now by induction on i.

The calculation of the period $\pi_{V(P,Q),p}$ of $V(P,Q)$, $Q \neq 1$ can be done similarly, and it can be shown that, in this case, $\pi_{V(P,Q),p} \mid p^2 - 1$.

It is important to realise that $V_k(P,1)$ (and in general $V_k(P,Q)$) can be calculated in $O(\log k)$ steps by square–and multiply techniques. In other words, one does *not* have to calculate $V_0, \ldots, V_{k-2}, V_{k-1}$ in order to be able to calculate V_k.

One possibility to calculate $V_k(P,1)$ in $O(\log k)$ steps is the following. Consider the 2×2 matrix

$$M = \begin{bmatrix} 0 & 1 \\ -1 & P \end{bmatrix},$$

and the matrix multiplication

$$\begin{bmatrix} a \\ b \end{bmatrix} = M^k \begin{bmatrix} 2 \\ P \end{bmatrix}.$$

It can be shown, [Vajda89], that $a = V_k(P,1)$ and $b = V_{k+1}(P,1)$. M^k (and therefore V_k) can be calculated in $O(\log k)$ steps by square–and multiply techniques.

A.2 Elliptic Curves

We only give a brief introduction into elliptic curves. The reader is referred to [Menezes93] for more details. We only consider elliptic curves over the field F_p or the ring Z_n, where $n = pq$, p, q two primes > 3.

An elliptic curve E is the set of solutions (x, y) to the affine Weierstrass equation

$$y^2 = x^3 + ax + b, \tag{1}$$

together with a point at infinity denoted by $\mathcal{O}$. If E is over F_p or if E is over Z_n, we denote the solutions to (1) by $E(F_p)$ or $E(Z_n)$, respectively. The number of solutions to (1) including $\mathcal{O}$ will be denoted by $\#E(F_p)$ or $\#E(Z_n)$, respectively.

If $4a^3 + 27b^2 \not\equiv 0 \bmod p$, then it can be shown that $E(F_p)$ is an abelian group by defining a suitable operation '+' on its points. $\mathcal{O}$ is the identity element. That is, $P + \mathcal{O} = \mathcal{O} + P = P$. For $P = (x_1, y_1)$, $Q = (x_2, y_2)$, $P \neq \mathcal{O} \neq Q$, $P + Q$ is defined as follows. If $x_1 = x_2$ and $y_2 = -y_1$, $P + Q = \mathcal{O}$. Otherwise $P + Q = R = (x_3, y_3)$, where

$$x_3 = \lambda^2 - x_1 - x_2, \quad y_3 = \lambda(x_1 - x_3) - y_1,$$

and

$$\lambda = \begin{cases} \frac{y_2 - y_1}{x_2 - x_1} & P \neq Q \\ \frac{3x_1^2 + a}{2y_1} & P = Q \end{cases}$$

Let E be an elliptic curve over F_p. It is well known that $E(F_p) \simeq Z_{n_1} \times Z_{n_2}$ where $n_2 \mid n_1$ and $n_2 \mid p - 1$. Furthermore, $\#E(F_p) = p + 1 + t$, where $t^2 \leq 4p$.

We can generalise these addition laws to the case $E(Z_n)$. Clearly, $E(Z_n)$ will not be a group, since the inversion step will not be possible if the denominator and n are not co-prime. Therefore, we call this operation *partial addition*. Whenever partial addition on $E(Z_n)$ is defined, we have for $P = (x, y) \in E(Z_n)$, $P_p = (x \bmod p, y \bmod p) \in E(F_p)$ and $P_q = (x \bmod q, y \bmod q) \in E(F_q)$. Therefore, this partial addition will have the following properties:

- if it is defined, it will yield a new point on $E(Z_n)$;
- if it is not defined, it will lead to the factorisation of n.

RSA Acceleration with Field Programmable Gate Arrays

Alexander Tiountchik[1] and Elena Trichina[2]

[1] Institute of Mathematics, National Academy of Sciences of Belarus,
11 Surganova str, Minsk 220072, Belarus
aat@im.bas-net.by
[2] Advanced Computing Research Centre, University of South Australia,
Mawson Lakes, SA 5095, Australia
elena.trichina@unisa.edu.au

Abstract. An efficient implementations of modular exponentiation, i.e., the main building block in the RSA cryptographic scheme, is achieved by first designing a bit-level systolic array such that the whole procedure of modular exponentiation can be carried out entirely by a single unit without using global interconnections or memory to store intermediate results, and then mapping this design onto Xilinx XC6000 Field Programmable Gate Array.

1 Introduction

Many popular cryptographic schemes, such as the RSA scheme [13], ElGamal scheme [6], Fiat-Shamir scheme [8], etc., make extensive use of modular exponentiation of long integers. However, it is a very slow operation when performed on a general purpose computer. A cheap and flexible modular exponentiation hardware accelerator can be achieved using Field Programmable Gate Arrays [2]. In this paper we do not compete with industrial-strength special purpose hardware for modular exponentiation. Rather we use a complexity of the problem as a benchmark for evaluating computing power of fine grained FPGAs, and for developing a more systematic methodology for their programming.

We propose a two-step procedure for an implementation of modular exponentiation on FPGAs. The main idea is as follows. Bit-level systolic arrays share many limitations and constraints with FPGAs; both favor regular repetitive designs with local interconnections, simple synchronisation mechanisms and minimal global memory access. While programming FPGAs is still pretty much an *ad hoc* process, there is a mature methodology of bit-level systolic systems design. Thus, to achieve a good FPGA implementation, it may be beneficial first to design a systolic array for a given application, and then map this array onto FPGAs in a systematic fashion, preserving the main properties of the systolic design.

In this paper an efficient systolic array for a modular exponentiation such that the whole exponentiation procedure can be carried out entirely by the single systolic unit without global interconnections or use of global memory to store intermediate results is designed first. This procedure is based on a Montgomery multiplication, and uses a high-to-low binary method of exponentiation. Moreover, this array is expected to be faster than similar devices performing exponentiation by repeated modular multiplications of an integer by itself [17,9].

The next step consists of a systematic mapping of the systolic array onto fine grained FPGAs. During this experiment a number of observations emerged, which we present in this paper. Our final design accommodates a modular exponentiation of a 132-bit long number on one Xilinx XC6000 chip comprising 64×64 elementary logic cells.

Reported in this paper hardware implementation relies on configurability of FPGAs, but does not use run-time reprogrammability or/and SRAM memory (intermediate results are stored in registers implemented within individual cells). This makes our design simpler and easy to implement. The price to pay is that more chips are needed to implement RSA with a longer key. 4 Kgates, or one XC6000 chip, is required for modular exponentiation of 132-bit long integers. 512-bit long integers need 4 XC6000 chips connected in a pipeline fashion, or 16 Kgates. The bit rate for a clock frequency of 25 MHz can be estimated to be approximately 800 Kb/sec for 512 bit keys, which is comparable with the rate reported in a fundamental paper of Shand and Vuillemin [15], and an order of magnitude better than that the ones in [9] and [12].

2 Modular Exponentiation of Long Integers

The main and most time consuming operation in the RSA algorithm is modular exponentiation of long integers. The RSA Laboratories recommended key sizes are now 768 bits for personal use, 1024 bits for corporate use, and 2048 bits for extremely valuable keys. A 768-bit key is expected to be secure until at least the year 2004.

A modular exponentiation operation $M^e \mod n$ cannot be implemented in a naive fashion by first exponentiating M^e and then performing reduction modulo n, since even if M and e have only 256 bits each, the intermediate result M^e contains $\approx 10^{80}$ digits. Hence, the intermediate results of the exponentiation are to be reduced modulo n at each step. The straightforward reduction modulo n involves a number of arithmetic operations (division, subtraction, etc.), and is very time consuming. Therefore, special algorithms for modular operations are to be used.

In 1985, P. L. Montgomery [10] proposed an algorithm for modular multiplication $AB \mod m$ without trial division. In [1] different modular reduction algorithms for large integers were compared with respect to their performance and the conclusion was drawn that for general modular exponentiation the exponentiation besed on Montgomery's algorithm has the best performance.

2.0.1 Montgomery multiplication

Let A, B be elements of $\mathbf{Z}_m$, where $\mathbf{Z}_m$ is the set of integers between 0 and $m-1$. Let h be an integer coprime to m, and $h > m$.

Definition. *Montgomery multiplication (MM) is an operation*

$$A \overset{h,m}{\otimes} B = A \cdot B \cdot h^{-1} \bmod m. \tag{1}$$

Implementation of this operation is much easier than a normal reduction modulo m ; and is based on some facts from number theory. The use of MM does not result in the desirable speed-up immediately. To compute $AB \bmod m$, a computation of MM is to be performed twice:

1. $C = A \overset{h,m}{\otimes} B = A \cdot B \cdot h^{-1} \bmod m$, and
2. $C \overset{h,m}{\otimes} (h^2 \bmod m) = ABh^{-1} \cdot h^2 \cdot h^{-1} \bmod m = AB \bmod m$,

where $h^2 \bmod m$ is computed in advance. The advantage of using two Montgomery multiplications instead of one operation of plain modular multiplication is uncertain.

2.0.2 Montgomery exponentiation

An efficient way to compute $AB \bmod m$ using MM is by exploiting special representations of A and B.

Definition. $\widehat{X}$ is called an *image* of X if $\widehat{X} = X \cdot h \bmod m$, $h > m$.

If h and m are relatively prime, then there exists a one-to-one correspondence between X and $\widehat{X}$. MM of $\widehat{A}$ and $\widehat{B}$ is isomorphic to the modular multiplication of A and B. Indeed, $\widehat{A} \overset{h,m}{\otimes} \widehat{B} = (Ah \bmod m \overset{h,m}{\otimes} (Bh \bmod m) = (AB)h \bmod m = \widehat{A \cdot B}$. The reduction of X to $\widehat{X}$ and vice versa can be carried out on the basis of MM:

$$X \overset{h,m}{\otimes} (h^2 \bmod m) = X \cdot h^2 h^{-1} \bmod m = \widehat{X}, \tag{2}$$

$$\widehat{X} \overset{h,m}{\otimes} 1 = X \cdot h \bmod m \cdot 1 \cdot h^{-1} \bmod m = X. \tag{3}$$

By virtue of the isomorphism of modular multiplication and MM, the use of the images is very convenient for exponentiation. Let $(\overset{h,m}{\otimes} X)^n$ denote $(n-1)$ MMs of X by itself. To compute $Y = X^n \bmod m$, we should perform three steps: first, convert X to $\widehat{X}$ by (2); next, realize $\widehat{Y} = (\overset{h,m}{\otimes} \widehat{X})^n = \widehat{X^n}$; and finally, convert $\widehat{Y}$ to Y by (3).

2.1 Algorithm for implementation of Montgomery multiplication

Several algorithms suitable for hardware implementation of MM are known [9,14,17,4,3]. In this paper, the design of a systolic array is based on the algorithm described and analysed in [17]. Let numbers A, B and m be written with radix 2:

$$A = \sum_{i=0}^{N-1} a_i \cdot 2^i, \qquad B = \sum_{i=0}^{M} b_i \cdot 2^i, \qquad m = \sum_{i=0}^{M-1} m_i \cdot 2^i,$$

where $a_i, b_i, m_i \in \mathbf{GF}(2)$, N and M are the numbers of digits in A and m, respectively. B satisfies condition $B < 2m$, and has at most $M + 1$ digits. m is odd (to be coprime to the radix 2). Extend a definition of A with an extra zero digit $a_N = 0$. The algorithm for MM is given below (4).

$$
\begin{aligned}
&s := 0; \\
&\textbf{For } i := 0 \textbf{ to } N \textbf{ do} \\
&\textbf{Begin} \\
&\qquad u_i := ((s_0 + a_i * b_0) * w) \bmod 2 \\
&\qquad s := (s + a_i * B + u_i * m) \mathrm{div} 2 \\
&\textbf{End}
\end{aligned}
\tag{4}
$$

Initial condition $B < 2m$ ensures that intermediate and final values of s are bounded by $3m$. The use of an iteration with $a_N = 0$ ensures that the final value $s < 2m$ [17]. Hence, this value can be used for B input in a subsequent multiplication. Since 2 and m are relatively prime, we can precompute value $w = (2 - m_0)^{-1} \bmod 2$. An implementation of the operations div2 and mod2 is trivial (shifting and inspecting the lowest digit, respectively). Algorithm (4) returns either $s = A \cdot B \cdot 2^{-n-1} \bmod m$ or $s + m$ (because $s < 2m$). In any case, this extra m has no effect on subsequent arithmetics modulo m. It should be noted, that the number of iterations in (4) affects h [17]. In our case, (4) presents the implementation of (1) with $h = 2^{N+1}$.

2.2   Graph model for Montgomery multiplication

Using standard methods for systolic systems design, first we construct a data dependency graph (also referred as DG, or graph model) for Algorithm (4). This graph is depicted in Fig. 1 (see also [17,16]). For $N-$ and $M-$digit integers A and B, a graph consists of $N+2$ rows and $M+1$ columns. The i-th row represents the i-th iteration of (4). Arrows are associated with digits transferred along indicated directions. Each vertex $v(j, i)$, $i \in \{0, ..., N\}, j \in \{0, ..., M\}$ is associated with the operation

$$
s_{j-1}^{(i+1)} + 2 \cdot c_{out} := s_j^{(i)} + a_i \cdot b_j + u_i \cdot m_j + c_{in},
$$

where $s_j^{(i)}$ denotes the j-th digit of the i-th partial product of s, c_{out} and c_{in} are the output and input carries. Rightmost starred vertices, i.e., vertices marked with "$*$", perform calculations of $u_i := ((s_0 + a_i * b_0) * w) \bmod 2$ besides an ordinary operation. Using standard notation, the vertex operations can be specified in terms of inputs/outputs as follows:

$$
s_{out} + 2 \cdot c_{out} := s_{in} + a_{in} \cdot b_{in} + u_{in} \cdot m_{in} + c_{in},
$$

$$
a_{out} := a_{in}, \qquad b_{out} := b_{in},
\tag{5}
$$

$$
u_{out} := u_{in}, \qquad m_{out} := m_{in},
$$

for plain vertices, and

$$
u_{out} := (s_{in} + a_{in} \cdot b_{in}) \cdot w_{in},
$$

$$c_{out} := \mathrm{maj}_2(s_{in}, a_{in} \cdot b_{in}, u_{in} \cdot m_{in}), \tag{6}$$

$$a_{out} := a_{in}, \qquad b_{out} := b_{in}, \qquad m_{out} := m_{in},$$

for starred vertices, where $\mathrm{maj}_2(s_{in}, a_{in} \cdot b_{in}, u_{in} \cdot m_{in})$ is 1 if at least two out of three entries are 1s; otherwise it is 0.

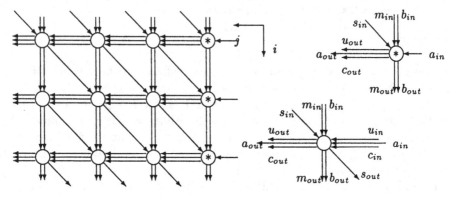

Fig. 1. Graph model for $A \overset{h,m}{\otimes} B$: case of $N = 2$, $M = 3$.

2.2.1   High-to-low binary method of exponentiation

If instead of digits A we input digits B both, at the topmost and rightmost vertices of the graph in Fig. 1, then the graph model represents a calculation of

$$B \overset{h,m}{\otimes} B = (\overset{h,m}{\otimes} B)^2,$$

called M-*squaring*. To represent the computation of $(\overset{h,m}{\otimes} B)^3$, two graphs can be joined in a single graph by connecting s_j-outputs of the first graph with b_j-inputs of the next (identical) graph, in which rightmost inputs a_i get digits of B as before. To compute $(\overset{h,m}{\otimes} B)^n$, we will need $n - 1$ joined graphs. The resulting graph model consists of vertices located in a rectangular domain $V_1 = \{v(i,j) | 0 \le i \le n \times (M + 2) - 1, \ 0 \le j \le M + 1\}$. The graph is almost homogeneous, with exceptional starred vertices in the rightmost column.

However, a faster way to compute $B^n \bmod m$ is by reducing the computation to a sequence of modular squares and multiplications [15]. Let $[n_0 \ldots n_k]$ be a binary representation of n, i.e., $n = n_0 + 2n_1 + + \cdots + 2^k n_k$, $n_j \in \mathbf{GF}(2)$, $k = \lfloor \log_2 n \rfloor$, $n_k = 1$. Let β denote a partial product. We start out with $\beta = B$ and run from n_{k-1} to n_0 as follows: if $n_j = 0$, then $\beta := \beta^2$; if $n_j = 1$, then $\beta := \beta^2 * B$. Thus, we need at most $2k$ operations to compute B^n. This algorithm has an advantage over a low-to-high binary method of exponentiation since, when implemented in hardware, it requires only one set of storage registers for intermediate results as opposed to two for a low-to-high method [15].

2.3 Graph model for squaring

To perform M-squaring the dependency graph for M-multiplication can be modified in such a way that all the b_j's inputs enter the graph only via the top-row vertices [16]. This eliminates rightmost a_i-inputs entirely. To deliver all b_js to the rightmost vertices, we have to pump them through the graph in a direction determined by vector $(1, -1)$. To do it, additional arcs x_j's for propagation of b_j's digits have to be added to a dependency graph in Fig. 1. Vertex operations are to be slightly modified to provide propagation of these digits: each non-starred vertex just transmits its x-input data to an x-output, while when arriving at the rightmost vertices, these data are "reflected" and propagated to the left as if they were ordinary a_i's input data. It is known that the output value $s < 2m$. Hence, we need at most $M + 1$ rows for the "reflected" factor and an additional row for the extension with an extra zero digit. A graph model for M-squaring is depicted in Fig. 2. Using standard notation, the vertex operations for M-squaring

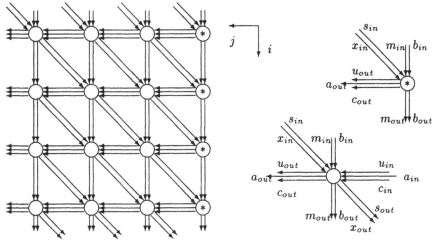

Fig. 2. Graph model for $\overset{h,m}{\otimes} B^2$: case of $M = 3$.

can be specified in terms of inputs/outputs as follows:

$$s_{out} + 2 \cdot c_{out} := s_{in} + a_{in} \cdot b_{in} + u_{in} \cdot m_{in} + c_{in},$$

$$a_{out} := a_{in}, \qquad x_{out} := x_{in}, \tag{7}$$

$$b_{out} := b_{in}, \qquad u_{out} := u_{in}, \qquad m_{out} := m_{in},$$

for plain vertices, and for starred vertices the operation is:

$$u := (s_{in} + x_{in} \cdot b_{in}) \cdot w_{in},$$

$$s_{out} + 2 \cdot c_{out} := s_{in} + x_{in} \cdot b_{in} + u \cdot m_{in}, \tag{8}$$

$$c_{out} := \mathrm{maj}_2(s_{in}, x_{in} \cdot b_{in}, u_{in} \cdot m_{in}),$$

$$u_{out} := u, \qquad a_{out} := x_{in}, \qquad b_{out} := b_{in}, \qquad m_{out} := m_{in}.$$

2.4 Linear systolic array for modular exponentiation

A graph model for an exponentiation as a whole is constructed as a composition of graphs for M-multiplication and M-squaring by joining outputs of one graph with corresponding inputs of the consecutive graph. There are at most $2k$ graphs altogether, and the precise number of required graphs for M-multiplication and M-squaring and the order in which they occur in the composition is fully determined only by the binary representation of n. The vertices of the resulting graph constitute a rectangular domain $V_2 = \{v(i,j)|0 \le i \le 2k \times (M+2), 0 \le j \le M+1\}$, where $k = \lfloor \log_2 n \rfloor$. [1]

The next stage of the systolic design is a space-time mapping of domain V_2 onto a one-dimensional domain of processing elements (PE). Spatial mapping is determined by a linear operator with matrix $P = (1\ 0)$ [16], which maps an indefinitely long composition of the cohered DGs onto a linear systolic array with $M + 1$ processing elements: each column of vertices is mapped onto one PE, as shown in Fig. 3. Hence, each PE in Fig. 3 has to be able to operate in two modes. To control the operation modes, a sequence of one-bit control signals τ is fed into the rightmost PE and propagated through the array. If $\tau = 0$ the PE implements an operation for M-multiplication, if $\tau = 1$, for M-squaring. The order in which control signals are input is determined by the binary representation of n. A timing function that provides a correct order of operations is $t(v) = 2i + j$ [16]. The total running time is thus at most $(4\lfloor \log_2 n \rfloor + 1)M + 8\lfloor \log_2 n \rfloor$ time units.

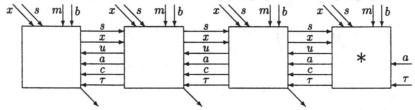

Fig. 3. Linear Systolic Array.

3 Logic Design of the FPGA Implementation of Montgomery Exponentiation

Our next step is to implement the systolic array on FPGAs. The purpose of this experiment is threefold: firstly, derive a systematic method of mapping systolic algorithms into a sea of cells; secondly, construct an efficient FPGA implementation of a particularly important application; and thirdly, investigate the limits of a fine grained FPGA chip for modular exponentiation. We conducted our experiments with Xilinx XC6000, comprising 64×64 logic cells.

3.1 Inputs and outputs

To meet limitations of FPGAs that input/output ports are located along the borders of the chip, we found the following ideas fruitful. The first step of any

---

[1] $2k \times (M+2)$ is the largest number of all possible rows in a resulting graph model.

exponentiation is always squaring, β^2; but this step can be implemented as multiplication $\beta \cdot \beta$ (where $\beta = B$, an input number). Since all s_i's are 0's at the first step of any multiplication and squaring, and for all other steps the s_i's are to be the results of the previous step, we can use registers to store intermediate s_i's, and instead of loading 0's from the host, just set all these registers to 0 initially. The dependency graph for M-multiplication does not have inputs x_i's, $i \in \{0, ..., M + 1\}$; hence, the final design does not need these inputs since input values for x_i's required for M-squaring will be generated later, and can be loaded from the registers containing the results s_j's of the previous stage of computations.

All inputs b_i's for the topmost row of the first graph for M-multiplication must receive corresponding bits of input B (the same as the rightmost inputs a_i's) while for all consecutive graphs these inputs are to be connected with s_j's- or b_j's-outputs of the previous graph, depending of whether this stage is multiplication or squaring. An additional control signal σ must be used to provide the correct assignment for registers associated with top row vertices. Thus, instead of having $M + 1$ "vertical" inputs for b_i's, we shall use registers and load them initially with corresponding bits b_i's from inputs a_i's; new values computed at later stages and used as inputs for the consequent graph, will be reassigned to these registers as described above. Hence, the only I/O ports actually needed in the design, are located at the rightmost and leftmost processing elements.

3.2 Logic design for the non-starred PE

Consider now the logic design for implementation of an individual PE in details. A minor optimisation first. Modes of the plain PE for multiplication and squaring differ only by the transmission or absence of the transmission of data x_i, and the control signal τ is used to distinguish these two modes. However, x_i's do not affect computations in the non-starred PEs; they are used only in the rightmost (starred) PEs. Therefore, we can ignore the existence of two modes for the plain PE and let it transmit x_i regardless τ. Hence, we do not need a control signal τ in the plain PEs; τ should be used only in the rightmost PE where it defines whether an input data x_i is to be used or ignored. Nevertheless, we need a control signal σ to ensure the correct initial assignments to x_i's depending on whether M-multiplication or M-squaring should be carried out: $x_{out} := \text{mux}(\sigma_{in} : x_{in}, s_{in})$.

Original input data b_i's are to be stored in the local memories of PEs for future M-multiplications. We use a special register $b_{in}^{<\text{old}>}$ for this purpose. As above, a control signal σ is used to provide the correct initial assignments to variables b_i's depending on whether PEs are supposed to perform multiplication or squaring: $b_{in} := \text{mux}(\sigma_{in} : b_{in}^{<\text{old}>}, s_{in})$.

A computational part of the main PE includes control over input data, two logic multiplications, $a_{in} \cdot b_{in}$ and $u_{in} \cdot m_{in}$, and addition of these products with an intermediate sum s_{in} and input carries. Evidently, four-element addition can generate two carries meaning that all main PEs will have two input carries, and produce two output carries; the first carry $c_{out}^{<1>}$ is to be used by the nearest neighbor PE, and the second carry $c_{out}^{<2>}$ is to be used by the PE followed after the nearest neighbor:

$$s_{out} + 2c_{out}^{<1>} + 4c_{out}^{<2>} = a_{in} \cdot b_{in} + u_{in} \cdot m_{in} + s_{in} + c_{in}^{<1>} + c_{in}^{<2>}.$$

We shall denote the carry that is just a transit from the right neighbor to the left one by $c^{<T>}$, hence $c_{out}^{<T>} := c_{in}^{<2>}$. It is not uncommon to implement addition of 5 entries using two full adders and one half adder, which can be found in a standard library XC6000 provided by EXACTStep6000, with the "communication" part surrounding this module. However, if the outputs of some gates are to be stored in registers, these gates and registers should not be at different hierarchical levels, because normally a gate–register pair may occupy only one cell but if the gate is embedded in a module, while the register is outside of this module they inevitably will be placed in different cells, and often rather far apart. Thus, if registers are to be used to store output data of a module, it is desirable to insert these registers inside the module. Fig. 4 presents the final design for a plain PE.

3.3 Logic design for the rightmost PE

The rightmost PE selects correct values for its b– and a–inputs, depending on control signals σ and τ, propagates data and signals to the left neighbor, computes value u and the sum $a_{in} \cdot b_{in} + u \cdot m_{in} + s_{in}$. For consistency, two zero carries should also be generated. Below we give a description of the rightmost PE, including the specification of data and control signals transmissions:

$a'_{in} = \text{mux}(\tau : x_{in}, a_{in});$
$b'_{in} = \text{mux}(\sigma_{in} : b_{in}, s_{in});$
$u_{in} = (a'_{in} \cdot b'_{in} \oplus s_{in}) \cdot w_{in};$
$s_{out} + 2c_{out}^{<1>} = a'_{in} \cdot b'_{in} + u_{in} \cdot m_{in} + s_{in};$
$u_{out} = u_{in}; \qquad a_{out} = a'_{in}; \qquad c_{out}^{<2>} = 0; \qquad c_{out}^{<T>} = 0.$

The main computational module of the rightmost PE after the optimisation and its structure as a whole are depicted in Fig. 5 and Fig. 6, respectively.

4 XACTStep 6000 Automatic Design and Its Optimisation

A high level of correspondence between the requirements of bit-level systolic arrays and FPGA designs provide an opportunity to implement a modular exponentiation algorithm on Xilinx XC6000 chips ensuring a very dense allocation of gates.

An ultimate design goal in our experiment was to find an absolute limit of the number of bits in Montgomery exponentiation, that can be handled by one 64×64 XC6000 chip without storing intermediate data in SRAM and without reprogramming the chip. By trial and error we found that automatic allocation provides successful routing for systolic arrays with a maximum of 67 PEs (1 starred, and 66 plain). Obviously, this is far from the limit. We decided to use it as a starting point for manual optimisation. Remote gates and registers were brought closer together so as to provide locality of interconnections and higher density of the overall design. For manual allocation of gates at the level of ViewLogic design, the RLOC (relative location) attribute has to be used. The attribute determines the coordinates of a gate inside its module.

To embed a long and narrow one-dimensional array of PEs constituting a systolic design into a XC6000 64 × 64 square of logic cells, a natural solution is to partition this array into blocks of PEs with respect to the width of the chip, so that every block can be allocated in a side-to-side line on a chip; and then combine these blocks in a "zig-zag" snake-like structure. The length of the block is determined empirically, and better to be estimated conservatively, so as to allow for some extra space to permit successful routing in the corners. In our case one block constitutes 13 PEs. It should be noted that an allocation of PEs inside the block must be manual since we want a long narrow band of the gates while an automatic allocation is trying to provide a square–like allocation.

To eliminate irregularity and criscross connections between PEs in every second block of the zig-zag, we had to design a mirror image for a block by reflecting the block itself. Every PE inside the reflected block has to be a mirror image under reflection of a regular PE with the same functionality; and two additional types of mirror images under rotation were used for the leftmost and the rightmost PEs in a block to ensure locality of logic connections where the "snake" turns. All this allows us to allocate 132 PEs successfully on XC6000 64 × 64 logic cells. In other words, we can exponentiate a 132-bit long integer on one Xilinx XC6000 chip. An allocation of 132 PEs on a chip and successful routing is presented in Fig. 7.

5 Summary

We presented a new implementation of a modular exponentiation algorithm based on a Montgomery multiplication operation on fine–grained FPGAs. With hand–crafted optimisation we managed to embed a modular exponentiation of 132-bit long integers into one Xilinx XC6000 chip, which is to our knowledge one of the best fine-grained FPGA designs for a modular exponentiation reported so far. 2,615 out of 4,096 gates are used for computations, and 528 for registers, providing 75% density. This array can be used for both, reducing B to $\widehat{B}$ by (2) and for reducing a final value $\widehat{B^n}$ to B^n by (3).

Hence, 4 Kgates (one XC6000 chip) is required for modular exponentiation of 132-bit long integers. 512-bit long integers need 4 XC6000 chips connected in a pipeline fashion, or 16 Kgates. Taking into account the total running time (see Chapter 2), we can estimate the bit rate for a clock frequency of 25 MHz being approximately 800 Kb/sec for 512 bit keys, which is comparable with the rate reported in a fundamental paper of Shand and Vuillemin [15], and an order of magnitude better than that one in [9] and [12]. Further improvement of the proposed implementation can be achieved by simplification of the operation performed by the starred vertices to an ordinary (non-starred vertex) operation due to shifting B up to make $b_0 = 0$ [5]. The reduction of complexity of starred vertices decreases an overall time and provides higher clock rate.

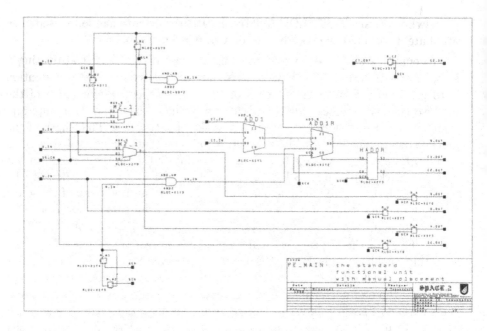

Fig. 4. Logic design for not-starred PE.

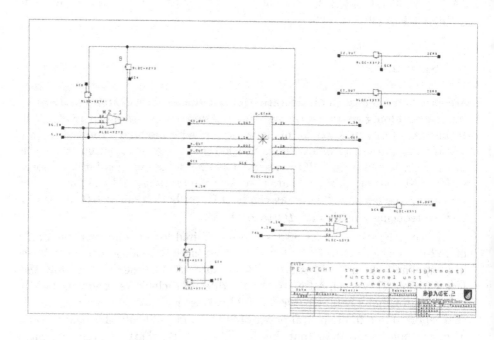

Fig. 5. Logic design for starred PE.

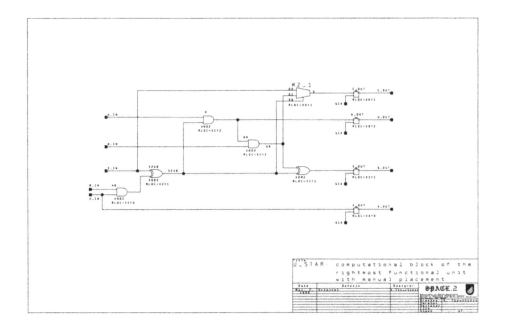

Fig. 6. Main computational block of starred PE.

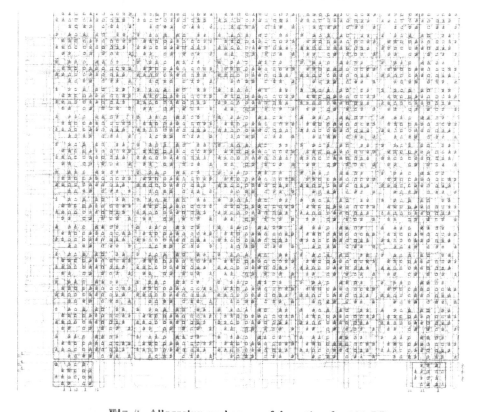

Fig. 7. Allocation and successful routing for 132 PEs.

Acknowledgement

We thank Raymond Keifer for continuous help and advice on XACTStep 6000 and for maintaining SPACE2 reconfigurable computer on which our experiments took place.

References

1. A. Bosselaers, R. Govaerts, and J. Vandewalle, Comparison of three modular reduction functions. pp 175–186
2. D. A. Buell, J. M. Arnold, and W. J. Kleinfelder (Eds.), Splash 2: FPGAs in a custom computing machine. IEEE Computer Society Press, 1996.
3. S. R. Dusse and B. S. Kaliski, A Cryptographic Library for the Motorola DSP56000, in *Advances in Cryptology - EUROCRYPT'90*, Spinger-Verlag, LNCS, vol. 473 (1990) 230–244.
4. S. E. Eldridge, A faster modular multiplication algorithm. Intern. J. *Computer Math.*, 1993 (40) 63–68.
5. S. E. Eldridge and C. D. Walter, Hardware implementation of Montgomery's modular multiplication algorithm. *IEEE Trans. on Comput.*, 1993 (42) 693–699.
6. T. ElGamal, A public-key cryptosystem and a signature scheme based on discrete logarithms. *IEEE Trans. Inform. Theory*, 1985 (31) 469–472.
7. S. Even, Systolic modular multiplication, in *Advances in Cryptology - Crypto'90*, Springer-Verlag, LNCS, vol. 537 (1990) 619–624.
8. A. Fiat and A. Shamir, How to prove yourself, in *Advances in Cryptology - Crypto'86*, Springer-Verlag, LNCS, vol. 263 (1986) 186–194.
9. K. Iwamura, T. Matsumoto and H. Imai, Modular Exponentiation Using Montgomery Method and the Systolic Array, IEICE Technical Report, vol. 92, no. 134, ISEC92-7, 1992, pp.49–54.
10. P. L. Montgomery, Modular multiplication without trial division. *Mathematics of Computations*, 1985 (44) 519–521.
11. Ç. K. Koç, RSA Hardware Implementation, TR 801, RSA Laboratories, 30 pages, April 1996. http://www.ece.orst.edu/ koc/vita/v22ab.html
12. H. Orup, E. Svendsen, E. And, VICTOR an efficient RSA hardware implementation. In: *Eurocrypt 90*, LNCS, vol. 473 (1991) 245–252
13. R. Rivest, A. Shamir and L. Adleman, A method of obtaining digital signatures and public key cryptosystems. J. +em Commun. of ACM, 1978 (21) 120–126.
14. J. Sauerbrey, A Modular Exponentiation Unit Based on Systolic Arrays, in *Advances in Cryptology - AUSCRYPT'93*, Springer-Verlag, LNCS, vol. 718 (1993) 505–516.
15. M. Shand, J. Vuillemin, Fast Implementation of of RSA Cryptography. In *Proc. of the 11th IEEE Symposium on Computer Arithmetics*, 1993. pp.252–259.
16. A. A. Tiountchik, Systolic modular exponentiation via Montgomery algorithm. J. *Electronics Letters*, 1998 (34).
17. C. D. Walter, Systolic Modular Multiplication. *IEEE Trans. on Comput.*, 1993 (42) 376–378.

Changing Thresholds in the Absence of Secure Channels*

Keith M. Martin** (Katholieke Universiteit Leuven),
Josef Pieprzyk, Rei Safavi-Naini and Huaxiong Wang
(University of Wollongong)

Katholieke Universiteit Leuven
Dept. Elektrotechniek - ESAT
Kardinaal Mercierlaan 94, B-3001 Heverlee, Belgium
keith.martin@esat.kuleuven.ac.be
and
Center for Computer Security Research
School of Information Technology and Computer Science
University of Wollongong
Northfields Avenue, Wollongong 2522, Australia
josef/rei/hw13@cs.uow.edu.au

Abstract. The ways the threshold parameter can be modified after the setup of a secret sharing scheme is the main theme of this work. The considerations are limited to the case when there are no secure channels. First we motivate the problem and discuss methods of threshold change when the dealer is still active and can use broadcasting to implement the change required. Next we study the case when participants themselves initiate the change of threshold without the dealer's help. A general model for threshold changeable secret sharing is developed and two constructions are given. The first generic construction allows the design of a threshold changeable secret sharing scheme which can be implemented using the Shamir approach. The second construction is geometrical in nature and is optimal in terms of the size of shares. The work is concluded by showing that any threshold scheme can be given some degree of threshold change capability.

Keywords: Secret Sharing, Threshold Changeable Secret Sharing, Shamir Secret Sharing, Geometrical Secret Sharing.

1 Introduction

A (t, n)-*threshold scheme* is a method of splitting a secret piece of information among n participants in such a way that any t of the participants can together

---

* This work was partially supported by the Australian Research Council under grant number A49703076

** This author was supported by the European Commission under ACTS project AC095 (ASPeCT)

recover the secret. They do this by pooling together their *shares*, which are secret values securely transmitted to them by a *dealer* on initialisation of the threshold scheme. Threshold schemes [1, 15] are special examples of *secret sharing schemes*, which allow more general combinations of participants to collectively engage in recovery of the secret [17]. Secret sharing schemes, and in particular threshold schemes, have become an indispensable basic cryptographic tool in any security environment where active entities are groups rather than individuals [6]. The group of participants involved in a threshold scheme is not necessarily static over time. The number of participants and the threshold parameter may fluctuate reflecting the current structure of the organisation to whom the participants belong and the sensitivity of the secret. New participants may enter an organisation and need to be incorporated into the security structure (*enrolment*). Current participants may leave the organisation, their shares may become compromised, or their access to the secret may be withdrawn for security reasons (*disenrolment*). A high threshold parameter established on initialisation due to a high degree of mutual distrust among the participants may be relaxed as the participants mutual trust grows over time (*threshold decrease*). Alternatively mutual trust may decrease over time, perhaps due to organisational problems or security incidents, and hence the threshold parameters may require tightening (*threshold increase*). The longer the lifetime of a secret, the greater the chances that any of these alterations to the security policy in place on scheme initialisation are to occur, and hence the greater the likelihood that the threshold parameters may need to be changed. Such a need is related, but quite distinct, to the notion of *proactivity* [10], where shares are refreshed at regular time intervals for security reasons, but where the threshold parameters do not change after each share refreshment. This motivates our interest in considering the problem of how to change the parameters of a (t, n)-threshold scheme after it has been initialised. In other words, how to obtain a (t', n')-threshold scheme from a (t, n)-threshold scheme. We assume that the secret is not reconstructed by the participants before the change of parameter. An obvious method of conducting such a change is for the dealer to issue new shares to all the participants in the new threshold scheme. This is an inefficient, and often impractical, solution as it involves the use of a secure communications from the dealer to each participant which may not be possible at the time the change of threshold is required. A possible method of enabling a change in the parameters of a threshold scheme is to conduct a secret *redistribution*. This technique was investigated for general secret sharing schemes in [7, 14]. A redistribution of the secret is conducted by the participants of the original scheme, and involves them communicating information among themselves, and among any new participants in the new scheme. Secret redistributions have two notable advantages in that they do not involve the dealer and that they can be conducted without any prior knowledge that a change of threshold parameters is required. However in general a redistribution requires the existence of secure communication links between the threshold scheme participants, which may be impossible or undesirable in many applications. In this paper we investigate how to change the parameters of a threshold scheme in the absence of either a secure link from the dealer to participants, or secure links between participants themselves. We restrict our attention to the cases of threshold increase and threshold decrease. Disenrolment in the absence of secure links has already been subject to investigation [2,13]. It does not seem likely that enrolment is possible in the absence of any secure links (unless enrolling participants have already been issued with some advance information and have been operating as "sleeping" participants, which arguably does not count as fresh enrolment). In the following discussion we note that procedures for changing threshold can be classified by the amount of preparation for change that is made on the initialisation of the original threshold scheme. We will consider cases where the exact change of threshold parameter is known on initialisation, where only knowledge that a change (but not which change) is known on initialisation, and where no advance preparation for change is made. The new threshold will be agreed upon by sending messages over public channels. We distinguish two cases: the case that the original dealer is still active and the case that the original dealer is no longer in existence and shareholders decide on the new threshold themselves. We assume that after such an agreement shareholders will behave honestly with respect to their agreed threshold and submit correct shares in reconstruction phase. A good example of a situation that change of threshold under the above conditions is required is when communication channels of t shareholders in a (t, n) threshold scheme are tapped by an enemy and hence an attempt to reconstruct the secret will enable the enemy to find the secret. By raising threshold to $t' > t$, the enemy will remain completely uncertain about the value of the secret. A second example is for distributing authority among a group of n participants and requiring two levels of collaboration, t and t', for two levels of security. This kind of multilevel security may also be seen as an option given to participants so that for more sensitive decisions a higher degree of agreement could be used. We also note that in some cases it may be desirable for the value of the secret to change when the threshold parameter changes. In general this is simply a matter of choice for threshold decrease. For threshold increase however, after the change of parameters certain sets that could previously access the secret may no longer be desired to. The paper is organised as follows. In Section 2, threshold schemes are introduced. Section 3 discusses general techniques for changing threshold by dealer broadcast. Section 4 introduces the model, derives bounds and proposes constructions for changing threshold without dealer assistance. Section 5 includes ideas on how an arbitrary threshold scheme can be made threshold changeable and Section 6 concludes the paper.

2 Threshold Schemes

Let $\mathcal{P} = \{P_1, \ldots, P_n\}$ be a group of n participants. Let S be the set of secrets and let the share of P_i come from set S_i. A (t, n)-threshold scheme is a pair of algorithms: the dealer and the combiner. For a given secret from S and some random string from $\mathcal{R}$, the dealer algorithm applies the mapping

$$\mathcal{D}_{t,n} : S \times R \to S_1 \times \ldots \times S_n$$

to assign shares to participants from $\mathcal{P}$. The shares of a subset $\mathcal{A} \subseteq \mathcal{P}$ of participants can be input into the combiner algorithm

$$\mathcal{C}_{t,n} : \bigcup_{P_i \in \mathcal{A}} \{S_i\} \to S,$$

which will return the secret if the set $\mathcal{A} \subseteq \mathcal{P}$ and $|\mathcal{A}| \geq t$, otherwise it fails. Each instance of the threshold scheme (pair (s, r), $s \in S$, $r \in R$) thus indexes a *distribution rule* and threshold scheme can be combinatorially represented by a matrix whose rows form the distribution rules, and columns are indexed by the secret and the participants. If we associate a probability with each $s \in S$ then a threshold scheme can also be described information theoretically using the entropy function [12]. More precisely, if $|\mathcal{A}| \geq t$ then $H(S|\mathcal{A}) = 0$, and if $|\mathcal{A}| < t$ then $H(S|\mathcal{A}) \neq 0$. A threshold scheme is *perfect* if $H(S|\mathcal{A}) = H(S)$ for any $|\mathcal{A}| < t$ (in other words groups of less than t participants learn no more information about the secret than is publicly known). Perfect threshold schemes with $H(S_i) = H(S)$ for all $i = 1, \ldots, n$ are said to be *ideal*. In general it can be assumed that in an ideal threshold scheme $S_i = S$ for each $i = 1, \ldots, n$. A consequence of the definition of a perfect threshold scheme is that the the size of shares is at least the size of the of the secret, that is $H(S_i) \geq H(S)$ [5]. If we reduce share size below that of the secret then it necessarily follows that the perfect property must be sacrificed. An example of threshold scheme that are not perfect are the so called *ramp schemes* [3,9] which offer a compromise between security and share size. A (c, t, n)-ramp scheme is a (t, n)-threshold scheme such that:

1. If $\mathcal{A} \subseteq \mathcal{P}$ and $|\mathcal{A}| \geq t$, then $H(S|\mathcal{A}) = 0$;
2. If $\mathcal{A} \subseteq \mathcal{P}$ and $c < |\mathcal{A}| < t$, then $0 < H(S|\mathcal{A}) < H(S)$;
3. If $\mathcal{A} \subseteq \mathcal{P}$ and $|\mathcal{A}| \leq c$, then $H(S|\mathcal{A}) = H(S)$.

In [9] a (c, t, n)-ramp scheme with the property that $H(S_i) = H(S)/(t - c)$ for each $i = 1, \ldots, n$ is shown to be *optimal* (where an optimal ramp scheme is a ramp scheme where $H(S|\mathcal{A}) = ((k - r)/(k - c))H(S)$ for $|\mathcal{A}| = r, c \leq r \leq t$, and shares are of minimal size). Such schemes have nice properties and are easily constructed (see [9] for details).

3 Changing Threshold by Dealer Broadcast

In this section we assume that the original dealer of the threshold scheme is still active, but no longer able to use the secure links that were used to initiate the scheme. All messages from the dealer must thus take the form of broadcasts, where we assume that a broadcast message is an insecure communication that can be read by all participants and any outsiders to the scheme. There are two general techniques that can be used to change threshold by means of a broadcast message.

1. *Advance key technique.* The dealer gives each participant a secret key as well as their share on initialisation. When the time comes to change threshold parameters, the dealer broadcasts new shares of the new threshold scheme, but encrypted under the secret keys issued to each participant. Unconditional security can be maintained by using a one-time pad to encrypt the information on this insecure channel.

2. *Advance share technique.* The dealer gives each participant shares in two different threshold schemes on initialisation. When the time comes to change threshold parameters, the dealer broadcasts specific shares of the second scheme that have the effect of changing the threshold parameters as required (see below).

The advance key technique would appear to be a somewhat trivial solution to the problem of changing thresholds by dealer broadcast. It does however suffer from the disadvantage that the size of the broadcast message is directly proportional to the number of participants in the scheme. The advance share technique can be used to reduce the broadcast size. A general example of the advanced share technique can be derived from techniques in [4, 13]. In this case, as well as their initial share in a (t, n)-scheme, on initialisation each participant is given a share in an $(n+1, 2n)$-scheme, which is defined on the n real participants, and n imaginary (*dummy*) participants. To realise a (t', n) scheme the dealer broadcasts $n - t' + 1$ shares of the $(n + 1, 2n)$-scheme belonging to $n - t' + 1$ dummy participants. The resulting scheme is an $(n + 1, 2n)$-scheme, contracted at $n - t' + 1$ participants: that is a $(t', n + t' - 1)$-scheme. However, $t' - 1$ of the shareholders are dummy participants and so the effective scheme is a (t', n)-scheme. The following comments apply to the two general techniques:

1. Both general techniques can be used when it is known on initialisation that a change of the threshold parameters may be needed, but not exactly what change will be necessary.

2. If the value of the secret changes when the threshold changes (i.e. the shares of the $(n + 1, 2n)$-scheme correspond to a different secret than the original shares) then both threshold increase and decrease are possible using these techniques. If the value of the secret stays the same then in the case of threshold increase, participants must be trusted to move onto the new shares and not use their original ones (see comments in Section 1).

We can refine the advance share technique for threshold decrease if it is known on initialisation exactly what change in threshold parameter may be required. Let $t' < t$. . Let $m = \max(n, n') + (t - t')$. On initialisation, the dealer issues shares of a $(t, n+t-t')$-scheme to the n participants. The remaining $t-t'$ shares correspond to dummy participants and hence the resulting scheme is a (t, n)-scheme. To change this to a (t', n)-scheme the dealer broadcasts the $t - t'$ shares belonging to dummy participants. The resulting scheme is a $(t, n+t-t')$-scheme, contracted at $t-t'$ participants: that is, a (t', n)-scheme. The advantages of this refinement are that it is no longer necessary to issue an extra share in advance to each participant, and the broadcast message will usually be much shorter than for the general techniques.

4 Changing Threshold without Dealer Assistance

For the rest of this paper we assume that the dealer is no longer able to provide assistance in changing the threshold parameter. In the absence of both an active dealer and any secure channels between participants it is clear that participants can only use the information sent to them on initialisation of the original scheme. Hence the original "shares" must contain the information necessary for deriving both the shares of the initial (t, n)-scheme and the shares of the future (t', n)-scheme (we refer to these two derived shares as *subshares*). Such a system is therefore restricted in its application to situations where participants are trusted to operate "honestly" in the sense that during a reconstruction of the secret they only use the subshare that is relevant to the threshold in current use (see Section 1). A number of trivial solutions to this problem exist. If it is known in advance exactly what threshold change will be required then the initial share given to each participant could consist of one subshare corresponding to a share in the original (t, n)-scheme, and a second subshare that consists of a share in the later (t', n)-scheme. In this naive construction the required storage for each participant is $2H(S)$ (assuming the two systems are ideal). In general the size of the stored shares for each participant grows linearly with the number of required threshold which makes this method very inefficient. Another possible solution is to use the broadcast techniques of Section 2 and rely on a publicly accessible directory containing transcripts of the relevant broadcast messages for certain types of threshold change. Since participants are required to behave with a degree of honesty then they can be trusted to read the relevant broadcast message at the appropriate time. These solutions do also generally involve more than one subshare being stored securely. We are thus interested in solutions that minimise the amount of information that each participant must store in order to derive both a (t, n) and (t', n)-scheme. The approach we will take is to construct (t, n)-schemes that can be changed into (t', n)-schemes through manipulation of the original shares. We will assume that $t' > t$ (threshold increase) and note that the schemes proposed could also be used for threshold decrease. For such schemes at least some advance knowledge of the future threshold change should be known on initialisation, since the schemes are designed to permit change. Later we consider some options for the much more difficult task of achieving some degree of change to an arbitrary threshold scheme (with no inbuilt mechanism in place to allow threshold change).

4.1 A Model for Threshold Change without Dealer Assistance

In this section we consider a basic model for schemes that permit threshold change without dealer assistance. We also discuss possible efficiency measures and then provide some constructions for such systems.

Definition 1. *A perfect (t, n)-threshold secret sharing with a dealer algorithm*

$$\mathcal{D}_{t,n} : S \times R \to S_1 \times \cdots \times S_n$$

is called threshold changeable to t' *if there exist publicly known functions* h_i : $S_i \rightarrow T_i = h_i(S_i)$, *for* $1 \leq i \leq n$, *such that* $H(S|T_A) = 0$ *for any* $|A| \geq t'$, *and* $H(S|T_A) < H(S)$ *for any* $|A| < t'$ *where* $A \subseteq \{1, \ldots, n\}$.

¿From this definition, if we combine the dealer algorithm $\mathcal{D}_{t,n}$ with the functions h_i, we obtain the function

$$\mathcal{D}' : S \times R \rightarrow T_1 \times \cdots \times T_n$$

defined by $\mathcal{D}' = (h_1 \times \cdots \times h_n)\mathcal{D}_{t,n}$. It has the obvious properties

$$H(S|T_A) = \begin{cases} 0 & \text{if } |A| \geq t'; \\ H(S) & \text{if } |A| < t, \end{cases}$$

for any $A \subseteq \{1, \ldots, n\}$. Thus we may regard $\mathcal{D}'$ as a new dealer algorithm for a secret sharing scheme with n participants. In this model the subshare used in the (t, n)-threshold scheme consists of the entire original share, and the subshare used in the (t', n)-threshold scheme is determined by the functions h_i.

4.2   Efficiency measures

We denote the (t, n)-threshold scheme by Π and the (t', n)-threshold scheme by Π'. The following lemma is fairly obvious.

Lemma 1. *Let* Π *be an ideal* (t, n)-*threshold scheme threshold changeable to* $t' > t$. *Then the resulting* (t', n)-*threshold scheme* Π' *is not perfect.*

Proof. By contradiction. Assume that the scheme Π' is ideal and perfect and any t' shares determine the secret. Thus $H(T_i) = H(S_i) = H(S)$. As the function h is deterministic we know that $H(T_i|S_i) = 0$. Since $I(S_i; T_i) = H(S_i) - H(S_i|T_i) = H(T_i) - H(T_i|S_i)$, $H(T_i) = H(S_i)$ and $H(T_i|S_i) = 0$, then $H(S_i|T_i) = 0$. This means that there is a one-to-one correspondence between shares from Π and Π'. This also says that the threshold of Π' must be t' which gives us our requested contradiction.

The efficiency of a perfect (t, n)-threshold scheme that is threshold changeable to t' can be measured by

1. the maximum and average size of the share which needs to be stored, given by $H(S_i)$, for $1 \leq i \leq n$,
2. the amount of information which needs to be delivered to the combiner at the pooling time expressed by $\sum_{i \in A} H(T_i)$ for $A \subseteq \{1, \ldots, n\}$ where $|A| = t'$,
3. the size of subshares to be sent to the combiner, given by $H(T_i)$, for $1 \leq i \leq n$.

Theorem 1. *Let* Π *be a perfect* (t, n)-*threshold scheme that is threshold changeable to* t' *using functions* $\mathcal{H} = \{h_i\}_{1 \leq i \leq n}$. *Then*

1. $H(S_i) \geq H(S)$ *for* $1 \leq i \leq n$;

2. $\sum_{i\in\mathcal{A}} H(T_i) \geq \frac{t'}{t'-t+1} H(S)$, for $\mathcal{A} \subseteq \{1,\ldots,n\}$ with $|\mathcal{A}| = t'$;

3. $\max_{1\leq i\leq n}\{H(T_i)\} \geq \frac{1}{t'-t+1} H(S)$.

Proof. Part 1. follows by definition of perfect threshold scheme. We next prove part 3. Assume that $\mathcal{A}$ is a t' subset of $\{1,\ldots,n\}$ and $\mathcal{B}$ is a subset of $\mathcal{A}$ such that $|\mathcal{B}| = t - 1$. We have $I(S; T_{(\mathcal{A}\setminus\mathcal{B})}|T_\mathcal{B}) = H(S|T_\mathcal{B}) - H(S|T_{(\mathcal{A}\setminus\mathcal{B})}, T_\mathcal{B}) = H(S|T_\mathcal{B}) - H(S|T_\mathcal{A}) = H(S|T_\mathcal{B}) = H(S)$. On the other hand, $H(S; T_{(\mathcal{A}\setminus\mathcal{B})}|T_\mathcal{B}) = H(T_{(\mathcal{A}\setminus\mathcal{B})}|T_\mathcal{B}) - H(T_{(\mathcal{A}\setminus\mathcal{B})}|T_\mathcal{B}, S) \leq H(T_{(\mathcal{A}\setminus\mathcal{B})}) \leq |\mathcal{A}\setminus\mathcal{B}| \max\{H(T_i; i \in \mathcal{A}\setminus\mathcal{B})\} = (t' - t + 1) \max\{H(T_i; i \in \mathcal{A}\setminus\mathcal{B}\}$, proving part 3. To see part 2., let $\mathcal{A}$ be a t' subset of $\{1,\ldots,n\}$. For any subset $\mathcal{B}$ of $\mathcal{A}$ with $|\mathcal{B}| = t-1$, from proving part 2. we know that $\sum_{i\in\mathcal{A}\setminus\mathcal{B}} H(T_i) \geq H(S)$. Let $\mathcal{F}$ be the collection of all $(t-1)$-subset of $\mathcal{A}$. We show that

$$\binom{t'-1}{t-1} \sum_{i\in\mathcal{A}} H(T_i) = \sum_{\mathcal{B}\in\mathcal{F}} \sum_{i\in\mathcal{A}\setminus\mathcal{B}} H(T_i).$$

Indeed, for each $i \in \mathcal{A}$, we denote $\mathcal{F}_i = \{\mathcal{B} \in \mathcal{F}; i \notin \mathcal{B}\}$. Then in the above equation $H(T_i)$ appears $|F_i| = \binom{t'-1}{t-1}$ times in the right-hand side for each $1 \leq i \leq n$, and so the equation follows. We then have

$$\binom{t'-1}{t-1} \sum_{i\in\mathcal{A}} H(T_i) = \sum_{\mathcal{B}\in\mathcal{F}} \sum_{i\in\mathcal{A}\setminus\mathcal{B}} H(T_i) \geq \binom{t'}{t-1} H(S).$$

and obtain $\sum_{i\in\mathcal{A}} H(T_i) \geq \frac{t'}{t'-t+1} H(\mathcal{S})$.

It is worth noting that item 2 shows that it is possible that the amount of information which needs to be delivered to the combiner at the pooling time is less than the original scheme $(tH(S))$ but of course the latter scheme is not perfect.

Definition 2. *A perfect (t,n)-threshold scheme Π that is threshold changeable to t' is called* optimal *if the bounds in Theorem 1 are met with equality.*

Corollary 1. *If a perfect (t,n)-threshold scheme Π that is threshold changeable to t' is optimal then Π is ideal and Π' is a $(t-1,t',n)$ optimal ramp scheme.*

Proof. By definition Π is ideal and Π' is a $(t-1,t',n)$ ramp scheme. ¿From Theorem 1 (Part 2.) it follows that $H(T_i) = \frac{1}{t'-t+1} H(S)$ for all $1 \leq i \leq n$, and hence that the ramp scheme is optimal (see Section 2).

4.3 A general construction from a ramp scheme

As noted earlier a naive (and very inefficient) method of allowing shareholders to choose among a number of thresholds is to give them independent subshares for each scheme. In this section we describe a much more efficient method of constructing a threshold scheme which can have a number of possible thresholds and has the property that original scheme is ideal. We give a general construction and then give the detail of an implementation based on Shamir polynomial scheme.

Theorem 2. *If there exists an optimal $((t-1)v, tv, nv)$-ramp scheme, then there exists a (t, n) threshold scheme that is threshold changeable to k for any integer k such that $k|vt$.*

Proof. Let Λ be an optimal $((t-1)v, tv, nv)$ ramp scheme. We can construct a (t, n) ideal threshold scheme Π from Λ as follows. As their initial share, give each participant in Π v different shares in Λ (we call these *component shares.* Since Λ is optimal, it is easy to verify that Π is a (t, n) ideal threshold scheme. We further define the conversion $\mathcal{H} = \{h_i\}_{1 \leq i \leq n}$ by letting the subshare of the (k, n)-scheme be formed by taking any vt/k component shares from the share of participant P_i (who has v component shares) for each $1 \leq i \leq n$. It is clear that k of these subshares will now be necessary to reconstruct the secret.

Let u denote the number of integer k such that $k|vt$. The reduction in the size of storage for each shareholder compared to the naive method is $(u - 1)H(S)$. A conceptually useful way of constructing ramp schemes suitable for use in Theorem 2 is to recall that by Theorem 9 [9], we know that if there exists a $(tv, nv+v-1)$ ideal threshold scheme then there exists an optimal $((t-1)v, tv, nv)$ ramp scheme. A simple construction method is thus to start with a Shamir threshold scheme [15], interpreted as a ramp scheme. Assume that $S = GF(q)^v$ is the set of shares and secrets.

Construction

1. Let $q \geq nv$. To share a secret $s = (s_1, \ldots, s_v) \in GF(q)^v$ The dealer randomly chooses a polynomial $F(x)$ of degree at most $tv - 1$ such that $F(x)$ satisfies

$$(F(1), \ldots, F(v)) = (s_1, \ldots, s_v).$$

   More precisely, $F(x)$ can be chosen in the following way. First select at random a vector $(s_{v+1}, \ldots, s_{tv}) \in GF(q)^{(t-1)v}$ and then use the Lagrange interpolation to compute the unique polynomial $F(x)$ of degree at most $tv-1$ satisfying $(F(1), \ldots, F(tv)) = (s_1, \ldots, s_{tv})$. Notice that the randomness of $(s_{v+1}, \ldots, s_{tv})$ results in the randomness of $F(x)$.
2. The dealer choose nv distinct numbers $x_1, \ldots, x_{nv}$ in $GF(q) \setminus \{1, \ldots, v\}$. Each participant P_i is assigned a subset $\mathcal{A}_i \subseteq \{x_1, \ldots, x_{nv}\}$ of v elements. $\mathcal{A}_i$ are public and unique for the participant P_i. Let $\mathcal{A}_i = \{x_{i_1}, \ldots, x_{i_v}\}$. The share of P_i is $S_i = F(\mathcal{A}_i) = (F(x_{i_1}), \ldots, F(x_{i_v}))$
3. At the pooling time, any t out of n participants can use the Lagrange interpolation to compute the polynomial $F(x)$ and so recover the secret $(F(1), \ldots, F(v))$.

The following comments apply to the above construction (and any other construction obtained using Theorem 2):

- Initially the scheme is clearly a (t, n)-threshold scheme. Any $t-1$ participants have no information about which of the q^v candidates for the secret has been selected.

- Any k participants, each submitting (vt/k) parts of their share can reconstruct the secret.
- Any $k-1$ participants A, each submitting (vt/k) parts of their share are left with $H(S|A) = (t/k)H(S)$, by definition of the ramp scheme.
- With respect to the bounds in Theorem 1, we have $H(S_i) = H(S)$, but $H(T_i) = (t/k)H(S)$. Thus such schemes will only be optimal in the degenerate case that $t = 1$.
- Each shareholder has $v \log q$ secret bits which is the same as the secret size.

4.4 An optimal geometrical construction

The previous construction is conceptually simple and easy to implement. It is not however optimal. We now give an example of an optimal perfect (t, n)-threshold scheme that is threshold changeable to t'. This construction is described in terms of projective geometry, a technique first used for secret sharing schemes in [16]. For background information on projective geometry, see [11].

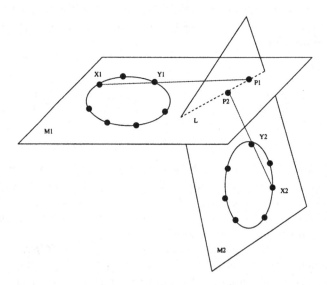

Fig. 1. AN OPTIMAL $(2, 7)$-SCHEME THAT IS THRESHOLD CHANGEABLE TO 3

First note that $(1, 3, n)$-ramp scheme can be constructed in finite projective space as follows.

1. Let Π be a publicly known plane and let each line contained in Π represent a possible secret.
2. Pick another plane $\Pi 1$ that meets Π in a line $\mathcal{L}$.

3. Pick n points on $\Pi 1$, but not on $\mathcal{L}$, such that no three of the points are collinear. Give one point to each participant as their share of the secret.

Any three shares consist of three non-collinear points, and thus knowledge of three shares is enough to generate the plane $\Pi 1$. Plane $\Pi 1$ can then be intersected with the public plane Π to recover the secret line $\mathcal{L}$. Any two shares $X1, Y1$ consist of two points which define a line $\langle X1, Y1 \rangle$. This line meets $\mathcal{L}$ in a unique point $P1$. Since it takes knowledge of two points on $\mathcal{L}$ to define $\mathcal{L}$, it follows that knowing two shares only reveals "half" of $\mathcal{L}$. Finally, any one share consists of one point not on $\mathcal{L}$, the span of which is naturally just that point and thus defines no points on $\mathcal{L}$. Hence knowledge of one share reveals nothing about the secret line $\mathcal{L}$. To see that such a configuration results in a set of mappings that fits the definition of ramp scheme in Section 2, see [8, 17]. Essentially there is one mapping for each plane $\Pi 1$ that meets plane Π in a line. Each secret line is represented by two points that generate that line. In each mapping, the share of a participant is one point, and the secret is two points, and hence $H(S_i) = H(S)/2$. In other words, the ramp scheme is optimal. We now extend this idea to construct an optimal perfect $(2, n)$-threshold scheme that is threshold changeable to 3.

1. Construct an optimal $(1, 3, n)$-ramp scheme on planes Π and $\Pi 1$ as before.
2. Pick another plane $\Pi 2$, distinct from Π and $\Pi 1$, that meets $\Pi 1$ (and Π) in line $\mathcal{L}$.
3. Construct an optimal $(1, 3, n)$-ramp scheme on plane $\Pi 2$. Each shareholder now holds a share that consists of two points, one on $\Pi 1$ and one on $\Pi 2$. The points of this second scheme must be allocated to shareholders in such a way that for any pair of shareholders, the unique point on $\mathcal{L}$ generated by their two points on $\Pi 1$ is distinct from the unique point on $\mathcal{L}$ defined by their two points on $\Pi 2$. Such an allocation of shares to shareholders is always possible (see closing remark in this section).

The resulting configuration is illustrated in Figure 1. Note that Π is not illustrated. In Figure 1 the share of participant X consists of points $X1$ and $X2$ (equivalently, line $\langle X1, X2 \rangle$), and the share of participant Y consists of points $Y1$ and $Y2$ (line $\langle Y1, Y2 \rangle$).

- Initially, shareholders use both their points to reconstruct the secret. Thus if shareholders X and Y try to reconstruct the secret then they can each use their point in each of the planes to generate the lines $\langle X1, Y1 \rangle$ and $\langle X2, Y2 \rangle$, which meet Π in points $P1$ and $P2$ respectively. Since $P1$ and $P2$ are distinct, the two shareholders use these points to generate the secret $\mathcal{L}$. Further, each of the lines $\langle X1, X2 \rangle$ and $\langle Y1, Y2 \rangle$ are skew to $\mathcal{L}$ and hence one shareholder can not generate any points of $\mathcal{L}$. Thus the initial configuration can be used to generate a perfect $(2, n)$-threshold scheme.
- If shareholders just use their points on plane $\Pi 1$ then the result is the configuration of a $(1, 3, n)$-ramp scheme, as described previously. Hence any three participants can generate the secret, any two learn "one half" of the secret, and one shareholder learns nothing about the secret.

- The conversion of such a configuration into a scheme satisfying Definition 1 is identical to the conversion process described in [8, 17] for geometric secret sharing. The function h_i is simply the function that extracts the point on $\Pi 1$ from the pair of points allocated to the ith shareholder.
- The secret is represented by a line (two points). Each shareholder has a share consisting of two points. If the threshold is changed to three, then each shareholder only submits one point, exactly one half of their share. Thus with respect to the bounds in Theorem 1, we have $H(S_i) = H(S)$, and $H(T_i) = H(S)/2$. The scheme is thus optimal.

The above scheme generalises to a configuration for an optimal perfect (t, n)-threshold scheme that is threshold changeable to t' as follows:

1. Replace each plane Π by a space of projective dimension $t' - 1$.
2. Take $t' - t + 1$ of these spaces (instead of just two in Figure 1) such that all the spaces Πj meet in a subspace $\mathcal{L}$ of projective dimension $(t' - t)$.
3. On each space Πj choose n points such that no t' points lie together in a subspace of projective dimension $(t' - 2)$. This defines a $(t - 1, t', n)$-ramp scheme on Πj. When the threshold is increased to t', shareholders will submit only their points on space $\Pi 1$.
4. Any t points on any Π_j define a subspace of projective dimension $t - 1$ that meets $\mathcal{L}$ in a point. By labelling the points on the spaces Πj carefully (see below) we ensure that the $t' - t + 1$ points on $\mathcal{L}$ defined by any t shareholders (one point on $\mathcal{L}$ for each space Πj) are all distinct, and hence together define $\mathcal{L}$. Thus the original scheme is a (t, n)-threshold scheme.
5. Each subshare is one point, the secret (and each share) is defined by $t' - t + 1$ points, and hence the scheme is optimal.

It remains to describe how to allocate the points on each space to shareholders in order to ensure the "distinctness" property described above. A summary of how this is done is as follows:

1. Let ξ be a Singer cycle on $\mathcal{L}$ (ξ permutes the points of $\mathcal{L}$ in a cycle whose length is the number of points on $\mathcal{L}$).
2. Extend ξ to an automorphism ϕ of $\Pi 1$.
3. Let the points on $\Pi 2$ be a projection of the points on $\Pi 1$. If shareholder i received point Xi on $\Pi 1$ then give shareholder i the projection of point $\phi(Xi)$ on $\Pi 2$.
4. More generally, let the points on $\Pi(j + 1)$ be a projection of the points on $\Pi 1$. If shareholder i received point Xi on $\Pi 1$ then give shareholder i the projection of point $\phi^j(Xi)$ on Πj.

The linearity relationships between the points on $\Pi 1$ are preserved by the automorphism ϕ and so the resulting configuration on $\Pi 2$ has the same properties as that on $\Pi 1$. Further, as ϕ restricted to $\mathcal{L}$ is ξ, we are guaranteed that the there are no points on $\mathcal{L}$ fixed by ϕ. Hence (considering the simple example) if points $X1, Y1$ generate point $Z1$ on $\mathcal{L}$, then points $\phi(X1), \phi(Y1)$ generate line $\phi(Z1)$ on $\mathcal{L}$, with $\phi(Z1)$ distinct from $Z1$. A similar argument applies to the other spaces Πj since ϕ^j is also an automorphism of $\Pi 1$ that fixes $\mathcal{L}$. It is interesting to note that the optimal geometrical construction can be used to reduce the amount of information which needs to be delivered to the combiner if we allow the threshold of participants who submit their (partial) shares to be increased. For example, in our optimal $(2, n)$ threshold changeable scheme, if two participants want to reconstruct the secret, they have to send their full shares (two points for each) to the combiner and the total amount of information is $2H(S)$. If three participants send their partial shares (one point for each), they can still recover the secret, but the total information delivered to the combiner is reduced to $1.5H(S)$.

5 Changing Threshold of an Arbitrary Threshold Scheme

We close by considering the problem of changing the threshold parameter of an arbitrary (t, n) threshold scheme, without dealer assistance or secure links. Thus we cannot guarantee that subshares can be deterministically derived from the original shares, as in the previous section. In reality this problem seems very difficult to solve with any degree of satisfaction, however we suggest two possible methods which could be further developed in a search for a solution. Both techniques involve releasing information about shares, instead of shares themselves.

5.1 Changing Thresholds via Probabilistic Shares

Instead of submitting shares to a combiner, this first idea is that participant give away some "hints" about their shares. This hint specifies a subset of values to which the share belongs (specification of particular bits, for example). Thus the information provided by P_i about the share s_i takes the form of a set $\mathcal{B}_i$ such that $s_i \in \mathcal{B}_i$. One approach to reconstruction is as follows. When trying to reconstruct the secret, each P_i submits their set (hint) $\mathcal{B}_i$ $(i = 1, \ldots, \ell)$ to the combiner. The combiner groups the sets into collections of size t, and from each such collection derives the set of all possible secrets corresponding to all the possible share allocations using these share hints. Using the following hints, and the corresponding possible secret sets S^i,

$$\mathcal{B}_1, \ldots, \mathcal{B}_{t-1}, \mathcal{B}_t \rightarrow S^t$$

$$\vdots$$

$$\mathcal{B}_1, \ldots, \mathcal{B}_{t-1}, \mathcal{B}_\ell \rightarrow S^\ell$$

the combiner can then precisely recover the secret if $|S^t \cap S^{t+1} \cap \ldots \cap S^\ell| = 1$. It is however clear that such a solution cannot guarantee the precise new value of the threshold. An open problem is thus to determine methods of selecting hints in order to be able to specify within a certain probability that the secret can be reconstructed uniquely.

5.2 Combiner Assisted Threshold Change

To avoid the uncertainty of the probabilistic method it is necessary to find a deterministic analogue of the probabilistic sharing idea. This may be possible if information about shares in a threshold scheme can be deterministically released in some manner. An idea is to negotiate a common encoding for delivery of information about participants' shares. The following provides an illustration of how this might work. Assume the original scheme is a (t, n) Shamir scheme based on polynomial $f(x)$ over $GF(q)$ of degree at most $t-1$. As usual a participant P_i; $i = 1, \ldots, n$ is assigned a public co-ordinate x_i and a share $s_i = f(x_i)$. The secret is $s = f(0)$. It is well-known that any t participants can collectively recover the secret as they can write t linearly independent equations and solve them. Let these t participants be $P_1, \ldots, P_t$, then they (or the combiner) can write

$$s_1 = f(x_1) = a_0 + a_1 x_1 + \ldots + a_{t-1} x_1^{t-1}$$

$$\vdots$$

$$s_t = f(x_t) = a_0 + a_1 x_t + \ldots + a_{t-1} x_t^{t-1}$$

Let the combiner impose the encoding scheme such that every integer $c_i \in GF(q)$ is represented as a vector of k co-ordinates so

$$c_i = c_{i,0} + b c_{i,1} + b^2 c_{i,2} + \ldots + b^{k-1} c_{i,k-1} = (c_{i,0}, \ldots, c_{i,k-1})$$

where b is the base (for binary representation $b = 2$). We assume that the representation is one to one. Note that if we encode s_i and a_j; $j = 1, \ldots, t-1$ then from the equation

$$s_i = f(x_i) = a_0 + a_1 x_i + \ldots + a_{t-1} x_i^{t-1}$$

we get a system of k independent and equivalent equations related to the corresponding co-ordinates. Now the combiner can ask participant P_i to use the base b to determine the required representation of their share. If the new threshold is t' ($t' > t$), the combiner requests α subshares $s_{i,j}$; $j = 1, \ldots, \alpha$ such that $t' \times \alpha = t \times k$, and the system of linear equations has a unique solution for vectors $a_i = (a_{i,0}, \ldots, a_{i,k-1})$. The combiner must get $t \times k$ linear equations and all $t \times k$ unknowns $a_{i,j}$ ($i = 0, \ldots, t-1$ and $j = 0, \ldots, k-1$) must be "covered". The role of the combiner is to ask the participants for "right" subshares so the combiner can cover all unknowns. The presented method can be applied in all linear secret sharing schemes. The encoding may be based on any vector space.

6 Conclusions

In this paper we considered the problem of changing threshold when there is no secure channel to be used for the purpose of threshold change. One of the main motivation for this study was to provide robustness in a system where communication channels to the combiner have been tapped. We gave a number of constructions of threshold changeable schemes, including one that is optimal with respect to storage and communication costs. We made some initial remarks on the interesting problem of enabling the threshold of an arbitrary threshold scheme to be changed. Finding efficient and practical solutions to this latter problem remains open. We acknowledge useful discussions with Christine O'Keefe and Peter Wild concerning the design and correctness of the geometric construction.

References

1. G. R. Blakley. Safeguarding cryptographic keys. *Proceedings of AFIPS 1979 National Computer Conference*, 48:313–317, 1979.
2. B. Blakley, G.R. Blakley, A.H. Chan and J. Massey. Threshold schemes with disenrolment. *Advances in Cryptology – CRYPTO '92, Lecture Notes in Comput. Sci.*, 740:540–548, 1993.
3. G. R. Blakley and C. Meadows. Security of ramp schemes. *Advances in Cryptology – Proceedings of CRYPTO '84, Lecture Notes in Comput. Sci.*, 196:242-268, 1985.
4. C. Blundo, A. Cresti, A. De Santis and U. Vaccaro. Fully dynamic secret sharing schemes. *Advances in Cryptology – CRYPTO '93, Lecture Notes in Comput. Sci.*, 773:110–125, 1993.
5. R. Capocelli, A. Santis, L. Gargano, and U. Vaccaro. On the size of shares for secret sharing schemes. *Advances in Cryptology - CRYPTO '91, Lecture Notes in Comput. Sci.*, 576:101–113, 1992. also, Journal of Cryptology, vol. 6, no. 3, pp. 157-167, 1993.
6. Y. Desmedt. Threshold cryptography. *European Transactions on Telecommunications*, 5(41):449–457, 1994.
7. Y. Desmedt and S. Jajodia. Redistributing secret shares to new access structures and its applications. *Preprint*.
8. W.-A. Jackson and K.M. Martin. Geometric secret sharing schemes and their duals. *Des. Codes Cryptogr.*, 4:83-95, 1994.
9. W.-A. Jackson and K.M. Martin. A combinatorial interpretation of ramp schemes. *Australasian Journal of Combinatorics*, 14:51–60, 1996.
10. A. Herzberg, S. Jarecki, H. Krawczyk, and M. Yung. Proactive secret sharing or: how to cope with perpetual leakage. *Advances in Cryptology - CRYPTO '95, Lecture Notes in Comput. Sci.*, 963:339–352, 1995.
11. J.W.P. Hirschfeld. *Projective geometries over finite fields*. Clarendon Press, Oxford, 1979.
12. E. Karnin, J. Greene, and M. Hellman. On secret sharing systems. *IEEE Transactions on Information Theory*, vol. IT-29: 35–41, 1983.
13. K.M. Martin. Untrustworthy participants in secret sharing schemes. *Cryptography and Coding III*, Oxford University Press, 255–264, 1993.
14. K.M. Martin, R.Safavi-Naini and H.Wang. Bounds and techniques for efficient redistribution of secret shares to new access structures. *Preprint*.
15. A. Shamir. How to share a secret. *Communications of the ACM*, 22:612–613, 1979.
16. G. Simmons. How to (really) share a secret. *Advances in Cryptology – CRYPTO '88, Lecture Notes in Comput. Sci.*, 403:390–448, 1990.
17. D.R. Stinson. An explication of secret sharing schemes. *Des. Codes Cryptogr.*, 2:357–390, 1992.

A Self-Certified Group-Oriented Cryptosystem Without a Combiner

Shahrokh Saeednia[1] and Hossein Ghodosi[2]

[1] Université Libre de Bruxelles, Département d'Informatique
CP 212, Boulevard du Triomphe, 1050 Bruxelles, Belgium, saeednia@ulb.ac.be

[2] University of Wollongong, Department of Computer Science
Northfields Ave., Wollongong 2522, Australia, hossein@uow.edu.au

Abstract. In a (t, n) group-oriented cryptosystem, collaboration of at least t participants is required to perform the group transformation. Two important issues in implementation of a such cryptosystems are:
1. the sender needs to collect authenticated public keys of the intended receivers;
2. the combiner needs a secure channel to collect (privately) the partial results from collaborating participants.

This paper discusses the above problems and proposes a (t, n) group-oriented cryptosystem that works with self-certified public keys, with no help of any combiner.

1 Introduction

Cryptography provides tools for the implementation of secure services that guarantee protection of legal rights of individuals and groups. In general, implementations of such services become more complex for groups than for individuals, as groups can exhibit different structures and richer relations among participants. Clearly, the security requirements can vary widely depending upon the size of the group and its internal structure.

The notion of society-oriented cryptography was introduced by Desmedt [1]. Unlike classical cryptography, society-oriented cryptography allows groups of cooperating participants to carry out cryptographic transformations. Of course, members of a group still perform some partial transformations independently. To obtain the group transformation, however, they need to cooperate by passing their partial transformations to the so-called *combiner*. If a subset of the cooperating participants is authorised, the combiner can successfully perform the required group transformation. A more precise definition of society-oriented cryptography may be stated as follows:

A society-oriented cryptographic system is a protocol which allows to distribute the power of performing a cryptographic operation among a group of participants such that:

1. only designated subsets (so called, the authorised sets) of the group can perform the required cryptographic operation, but unauthorised sets cannot do so.

2. the knowledge of partial transformations corresponding to an authorised set of participants (in performance of a particular cryptographic transformation) must not help an unauthorised set to perform any other cryptographic transformation relating to the group.

Society-oriented cryptographic systems can be classified into two broad classes. If the group that performs the cryptographic operation is with anonymous membership, then the society-oriented cryptographic system is called a *threshold cryptographic system*, (even though the internal structure of the group is not a threshold structure). On the other hand, if the group is with known members, then the society-oriented cryptographic system is called a *group-oriented cryptographic system*.

Although only a small fraction of all groups in our society are groups with known members, there exists numerous examples to justify the needs for group-oriented cryptography. For example, suppose the Federal Bank wishes to send a message such that a particular set of banks according to an access structure [1] can decrypt a cryptogram and hence read the message. In this and many other similar examples, the intended group is a group with known members. Each member of the intended group is either an individual or a group with anonymous membership (from cryptographic point of view, groups with anonymous membership act as individuals).

There has not been much research on group-oriented cryptography. Hwang [7] proposed a shared decryption system in which the sender knows the set of receivers. The Hwang system utilises the Diffie-Hellman [2] key distribution scheme, and concatenates the Shamir [11] secret sharing scheme with a *predetermined cryptographic system*. Franklin and Haber [4] also discussed group-oriented cryptosystems. Their system uses the ElGamal cryptosystem and is more efficient than Hwang's system. In [5] a group-oriented decryption system based on the RSA cryptosystem is proposed. This scheme works with the assumption that the authenticated public keys are available from a central key authority or from "White Pages".

2 Group-Oriented Cryptography

Let $\mathcal{U} = \{U_1, \ldots, U_\ell\}$ be the collection of all users in the system. A public-key cryptosystem is associated with each user. That is, k_i and K_i are the public and the secret keys corresponding to the user U_i ($1 \leq i \leq \ell$). The set of all encryption keys is denoted by $\mathcal{E} = \{k_1, \ldots, k_\ell\}$. By $\mathcal{M}$ and $\mathcal{C}$, we denote the set of all messages and cryptograms, respectively.

---

[1] The group of intended receivers and the access structure that determines how the cryptogram can be decrypted are chosen by the sender.

A group-oriented cryptosystem is implemented by the sender. It is at the sender's discretion to create a subgroup $\mathcal{P} \subseteq \mathcal{U}$ of users for whom he encrypts a message. In addition, the sender determines a subgroup $\mathcal{A} \subseteq \mathcal{P}$ of intended receivers who are able to decrypt (collectively) a cryptogram generated by the sender. The sender also determines the access policy in the intended group.

An interesting class of all access structures is the threshold access structure. In this paper, we assume that the access policy in the intended group is threshold. A set $\mathcal{A} \subseteq \mathcal{P}$ retrieves the message only if $|\mathcal{A}| \geq t$ (t is chosen by the sender). More precisely, a (t, n) group-oriented cryptosystem is such that:

- any set of t or more participants makes the required cryptographic operation easily computable;
- any set of $t - 1$ or fewer participants cannot perform the required cryptographic operation;
- knowledge of partial transformations corresponding to an authorised set of users to perform a particular cryptographic transformation, does not help an unauthorised set of users to perform any other cryptographic transformation regarding to the group.

2.1 The Problems

A (t, n) group-oriented cryptographic system is a collection of two main algorithms:

1. sender, who composes the group $\mathcal{P} \subseteq \mathcal{U}$ of intended receivers (without loss of generality, we assume that the n first indexes are chosen; that is, $\mathcal{P} = \{U_1, \ldots, U_n\}$), selects the threshold parameter t, collects authenticated public keys $\{k_1, \ldots, k_n\} \in \mathcal{E}^n$ of users of the group $\mathcal{P}$, and applies the encryption function

$$E : \mathcal{M} \times \mathcal{E}^n \to \mathcal{C}.$$

The sender dispatches the cryptogram $C \in \mathcal{C}$ to the members of the group $\mathcal{P}$.

2. combiner, who collects partial decryptions from a set $\mathcal{A} \subseteq \mathcal{P}$ (for the sake of simplicity assume that $\mathcal{A} = \{U_1, \ldots, U_d\}$) and decrypts the cryptogram as

$$f_{COM} : \Delta_1 \times \ldots \times \Delta_d \to \mathcal{M}$$

where Δ_i is the set of partial decryptions for U_i ($i = 1, \ldots, d$). The decryption is always successful if the number of cooperating participants is equal to or greater than the threshold parameter; that is, $d \geq t$.

Two important issues in implementation of a group-oriented cryptosystem is to handle the following problems:

1. how the sender collects *authenticated public keys*?
2. how the combiner privately collects *partial decryptions*?

Problem with collecting authenticated public keys When an individual wishes to encrypt a message for a group of users, he has first to collect their public keys (that are assumed to be stored in a public directory) and make sure that they actually correspond to those users. This assurance may clearly not be obtained, if each user is responsible for creating his pair of keys and publishing his public key in a directory, because with such a system, nothing can prevent adversaries to make fake keys related to a given user[2].

The obvious solution to this problem is to provide authenticated public keys by connecting users' public keys to their identities. There are three known approaches that require the existence of a trusted authority.

In the simplest approach, which is often called *certificate-based*, the authority creates a *certificate* for each user, after having checked carefully his identity. In this case, each user visiting the authority is given a certificate of the form $R = S(k, I)$, where I is an identification string based on the user's identity (prepared by the authority), k is the user's public key and S is the authority's signature. The certificate will then be registered in a public directory together with user's public key and his identity. Whenever a user A needs to encrypt a message for another user B, he gets (R_B, k_B, I_B) from the directory and checks the validity of the authority's signatures on the pair (k_B, I_B), using the authority's public key (that everybody is assumed to know). This approach, though having the advantage that even the authority does not know users' secret keys, requires a large amount of storage and computation (which essentially depends on the signature scheme in use).

Another approach, known as *identity-based*, is proposed by Shamir [12] and has been adopted in many public key schemes. The advantage of this method is that the user's identity serves as his public key and the related secret key is computed by some trapdoor originated by the authority, so that nobody can determine a valid pair of public and secret keys without knowing that trapdoor. This leads to a scheme that needs no certificate and no verification of signatures, hence, reducing the amount of storage and computation. This method has, however, the disadvantage that the secret keys are known to the authority.

A more sophisticated technique combining the advantages of certificate-based and identity-based methods is proposed by Girault [6], which is known as *self-certified*. In this approach, (contrary to identity-based schemes) each user chooses his secret key and creates a shadow w of that secret key using a one-way function and gives it to the authority. Then, (in contrast to certificate-based schemes) instead of creating a certificate, the authority computes the public key k from the pair (w, I), in such a way that k may not be computed without the knowledge of some trapdoor, while w may be easily determined from k, I.

In this paper, we adopt the latter approach to guarantee the authenticity of the public keys.

---

[2] Even if there is an authority that controls the public directory and protect the write access to it, an adversary can still substitute a public key on the transmission line between the user who is asking that public key and the server which supports the public directory.

Problem with collecting partial decryption It is well known that in society-oriented (threshold or group-oriented) systems everyone who knows the partial results computed by at least t authorised users can also compute the final result. Consequently, it is very important to send partial results to the combiner privately. In some situations, where collaborating participants belong to a closed organisation (e.g., they work together in the same building) this may not be a serious problem, since they usually have no problem for sending their partial results to the combiner (that can be a member of that organisation as well) via internal mail or personally and in private.

However, this is not the case in most group-oriented cryptographic systems in which the participants of the intended group are either individuals or organisations far in distance. Therefore, in group-oriented cryptosystems, in order to transmit the partial decryptions to the combiner a secure channel is usually needed between the collaborating participants and the combiner. Of course, providing the secure channel is expensive and it may not be available when the group decryption is required.

3 The Scheme

In order to avoid the above mentioned problems, we present a group-oriented cryptosystem which utilises self-certified public keys and works with no help of any combiner.

3.1 Implementation of Self-Certified Public Keys

As in all self-certified schemes, our system assumes the existence of an authority that delivers certified public keys to the legitimate users.

Setup Phase: In this phase, the authority chooses:

- an integer N as the product of two large distinct random primes p and q of almost the same size such that $p = 2p' + 1$ and $q = 2q' + 1$, where p' and q' are also prime integers,
- a prime $F > N$,
- a base $\alpha \neq 1$ of order $r = p'q'$ modulo N, and
- a one-way hash function h, that outputs integers less than the minimum value of p' and q', that is, $h(m) < \min(p', q')$.

The authority makes α, h, F and N public, keeps r secret and discards p and q.

Key Generation: Now, every legitimate user, who wishes to receive messages, chooses his secret key x, computes the shadow $z = \alpha^x \pmod{N}$ and gives it to the authority. The authority first interrogates the user about his secret key using an authentication protocol (e.g., a variation of the Schnorr authentication scheme [10] with composite modulus) who must prove his knowledge of x, which is required to be a positive integer. If the authority is convinced of this fact, it prepares a string I corresponding to the user's identity (his name, his address, ...) and computes $ID = h(I)$. Then, it computes the user's public key as

$$y = (z^{-1} - ID)^{ID^{-1}} \pmod{N}.$$

Note that the inverse of ID modulo r always exists,
   due to the fact that h outputs integers less than p' and q', which guarantees that ID is co-prime to r, for any I.
   Note also that, the user's proof of knowledge of his secret key and the fact that it should be a positive integer is very important, as we will see further in this paper.

3.2 Implementation of a (t, n) Group-Oriented Cryptosystem

Suppose an individual wants to send a message $0 \le m < N$ to a group $\mathcal{P} = \{U_1, \ldots, U_n\}$ of n users of his choice, such that cooperation of any t members of the group is sufficient to retrieve the message.

Encryption: The sender,

- randomly chooses an integer k and computes $c = (\alpha^{-1})^k \pmod{N}$,
- forms at random a polynomial $g(x) = a_0 + a_1 x + \ldots + a_{t-1} x^{t-1}$ in $GF(F)$ such that $g(0) = a_0 = \alpha^{h(m)} \pmod{N}$,
- computes for $i = 1, \ldots, n$

$$
\begin{aligned}
w_i &= y_i^{ID_i} + ID_i \pmod{N} \\
s_i &= w_i^k \pmod{N} \\
d_i &= g(s_i) \\
e_i &= m \cdot w_i^{h(m)} \pmod{N}
\end{aligned}
$$

and sends (t, c, d_i, e_i) to each U_i.

Decryption: Upon receiving the cryptogram, every group, $\mathcal{A} \subseteq \mathcal{P}$, of at least t intended receivers can cooperate to retrieve the plaintext message m. That is, each $U_i \in \mathcal{A}$ first calculates,

$$s_i = c^{x_i} \pmod{N},$$

and broadcasts the pair (d_i, s_i). When t values of such pairs are broadcasted, each U_i can recover $v = \alpha^{h(m)} \pmod{N}$, which allows him to compute the plaintext message as,

$$m = v^{x_i} e_i \pmod{N}.$$

Verification: Since a group of cheating participants can broadcast false pairs (d_i, s_i) to prevent the honest participants to compute the plaintext message, each participant needs to verify the correctness of the message that he has computed. For this purpose, after having computed the message m, each U_i checks,

$$\alpha^{h(m)} \stackrel{?}{\equiv} v \pmod{N}.$$

If the equation holds true, the retrieved message is valid otherwise another collaboration of the intended group can recover the secret, if there exists at least t honest participants in the group.

4 Security Analysis

In this section we briefly consider two main issues regarding the above cryptosystem, i.e., forging identities and the ability of decrypting messages by adversaries.

Theorem 1. *Under the assumption that factoring large intergers and computing discrete logarithms are difficult, it is computationally infeasible to create a pair of related secret and public keys for a given ID.*

Proof. (sketch) After computing $z = \alpha^x \pmod{N}$, for a given *ID*, the corresponding y may be computed from the relation

$$y^{ID} \equiv z^{-1} - ID \pmod{N}.$$

However, this means to break an instance of the RSA cryptosystem [9], which is believed to be equivalent to factoring N.

On the other hand, if one first fixes y, then z can be computed from the pair (y, ID) as

$$z = (y^{ID} + ID)^{-1} \pmod{N}.$$

However, in order to determine the related x, one has to solve a hard instance of the discrete logarithm problem with composite modulus, i.e.,

$$\alpha^x \pmod{N} = z.$$

It is interesting to notice that, the authority can still create a pair of forged keys for a given identity, but the existence of more than one public key for a user means that the authority has cheated, since this may only be done by the authority. This is exactly why we proposed to compute the public key as $y = (z^{-1} - ID)^{ID^{-1}} \pmod{N}$ and not $y = z^{-ID^{-1}} \pmod{N}$, because in the latter case any user having a pair of keys (x, y) can create new pairs (kx, y^k) for any value of k. As a result, a cheating authority could not be distinguished from a cheating user.

Theorem 2. *No group of less than t intended receivers can decrypt a message if both problems of factoring large integers and computing discrete logarithms are difficult.*

Proof. (sketch) To decrypt a message, it is essential to know at least

$$v = \alpha^{h(m)} \pmod{N}.$$

Hence, we utilised Shamir's (t, n) threshold scheme for sharing this value as a secret. This means that the calculation of v needs the knowledge of at least t pairs (d_i, s_i). So, if $t - 1$ participants $\{U_1, \ldots, U_{j-1}, U_{j+1}, \ldots, U_t\}$ try to recover v, then they need to know s_j which is actually equal to

$$\alpha^{-k x_j} \pmod{N}.$$

However, knowing that

$$c = \alpha^{-k} \pmod{N} \qquad \text{and} \qquad z_j = \alpha^{x_j} \pmod{N}$$

but without the knowledge of neither x_j nor k, one has obviously to solve a Diffie-Hellman problem with composite modulus which is proven to be equivalent to factoring N and computing discrete logarithms modulo each prime factor[3].

Note that, without using an authentication protocol at the key generation phase to verify the knowledge of the secret keys, a cheating user C may join the system in a very special way in order to take advantage of some particular situations that we discuss hereafter.

Instead of computing z with the predetermined protocol, C who knows two public keys y_1 and y_2 already in use, computes

$$y_i^{ID_i} + ID_i = w_i \pmod{N}, \qquad i = 1, 2$$

and sets his own shadow to be

$$z = (w_1 w_2)^{-1} \pmod{N}.$$

Now, C presents z to the authority, which delivers as usual C's public key as $y = (z^{-1} - ID)^{ID^{-1}} \pmod{N}$.

Although C does not know the secret key corresponding to shadow z, when a message is sent to a group including C and the two users U_1 and U_2 corresponding to y_1 and y_2, C may decrypt the message. To do so, C sees e_1 and e_2 transmitted to them and gets his own message data, including $e = m \cdot z^{-h(m)} \pmod{N}$. Thus, C computes

$$e_1 e_2 e^{-1} \pmod{N} = m \cdot (w_1 w_2)^{h(m)} \cdot z^{h(m)} = m$$

without needing partial results from other participants.

This attack is very useful in situations where the quorum of t honest participants is not reached, which means that other members of the group cannot decrypt the message.

---

[3] This problem has been considered by McCurley [8] and is proven to be hard as long as at least one of the problems of computing discrete logarithms and factoring large integers remains intractable.

When the authority requires a proof of knowledge of the secret key, then C fails because he does not know the discrete logarithm of z he has computed as above. However, the attack would still work if C cooperates with U_1 and U_2. In this case, the discrete logarithm of z is obviously $-(x_1 + x_2)$ that is a negative integer. To compute a positive integer equivalent to this, one has to know r that is authority's secret. This is why we required that x be a positive integer.

Theorem 3. *It is computationally infeasible to decrypt a message without knowing one of the x_j's.*

Proof. (sketch) Although broadcasting the pairs (d_i, s_i) enables everyone to compute $v = \alpha^{h(m)} \pmod{N}$, the knowledge of v cannot help the adversaries to recover m. Without knowing one of the x_j's, computing the message m from the pair v and e_j is straightforwardly equivalent to breaking the ElGamal cryptosystem [3] with composite modulus, which is known to be equivalent to factoring large integers and solving discrete logarithms.

5 Conclusions

The paper proposed a (t, n) group-oriented cryptosystem that utilises self-certified public keys and works with no help of any combiner. We showed that in order to decrypt a message one needs to know at least t pairs (d_i, s_i). However, it is still possible to cheat if there does not exist t honest participants in the group. In fact, if $t - 1$ participants transmit their shares then any of the other $n - (t - 1)$ participants have enough information to recover the original message while none of those $t-1$ participants may decrypt the message successfully. In the full paper, we show how to prevent this problem.

Acknowledgements

The authors wish to thank anonymous referees for their helpful suggestions. The second author also would like to thank the University of Tehran for financial support of his study.

References

1. Y. Desmedt, "Society and group oriented cryptography: A new concept," in *Advances in Cryptology - Proceedings of CRYPTO '87* (C. Pomerance, ed.), vol. 293 of *Lecture Notes in Computer Science*, pp. 120–127, Springer-Verlag, 1988.
2. W. Diffie and M. Hellman, "New Directions in Cryptography," *IEEE Trans. on Inform. Theory*, vol. IT-22, pp. 644–654, Nov. 1976.
3. T. ElGamal, "A Public Key Cryptosystem and a Signature Scheme Based on Discrete Logarithms, " *IEEE Trans. On Inform. Theory*, vol. 31, pp. 469-472, 1985.
4. M. Franklin and S. Haber, "Joint Encryption and Message-Efficient Secure Computation," in *Advances in Cryptology - Proceedings of CRYPTO '93* (D. Stinson, ed.), vol. 773 of *Lecture Notes in Computer Science*, pp. 266–277, Springer-Verlag, 1994.

5. H. Ghodosi, J. Pieprzyk, and R. Safavi-Naini, "Dynamic Threshold Cryptosystems: A New Scheme in Group Oriented Cryptography," in *Proceedings of PRAGOCRYPT '96 –International Conference on the Theory and Applications of Cryptology* (J. Přibyl, ed.), (Prague, Czech Republic), pp. 370–379, CTU Publishing house, ISBN: 80-01-01502-5, 1996.

6. M. Girault, "Self-Certified Public Keys," in *Advances in Cryptology - Proceedings of EUROCRYPT '91* (D. Davies, ed.), vol. 547 of *Lecture Notes in Computer Science*, pp. 490–497, Springer-Verlag, 1991.

7. T. Hwang, "Cryptosystem for Group Oriented Cryptography," in *Advances in Cryptology - Proceedings of EUROCRYPT '90* (I. Damgård, ed.), vol. 473 of *Lecture Notes in Computer Science*, pp. 352–360, Springer-Verlag, 1991.

8. M. McCurley, "A Key Distribution System Equivalent to Factoring," *Journal of Cryptology*, vol. 1, no. 2, pp. 95–105, 1988.

9. R. Rivest, A. Shamir, and L. Adleman, "A Method for Obtaining Digital Signatures and Public-Key Cryptosystems," *Communications of the ACM*, vol. 21, pp. 120–126, Feb. 1978.

10. C. Schnorr, "Efficient Signature Generation by Smart Cards, " *Journal of Cryptology*, vol. 4, no. 3, , pp. 161–174, 1991.

11. A. Shamir, "How to Share a Secret," in *Communications of the ACM*, vol. 22, pp. 612–613, Nov. 1979.

12. A. Shamir, "Identity-Based Cryptosystems and Signature Schemes, " in *Advances in Cryptology - Proceedings of Crypto '84* (G. Blakley and D. Chaum, eds.), vol. 196 of *Lecture Notes in Computer Science*, pp. 47–53, Springer-Verlag, 1985.

Companion Viruses and the Macintosh: Threats and Countermeasures

Jeffrey Horton and Jennifer Seberry

Centre for Computer Security Research
School of Information Technology and Computer Science
University of Wollongong
Northfields Avenue, Wollongong
{jeffh, j.seberry}@cs.uow.edu.au

Abstract. This paper reports on how some features of the Macintosh operating system, versions 7.1 through 8.1 and perhaps later versions, could be used to implement a virus attack unlike any seen previously on the Macintosh, but which bears some resemblance to a "Companion Virus" style of attack as seen under MS-DOS. We briefly discuss some methods used in the implementation of companion viruses under MS-DOS, and also examine techniques used by other Macintosh viruses. Following an examination of the details of our attack, we discuss generic countermeasures to a virus using the attack, one of which in particular appears very effective against the attack.

1 Introduction

The Macintosh virus world is not as active as that of PC and PC-compatible computers. There are only a few dozen Macintosh viruses and variants of those viruses known, not counting macro viruses. To the best of the authors' knowledge, the techniques described here are not employed by any existing Macintosh virus.

A "companion virus" is a variety of computer virus which avoids modifying the files that it "infects". Having discovered what we considered a weakness in the Macintosh operating system, which could potentially be exploited to construct a computer virus of this type which has been previously unknown on the Macintosh, we decided to explore the consequences of this in more detail, and to attempt to devise some countermeasures to the attack that could be implemented by anti-virus software to enhance its effectiveness against a virus employing these techniques. Macintosh users and anti-virus vendors should be aware of the possibilities we outline.

Implementations of companion viruses under MS-DOS will be briefly explained in Section 1.2. The dangers posed by a companion virus attack are outlined in Section 1.3. Section 2 gives an overview of common techniques used in viruses on the Macintosh. Background on workings and features of the Macintosh operating system exploited by the attack we describe is covered in Section 3.

Details of the attack and some thoughts on detecting and countering the attack are covered in Section 4.

In the interests of not supplying sufficient information to allow the easy implementation of a functioning virus, only the basic ideas behind the attack will be discussed. We feel that the security community is better able to respond to a potential security problem of this nature with some degree of foreknowledge of the problem. We present some ideas on how it might be combated.

1.1 What is a Computer Virus?

The formal definition of a computer virus, due to Dr. F. Cohen, has been used to prove a variety of interesting results [1, pp. 164–187][2]. However, a more accessible English definition that is still thought to describe the essential elements of computer viruses in practice is:

> We define a computer 'virus' as a self-replicating program that can 'infect' other programs by modifying them or their environment such that a call to an 'infected' program implies a call to a possibly evolved, and in most cases, functionally similar copy of the 'virus'. [3]

The term "infect", where used, is used with respect to computer viruses in the sense of the definition above throughout the remainder of this document.

Computer viruses fall into a number of different classes, with some degree of overlap, such as **file infectors**, which modify various executable objects, for example .EXE and .COM files under MS-DOS, to contain the viral code, or **boot sector infectors**, which replace or modify the machine instructions stored on disk and executed as part of system startup.

Another of the varieties of computer virus is the **companion virus**.

1.2 What is a Companion Virus?

A companion virus is of interest because it does not modify any of the files which it infects. Instead, it creates a separate executable file to hold the virus body. Implementations of such a virus depend on the operating system; two basic types of companion virus which could be created under MS-DOS are [4, 5]:

Regular Companion [4] or Corresponding File Virus [5]:
Creates a file in the same directory as the target of infection but with a filename extension which the operating system chooses to execute before that of the original file when the extension is not explicitly specified (for example, under MS-DOS a .COM file with the same name as a .EXE file and in the same directory is executed before the .EXE file if the file extension is not specified).

PATH Companion:
Create a file with any executable extension in a directory that is searched for executable files before the directory containing the target of infection. Named after the PATH environment variables found in operating systems such as MS-DOS and UNIX.

Magruder [5] also discusses "surrogate file viruses", a type of companion virus which renames the executable file being infected and replaces it with a copy of the virus program.

The Macintosh, however, does not have the concept of a "path" which is followed when searching for executable files, relied upon by the path companion virus, or the notion of filename extensions, relied upon by a regular companion virus. However, several features of the Macintosh operating system enable an attack that appears very similar in conception if not in execution.

1.3 Dangers of Companion Viruses

Bontchev [4] describes companion viruses as one possible attack against an anti-virus measure known as an **integrity checker**. Magruder [5] also discusses the possibility that a companion virus infection may be missed by an integrity checker that is not aware of this type of attack.

An integrity checker works by computing some variety of hash or checksum (a "signature") of files believed to be at risk of infection by a virus. These signatures are stored, and at some future date may be recomputed and compared to the originals; if there is a difference, then the file corresponding to that signature has changed, and this change may be the result of a virus infection — many common viruses infect executable code by altering it in some way, and an integrity checker detects the modifications made by the virus. They can be useful in detecting the presence of known and unknown viruses.

However, integrity checkers are not able to detect companion viruses by this approach, as these viruses do not alter any file which is a target of infection. Instead, they alter the environment of the file. So to detect this type of virus, an integrity checker must be modified to also monitor changes in a file's environment. For example, under MS-DOS the appearance of a .COM file in the same directory as a .EXE file, where none had been observed previously, would be a suspicious occurrence that an integrity checker could detect. Checking directory modification times might also prove useful. A virus-specific anti-virus measure could then be applied to determine if the suspicious occurrence is the result of a virus.

2 How Macintosh Viruses Work

Most existing Macintosh viruses infect executable code intended to run on a Macintosh based on one of the Motorola MC680x0 series of microprocessors. The first Macintosh computers based on PowerPC microprocessors were introduced in 1994, ultimately replacing the 680x0 in new computers. Programs containing code only for 680x0-based Macintoshes continue to function because operating system software running on the new microprocessors provides an emulator for 680x0 code [6, Ch. 1]. Most viruses are written for 680x0-based Macintoshes; they continue to be a threat to 680x0-based applications on PowerPC-based Macintoshes as a consequence of the compatibility provided by this emulator.

The following discussion relating to the organization of executable code on a Macintosh applies only to applications containing code intended for a 680x0-based Macintosh.

Every Macintosh file is composed of two forks, a data fork and a resource fork. The data fork contains a file's data — for example, a text file would contain ASCII text in the data fork. The resource fork contains a file's **resources**. An application program's resource fork contains the application's executable code [7, p. 1-4]. Resources within a particular file are described by a resource type (a four-letter code), and an ID number (2-byte signed integer).

The executable code for an application is usually divided up into a number of segments, each segment stored in a "CODE" resource. Only some of these must be in memory at certain times; code segments will be loaded when needed and may be unloaded when not required. This enables large application programs to be run in limited memory. Segment loading, and references from one segment to a routine located in another segment are coordinated using a table created when the executable code is linked by a compiler. This table, the **jump table**, is stored as the "CODE" resource of ID 0 [8, Ch. 7]. The first entry in the jump table specifies the first code that will be executed when an application is run.

A virus that infects an application program then has two ways in which it may proceed. First, it may add a new code segment to the application's resource fork, and adjust the jump table to refer to the new segment, usually as the first code that is called when the application starts executing. Having performed its startup tasks, the virus can replace the original jump table entry, saved during the infection process, and jump to it. This strategy is used by the nVIR family of viruses [9] and also by the INIT 29 virus [10], among others.

Second, a virus might instead choose to append its code to an existing code resource, perhaps not modifying the jump table at all. Complications can arise due to resource size limitations, however. The ZUC family of viruses are an example of the use of this strategy [11].

Such a virus is presented with a problem in becoming permanently resident in memory, and arranging for calls to virus code at a later time. Patches may be applied to many calls provided by the Macintosh operating system, but will only have global effect when applied at system startup [12, p. 8-9]. So many viruses that infect application programs also infect the operating system, either directly or by infecting a system extension that loads at startup, so that virus code is executed when the computer is rebooted. Otherwise, the virus will cease to be effective once an application exits. The nVIR family [9] and INIT 29 [10] are examples of viruses that behave this way. Viruses of the ZUC family infect applications only, not the operating system, however [13].

Patching can also be used by anti-virus programs, to attempt to detect signs of virus activity. The suspicious activity could perhaps be blocked, logged, or reported to the user.

Other viruses work by modifying or overriding code used by the operating system. The WDEF virus worked by overriding the code used by the operating system to draw windows on the screen, and did not involve making any modifications to application programs or making direct modifications to the operating system [14]. Some of these viruses are no longer effective, as operating system features on which they depended were changed or removed [15].

One recent virus-like program, the **AutoStart** worm [16], uses techniques not seen previously in Macintosh viruses. It relies on a feature of **QuickTime**, Apple Computer's software architecture for creating and viewing digital media. The AutoStart feature allows an application to be designated for automatic execution whenever disks are mounted. When the virus is executed, the operating system is infected. The virus becomes active on the next reboot, searching periodically for other media, like floppy disks, to infect. This virus/worm spreads well, but is easy to remove by hand. The AutoStart feature may be disabled to prevent future infection.

We describe here techniques which could potentially be used by a virus, which do not involve any modification of application programs or the operating system during the process of infection, unlike most of the techniques outlined above. We feel the style of the attack is very similar to that employed by companion viruses under an operating system such as MS-DOS; hence the name.

3   More Macintosh Basics

This section explains some aspects of the Macintosh file system and operating system which will be required to understand the description of the attack to follow. These details, and the attack description, are valid with respect to versions of the Macintosh operating system from 7.1, which is now several years old, to 8.1, the latest available to the authors when this paper was prepared.

3.1   File Types and Creators

Every file used on a Macintosh computer has both a **file type** and **file creator** associated with it.

The **file creator** is a four-byte code, usually a combination of various ASCII characters, which is identical to that of the application program (the package of executable code which is executed directly by the computer user in a variety of possible ways; henceforth it will be referred to simply as the "application") responsible for creating that particular file. Each application in turn defines a number of **file types**, each of which is another four-byte code, again usually a combination of various ASCII characters, that describes the nature of the data stored in the file. These codes need have meaning only to the application concerned.

Files of certain types may be used by many different applications. For example, files of type TEXT are files that consist of plain ASCII text that requires no special handling, so that they may be viewed and altered by applications other than the creating application. A file of type APPL is the common variety of executable program file of most interest to a computer user (there are several other types of executable files which are not of interest here).

An application typically defines an **icon**, or small graphical symbol, for each file type which can be created by that application, to help users easily determine which application was responsible for creating the file.

3.2 The Desktop Database

The Desktop Database is a collection of information maintained and used by the operating system. Its format does not appear to have been publicly documented. The function of the Desktop Database which is of interest is that it stores information about the location and creation date of applications. Information about the icons used by files created by particular applications is also stored here.

Not every type of disk has a Desktop Database. For example, floppy disks (storing about 1.4 megabytes) do not have a Desktop Database, but instead have a simpler structure which performs similar functions. Our attention here is confined to disks which do have Desktop Databases, such as hard disks, or for which one is created, such as AppleShare volumes [17, pp. 9-3–9-4].

The Desktop Database is used when the operating system creates its graphical display of windows and icons — the icon that should be displayed for a file with a certain type and creator may be determined using the Desktop Database.

It is also of use when determining which application program should be started when the user opens a file, if an application with the appropriate creator code is not already executing. Commonly this is done by double-clicking on the file concerned using the mouse, although there are other methods which achieve the same effect. In order to make use of this file, the operating system must start an application which can interpret the contents of the file.

Usually there will be a single application with a certain creator code on a disk. However, it is possible to have several applications with the same creator code on the one disk. Although according to a technical note [18] the application which is the "first choice" is the one with whose information the Desktop Database was last updated, correcting earlier documentation stating that the "first choice" application was the one with the most recent creation date [17, p. 9-5], it appears that in most cases the application selected will be the one with the most recent creation date. Even after rebuilding the Desktop Database, a process that may be initiated by the user and which is sometimes useful in troubleshooting, the application selected is the one with the most recent creation date. It is critical to the attack described in Section 4 that the application selected for execution be the viral application.

3.3 Starting an Application

When the user starts an application by opening a file or files in some manner, the application is notified by the operating system of the files that were selected by the user.

This is accomplished using an **Apple Event**, which is a type of high-level event commonly used for interapplication communication. There are many different types of Apple Event, and applications may define their own. In the case being considered here, the operating system sends an "Open Document" (odoc) Apple Event to the application when it has started executing to inform the application of the location of the files that the user wishes to open using that application.

Not all application programs support receiving Apple Events; a program that does not support these events is not a candidate for infection by the method we will describe. Applications may provide Apple Event support but don't themselves "own" any files; as will be seen, such applications are not good candidates for infection. However, many common application programs that create files that are "owned" by that application support these events, and would be more difficult for users to work with if they did not.

4   A Macintosh "Companion Virus"

How might these facilities provided by the operating system be used to implement a viral attack? If the application required is not already running and is not specified, only the documents that are to be processed, then the operating system must identify and execute the appropriate application(s) itself, passing an event to the application to inform it of the documents it is to process. When there exists more than one application on a given disk with the particular creator code, the operating system selects the one with the most recent creation date.

So it suffices to infect an application by creating an application program with the same creator code as the other application that is the target of infection, but with a more recent creation date, such that the operating system executes the viral application in preference to the application which is the target of infection.

Then, when an infected application is launched, to make it seem as though everything is normal, the viral application performs the following tasks:

1. Intercepts the event intended for the infected application which is sent by the operating system; and
2. Runs the infected application and forwards it the intercepted event; soon after completing this step, the viral application would exit, to avoid easy detection.

There are a number of other details which must be handled to create an effective virus. As an example of these details, it is useful to preserve the original application icon information, which is usually overridden by the icons applicable to the more recently created application, so that visual displays look unchanged. We are reluctant to discuss solutions to such problems here, in the interests of not revealing enough information to easily create an effective virus.

It is possible to extend the implementation to handle Apple Events sent to a newly-launched application under other circumstances and that require different handling. However, the presence of the viral application can result in behaviour that differs slightly from that of the pre-infection state.

Cooperating applications might use other types of high-level events that are not Apple Events. We consider this to be sufficiently uncommon that the possibility is not addressed here.

Clearly this attack bears some resemblance to a companion virus style of attack as described in Section 1.2.

It should be noted that it is certainly possible to specify exactly which application program is to be used to manipulate a particular file or files; such a virus would rely on the fact that it is more convenient to permit the operating system to identify and run an application than to perform this task manually.

Some consideration has been given to how such a virus might become resident in memory; that is, how it might place viral code somewhere in memory and arrange for it to be executed at some time in the future, long after the viral application itself has ceased to run. Installing a device driver is one possible option. Device drivers are not required to deal with devices at all; other uses have been found for them. A device driver can elect to receive calls from the operating system to perform periodic tasks — in the case of a companion virus, such a periodic task could be searching the list of currently running application programs, infecting any that appear to be uninfected.

4.1 Detection

The mere presence of several applications with the same creator code on a Macintosh computer system is not something which should cause any alarm, and is not enough to conclude that an application program has been infected by a companion-type virus. This situation commonly arises when, for example, a new version of an application package is installed without removing the previous version. An integrity checker would need to monitor other information to help it decide how alarming the presence of multiple applications with the same creator code is. For example, as a companion virus would most likely be a much smaller file and of a simpler structure than an application that has some more useful functionality, the presence of two application programs with the same creator code but very different sizes or structures might be considered suspicious.

It would be useful for an integrity checker to keep track of the locations of legitimate applications, and require authorisation from the user to recognise a new or moved application. An integrity checker that is aware of legitimately installed applications can consult the Desktop Database for a specific creator code to determine if any new applications have been added.

There are a number of system calls which may be of use in implementing such a virus and which may be considered suspicious by a behaviour monitoring program. A behaviour that is a characteristic of such a virus is a need to launch the infected application. As the viral application and infected application have the same creator codes, if a patch were installed on the operating system routine responsible for launching an application, it could check the creator code of the application originating the request against the creator code of the application being launched, and refuse to launch an application having the same creator code as the one making the request; an indication to the user that suspicious activity has been detected would certainly be appropriate. There are various ways that might be used by a virus to circumvent such a check, but employing this check cuts off the simplest and most straightforward way for one application to launch another application. An occasion where one application might legitimately need to launch another with the same creator code seems most unlikely.

As the virus exists as an application separate to the infected application, checks on the creation of applications may also be effective. Some anti-virus applications will likely include such checks, at least as an option, as it may be effective against other varieties of virus. However, this is not as specifically targeted against a companion virus attack as the previous countermeasure, and would not seem to be appropriate to as wide an environment — for example, people working with compilers may find checks on creation of application programs produce many false alarms.

Under OS 8.0 and 8.1, application files may be marked as "invisible" or be located within invisible directories, and still be executed successfully when a document is double clicked. Under most earlier versions of the operating system, this is not the case[1]. Although under some OS versions applications may be hidden, as there would seem to be no good reasons for this, the presence of such concealed applications could even be seen by an anti-virus program as being suspicious. Substituting a non-hidden application if available for a hidden one at time of execution is a potentially useful strategy. Fixing the operating system to ignore hidden applications would also be a useful strategy.

The possible utility that a device driver might have for a companion virus is discussed in Section 4. There are many legitimate reasons that a program might wish to install a device driver[2]. As a device driver is potentially of use in a virus attack, it would be useful to check drivers for suspicious code that might perform virus-like actions when installed.

Other calls by the virus may also be able to be monitored. For example, the companion virus might use the PBDTAddAPPL call to update the Desktop Database with information about the newly created viral application when performing an infection, rather than waiting for the operating system to update the Desktop Database with information about the new application at some time in the future. Apple documentation discourages the practice of making modifications to the Desktop Database [17, p. 9-3], so it might also be viewed as a suspicious event.

4.2 Demonstration Program

A non-viral application program demonstrating this attack has been created by the authors. The demonstration program has been found to work appropriately in a variety of environments — single and multiple partition Macintosh hard drives, removable media such as Zip disks, and a simple network consisting of two Macintosh computers.

---

[1] Sometimes invisible applications will be launched under earlier versions of the operating system where this is not normally the case, but apparently only just after the application has been made invisible. This appears to be due to stale catalog information being read from the disk; this behaviour passes quickly.

[2] For example, they are commonly used to implement virtual disk schemes, where the raw disk data resides in a large container file.

4.3   Dangers Posed?

Having discussed a method by which a companion virus for the Macintosh might be written, some consideration ought to be given to the dangers posed by an attack of this nature.

It is more difficult for a virus constructed in this manner to remain unde-tected and to spread between systems. Under most OS versions prior to 8.0, this variety of virus must exist as a distinct non-invisible file on the disk if it is to be executed, and is noticeable by an observant user. Furthermore, in the inter-ests of surviving to multiply, such a virus if visible would place itself somewhere not associated with the infected application, and so would be unlikely to spread through distribution of software archives.

Under OS versions after and including 8.0, this variety of virus has more options. It could even conceal itself in the same directory as the application which is the target of infection, which enhances its chances of distribution via software archive.

Such a virus may be able to spread via a local area network to another Macintosh. Its ability to spread across a network could of course be slowed by proper configuration of user permissions. In particular, users should not have permission to make changes on network volumes unless absolutely necessary.

The attack is rendered considerably more potent if the virus is able to become resident in memory. One way that this might be accomplished is outlined.

The attack is perhaps most dangerous if the virus so constructed is capable of two modes of infection. For example, one time in ten the virus might infect by modifying the target program in the manner of a file-infecting virus; although it would be readily detected by an integrity checker, and perhaps by a behaviour monitor, this would improve its chances of spreading to another computer. The undetected copies of the virus which infect using the "companion" strategy would form a reservoir for future infections.

5   Conclusion

We have considered a possible virus attack that could be implemented under the Macintosh operating system. The attack has a good resemblance to a companion virus style of attack.

The authors know of no Macintosh viruses implementing an attack such as we describe here. The attack is not believed to pose as great a danger as other varieties of computer virus, due to limitations of the implementation described. It could, however, avoid detection by an integrity checking program or other generic anti-virus measures that were not aware of the possibility of this implementation of the companion virus strategy.

We discuss various countermeasures that might be employed against such a virus. We believe that the most effective of these measures is to check the creator code of the application attempting to launch another against that of the application being launched, and to abort the request if the creator codes match. Infection is not prevented, but is readily detected.

References

1. F. Cohen. *A Short Course on Computer Viruses.* John Wiley & Sons, Inc., 1994.
2. F. Cohen. Computational aspects of computer viruses. *Computers & Security,* 8:325–344, 1989.
3. V. Bontchev. Are 'good' computer viruses still a bad idea? In *Proceedings of the EICAR '94 Conference,* pages 25–47, 1994. Available online from ftp://ftp.informatik.uni-hamburg.de/pub/virus/texts/viruses/goodvir.zip.
4. V. Bontchev. Possible virus attacks against integrity programs and how to prevent them. In *Proc. Second International Virus Bulletin Conf.,* pages 131–141, 1992. Available online from ftp://ftp.informatik.uni-hamburg.de/pub/virus/texts/viruses/attacks.zip.
5. S. Magruder. High-level language computer viruses — a new threat? *Computers & Security,* 13(3):263–269, 1994.
6. Apple Computer Inc. *Inside Macintosh: PowerPC System Software.* Addison-Wesley Publishing Company, 1994.
7. Apple Computer Inc. *Inside Macintosh: Files.* Addison-Wesley Publishing Company, 1992.
8. Apple Computer Inc. *Inside Macintosh: Processes.* Addison-Wesley Publishing Company, 1992.
9. David Ferbrache. Virus Analysis: nVIR and its Clones. *Virus Bulletin,* pages 13–14, October 1989.
10. David Ferbrache. Macintosh Viruses: INIT 29 — Infectious, but your data is safe. *Virus Bulletin,* pages 8–9, December 1989.
11. Known Apple Macintosh Viruses. *Virus Bulletin,* pages 12–13, August 1992.
12. Apple Computer Inc. *Inside Macintosh: Operating System Utilities.* Addison-Wesley Publishing Company, 1994.
13. Mac viruses: An update. *Virus Bulletin,* pages 14–15, May 1995.
14. David Ferbrache. Virus Report: WDEF — The Hidden Virus. *Virus Bulletin,* page 14, January 1990.
15. David Ferbrache. Dirty Macs. *Virus Bulletin,* pages 17–18, February 1992.
16. Craig Jackson. Worms in the ripe apple. *Virus Bulletin,* pages 6–8, July 1998.
17. Apple Computer Inc. *Inside Macintosh: More Macintosh Toolbox.* Addison-Wesley Publishing Company, 1993.
18. TB 19 — How PBDTGetAPPL chooses which copy of an App to launch. Available online from http://developer.apple.com/qa/tb/tb19.html.

An Implementation of a Secure Version of NFS including RBAC

Paul Ashley[1], Bradley Broom[1], and Mark Vandenwauver[2]

[1] Information Security Research Centre, School of Data Communications,
Queensland University of Technology, GPO Box 2434, Brisbane - AUSTRALIA
ashley,broom@fit.qut.edu.au
[2] Katholieke Universiteit Leuven, Dept. Elektrotechniek, ESAT-COSIC
Kardinaal Mercierlaan 94, B-3001 Heverlee - BELGIUM
mark.vandenwauver@esat.kuleuven.ac.be

Abstract. The NFS protocol provides transparent remote access to shared file systems across networks. It is very popular particularly in Unix networks where it is probably the most common distributed file system technology. NFS however is rarely used outside closed protected networks, because its security is notoriously weak. In 1998 Sun Microsystems released what is considered the first attempt at providing comprehensive security to NFS: a security flavour called RPCSEC_GSS based on Kerberos V5 and the GSS-API. The main benefit of this version over previous versions is that for the first time each NFS file access call could be protected. This paper outlines our efforts to secure NFS producing a security solution with even greater functionality. The major new functionality is that users may optionally use an access control system based on role based access control (RBAC). RBAC allows users to log in, be provided with a role, and use this to transparently access their remote files through secure NFS. There are also other advantages provided, for example security for the mount protocol and the option of public-key technology for authentication and key distribution. NFS has been secured with SESAME V4 and the practicality and performance of this mechanism has been demonstrated by modifying the Linux kernel and NFS utilities.

1   Introduction

The NFS protocol provides transparent remote access to shared file systems across networks [6]. It is designed to be hardware, operating system, and network independent. The independence is achieved through the use of the Remote Procedure Call (RPC) [20] and the External Data Representation (XDR) [21]. NFS Version 2 is specified in RFC1094 [17] and the more recent NFS Version 3 is specified in RFC1813 [3].

The security of NFS relies on the underlying RPC implementation. RPC provides a number of security alternatives called *authentication flavors*. In the case of NFS the important flavors are:

- **AUTH_SYS**: When this flavor of authentication is used, the server receives on each call the client's effective user identifier (UID), effective group identifier (GID), and supplemental group identifiers. The server uses these identifiers to determine if access can be granted. It is assumed that the same UIDs and GIDs are used on both client and server, or that there is some mapping in place. AUTH_SYS is the most common authentication flavor used for NFS but is notoriously weak. The scheme doesn't authenticate the users to the NFS Server, and there is no security for the NFS file access calls [2].

- **AUTH_DH** and **AUTH_KERB4**: These flavors provide greater strength in authentication and use Diffie-Hellman [4] in the case of AUTH_DH and Kerberos authentication [22] for AUTH_KERB4. The client and server must agree on particular names. This name is more operating system independent than the UID/GID scheme. Both users and NFS server are authenticated. Unfortunately the scheme also provides no security for NFS file access calls.

- **RPCSEC_GSS**: This is the most recent flavor announced and was released by Sun Microsystems in 1998 [6]. The implementation is based on using Kerberos V5 [14] and the Generic Security Services Application Programming Interface (GSS-API) [15,16]. Sun first announced provision for Kerberos V5 security using the GSS-API in its RPC implementation in [7,8], following on similar work done at OpenVision [12]. The identification is based on names. The RPCSEC_GSS is a big improvement on the previous releases because it provides the additional option of security for the NFS file access calls.

This paper describes an implementation of RPCSEC_GSS security based on SESAME V4 (described in Appendix B). Similarly to Sun's implementation the system is based on using SESAME's GSS-API to secure the RPC. During the implementation RFC2203 [7] was followed which describes Sun's RPCSEC_GSS flavor for RPC. The fact that this could be accomplished reinforces the GSS-API's claim to mechanism independence. A detailed description and performance figures of the SESAME GSS-API RPC is outside of the scope of this paper and can be found in [1].

Because SESAME V4 was used instead of Kerberos V5, the implementation differs in a number of ways from Sun's implementation. SESAME V4 provides an access control service based on RBAC. This allows a user to acquire credentials containing their role(s). Hence access control decisions can be based on the user's role. SESAME V4 also provides other differences for example authentication and key distribution services using public-key technology.

Additionally, the NFS mount protocol has been secured. This allows the system to detect whether there is any masquerading by NFS Client or NFS Server at the point of mounting. The mount protocol has not been secured with any previous flavor of NFS.

The aim of this paper is to describe the design and implementation decisions that were made in building a SESAME V4 secured NFS. The system was implemented on Linux. The performance figures are included so the reader can determine the impact of adding security. For the rest of this paper SESAME is used to refer to SESAME V4.

The paper is set out as follows. The next section describes how SESAME was used to secure the mount protocol. Section 3 includes an outline of how file accesses were secured with SESAME. This emphasizes the difficult decisions involved with putting SESAME security into the operating system. Section 4 then describes the major innovation achieved with SESAME: using RBAC for NFS access control. The paper finishes with our conclusions.

2   Implementation of SESAME Security for *mount*

The basic NFS system is explained in Appendix A. There are two main limitations to the current mount protocol (note that none of the existing authentication flavours secure the mount protocol):

- The NFS *file handle* can be eavesdropped as it passes from NFS Server to NFS Client. Since the NFS Client uses this *file handle* to access the mounted filesystem it should be protected.
- There is no authentication of the NFS Client or NFS Server.

The *mount* protocol was modified to provide SESAME mutual authentication of NFS Client and NFS Server and SESAME protection of the NFS *file handle* during transfer from NFS Server to NFS Client.

Before the *mount* protocol begins, the *mount* program and *mountd* must have access to the appropriate SESAME credentials. In the case of the *mount* program it uses the *root* user's credentials that have been acquired through logging into the SESAME domain security server. *mountd* has credentials allowing it to act as a server once it has been defined in the SESAME database and given access to the appropriate cryptographic information. Using these credentials, the NFS Client and NFS Server (through *mount* and *mountd*) mutually authenticate and establish a security context using calls to the GSS-API. Within this security context the request and NFS *file handle* response are protected using the GSS-API data protection routines.

The system also works if mounting occurs at boot time, or if an automounter is used, as long as the SESAME Security Servers are started first, and a boot script logs in the *root* user to SESAME.

The advantage of securing the *mount* protocol is that the NFS system knows whether the NFS client or NFS Server are being masqueraded at the point of mounting, and the NFS *file handle* cannot be eavesdropped.

3   Implementation of SESAME Security for File Access

When a user on an NFS Client tries to access a file on a mounted file system there are a number of security considerations:

- The user and NFS Server should be mutually authenticated.
- The file system calls between the NFS Client and NFS Server should be data protected.

– The NFS Server should be able to validate the user's privileges.

SESAME provides all three security services. Note however there is an additional complexity for the file accesses. Some of the NFS services are provided by the kernel (the kernel level NFS Client program) and hence SESAME may be required in the kernel. The implications of this are discussed by describing three options for the implementation:

– **All SESAME client code inside the kernel**: In this option all of the SESAME client code is placed inside the Linux kernel as part of the kernel level NFS Client program. This option is the optimal solution if speed is the only requirement. The disadvantage of putting the SESAME client code in the kernel is that it would become a much larger kernel. This is a problem because the kernel can't be swapped out of main memory, and the larger the kernel the more run-time memory is used, and the less memory is available for applications. Hence bloating the kernel unnecessarily is poor programming practice. There is no doubt that putting all of the SESAME client code in the kernel would bloat the kernel above acceptable limits.

– **A separate security daemon for all NFS client security operations**: In this option a separate user level daemon is used at the client to perform the SESAME functions. The kernel level NFS Client program would make requests to the daemon for all SESAME security (security context establishment followed by data protection). The advantage of this option is that the kernel is relatively unchanged in size because all of the SESAME code is in the User level daemon. The main disadvantage is that the system is much slower. There are user level NFS Clients available, but these are rarely used in place of kernel level ones, because of the performance reduction. It is far too slow to put all NFS operations outside of the kernel.

– **Compromise: security context outside the kernel, data protection inside the kernel**: In this protocol a separate daemon at the client is used to perform the SESAME context establishment, but the SESAME wrapping functions are placed in the kernel. This option is therefore a compromise between putting all of the SESAME client code in the kernel as in the first option, and putting all of the SESAME client code outside the kernel as in the second option. This option uses a user level daemon to perform context establishment with mutual authentication of the user and *nfsd*. This is slower than using the kernel but moves a lot of the SESAME client code out of the kernel. Also context establishment only occurs once for each user accessing each file system, so performance delays are for the first access only. The protection of the individual file requests occur inside the kernel using SESAME calls. The increase in size of the kernel is reasonably small (a few percent of the kernel size), with the speed benefit of running inside the kernel. Placing the data protection calls inside the kernel also results in a minimal overhead to the performance of all but the first NFS operations.

Because of the balance between a mild increase in kernel size and a reasonable decrease in performance, the compromise scheme was implemented.

4 Role Based Access Control

RBAC is a relatively new access control paradigm that provides an alternative to traditional Discretionary Access Control (DAC) and Mandatory Access Control (MAC) models. The aim of RBAC is to simplify security management by providing access control that more closely aligns to most organizational structures.

SESAME provides an RBAC service that has the potential to simplify the security management of file systems. To test this, an access control service for NFS based on SESAME RBAC was implemented.

The central notion of RBAC [19] is that access permissions are associated with roles, and users are given the ability to act in certain roles. This is a change from most traditional access control schemes where permissions are associated with users. The comparison is shown in Figure 1, with the top of the figure showing the traditional model, and the bottom part of the figure showing the RBAC model. Note also on the figure the use of the terms *user manager* and *resource manager*. They are used throughout the remainder of this paper.

To help describe the RBAC requirements and design decisions that were made, a reference role based model created by the authors is used.

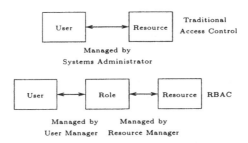

Fig. 1. Traditional Versus Role Based Access Control

4.1 Reference RBAC Model

Figure 2 shows the reference role based model. Obviously, it is a subset of a full medical role based model, but it includes many of the important features of a role based implementation (we use the terminology introduced by Sandhu et al. in [19]):

1. **Inheritance**: The medical model requires inheritance of privileges between roles and this is shown in the figure as a *role hierarchy*. In the hierarchy depending on where your role(s) are in the tree you automatically get the privileges of those roles lower in the tree (on the same branch). For example a pharmacist can access those objects accessible by the pharmacist role, and also automatically those objects accessible by the employee role (unless explicitly denied access).

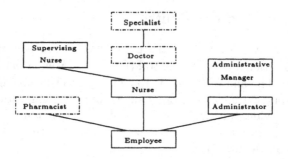

Fig. 2. Medical Role Based Model

2. **Constraints**: The medical model requires constraints on privileges between roles. The particular type of constraint required is *separation of duties*. In the model for example, a person cannot both act as a doctor or specialist (a person who prescribes medication) and a pharmacist (a person who dispenses medication).

Table 1. Rules for Medical Resources

Resource	Controller	Role	Affiliation	Operations
Employee Form	Resource Manager	employee		rw
Patient Daily Log	Resource Manager	nurse	ward	rw
		supervising nurse		r
		doctor	ward	r
		specialist	ward	r
Patient Medical Record	Resource Manager	nurse	ward	r
		doctor	ward	rw
		specialist	ward	rw
Patient Admin Record	Resource Manager	administrator		rw
		admin-manager		r
Patient Medicine Script	Resource Manager	doctor	ward	rw
		specialist	ward	rw
		pharmacist	ward	r
Personal Files	Creator	undefined		

There are additional requirements not obvious from the figure but they can be identified if specific medical resources are examined (see Table 1):

3. **Role Affiliation**: In many organizations the term role *affiliation* is very useful [10, 18]. For example, although a Nurse may have access to a patient's daily logs, it may only be for patients in the Nurse's ward.
4. **Flexibility for Users**: RBAC by its nature is non-discretionary [9]. That is, the *resource managers* decide the permissions of all objects in the system. In most cases a weakening from those strict requirements is more suitable in that there is a need to support two types of files in the system: *organization*

files would be non-discretionary in that the permissions on those files would be set by the *resource manager*, and *personal files* would be discretionary in that the creator of those files would set the permissions on them.

4.2 Implementing RBAC Using Unix Access Control

Unix provides the group mechanism which has some similar concepts to a role. Users can be members of groups, and permissions on objects can be set for the group rather than particular users. There are therefore two sets of databases: users and groups, and for each object groups and permissions.

There are essential differences though between RBAC and the Unix group mechanism. The first is who can modify the permissions on the resources. Unix has a discretionary access control system (in that the creator of the object sets the permissions) whereas RBAC is essentially non-discretionary (in that the *resource manager* should set the permissions). Another difference is that to implement a role hierarchy, it may be necessary to translate a single role into multiple Unix groups.

To implement RBAC with groups each role can be translated into a corresponding group (or into a number of groups to implement the hierarchy) and an additional mechanism needs to enforce the non-discretionary nature. Unix provides a simple solution for this. For each object in the system, the owner is identified, and Unix allows only the owner to set the permissions. Therefore if the owner could be set to be the *resource manager* and the permissions set according to the *resource manager* requirements, RBAC can be implemented with Unix groups.

4.3 Implementing Roles as Groups

Table 2 shows how to implement the RBAC model from Figure 2 with Unix groups. Each role is directly translated into a group, and the role hierarchy can be easily implemented by translating a role into multiple groups. One of the limitations though of the traditional Unix permission structure is that there is only one group implemented for each object. For example, typical Unix permissions on a file called *project* could be:

```
-rw-r----- 4 resource nurse 512 Sep 25 1998 project
```

This indicates that the owner is *resource* (the *resource manager*) and the group is *nurse*. All members of the group *nurse* have read access to the file. These single group permissions have been seen as too restrictive for some time, and many new versions of Unix are implementing multiple group permissions (for example newer versions of Sun Microsystem's Solaris operating system provide ACLs for each object).

Assuming the implementation is done on a newer version of Unix with the ability to list multiple group permissions per file, the medical RBAC model could

Table 2. Implementing Roles With Unix Groups

Groups	Members
employee	pharmacist, nurse, super_nurse, doctor, specialist, admin, admin_manager
pharmacist	
nurse	super_nurse, doctor, specialist
super_nurse	
doctor	specialist
specialist	
admin	admin_manager
admin_manager	

Table 3. Implementing the Medical Model with Unix Permissions: Multiple Groups

Resource	UID	GID1	GID2	GID3
Employee Form	Resource Manager	employee		
Patient	Resource Manager	nurse	super_nurse	doctor
Daily Log		rw	r	r
Patient	Resource Manager	nurse	doctor	
Medical Record		r	rw	
Patient	Resource Manager	admin	admin_manager	
Admin Record	.	rw	r	
Patient	Resource Manager	doctor	pharmacist	
Medicine Script		rw	r	
Research	Creator	doctor		
Files		r		

be implemented as shown in Table 3. The first column gives the file types from Table 1, and the next columns give the Unix permissions that would be necessary to implement the RBAC scheme. With the role hierarchy implemented, and using the resource example, up to three groups for each object would be required to implement the system.

Note also the use of the Unix UID field. In Unix this field is used to denote the owner of the file, and this owner has the right to change the permissions on the file. In the medical context the permissions on most files should only be modifiable by the *resource manager* with fewer files being modifiable by the creator. This is indicated in the table with the appropriate UID.

Suppose the model was implemented on a traditional Unix system with only one group. In this case the *others* field must be used which gives more access than was originally intended.

4.4 Implementation of Non-Discretionary Access Control

As stated previously, non-discretionary access control is required for the organizational files. This entails:

- That the owner of the file be set to the *resource manager's* UID (so that only the *resource manager* can modify the permissions).
- That the permissions on the files be set to those required by the *resource manager* (similar to Table 1).

The scheme was implemented by modifying the NFS Server functions for creating files and directories. For each of the different resource types the system enforces that the files are created in particular directories (for example the daily logs in the directory for daily logs). Inside this directory is a hidden file, created by the *resource manager*, that has an entry indicating the permissions for files in that directory.

For example, taking the case of the daily log, a directory */usr/daily* has a file *.rbac* with the following entry: nurse(rw),others(r). When a file is created in a directory, or a subdirectory is created, the NFS Server must check for the *.rbac* file, and if it exists ensure it is valid. There are two checks required to validate the *.rbac* file:

- The owner of the *.rbac* file must be the same as the owner of the directory it is in.
- The owner must be a member of any groups specified by the entries in the *.rbac* file. For example, if the *.rbac* file has an entry nurse(rw), then the owner of the *.rbac* file must be a member of the nurse group.

If either of these conditions are not satisfied then the create does not occur and an error is returned. There is one exception to this, if the user creating the file or directory is the same as the owner of the directory (*resource manager*) then the create will always occur. If the *.rbac* file exists and it is valid, then the NFS Server creates a file as follows:

- The UID of the file is set to the same as the *.rbac* file in the directory (the *resource manager's* UID).
- The GID and others fields is set as specified in the *.rbac* file.

For creating directories, the same scheme applies. The *.rbac* file from the parent directory is copied into the sub-directory with the same permissions. The system also supports personal files. If the *.rbac* file does not exist the NFS Server create functions behave exactly as for the traditional Unix system.

4.5 Implementation of Role Constraints

The important role constraint for the medical role model is separation of duties. Implementation of role constraints can occur at two different levels:

- The *user manager* can ensure that users are never given access to mutually exclusive roles.
- The *resource manager* can ensure that permissions on resources never disobey the constraints.

The integrity of the system therefore depends on the *user manager* and *resource manager*. This can be achieved by user level tools that automate the process.

4.6 Implementation of Role Affiliation

Role affiliation is a constraint applied to the role. For example in the medical system, a nurse can only access the daily log of wards the nurse is currently working in. Affiliations can be due to a number of reasons, for example location of access and time. Parker and Sundt [18], and Hilchenbach [10] believe that roles and affiliations should be considered separately, and both active roles and affiliations should be used to determine what access is given.

An alternative implementation to separation of role and affiliation is to increase the number of roles to cover all possible affiliations. This is the scheme implemented with SESAME NFS.

4.7 Performance

Obviously it is an important objective to have similar performance with RBAC NFS as with traditional NFS. The overhead for the complete system is shown in Table 4. The timing is for two 200MHz 64M RAM Pentiums on a LAN.

Table 4. Overhead to Traditional NFS

Test Scenario		Overhead
1	First Access by the user to the NFS Server (Handshake including PAC transferred)	235 ms
2	Subsequent Access (GID is looked up in a UID/GID cache)	8 μs
3	Create File (.rbac file does not exist)	1.2 ms
4	Create File (.rbac file does exist and is valid)	7.3 ms
5	Create Directory (.rbac file does not exist)	2.7 ms
6	Create Directory (.rbac file does exist and is valid)	9.9 ms

5 Conclusions

A comprehensive security mechanism for NFS has been developed based on SESAME. This includes strong authentication of users and NFS servers, security for all NFS file accesses, and an access control system based on RBAC. Implementation of the authentication and file access security was relatively straight forward (although modifying a Unix kernel is always a challenge) and work well. The RBAC system was implemented using Unix groups, by modifying the NFS Server to translate roles into groups and implement non-discretionary access control of files. Although this system is a workable RBAC file system, the single group Unix permissions and the need for non-discretionary behaviour results in the system having a number of constraints.

References

1. P. Ashley and M. Vandenwauver. *Practical Intranet Security: An Overview of the State of the Art and Available Technologies.* Kluwer Academic Publishers, 1999.
2. B. Broom and G. Gaskell. On the Recent Attacks Against WWW Systems. In *Proceedings of the 2nd Joint Conference of AUUG and Asia Pacific World Wide Web*, pages 28–36, September 1996.
3. B. Callaghan, B. Pawlowski, and P. Staubach. NFS Version 3 Protocol Specification, 1995. RFC1813.
4. W. Diffie and M. Hellman. New Directions in Cryptography. *IEEE Transactions on Information Theory*, 22(6):644–654, 1976.
5. ECMA 219. ECMA-219 Security in Open Systems - Authentication and Privilege Attribute Security Application with Related Key Distribution Functionality, 2nd Edition, March 1996. European Computer Manufacturers Association.
6. M. Eisler. NFS Version 2 and Version 3 Security Issues and the NFS Protocol's Use of RPCSEC_GSS and Kerberos V5, April 1998. Internet Draft.
7. M. Eisler, A. Chiu, and L. Ling. RPCSEC-GSS Protocol Specification, September 1997. RFC2203.
8. M. Eisler, R. Schemers, and R. Srinivasan. Security Mechanism Independence in ONC RPC. In *Proceedings of the 6th USENIX Security Symposium*, San Jose, CA., July 1996.
9. D.F. Ferraiolo and R. Kuhn. Role-Based Access Control. In *Proceedings of the 15th NIST-NSA National Computer Security Conference*, Baltimore, MD., October 1992.
10. B. Hilchenbach. Observations on the Real-World Implementation of Role-Based Access Control. In *20th National Information Systems Security Conference*, pages 341–352, October 1997.
11. ITU. ITU-T Rec. X.509 (revised). The Directory - Authentication Framework, 1993. International Telecommunication Union, Geneva, Switzerland.
12. B. Jaspan. GSS-API Security For ONC RPC. In *Proceedings of the Symposium on Network and Distributed System Security*, pages 144–151, San Diego, CA., February 1995.
13. P. Kaijser. A review of the SESAME Development. In C. Boyd and E. Dawson, editors, *Proceedings of the 3rd ACISP Conference - LNCS 1438*, pages 1–8. Springer-Verlag, 1998.
14. J. Kohl and C. Neuman. The Kerberos Network Authentication Service V5, September 1993. RFC1510.
15. J. Linn. Generic Security Services Application Program Interface, September 1993. RFC1508.
16. J. Linn. Generic Security Service Application Program Interface Version 2, January 1997. RFC2078.
17. B. Nowicki. NFS : Network File System Protocol, 1989. RFC1094.
18. T. Parker and C. Sundt. Role Based Access Control in Real Systems. In *Compsec '95*, October 1995.
19. R. Sandhu, E.J. Coyne, H.L. Feinstein, and C.E. Youman. Role-Based Access Control Models. *IEEE Computer*, pages 38–47, February 1996.
20. R. Srinivasan. Remote Procedure Call Protocol Specification Version 2, 1995. RFC1831.
21. R. Srinivasan. Xdr: External data respresentation standard, August 1995. RFC1832.

22. J. Steiner, B. Neuman, and J. Schiller. Kerberos: An Authentication Service for Open Network Systems. In *Proceedings of the USENIX Winter Conference*, pages 191–202, Dallas, Tx., February 1988.

A   Network File System

Figure 3 shows how NFS works from an implementation point of view. The Linux kernel V 2.1 was used for the implementation, and this version includes the NFS Client inside the kernel, and the NFS Server outside of the kernel (as shown on the Figure). In other operating systems the NFS Server may be inside the kernel. The diagram also shows Client operations that occur on the left hand side of the figure, and Server operations that occur on the right hand side of the figure.

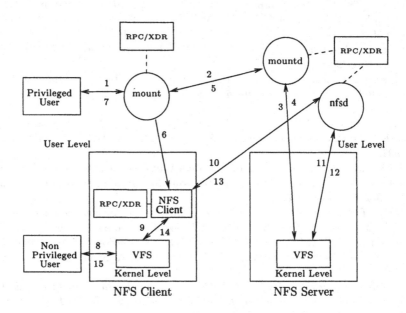

Fig. 3. The Internal Operation of NFS

The NFS process has two main phases. The first phase is the NFS Client mounting the NFS Server's file system (note the numbers relate to Figure 3):

1. A privileged user on the NFS Client (for example the *root* user on Linux) performs the *mount* operation. The privileged user is actually requesting an NFS *file handle* from the NFS Server. The *mount* program exists outside the kernel.
2. The *mount* program contacts the *mount daemon* on the NFS Server called *mountd* requesting the NFS *file handle*. Note that both *mount* and *mountd* use the RPC/XDR user level library for their transport mechanism. *mountd* also exists outside the kernel.

3. *mountd* then sends a request to the NFS Server Virtual File System (VFS) to return a NFS *file handle*.

4. The VFS returns a NFS *file handle* to *mountd* if the request was valid.

5. *mountd* returns the NFS *file handle* response back to the NFS Client's *mount* program.

6. The *mount* program then passes the NFS *file handle* to the kernel level NFS Client program that stores it for future use. Note also that the *mount* program can optionally pass the authentication flavor flag to the kernel level NFS Client program. If the flavor is the AUTH_SYS then no flag is required (the NFS Client program assumes AUTH_SYS as the default), if it is any other flavor, then the appropriate flag must be passed.

7. The *mount* program indicates to the privileged user if the mount operation was successful.

The second phase is a user (either privileged or non-privileged) on the NFS Client requesting to perform a file system operation (again the numbers relate to Figure 3):

8. A user on the NFS Client makes a request to the VFS to perform an operation on a mounted file system.

9. The VFS determines the request is for a remote file system and forwards the request to the kernel level NFS Client program for transmission across the network. Note that the NFS Client program uses a kernel level RPC/XDR library.

10. The NFS Client program forwards the request to the NFS Server daemon called *nfsd*. *nfsd* lives outside the kernel and uses a user level RPC/XDR library for its network transport.

11. *nfsd* forwards the request to the NFS Server's VFS that accesses its local file system (not shown on the diagram).

12. The NFS Server's VFS returns the result to *nfsd*.

13. *nfsd* returns the result back to the NFS Client program.

14. The NFS Client program returns the result to the NFS Client VFS.

15. Finally the result is returned to the user.

All of the second phase occurs transparently to the user. As far as the user is concerned it appears a file on a local file system is being accessed. When the NFS client no longer wants to access the NFS Server, the privileged user uses the *umount* program that un-mounts the file system (not shown on the figure). After un-mounting, users can no longer access the file system.

B SESAME

SESAME [1] is the name of a security architecture. It is the result of a collaboration of Bull, ICL and Siemens together with some leading European research groups [13]. The project was partly funded by the European Commission under the auspices of its RACE program. SESAME is an acronym for *"A Secure European System for Applications in a Multi-vendor Environment"*. Figure 4 gives an overview of the SESAME architecture. At first glance it might look very complex but it is possible to distinguish four boundaries in the architecture: the client, the domain security server, the (application) server, and the support components.

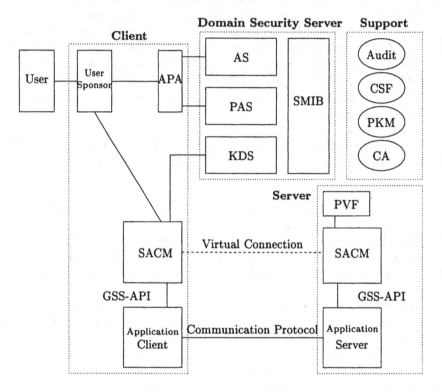

Fig. 4. The SESAME components

The client system incorporates the User, User Sponsor (US), Authentication Privilege Attribute (APA) Client, Secure Association Context Manager (SACM) and client application code. The User Sponsor gives the user the interface to the SESAME system, and allows the user to logon. The APA is used by the User Sponsor for the communication with the domain security server. The SACM provides the data protection services (data authentication, data confidentiality, non-repudiation) for the client-server interaction.

The Domain Security Server is very similar to Kerberos [14]. The main difference is the presence of the Privilege Attribute Server (PAS) in SESAME. This server has been added to manage the access control mechanism that is implemented by SESAME. Because role based access control has many advantages over traditional access control schemes, SESAME has chosen to adopt it. The scheme is enforced using Privilege Attribute Certificates (PACs) [5]. The function of the Authentication Server (AS) and Key Distribution Server (KDS) (ticket granting server in Kerberos) are similar to their Kerberos counterparts: providing a single sign-on and managing the cryptographic keys. A major difference with Kerberos is that SESAME also supports public-key based authentication using the X.509 authentication mechanism [11].

When the application server receives a message from an application client indicating that it wants to set up a secure connection, it forwards the client's credentials and keying material (an encrypted session key) to the PAC Validation Facility (PVF), which checks whether the client has access to the application. If this check is successful, it decrypts the keying material and forwards the session keys (SESAME uses independent keys for providing data authentication and data confidentiality) to the SACM on the server machine. Through this the application server authenticates to the client (mutual authentication) and it also enables the application server to secure the communication with the client.

The SESAME architecture provides a number of support components used throughout the system. These include the Audit facility (providing detailed audit logs), Cryptographic Support Facility (CSF) (providing the various cryptographic primitives), Public Key Management (PKM) facility and a Certification Authority (CA).

A detailed description of SESAME can be found in [1].

Group Signatures and Their Relevance to Privacy-Protecting Off-Line Electronic Cash Systems

Jacques Traoré

France Télécom - Branche Développement
Centre National d'Etudes des Télécommunications
42, rue des Coutures, B.P. 6243
14066 Caen Cedex, France
jacques.traore@cnet.francetelecom.fr

Abstract. A group signature scheme allows members of a possibly large group to sign messages anonymously on behalf of the group. Only a *designated entity* can determine the identity of the group member who issued a given signature. Group signatures, and particularly group blind signatures [28, 35] (which incorporate the properties of both blind signatures and group signatures), have many applications such as e-commerce.

In this paper, we first propose a new group signature scheme, suitable for large groups (i.e., the group's public key and the signatures are fixed-size regardless of the number of memberships). Furthermore, we show how to use our group signature scheme to construct a practical privacy-protecting off-line electronic cash system. Our group signature scheme is more efficient than previous ones and the resulting electronic cash system is characterized by a high computational efficiency in the withdrawal protocol[1].

Then, we show some weaknesses in the design of an electronic cash system based on a group signature scheme [28, 35][2]. Finally, we describe some weaknesses of recently proposed group signature schemes [1, 2, 10, 28].

1 Introduction

1.1 Group Signatures

At Eurocrypt'91, Chaum and Van Heijst introduced the concept of group signature schemes. Such a scheme allows any member, of a possibly large group, to sign messages on behalf of the group. Group signatures, like ordinary ones, are publicly verifiable and can be verified with respect to a single group public key.

Group signatures have the additional property of being anonymous. However, only a designated entity can (if needed) revoke the anonymity of a group signature and consequently find out the identity of the originator of a given signature.

In [17], Chaum and Van Heijst proposed four realizations of group signature schemes. Various improvements of their schemes were later proposed [7, 18, 34].

---

[1] Such protocol involves a bank and a customer. The bank is the processing and communications bottleneck in such payment systems. Therefore, it is important to minimize bank's workload when it is involved.

[2] Our cash system avoids the weaknesses found in the (group signature based) anonymous payment system described in [28].

The drawback of these solutions [7, 18, 34] is that the length of the signatures and/or the size of the group's public key depend on the size of the group. This limits the applicability of such schemes to only small groups.

Recently, Camenisch and Stadler have presented new group signature schemes which remain practical even for large groups. In their schemes, the group's public key and the signatures are fixed-size regardless of the number of memberships.

Recent improvements, in terms of efficiency and security, have been made on group signature schemes (suitable for large groups) by Camenisch and Stadler [10], Camenisch and Michels [8] and by Ateniese and Tsudik [1, 2].

1.2 Blind Signatures and Privacy-Protecting Electronic Payment Systems

The concept of blind signature schemes was introduced by Chaum in 1982 [13]. A blind signature scheme is a cryptographic protocol involving two entities: a sender and a signer. This protocol allows the sender to choose a message and obtain a digital signature of this message from the signer, in such a way, that the signer learns nothing about the content of the message that he has signed. Moreover, if the signer later sees a message he has signed, he won't be able to determine when or for whom he signed it.

Blind signature schemes can be used in applications where anonymity is required, such as anonymous prepaid electronic payment systems.

Recent anonymous prepaid electronic payment systems, based on the blind signature technique, 'emulate' physical cash. In these systems, the users withdraw electronic coins which consist of numbers, generated by users, and *blindly* signed by an electronic money issuer (a bank). Each signature represents a given amount. These coins are then spent (released) in shops which can authenticate them by using the public signature key of the bank. The users retain anonymity in any transaction since the coins they use have been blindly signed.

1.3 Group Blind Signatures

At Financial Cryptography'98, Lysyanskaya and Ramzan introduced the concept of group blind signature schemes and proposed the first realizations of such schemes. Group blind signatures incorporate the properties of both blind signatures and group signatures. They can be used in many of the settings where blind signatures are used. Particularly, they can be used to design privacy-protecting electronic payment systems. As an application, Lysyanskaya and Ramzan showed how to use their new schemes to achieve a (off-line) payment system in which 'multiple'[1] banks can securely dispense 'anonymous' and 'untraceable' electronic cash[2]. In this system no one, except the *designated entity* (e.g., the country's Central Bank), can identify the bank who issued a given coin (thus providing users with an extra layer of anonymity).

---

[1] Previous realizations of electronic cash systems focused on models in which a single bank issues all the electronic coins.

[2] In this system all the banks form a group and the *designated entity* is the country's central bank.

Our results: In this paper, we first propose a new group signature scheme, suitable for large groups (i.e., the group's public key and the signatures are fixed-size regardless of the number of memberships). Furthermore, we show how to use it to construct a practical privacy-protecting off-line electronic cash system.

Our group signature scheme is more efficient than previous ones [7, 10, 9][1] (and relies on different security assumptions than these previous schemes). Moreover, our electronic cash system is characterized by a high computational efficiency in the withdrawal protocol. Then, we show some weaknesses in the design of an electronic cash system based on a group signature scheme [28, 35]. Finally, we describe some weaknesses of recently proposed group signature schemes [1, 2, 10, 28].

Organization of the paper: In section 2, we define the notations we use in this paper and introduce the assumptions on which the security of our schemes relies. Then, we present the non-interactive proofs of knowledge that will be useful in the sequel. In section 3, we describe our new group signature scheme and the resulting electronic cash system. In appendix A, we examine the security of this cash system. In appendices B and C, we describe some weaknesses of recently proposed group signature schemes.

2 Notations, Assumptions and Basic Tools

The security of our scheme is based on assumptions relating to the difficulty in solving certain problems. In this section, we define these assumptions, explain our notations and introduce the background of the key techniques that will be useful in the sequel.

2.1 Notations

Throughout the paper we will use the following notations:

The symbol $\|$ will denote the concatenation of two strings. The symbol $\tilde{\varepsilon}$ will denote the empty string. The notation '$x \in_R E$' means that x is chosen uniformly at random from the set E. The notation '$x \overset{?}{=} y$', used in a protocol, means that the party must check whether x is equal to y.

N will denote the following set: $N = \{n \mid n = pq, p<q, p = 2p'+1, q = 2q' + 1$ where p, q, p', q' are all prime numbers and p' and q' are of equal length$\}$.

For an integer N, Z_N denotes the residue class ring modulo N and Z_N^* denotes the multiplicative group of invertible elements in Z_N.

For an element $\alpha \in Z_N^*$, we denote by $ord(\alpha)$ the order of α in Z_N^*. The subgroup generated by an element $\alpha \in Z_N^*$ is denoted by $\langle \alpha \rangle$. For two integers a and b, we denote by $[a, b]$ the following set: $[a, b] \overset{def}{=} \{a, a+1,......, b-1, b\}$.

H will denote a one-way hash function that maps $\{0,1\}^*$ to Z_{2^k} (where k denotes a security parameter). Other notations and definitions will be set as needed.

---

[1] Our group signature scheme is slightly more efficient than [9].

2.2 Number Theoretic Preliminaries and Assumptions

Let G be a cyclic group of order n and g and h two distinct generators of this group (in our protocol, n will designate an RSA modulus of unknown factorization). The discrete logarithm of $y \in G$ to the base g is the smallest positive integer x satisfying $g^x = y$. A representation of $y \in G$ to the bases g and h is a pair (a,b) satisfying $y = g^a h^b$ (see [4] for a discussion of the representation problem). In the sequel, the parameters n, G and g should be chosen such that computing discrete logarithms in G to the base g is computationally infeasible.

Let us now introduce two lemmas that will be useful in the construction of our cash system (these lemmas have been introduced in [22]).

Lemma 1. Let $N = PQ$, where $P<Q$, $P = 2P'+1$, $Q = 2Q'+1$ and P, Q, P', Q' are all prime numbers (i.e., $N \in \mathbb{N}$). The order of elements in Z_N^* is one of the set $\{1, 2, P', Q', 2P', 2Q', P'Q', 2P'Q'\}$. Given an element $\alpha \in Z_N^* \setminus \{-1,1\}$, such that $ord(\alpha) < P'Q'$ then $gcd(\alpha -1, N)$ is a prime factor of N.

Following [22], we will assume in our protocol, as a consequence of the above lemma, that any value (different from 1 or -1) found by a party that does not know the factorization of N must be of order at least $P'Q'$ in Z_N^*.

Lemma 2. Let N be as in lemma 1. Given an element α such that $ord(\alpha) \in \{P'Q', 2P'Q'\}$ then for every $m \in Z_N^*$ it holds that $m^4 \in \langle \alpha \rangle$.

Note: The proofs of these lemmas do not appear in [22] (they appear in an extended version of this paper [23]). Lemma 2 is true but incomplete. Indeed, it is possible to prove 'more' than what is claimed in Lemma 2: in fact, we can prove that $m^2 \in \langle \alpha \rangle$ (the proof of this 'new' lemma will appear in the full paper).

The following assumption is needed for the proof of *soundness* of one of our underlying building blocks.

Assumption 1 (Modified RSA Assumption [21])

Given as inputs an element $N \in \mathbb{N}$ (of unknown factorization) and $Y \in Z_N^*$ (such that Y is not a power in Z), it is hard to find X and e ($e \geq 2$) such that $Y \equiv X^e \pmod{N}$. (see [21] for a general and formal definition of this assumption).

The security of our electronic cash system also relies on the following two assumptions:

Assumption 2 (Decision Diffie-Hellman Assumption[1])

Let $N \in \mathbb{N}$. Let α be a *quadratic residue* modulo N that has a large order in Z_N^*. Let $G = \langle \alpha \rangle$. Given as input a triplet $T = (\alpha^a, \alpha^b, \alpha^c)$ in G^3, it is hard to *decide* whether T is a Diffie-Hellman triplet (that is $T = (\alpha^a, \alpha^b, \alpha^{ab})$) or a random triplet. (see [3] for a general and formal definition of this assumption and also for a

---

[1] or perfect-Decision Diffie-Hellman assumption using the terminology of [3]. The perfect-Decision Diffie-Hellman assumption is, in some groups, equivalent to the Decision Diffie-Hellman assumption (not perfect).

discussion of the Decision Diffie-Hellman assumption in groups in which only an upper bound on size of the group is given).

Assumption 3 (Computation of approximate e-th roots modulo a composite number) Let e be an integer ($e \geq 4$). Given as inputs an element $N \in \mathbb{N}$ (of unknown factorization) and a (suitably chosen)[1] element $C \in Z_N^*$, it is hard to find two integers X and δ such that: $X^e \equiv C + \delta \pmod{N}$ and $\delta \in [a,b]$ (where a and b are two integers satisfying: $0 \leq a < b < N^{\frac{2}{3}}$).

Note: The security of the Okamoto-Shiraishi signature scheme [33] is based on the same assumption (i.e., on the assumption that computing approximate e-th roots modulo a composite number is hard when the factorization of this number is unknown). In their scheme, the composite number N is equal to $p^2 q$, where p and q are two distinct primes. N is the public key and the factorization of N constitutes the secret key. A signature s (with s not too small) is considered as valid for a message m if: $h(m) \leq s^e \pmod{N} \leq h(m) + O(N^{\frac{1}{3}})$ (where h is a given one-way hash function). This scheme has been broken when the exponent e is equal to 2 or 3 [6, 26, 39]. But, till now, no attack is known against higher degree versions of the Okamoto-Shiraishi scheme, and when the exponent e is superior or equal to 4, the Okamoto-Shiraishi scheme is considered as robust.

Other assumptions will be set as needed.

2.3 Building Blocks: Proofs of Knowledge

In this section, we describe the building blocks necessary for the design of our group signature scheme (and also for the resulting off-line electronic cash system).

These building blocks are signature schemes derived from 'zero-knowledge' proofs of knowledge using the Fiat-Shamir heuristic [20].

The first building block is a proof of knowledge of a representation. As proof of knowledge of a representation we are inspired by a proof given by T. Okamoto [31].

Proof of Knowledge of a Representation. Let G be a cyclic group of order n and g_1 and g_2 be two distinct generators of this group (in our protocol, n will designate an RSA modulus of unknown factorization).

Definition 1 (*Proof$_{REP}$*) A (message-dependent) proof of knowledge of a representation of h with respect to (g_1, g_2) is a tuple $(c, r_1, r_2) = Proof_{REP}(M, g_1, g_2, h)$, where $c = H(M \| g_1 \| g_2 \| h \| g_1^{r_1} g_2^{r_2} h^c)$. Since the proof involves the message M, it is called *message-dependent*. This message may be the empty string $\tilde{\varepsilon}$.

The prover who knows the representation (x_1, x_2) of h with respect to (g_1, g_2) can construct such a proof. For this purpose, he chooses two random numbers $(a_1, a_2) \in_R Z_n^{*2}$ and computes $c = H(M \| g_1 \| g_2 \| h \| g_1^{a_1} g_2^{a_2})$. Then, he computes $r_i = a_i - c \, x_i \bmod n$ for $1 \leq i \leq 2$. To verify such a proof, the verifier checks whether c is equal to $H(M \| g_1 \| g_2 \| h \| g_1^{r_1} g_2^{r_2} h^c)$.

---

[1] See [27] for example.

Note: According to the definition of [19], Proof$_{REP}$ is not a proof of knowledge. However, it is assumed that this proof does not leak any information about the representation that the prover knows.

The second building block is used to prove that the discrete logarithm of an element is equal to the second coordinate of a representation.

Proof of Equality of Discrete Coordinates. This proof is related to the proof of equality of two discrete logarithms described in [16]. Let G be a cyclic group of order n and g, g_1 and g_2 be three distinct generators of this group (in our protocol, n will designate an RSA modulus of unknown factorization).

Definition 2 (*Proof$_{REP+LOGEQ}$*) A (message-dependent) proof of knowledge of a representation of h_1 with respect to (g_1, g_2), which also proves that the exponent of g_1 in this representation is equal to $\log_g h$ is a tuple $(c, r_1, r_2) = Proof_{REP+LOGEQ}(M, g_1, g_2, h_1, g, h)$, where $c = H(M \| g_1 \| g_2 \| h_1 \| g \| h \| g_1^{r_1} g_2^{r_2} h_1^c \| g^{r_1} h^c)$. As before, M is a (possibly empty) message associated to the proof. The prover who knows the representation (x_1, x_2) of h_1 with respect to (g_1, g_2) and $\log_g h = x_1$, can construct such a proof. For this purpose, he chooses two random numbers $(a_1, a_2) \in_R Z_n^{*2}$ and computes $c = H(M \| g_1 \| g_2 \| h_1 \| g \| h \| g_1^{a_1} g_2^{a_2} \| g^{a_1})$. Then he computes $r_i = a_i - c x_i \bmod n$ for $1 \le i \le 2$. The verifier of this proof checks whether c is equal to $H(M \| g_1 \| g_2 \| h_1 \| g \| h \| g_1^{r_1} g_2^{r_2} h_1^c \| g^{r_1} h^c)$.

The following building block is used to prove the knowledge of the e-th root of the first coordinate of a representation.

Proof of Knowledge of Roots of Representations. Let G be a cyclic group of order n and g_1 and g_2 be two distinct generators of this group (in our protocol, n will designate an RSA modulus of unknown factorization).

Definition 3 (*Proof$_{REP+ROOT}$*) $Proof_{REP+ROOT}(M, e, g_1, g_2, h)$ denotes a (message-dependent) proof of knowledge of the e-th root of the g_1-part of a representation of h with respect to (g_1, g_2).

For this proof, we adopt a proof of knowledge presented by Camenisch and Stadler in [10].

Proof that a Secret Lies in a Predetermined Interval. The following building block is used to prove that a secret lies in a predetermined interval. Our building block is related to the *Range Bounded Commitment* protocol (RBC for short) of Chan et al. [11 and also 37]. It is also related to a protocol given by Camenisch and Michels [8].

Note: The RBC protocol is not secure. More precisely, this protocol does not prove that a secret lies in a predetermined range (counter-examples are easy to find). We have informed the authors of this fact. They were aware of this mistake [38]. An updated version of [11], with a new RBC, is available at [12]. Our building block is related to this new version of the RBC.

Let us now define our building block (we freely borrow the notations of the similar building block described in [8]).

Let G be a cyclic group of order n and g, g_1 and g_2 be three distinct generators of this group (in our protocol, n will designate an RSA modulus of unknown factorization).

Let N be an element of N of unknown factorization. Let α be a *quadratic residue* modulo N that has a large order in Z_N^*. Let l_N denotes the bit-length of N. Let $\varepsilon > 1$ be a security parameter and let l_1 and l_2 denotes lengths. Let H be a one-way hash function that maps $\{0,1\}^*$ to Z_{2^k} (where k denotes a security parameter).

Definition 4 (*Proof$_{LOG+RANGE}$*) A (message-dependent) proof of knowledge of the discrete logarithm of h with respect to g and of δ with respect to α, which also proves that $\log_g h = \log_\alpha \delta$ and that $\log_g h$ is in $I_{extended} = [\, 2^{l_1} - 2^{\varepsilon(l_2+k)+1}, 2^{l_1} + 2^{\varepsilon(l_2+k)+1}\,]$, is a pair $(c,r) = Proof_{LOG+RANGE}(M, g, h, \alpha, \delta, l_1, l_2, l_N, \varepsilon, k)$, where:

$c = H(M \| g \| h \| \alpha \| \delta \| g^{r-c2^{l_1}} h^c \| \alpha^{r-c2^{l_1}} \delta^c)$ and r is in $[\, -(2^k - 1)(2^{l_2} - 1), 2^{\varepsilon(l_2+k)}\,]$.

Such a proof can be obtained, if the prover *knows an element x in $I = [\, 2^{l_1}, 2^{l_1} + 2^{l_2} -1]$* such that $h = g^x$ and $\delta = \alpha^x$ holds.

To construct the proof, the prover chooses $a \in_R \{0,1\}^{\varepsilon(l_2+k)}$ and computes $c = H(M \| g \| h \| \alpha \| \delta \| g^a \| \alpha^a)$ and $r = a - c(x - 2^{l_1})$ (in Z). To verify such a proof, the verifier checks whether:

- c is equal to $H(M \| g \| h \| \alpha \| \delta \| g^{r-c2^{l_1}} h^c \| \alpha^{r-c2^{l_1}} \delta^c)$
- r is in $[\, -(2^k - 1)(2^{l_2} - 1), 2^{\varepsilon(l_2+k)}\,]$.

We assume that $n < N$ and that $I_{extended} \subset [1, n-1]$.

Lemma 3: If Assumption 1 holds and $\varepsilon > 1$ then the interactive protocol underlying *Proof$_{LOG+RANGE}$* is a statistical honest-verifier zero-knowledge proof of knowledge of an integer x in $[\, 2^{l_1} - 2^{\varepsilon(l_2+k)+1}, 2^{l_1} + 2^{\varepsilon(l_2+k)+1}\,]$ such that $h = g^x$ and $\delta = \alpha^x$.

Proof: See [21] and also [8] for the *proof of soundness*. See [8, 36] for the proof that the protocol is statistical honest-verifier zero-knowledge for any $\varepsilon > 1$.

Definition 5 (*Proof$_{REP+RANGE}$*) A (message-dependent) proof of knowledge of a representation of h_1 with respect to (g_1, g_2), which also proves that the exponent of g_1 in this representation is in $[\, 2^{l_1} - 2^{\varepsilon(l_2+k)+1}, 2^{l_1} + 2^{\varepsilon(l_2+k)+1}\,]$ and is equal to $\log_\alpha \delta$ is denoted by $Proof_{REP+RANGE}(M, g_1, g_2, h_1, \alpha, \delta, l_1, l_2, l_N, \varepsilon, k)$.

This building block is an easy variant of the previous building block.

3 The Proposed Group Signature Scheme and the Resulting Anonymous Off-Line Electronic Cash System

Due to space limitations, we will not (in this section) describe in detail our group signature scheme. Rather, we will present a practical electronic cash system based on our group signature scheme.

In this section, we show how to use the basic tools described in the previous sections, to construct a practical off-line electronic cash system satisfying various requirements concerning privacy and security.

Usually, the desired properties for an electronic cash system are the following:
- Security: coins must be unforgeable and it must be impossible to use the same coin twice without being identified.
- Privacy: The purchases must be untraceable and it must be impossible for anyone to determine whether two payments were made by the same user.

In the simplified model of off-line electronic cash system that we use, three types of parties are involved: the customers (or 'users'), the shops and a bank. Three possible transactions may occur between them: the withdrawal (by a user from the bank), the payment (by a user to a shop), and the deposit (by a shop to the bank). In the withdrawal protocol, the user withdraws electronic coins from the bank while his account is being debited. In the payment protocol the user pays the shop with the coins he has withdrawn. In the deposit protocol, the shop deposits the coins it has received in the bank and the shop's account is credited.

In our system, the users form a group. A trusted authority acts as the manager of this group. We will call this trusted authority *GR* (for group manager). The role of *GR* is to fill, only once, each user's device (not necessarily tamper-resistant) with a special string. The only constraint is that *GR* is trusted to produce only one such string per user. We will call such string a license[1] (or membership certificate using the terminology of [1, 2]).

Our scheme is an anonymous payment system, however the customers' anonymity may be revoked by a proper trusted authority. We will call this trusted authority the revocation manager (*RM* in short). The customers' anonymity can be revoked in the following way:
- *owner tracing:* the bank provides the trusted authority with data of a (suspect) payment (in fact the deposit) and asks for the identity of the customer who has withdrawn the money used in this (suspect) payment.

3.1 The Set-up of the System

For the sake of simplicity, we assume that there is only one coin denomination in the system (extension to multiple denominations is easy).

The Group Manager. The group manager computes the following values:
- an element $n \in$ N. For this purpose, *GR* selects random primes p, q, p' and q' ($p < q$), such that $p = 2p'+1$, $q = 2q' + 1$ (where p' and q' are of equal length).

---

[1] This concept was first introduced in [32].

- GR computes $n = pq$. Let l_n denotes the bit-length of n.
- a public exponent $e > 4$ such that e is relatively prime to $\varphi(n)$.
- a prime number P such that n divides $P-1$[1].
- g an element of Z_P^* of order n. Let $G = \langle g \rangle$.
- an element $h \in G$ whose discrete logarithm to the base g must not be known.
- a (suitably chosen)[2] element $C \in Z_n^*$.
- N another element of N. ($N = P_1 Q_1$, where $P_1 < Q_1$, $P_1 = 2P'+1$, $Q_1 = 2Q'+1$ and P_1, Q_1, P', and Q' are all prime numbers). Let l_N denotes the bit-length of N.
- an element $\beta \in Z_N^*$ of large multiplicative order modulo both primes factors of N.
- $\alpha \in Z_N^*$ such that $\alpha \equiv \beta^2 (\bmod N)$. (Note that α is a quadratic residue modulo N).
- three constants l_1, l_2 and $\varepsilon > 1$. (These parameters are required for the proofs of knowledge $Proof_{LOG+RANGE}$ and $Proof_{REP+RANGE}$).

Then, GR publishes the group's public key P_{group}:

- $P_{group} = (n, e, g, h, C, l_n, l_N, \varepsilon, l_1, l_2, N, \beta, \alpha)$.

Finally, GR publishes a one-way hash function H that maps $\{0,1\}^*$ to Z_{2^k} (where k is an appropriate security parameter). An example of choosing the parameters k, l_1, l_2, ε, l_n and l_N is given in appendix A.

In practice, components of P_{group} must be verifiable to prevent framing attacks. For instance, to verify that β has large order in Z_N^*, it is enough to test whether $\beta \neq -1$ and 1 and that $\gcd(\beta - 1, n) = 1$ (Lemma 1). This proves that β has order at least $P'Q'$. Consequently, α which is equal to $\beta^2 (\bmod N)$ has order $P'Q'$. GR also needs to provide a proof that N belongs to N (i.e., $N = P_1 Q_1$, where $P_1 < Q_1$, $P_1 = 2P'+1$, $Q_1 = 2Q'+1$ and P_1, Q_1, P', and Q' are all prime numbers). See [24] or [22] for efficient methods providing this kind of proof.

The Revocation Manager

1. RM chooses a secret value $x_R \in Z_n^*$.
2. RM publishes $h_R = h^{x_R} (\bmod P)$.

The Bank

1. The bank B chooses an RSA modulus N_B, a public exponent e_B and the corresponding RSA private key d_B (i.e., $e_B \cdot d_B \equiv 1 \bmod \varphi(N_B)$).
2. B publishes e_B and N_B.

---

[1] One way to achieve this is first to generate n and then find by exhaustive search $P = \omega \cdot n + 1$ (where ω is an integer) as small as possible. In [40], it is argued that given a random n, P can be expected to be less than $n \cdot \log_2^2 n$).

[2] See [27] for example.

Finally, B publishes two one-way hash functions H_1 and H_2.

H_1: $\{0,1\}^* \rightarrow Z_{N_B}$ and H_2: $\{0,1\}^* \rightarrow Z_N$.

Beforehand, every user must obtain a license (membership certificate) from GR.

3.2 Obtaining a License

The first step in our system is obtaining a license from GR. A license in our scheme consists of a pair of integers (X, δ) satisfying:

$$X^e \equiv C + \delta \ (\text{mod } n) \text{ and } \delta \in I = [2^{l_1}, 2^{l_1} + 2^{l_2} - 1]. \tag{1}$$

To obtain his license, each user U_i must perform the following protocol with GR.

1. U_i randomly selects an element x_i in $I = [2^{l_1}, 2^{l_1} + 2^{l_2} - 1]$ and computes $ID_{U_i} = g^{x_i} (\text{mod } P)$ and $id_{U_i} = \alpha^{x_i} (\text{mod } N)$. ($x_i$ can be jointly determined by U_i and GR).

2. Then, U_i must prove to GR that he knows $\log_g ID_{U_i}$ and that this value is in $I_{extended}$ (see definition 4). For this purpose, U_i generates $U = Proof_{LOG+RANGE}(\tilde{\varepsilon}, g, ID_{U_i}, \alpha, id_{U_i}, l_1, l_2, l_N, \varepsilon, k)$. Then, he computes $y = g^{C+x_i} (\text{mod } P)$.

3. Next, U_i chooses $r \in_R Z_n^*$ and computes $z = r^e(C + x_i) \mod n$. He then chooses $a \in_R Z_n^*$ and computes $A = g^z h^a = y^r h^a$. U_i then generates $V = Proof_{REP+ROOT}(\tilde{\varepsilon}, e, y, h, A)$.

4. U_i then sends y, z, U and V to GR.

GR verifies these proofs and if the verifications are successful sends to U_i:

- $\tilde{z} = z^{1/e} (\text{mod } n) = r(C + x_i)^{1/e} (\text{mod } n)$.

U_i computes $X = \tilde{z}/r = (C + x_i)^{1/e} \mod n$.

(X, x_i) is the license of U_i.

Note: this license has been issued in a blind manner (using the blind RSA-signature scheme of Chaum [14]). Consequently, at the end of the protocol, GR does not know (X, x_i).

GR creates a new entry in the *group database* and stores ID_{U_i} and id_{U_i} (U_i's account number) in the new entry.

Remark: If there exists t users in the system, then GR must issue t distinct solutions of the particular equation (1). So, let us introduce another assumption.

The security of our scheme relies on the following assumption: given one or more licenses, it is hard to compute a new license without the help of the group manager.

This assumption does not hold when $l_2 > l_n^{\frac{1}{2}}$ ([25, 29, 30]). An example of choosing the parameters l_2 is given in appendix A. (Our choice is based on the recommendations given in [29, 30]).

3.3 The Withdrawal Protocol

Each user that has an account and a license can ask for coins from the bank. Below we will describe the two move protocol that allows a user U_i to withdraw a coin $C_\$$. Before the user and the bank begin the protocol, U_i must authenticate itself to the bank, so that B is sure that U_i is the owner of the corresponding account.

This can be done by any (fast) standard authentication protocol. If the authentication is successful, then U_i sends a *blind* string s to the bank and the bank returns an RSA-signature on s^1. Then U_i extracts the blind factor and obtains a coin $C_\$$ of the form $(x, S(x))$ (where $S(x)$ is the bank's signature on x). If smart cards are used, the elements necessary to produce the string s can be computed in a preprocessing mode during the idle time of the processor and not necessarily during the withdrawal. For this reason, the withdrawal protocol is very practical.

Let (X, x_i) be the license of U_i. ($X^e \equiv C + x_i \pmod{n}$).

More formally, U_i performs the following protocol with B.

1. U_i chooses $(a, b, z) \in_R Z_n^{*3}$ and $r \in_R Z_{N_B}^*$. He then computes:

    - $A = g^{x_i} h^z \pmod{P}$
    - $ot = h_R^z \pmod{P}$
    - $D = g^a h^b \pmod{P}$
    - $E = h_R^b \pmod{P}$. Let M be the following message: $M = A \parallel ot \parallel D \parallel E$.
    - $s = r^{e_B} H_1(M) \bmod N_B$.

U_i sends s to B.

2. B computes $s^{d_B} \bmod N_B$ and sends this value to U_i.

U_i computes $H_1(M)^{d_B} \bmod N_B = \dfrac{s^{d_B}}{r} \bmod N_B$. $C_\$ = (M, H_1(M)^{d_B} \bmod N_B)$.

Note: the message $M = A \parallel ot \parallel D \parallel E$ (disclosed during the payment protocol) is intended to both assure *owner-tracing* (thanks to the '*ownertrace*' $ot = h_R^z \pmod{P}$) and prevent future *double-spending* of the coin (thanks to $D = g^a h^b \pmod{P}$ and $E = h_R^b \pmod{P}$).

3.4 The Payment Protocol

The user U_i wants to spend the coin $C_\$$ in the shop S. We assume that the shop S is known under Id_s (its account number for example), and define 't' to be the payment (date and) time. Let $msg = (Id_s \parallel t)$.

Payment consists of two stages: coin authentication and proof phase. During the coin authentication phase, the shop verifies that the coin $C_\$$ bears the bank's signature. In the proof phase, the user tries to convince the shop that his license is 'embedded' in his coin.

Let us describe the proof phase:

1. U_i computes $F = A \cdot g^C = g^{x_i + C} h^z = g^{X^e} h^z \pmod{P}$.

---

[1] Any other blind signature scheme can be used.

He then generates $U = Proof_{REP+ROOT}(\tilde{\varepsilon}, e, g, h, F)$.

Let $m \in {}_R Z_N^*$ (for example $m = H_2(msg\|M)$) and $\delta = m^2 \bmod N$. We know that $\delta \in \langle \alpha \rangle$ (Lemma 2 *improved*).

U_i computes $T = \delta^{\tau_i} \bmod N$ and generates $V = Proof_{REP+RANGE}(\tilde{\varepsilon}, g, h, A, \delta, T, l_1, l_2, l_N, \varepsilon, k)$. (this proof will convince the shop that the g-part of the representation of A with respect to (g, h) is in $I_{extended}$ (see definition 4)).

Finally, U_i uses the commitments D and E to generate :

$Proof(ot) = Proof_{REP+LOGEQ}(msg, h, g, A, h_R, ot)$ (for *owner tracing*). More precisely, $Proof(ot) = (c, r_1, r_2)$, where: $c = H(msg \| h \| g \| A \| h_R \| ot \| D \| E)$, $r_1 = b - c z \bmod n$ and $r_2 = a - c x_i \bmod n$, with (a, b) from the withdrawal (section 3.3). U_i sends $C_\$$, U, V and $Proof(ot)$ to the shop.

2. S verifies the bank's signature and the proofs and, if the verifications hold, accepts the payment.

Note: U and V will convince the shop that a license is 'embedded' in $C_\$$.

3.5 The Deposit Protocol

To be credited with the value of this coin, the shop sends the transcript of the execution of the payment protocol to the bank, which verifies, exactly as the shop did, that the coin $C_\$$ bears the bank's signature and that the other responses are correct.

Acknowledgments. We would like to thank Marc Girault for fruitful discussions and suggestions. We also thank Guiseppe Ateniese, Zulfikar Ramzan and Yiannis Tsiounis for their useful comments.

References

1. G. Ateniese and G. Tsudik, Group signatures à la carte, ACM Symposium on Discrete Logarithms, (to appear) January 1999. Available at http://www.isi.edu/~gts/pubs.html.
2. G. Ateniese and G. Tsudik, A coalition-resistant group signature, available as ISI Technical Report at: http://www.isi.edu/~gts/pubs.html.
3. D. Boneh, The decision Diffie-Hellman problem, *Proceedings of* the third Algorithmic Number Theory Symposium, Lecture Notes in Computer Science, Vol. 1423, Springer-Verlag, pp. 48-63.
4. S. Brands, An efficient off-line electronic cash system based on the representation problem, Technical Report CS-R9323, CWI, April 1993.
5. S. Brands, Untraceable off-line cash in wallets with observers, *Proceedings of* CRYPTO'93, Lecture Notes in Computer Science, Vol. 773, Springer-Verlag, pp. 302-318.
6. E. F. Brickell and J. M. DeLaurentis, An attack on a signature scheme proposed by Okamoto and Shiraishi, *Proceedings of* CRYPTO'85, Lecture Notes in Computer Science, Vol. 218, Springer-Verlag, pp. 28-32.
7. J. Camenisch, Efficient and generalized group signatures, *Proceedings of* EUROCRYPT'97, Lecture Notes in Computer Science, Vol. 1233, Springer-Verlag, pp. 465-479.
8. J. Camenisch and M. Michels, A group signature scheme with improved efficiency, *Proceedings of* ASIACRYPT'98, Lecture Notes in Computer Science, Vol. 1514, Springer-Verlag, pp. 160-174.
9. J. Camenisch and M. Michels, A group signature scheme with improved efficiency. *Revised extended abstract*.
10. J. Camenisch and M. Stadler, Efficient group signatures for large groups, *Proceedings of* CRYPTO'97, Lecture Notes in Computer Science, Vol. 1296, Springer-Verlag, pp. 410-424.
11. A. Chan, Y. Frankel, and Y. Tsiounis, Easy come - easy go divisible cash, *Proceedings of* EUROCRYPT'98, Lecture Notes in Computer Science, Vol. 1403, Springer-Verlag, pp. 561-575.

12. A. Chan, Y. Frankel, and Y. Tsiounis, Easy come - easy go divisible cash. *Updated version with corrections on the Range Bounded Commitment protocol.* Available at http://www.ccs.neu.edu/home/yiannis/pubs.html.

13. D. Chaum, Blind signatures for untraceable payments, *Proceedings of* CRYPTO'82, Plenum Press, 1983, pp. 199-203.

14. D. Chaum, Blind signature systems, *Proceedings of* CRYPTO'83, Plenum Press, 1984, page 153.

15. D. Chaum, A. Fiat and M. Naor, Untraceable electronic cash, *Proceedings of* CRYPTO'88, Lecture Notes in Computer Science, Vol. 403, Springer-Verlag, pp. 319-327.

16. D. Chaum and T. Pedersen, Wallet databases with observers, *Proceedings of* CRYPTO'92, Lecture Notes in Computer Science, Vol. 740, Springer-Verlag, pp. 89-105.

17. D. Chaum and E. van Heijst, Group signatures, *Proceedings of* EUROCRYPT'91, Lecture Notes in Computer Science, Vol. 547, Springer-Verlag, pp. 257-265.

18. L. Chen and T. Pedersen, New group signature schemes, *Proceedings of* EUROCRYPT'94, Lecture Notes in Computer Science, Vol. 950, Springer-Verlag, pp. 171-181.

19. U. Feige, A. Fiat and A. Shamir, Zero-knowledge proofs of identity, Journal of Cryptology, 1 (2), pp. 77-94, 1988.

20. A. Fiat and A. Shamir, How to prove yourself, *Proceedings of* CRYPTO'86, Lecture Notes in Computer Science, Vol. 263, Springer-Verlag, pp. 186-194.

21. E. Fujisaki and T. Okamoto, Statistical zero knowledge protocols to prove modular polynomial relations, *Proceedings of* CRYPTO'97, Lecture Notes in Computer Science, Vol. 1294, Springer-Verlag, pp. 16-30.

22. R. Gennaro, H. Krawczyk, and T. Rabin, RSA-based undeniable signatures, *Proceedings of* CRYPTO'97, Lecture Notes in Computer Science, Vol. 1294, Springer-Verlag, pp. 231-234.

23. R. Gennaro, H. Krawczyk and T. Rabin, RSA-based undeniable signatures, *Final version.* Available at http://www.research.ibm.com/security/papers1997.html.

24. R. Gennaro, D. Micciancio, and T. Rabin, An efficient non-interactive statistical zero-knowledge proof system for quasi-safe prime products. To appear in the *Proceedings* of the Fifth ACM Conference on Computer and Communications Security, 1998.

25. M. Girault and J.F. Misarsky, Selective forgery of RSA signatures using redundancy, *Proceedings of* EUROCRYPT'97, Lecture Notes in Computer Science, Vol. 1233, Springer-Verlag, pp. 495-507.

26. M. Girault, P. Toffin, and B. Vallée, Computations of approximate L-th roots modulo n and application to cryptography, *Proceedings of* CRYPTO'88, Lecture Notes in Computer Science, Vol. 403, Springer-Verlag, pp. 100-117.

27. L.C. Guillou, J.J. Quisquater, M. Walker, P. Landrock, and C. Shaer, Precautions taken against various potential attacks in ISO/IEC DIS 9796, Digital signature scheme giving message recovery, *Proceedings of* EUROCRYPT'90, Lecture Notes in Computer Science, Vol. 473, Springer-Verlag, pp. 465-473.

28. A. Lysyanskaya and Z. Ramzan, Group blind digital signatures: A scalable solution to electronic cash, *Proceedings of* the 2nd Financial Cryptography conference, Anguilla, BWI, February 98. Springer-Verlag. To appear.

29. J. F. Misarsky, A multiplicative attack using LLL algorithm on RSA signatures with redundancy, *Proceedings of* CRYPTO'97, Lecture Notes in Computer Science, Vol. 1294, Springer-Verlag, pp. 231-234.

30. J.F. Misarsky, How (not) to design RSA signatures schemes, *Proceedings of* PKC'98, Lecture Notes in Computer Science, Vol. 1431, Springer-Verlag, pp. 14-28.

31. T. Okamoto, Provably secure and practical identification schemes and corresponding signature schemes, *Proceedings of* CRYPTO'92, Lecture Notes in Computer Science, Vol. 740, Springer-Verlag, pp. 31-53.

32. T. Okamoto and K. Ohta, Disposable zero-knowledge authentications and their applications to untraceable electronic cash, *Proceedings of* CRYPTO'89, Lecture Notes in Computer Science, Vol. 435, Springer-Verlag, pp. 481-497.

33. T. Okamoto and A. Shiraishi, A fast signature scheme based on quadratic inequalities, *Proceedings of* IEEE Symposium on Security and Privacy, pp. 123-132, 1985.

34. H. Petersen, How to convert any digital signature scheme into a group signature scheme. In *Security Protocols Workshop*, Paris, 1997.

35. Z. Ramzan, Group blind signatures à la carte, unpublished, available at http://theory.lcs.mit.edu/~zulfikar/homepage.html.

36. M. Stadler. Cryptographic protocols for revocable privacy. PhD thesis, ETH Zürich, 1996. Diss. ETH No. 11651.
37. Y. Tsiounis, Efficient electronic cash: new notions and techniques. PhD thesis, College of Computer Science, Northeastern University, Boston, MA, 1997. Available at http://www.ccs.neu.edu/home/yiannis/pubs.html.
38. Y. Tsiounis, *Personal communication.*
39. B. Vallée, M. Girault, and P. Toffin, How to guess l-th roots modulo n by reducing lattice bases, *AAECC-6*, Lecture Notes in Computer Science, Vol. 357, Springer-Verlag, pp. 427-442.
40. S.S. Wagstaff Jr, Greatest of the Least Primes in Arithmetic Progression Having a given modulus, Mathematics of computation, 33 (147), pp. 1073-1080.

Appendix A: The Security of the Scheme

Let us analyze, informally speaking, the security of our scheme. (Due to space limitations, the description of the tracing mechanisms is omitted).

Security for B (unforgeability). The security of our cash system is based on the security of the RSA signature scheme and on the assumption that computing a valid license is infeasible if the factorization of the modulus n is unknown.

Anonymity. The blind RSA-signature scheme is a perfect blind signature scheme. (Consequently, it prevents linking the withdrawal of a coin to the payment made with this coin). So, in our system only $T = \delta^{x_i} \bmod N$ could help to establish a link between a payment and an account number $id_{U_i} = \alpha^{x_i} \bmod N$. However, if the decision Diffie-Hellman assumption holds, it is hard to establish such a link. Moreover, U, V and $Proof(ot)$ leak no information that seem useful to establishing a link between a payment and an account number.

Blacklist (see also Appendix B). Let $(\widetilde{X}, \widetilde{x})$ be the license of a multiple spender. Then, this license can be put on a blacklist. This blacklist can be sent to the vendors. At the time of a payment, the vendor can check whether the customer's license is on the blacklist or not. For this purpose, he must perform the following test (for each $\widetilde{x}$ in the blacklist[1]): $T \stackrel{?}{=} \delta^{\widetilde{x}} \bmod N$ (see the payment protocol for the signification of T).

Systems parameters. We propose to use our system with the following parameters: $e = 5$, $\varepsilon = 4/3$, $k = 80$, $l_1 = 325$, $l_2 = 160$, $l_n = 800$, $l_N = 1200$.

Appendix B: Weaknesses of the Lysyanskaya-Ramzan Trustee Based Anonymous Off-line Electronic Cash system

In this section, we describe some weaknesses in the design of the *group based* anonymous *off-line* electronic cash system of Lysyanskaya and Ramzan [28]. Borrowing freely from the exposition in [28], we now recall how their cash system works.

In their schemes, all the banks form a group and the *designated entity* with respect to this group is (for example) the country's Central Bank. The users (spenders) in their system form a group too. A trusted third party (TTP for short) acts as the *designated entity* of this group. When a user wants to withdraw e-cash from his bank, he first creates an electronic coin C.

---

[1] If the licenses are stored in tamper-resistant smart cards, the blacklist will contain only few values.

His bank applies a *group blind signature* to C and withdraws the appropriate amount from the user's account. The user can now spent his coin C in a shop. For this purpose, he applies the *user group* signature to C (now, no one, except the TTP can determine the identity of the spender). He now gives C, both the bank's and the user's signature on C to a vendor. The vendor uses the *banks' public key* to verify the bank's signature on C. He also checks that the user's group signature is authentic (by using the *users' public key*). If the coin is valid, the vendor gives Alice her merchandise, and gives the coin to his bank. If there are any conflicts (e.g., the user has double-spent his coin), then the TTP can intervene and determine the identity of the user.

The weakness of this approach comes from not embedding (in a way or another) the user's identity in the coin he withdraws. This leads to the following collusion attack: Let Alice and Bob be two (colluding) users. Let s_B be Bob's private key with respect to the *users' public key*. Bob can withdraw a coin C and spend it several times in different shops. This fraud will be detected, Bob will be identified and (probably) not allowed in future to make new withdrawals. But this by no means prevents him from giving his private key s_B to Alice, who can use s_B to sign coins $\tilde{C}$ she (legitimately) withdrew at her bank...and spend it as many times as she likes - since the fraud will be attributed forever to Bob ! Still worse: even if s_B were disclosed and put on a blacklist, this would be of no help since there is no way the merchant can detect that s_B has been used (group signatures are untraceable and unlinkable). Note that collusion is even not required: Bob may be a honest user whose key has been compromised or lost (and which is fraudulently used by Alice). So the problem the TTP has to solve is to find a method of stopping such a fraud. In section 3, we will give a solution to this problem.

Note: In traditional electronic cash systems [4, 15] (i.e., not based on a group signature scheme) such a fraud is not possible.

Appendix C: Weaknesses of some Group Signature Schemes

In this appendix, we describe some weaknesses of recently proposed group signature schemes [1, 2, 10, 28][1]. In [1], Ateniese and Tsudik presented an efficient group signature scheme. However they do not address the issue of 'coalition resistance' (an important security requirement for group signature schemes). They have studied this problem in the appendix to their original paper [1] and also in a separate paper [2]. In this section, we will focus on this issue. The group signature scheme described in [1] is clearly not coalition-resistant. So, we will examine their second scheme [2].

More precisely, we will show that three colluding members of the group can generate a valid *membership certificate* without the help of the *group manager*. As a consequence, these colluding members can generate valid group signatures which are *perfectly* untraceable (that is, the *revocation manager* is unable to determine the originator of such signatures).

Let us briefly describe the Ateniese-Tsudik group signature scheme.

In the setup phase, the group manager (which is also the revocation manager) must perform the following operations: he creates an RSA modulus $n = pq$, $p = 2p'+1$, $q = 2q'+1$ where p, q, p', q' are primes (only the group manager knows p, q, p' and q').

---

[1] Due to space limitations, we will only describe an attack on [2].

Then, he chooses two elements $a, b \in Z_n^*$ of large multiplicative order modulo both prime factors of n. Finally, he selects two secret random exponents y, z, and a public prime v and computes: $Y = a^{-y}$ and $Z = a^z$. The group public key is: $\Psi = (n, v, a, b, Y, Z)$.

If a user M wants to join the group he has to pick certain parameters and engage in a protocol with the group manager in order to obtain a *membership certificate*.

The user chooses a value x such that $0 < x < v$ and at the end of the protocol, he will obtain a membership certificate (A, B) where: $A = a^{(x+y)v^{-1}}$, $B = b^{x^2 v^{-1}}$. x is the private key of the user M. (In fact, the value x is jointly chosen by the member and the group manager. However, only the member knows x). To sign on behalf of the group requires the knowledge of a value x and a corresponding membership certificate $A = a^{(x+y)v^{-1}}$, $B = b^{x^2 v^{-1}}$.

The coalition resistance of the Ateniese-Tsudik protocol [2] is based on the following assumption: given one or more certificates of the form ($A = a^{(x+y)v^{-1}}$, $B = b^{x^2 v^{-1}}$), it is hard to generate a new membership certificate without the help of the group manager.

Let M_1, M_2, M_3 be three *colluding* members of the group.

Let (A_i, B_i) be the certificate of the member M_i ($i \in \{1, 2, 3\}$).

So, $A_i = a^{(x_i + y)v^{-1}}$, $B_i = b^{x_i^2 v^{-1}}$, where x_i is known by M_i and is such that: $0 < x_i < v$.

Suppose (for the sake of simplicity) that $0 < x_1 < x_2 < x_3 < v$.

Let $\tilde{x} = x_3 - x_2 + x_1$. We have $0 < \tilde{x} < v$.

Let $d = \gcd(x_1, x_2, x_3)$. Let $y_i = x_i / d$ ($i \in \{1, 2, 3\}$).

We have: $d^2 = \gcd(x_1^2, x_2^2, x_3^2)$. So, we can find three integers, α, β and δ such that: $\alpha \cdot x_1^2 + \beta \cdot x_2^2 + \delta \cdot x_3^2 = d^2$. Let $C = B_1^\alpha \cdot B_2^\beta \cdot B_3^\delta$. This implies that: $C = b^{d^2 v^{-1}}$. Recall that: $\tilde{x} = x_3 - x_2 + x_1 = y_3 \cdot d - y_2 \cdot d + y_1 \cdot d = d \cdot (y_3 - y_2 + y_1)$. So, $\tilde{x}^2 = d^2 \cdot (y_3 - y_2 + y_1)^2$. Let $\tilde{A} = A_3 \cdot A_1 \cdot A_2^{-1}$ and $\tilde{B} = C^{(y_3 - y_2 + y_1)^2}$.

This implies that: $\tilde{A} = a^{(\tilde{x} + y)v^{-1}}$, $\tilde{B} = b^{\tilde{x}^2 v^{-1}}$. So $(\tilde{A}, \tilde{B})$ is a **valid** membership certificate that cannot be traced. Consequently, the proposed scheme is not coalition-resistant[1].

---

[1] We have informed Ateniese and Tsudik of our attack. They have modified their scheme in order to thwart our attack. In their new scheme a membership certificate is of the form: $A = a^{(x+y_1)v^{-1}}$, $B = b^{(x^2 + y_2)v^{-1}}$, where y_1 and y_2 are two secret exponents. Unfortunately, this new scheme is vulnerable to an attack similar to the one described in Appendix C.

We point out that a similar attack to the one described in Appendix C also applies to the first group signature scheme described in [10], as also observed independently by Ateniese and Tsudik [2]. This scheme is also used in [28]. Due to space limitations, we will only describe the attack on this scheme [10] in the full paper, in which we will also propose two heuristic methods to thwart this attack.

Efficient Electronic Cash Using Batch Signatures

Colin Boyd, Ernest Foo*, and Chris Pavlovski

Information Security Research Centre
School of Data Communications
Queensland University of Technology
Brisbane, Australia
{boyd,ernest,pavlovsk}@fit.qut.edu.au

Abstract. All known anonymous electronic cash protocols are inefficient compared to other electronic payment protocols. This is because much of the complexity of the protocols is devoted to ensuring the anonymity of the consumer. This problem is addressed with an extension of Brands' electronic cash payment protocol using batch cryptography. Batch signature generation is used to improve the efficiency of the withdrawal process so that multiple coins can be withdrawn for almost the cost of only one Brands' coin withdrawal. As a consequence coins withdrawn together can be linked. Batch verification is also used to increase the efficiency of payment. We show that the security of the original scheme is maintained and the level of privacy provided by the cash scheme can be determined by the customer.

1 Introduction

For the last few years, anonymous off-line electronic payment has seen growing interest from both the research and the business communities. In its simplest form electronic payment consists of three remote entities: the merchant, the customer and the bank. These entities participate in four secure protocols conducted over insecure communications channels. During execution of these protocols an electronic coin (a series of bits representing commitment to value) is transmitted between the three entities. These protocols are called registration, withdrawal, payment and deposit. The customer identifies herself to the bank in the registration protocol and establishes necessary cryptographic keys. The customer obtains an electronic coins from the bank in the withdrawal protocol. The customer exchanges electronic coins for goods from the merchant during payment. The merchant returns the coins to the bank during deposit.

An electronic payment scheme is *anonymous* if the merchant and the bank cannot determine the identity of the customer involved in a transaction during payment or when the electronic coin is deposited. An electronic payment protocol is *off-line* if the customer and the merchant conduct the payment protocol without the participation of the bank. Brands' protocol [3] is both anonymous (no matter how computationally powerful any of the entities are) and off-line.

---

* Sponsored by Commonwealth Bank and the Australian Research Council

In addition, it provides *single-term* coins which can only be spent once before being deposited back to the bank. All these properties will be inherited by the scheme proposed in this paper, except that the strength of anonymity will become tuneable in a way that we will specify.

Despite the similarities between electronic payment and physical payment, the number of practical anonymous off-line electronic payment schemes which have been implemented for long-term use is surprisingly low. There are still some major issues which must be addressed before anonymous electronic payment is widely accepted. One of these issues is consumer confidence in the security of the transaction and in the privacy of the transaction. Another issue which is important is the efficiency of the protocols used both in terms of data transmitted and in computation. All proposed schemes expend a large computational effort in providing the customer with anonymity from the bank and the merchant. Banks do not want to spend a lot of computations achieving a withdrawal especially when large numbers of transactions have to be accommodated. Customers and merchants do not want to spend a lot of time conducting payments or storing large amounts of information as electronic coins.

We address the issue of efficient electronic payment systems in this paper while still maintaining the anonymous and off-line properties. We are particularly interested in reducing computation for the bank during withdrawal, since the bank is the 'central server' that will have the highest computational load.

1.1 Previous Work

There have been numerous anonymous electronic payment schemes presented in the literature. Chaum [7] was the first to use a blind signature mechanism (also introduced by Chaum [6]) to construct an anonymous payment scheme. Chaum's first scheme granted the customer unlimited anonymity which would allow the possibility for abuse of the system by spending coins many times. Several subsequent protocols provided anonymity revocation on the detection of double spending or some other protocol breach [9, 11, 14, 16, 20, 10]. Unfortunately most of these schemes were too complex and computationally intensive to be practical. It wasn't until Brands [3] presented his untraceable off-line cash scheme based on Schnorr signatures [22] that a practical anonymous scheme became available. Since then many proposed anonymous payment schemes have been variations of Brands' original protocol [2, 13, 17, 8, 18, 4]. However, even Brands' scheme is much more computationally intensive than we would like, particularly for the bank which is likely to have to serve large numbers of customers simultaneously when electronic cash becomes popular. Our payment scheme is based on Brands' too and changes the withdrawal and payment phases to improve efficiency.

There are a number of divisible cash schemes in the literature [20, 9, 19, 5]. The basis of all these protocols is that the value of a single coin can be split so that an exact value is used in a transaction. This can be compared with our protocol in that we also enable many payments from a single withdrawal, although our protocol is not a truly divisible cash protocol. The problem with the known divisible cash schemes is that they all appear to have a computationally expensive setup process which severely limits their overall efficiency.

Brands' protocol and most of its variations have the same structure. During withdrawal the bank and the customer exchange information (including the identity of the customer) which is used to generate a representation of the electronic coin for the customer to commit to. This data is blinded by the customer and sent to the bank. In this way, the customer hides her identity from the bank and others. Once the bank is convinced the coin has been constructed correctly and that it does contain the identity of the customer, he sends the signed coin back to the customer.

During payment the customer transfers the bank signed customer commitment as the coin to the merchant. The merchant provides some information to link the coin to a particular transaction. The coin and transaction data are finally returned to the bank by the merchant during deposit. Then the bank verifies that the transaction has been conducted correctly. If double spending of the coin is detected then the bank can revoke the anonymity of the coin by revealing the identity of the customer. The bank is unable to do this unless the customer has actually spent the coin twice.

The most complex and computationally expensive component of the entire scheme is not the payment protocol but the withdrawal process. The protocol which we present addresses this weakness by allowing multiple coins to be withdrawn in a protocol which is based on a Brands' protocol for withdrawal of a single coin. In addition, we show how the merchant can also save in computation by checking the validity of several coins at the same time.

1.2 Our Approach

In this paper, an extension to Brands' untraceable off-line cash protocol [3] is presented. The main idea is to use techniques from *batch cryptography* to streamline the processing required. Batch signature generation increases the efficiency of the blind signature generated by the bank in the withdrawal protocol. In effect batch signatures allow many coins to be withdrawn using the one withdrawal procedure. The computational expense for this process is equivalent to just one blind signature! The cost is a small increase in the size of coins, which increases linearly with the number of coins withdrawn. We use another batch technique during payment, to reduce the cost to the merchant of verifying many coins together. By allowing multiple coins to be exchanged in a single payment we can use our protócol to conduct transactions of exact change. We regard the following as the main contributions of the current paper.

- The use of a batch signature generation algorithm in conjunction with a (blinded) Schnorr signature scheme.
- A new anonymous electronic cash scheme which is more efficient than other similar anonymous payment schemes but still provides the same security as Brands' untraceable off-line cash protocol.

In section 2 we provide an overview of the new payment scheme. In section 3 we discuss the security of this new scheme and compare its security with Brands' scheme. In section 4 we comment on the performance of our new scheme. In the appendix of this paper describe batch signature generation based on the Schnorr signature scheme which is the basis of the coins used in our scheme. We also prove the security of these batch signatures.

2 The New Cash Protocol

We must define some parameters. In most cases these are the same as those used by Brands and we keep the notation the same as far as possible. Let the bank choose the large primes p, q as public keys where q is a factor of $p - 1$ and a private key $x \in_R \mathbb{Z}_q$. The bank also publishes a set of random public generators g, g_1, g_2. Here the value g_2 is a new parameter which varies according to the specific number of coins n within a batch. In this way all the entities in the transaction can verify that the correct number of coins are contained within each batch coin. The bank has an additional public key $h = g^x$. Let $\mathcal{H}$ and $\mathcal{H}_0$ be publicly known collision-free functions.

We shall use a batched version of the signature used by Brands, which is in turn a variant of Schnorr's signature. (The batched version of Schnorr's signature is described in the appendix and its security is proven.) We shall say that the tuple $(h_1, \ldots, h_n, z, a, b, r, i)$ is a signature of the pair A, B_i if

$$g^r = h^c a \qquad \text{and} \qquad A^r = z^c b$$

where $h_i = \mathcal{H}_0(B_i)$ and $c = \mathcal{H}(A \| h_1 \| \ldots \| h_n) \| z \| a \| b)$.

We will refer to this signature as $sign(A, B_i)$. This can be extended in the obvious way to any subset of B_i values which are signed with the same z, a, b, r values.

Before any protocol can be conducted, the customer must register her identity with the bank. This is equivalent of opening an account with the bank in the physical world. During the registration process the customer and the bank securely exchange a value $I = g_1^{u_1}$ which uniquely identifies the customer to the bank. The value u_1 is a secret kept by the customer.

2.1 Withdrawal

During the payment protocol (see figure 1) the customer is able to generate a valid electronic coin with the assistance of the bank. As in Brands' cash protocol, it is assumed that when a customer wishes to withdraw an electronic coin from the bank, she has previously proven that she has a valid account at the bank.

The bank, on determining that the customer owns a valid account, chooses a random number $\omega \in_R \mathbb{Z}_q$. The bank also calculates the values $z = (Ig_2)^x$, $a = g^\omega$ and $b = (Ig_2)^\omega$. The value a represents the witness value which is normally generated by the Schnorr signature. The values b and z are to be used to build a representation of the electronic coin which hides the customer's identity. The values a, b and z are transmitted to the customer.

At the same time, or at a previous time off-line, the customer chooses several random numbers $s, x_{1_1}, \ldots, x_{1_n}, x_{2_1}, \ldots, x_{2_n} \in_R \mathbb{Z}_q$ where n is the number of coins to be withdrawn from the bank during this withdrawal protocol run. These values are to be used to build a unique representation of the coin and to hide the customer's identity within the coin. The customer generates the coins' representations by computing $A = (Ig_2)^s$, $B_1 = g_1^{x_{1_1}} g_2^{x_{2_1}}, \ldots, B_n = g_1^{x_{1_n}} g_2^{x_{2_n}}$ and $z' = z^s$.

On receiving a, b and z from the bank, the customer chooses the random blinding factors u and v. The customer then computes $a' = a^u g^v$ and $b' = b^{su} A^v$. Then she calculates the challenge $c' = \mathcal{H}(A, \mathcal{H}_0(B_1), \ldots, \mathcal{H}_0(B_n), z', a', b')$ and sends the blinded challenge $c = c'/u$ to the bank.

The bank returns the appropriate response $r = cx + \omega$ to the customer and debits the customer's account by the appropriate amount.

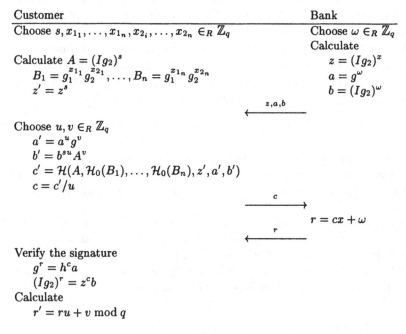

Fig. 1. The withdrawal protocol

The customer now checks that the bank has correctly signed the coin by verifying that $g^r = h^c a$ and $(Ig_2)^r = z^c b$. Once the customer is satisfied she calculates $r' = ru + v \bmod q$. It is straightforward to check that $(\mathcal{H}_0(B_1), \ldots, \mathcal{H}_0(B_n), z', a', b', r', i)$ is a batch signature on the pair (A, B_i), and that the verification mentioned above is equivalent to the verification of this signature.

The customer can now construct the coins which have been withdrawn from the bank. The ith coin and its signature may be denoted by:

$$(A, B_i, \mathcal{H}_0(B_1), \ldots, \mathcal{H}_0(B_{i-1}), \mathcal{H}_0(B_{i+1}), \ldots, \mathcal{H}_0(B_n), z', a', b', r', i).$$

The string $\mathcal{H}_0(B_1), \ldots, \mathcal{H}_0(B_n), z', a', b', r', i$ represents the bank's blinded signature of A, B_i. The customer is able to generate n of these coins which she can spend separately. Each coin is uniquely identified by B_i. As each coin is spent the customer can delete B_i from memory but the customer must retain the values $\mathcal{H}_0(B_1), \ldots, \mathcal{H}_0(B_n)$ until the last coin in the batch has been spent.

Because B_i is transferred in the coin it is not necessary for $\mathcal{H}_0(B_i)$ to be also transferred with the coin. If this option is chosen, the value i must also be included in the coin so that the merchant can insert $\mathcal{H}_0(B_i)$ in the correct order during the payment verification.

Note that because each coin has the same signature, all the coins constructed from a single withdrawal process can be linked, although the identity of the customer who withdrew the coins is still hidden. If the customer was worried about her purchases being tracked with the linked coin she has the option of spending the coins with a single specific merchant or withdrawing one coin with each batch. This will allow the customer to tune the amount of linkability she requires. In practice, banks would probably charge for each withdrawal. This could prove to be costly for a customer who desires no linkability.

2.2 Payment

This protocol (see figure 2) describes the process in which the customer securely transfers an electronic coin to the merchant. It is assumed that once the merchant has verified the receipt of the coin that he sends the correct goods to the customer.

By using batch signatures, the customer can spend more than one coin during a withdrawal protocol and thus an exact change transaction can be conducted. A group of multiple coins is uniquely identified by $B_i, \ldots, B_j$. It is not necessary that these coins be spent in a consecutive manner.

The customer sends a group (or a single one) of her batch signed coins $(A, B_i, \ldots, B_j, sign(A, B_i, \ldots, B_j))$ to the merchant. At this stage the merchant is not sure if this coin is valid or not. So he returns a unique challenge $d = \mathcal{H}(A, B_i, \ldots, B_j, I_M, date/time)$ to the customer. I_M represents the merchant's identity and $date/time$ the recorded date and time of the transaction.

The customer generates the correct responses $r_{1_i} = du_1 s + x_{1_i}, \ldots, r_{1_j} = du_1 s + x_{1_j}$ and $r_{2_i} = ds + x_{2_i}, \ldots, r_{2_j} = du_1 s + x_{2_j}$, for each coin that is to be spent in this transaction. These responses are returned to the merchant.

The merchant must now verify that each of the values $B_i, \ldots, B_j$ has indeed been signed in the batch signature and thus is linked to the signature provided in the coin. To do this he must ensure that the correct B value is used to compute the appropriate $\mathcal{H}_0(B)$ value. If this is true then the merchant can check that $sign(A, B_i, \ldots, B_j)$ is valid by verifying that $g^{r'} = h^{\mathcal{H}(A, \mathcal{H}_0(B_1), \ldots, \mathcal{H}_0(B_n), z', a', b')} a'$

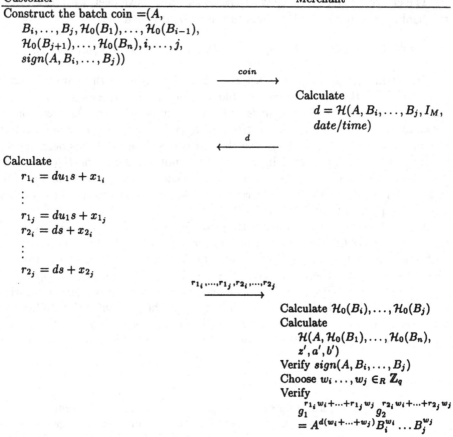

Fig. 2. The payment protocol

and $(Ig_2)^{r'} = z'^{\mathcal{H}(A,\mathcal{H}_0(B_1),...,\mathcal{H}_0(B_n),z',a',b')}b'$. The merchant must also check the representation of the coin and ensure that the customer has not forged the r' values. This is done by choosing random numbers $w_i \ldots, w_j \in_R \mathbb{Z}_q$ and verifying that $g_1^{r_{1_i}w_i+...+r_{1_j}w_j} g_2^{r_{2_i}w_i+...+r_{2_j}w_j} = A^{d(w_i+...+w_j)}B_i^{w_i} \ldots B_j^{w_j}$ before accepting the coin as payment. Without the random numbers $w_i, \ldots, w_j$ it is possible for the customer to choose any values $r'_{1_i}, \ldots, r'_{1_j}$ and $r'_{2_i}, \ldots, r'_{2_j}$ and provided the sum of these values is valid the merchant would be unable to detect the subterfuge. The size of the random values $w_i, \ldots, w_j$ can be chosen to be only 2^{15} bits which allows more efficient modular exponentiations. The security of this choice is analysed by Yen and Laih [23] in their own batch signature verification scheme.

2.3 Deposit

In the deposit protocol (see figure 3) the electronic coin, the values $r_{1_i}, \ldots, r_{1_j}$ and $r_{2_i}, \ldots, r_{2_j}$, the date and time of the transaction and the merchant's identity I_M are returned to the bank by the merchant.

The bank verifies the coin by reconstructing d using the date and time of the transaction and the merchant's identity I_M. The bank can now go through a similar process of verification executed by the merchant during the payment protocol. The link between the batch signature and $B_i, \ldots, B_j$ is verified. If this is valid the batch signature is checked. And if this is valid the coin's representation is verified.

When the verification process is successfully completed the bank can credit the merchant's account the value of the coin.

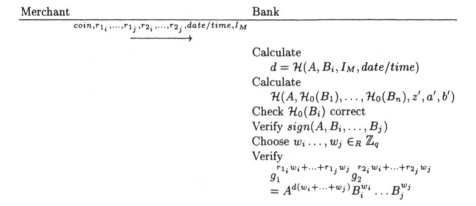

Fig. 3. The deposit protocol

As in Brands' protocol, the identity of the customer can be recovered if the user is found to have double spent the coin. To detect double spending it is necessary that the bank store $(B_i, \ldots, B_j, date/time, I_M, r_{1_i}, r_{2_i})$ from previously spent coins. The bank detects double spent coins by checking for duplicate B's. For example, if a duplicate value, B_i, is found, the bank generates d, r_{1_i} and r_{2_i} from the new information and d', r'_{1_i} and r'_{2_i} from the stored coin information. The bank determines that the merchant has double spent by checking if $d = d'$. Otherwise we assume that the customer has double spent. The customer's identity can be recovered by calculating $g_1^{(r_{1_i} - r'_{1_i})/(r_{2_i} - r'_{2_i})}$ which reveals the customer's identity I.

3 Protocol Security

Our scheme can be viewed as a straightforward variation of Brands' scheme in which the signature and coin verification equations have been changed to batched versions. It is shown in the appendix that the batched Schnorr signature scheme is secure as long as Schnorr's signature scheme is. But forgery of a coin is equivalent to a forgery of the batch Schnorr signature scheme with a modified hash function. The security of the verification procedure also follows from the analysis of similar schemes given by Yen and Laih [23] and Bellare et al. [1].

A *representation* of a value X, with respect to the bases g_1 and g_2, consists of exponents e_1 and e_2 such that $X = g_1^{e_1} g_2^{e_2}$. Following Brands, we say that a customer knows a *representation* of a coin $A, B_i, \mathcal{H}_0(B_1), \ldots, \mathcal{H}_0(B_n)$ if she knows a representation of A and B_i in the with respect to g_1 and g_2. Because $A = g_1^{u_1 s} g_2^s$ and the B_i are chosen as representations in the withdrawal protocol, the following holds.

Proposition 1. *If the customer accepts in the withdrawal protocol, then each (A, B_i) pair is a batched coin of which she knows a representation.*

In the payment protocol the merchant accepts the coins only if (with overwhelming probability) $g_1^{r_{1i}} g_2^{r_{2i}} = A^d B_i$. It is straightforward to show that if the customer can solve this equation for two different values of d then she must know a representation of A and B_i. This can be summarized in the following.

Proposition 2. *A customer can spend a batched coin if and only if she knows a representation of it.*

The arguments given for security of the batch Schnorr scheme imply that existential forgery of a coin is possible only if Schnorr's signature scheme is existentially forgeable. Together with the above results this means that a coin may only be spent by the customer that withdraws the coin.

4 Protocol Efficiency

The efficiency of the scheme may be directly correlated to the savings in computations due to the batch signature generation. There are, however, some additional storage and communication overheads introduced. To consider the storage and communication overheads, we compare a batch coin (A, B_i) and its signature $(\mathcal{H}_0(B_1), \ldots, \mathcal{H}_0(B_n), z', a', b', r', i)$ to a basic coin (A, B) and associated signature (z', a', b', r').

For batch size n, the size of the coin will increase by $160n$ bits (assuming the $\mathcal{H}_0$ function produces 160 bits), plus $\lceil \log n \rceil$ additional bits for i. For example, where p and q are 1024 and 160 bits respectively, a basic coin will be 5270 bits in length[1], whilst, a batch of 10 coins would be 6710 bits, an increase of only 27%. On the other hand, if the coins were individually generated using the basic scheme, this would be 56320 bits! Thus, a comparative assessment based upon the number of coins withdrawn suggests that the batch protocol is lighter. In spite of this, each batch coin will be of the same, increased, size and thus a communications penalty is incurred.

---

[1] $B = 1024$, $A = 1024$, $z' = 1024$, $a' = 1024$, $b' = 1024$, $r' = 160$

In addition to this small increase in coin size, there are some additional computations performed. These will now be viewed from the perspective of each interacting party in respect to the original Brands' scheme when withdrawing n coins.

Bank. The scheme is specifically designed to reduce the computational load imposed on the bank during coin withdrawal. The cost of withdrawing one coin is exactly the same as the cost of withdrawing n coins. The bank performs exactly the same processing steps when signing a batch of coins, with respect to signing a single coin! This could provide large savings to the bank as the batch size increases. For example, a batch of 10 coins would improve the efficiency by 90% over the original scheme.

Later, when the merchant deposits the coin, the bank is required to store the additional $160n$ bits per coin. It is possible, however, that upon detection of the associated batch, the bank may store the spent coin with its parent batch and hence reduce the common storage overheads.

The exponentiation $B_i^{w_i}$ is added to the bank's computations. However, since the w_i are only 15 bits in length this adds only a small amount of computation over that which is required to verify a single coin in Brands original scheme. The additional computation required for each w_i value can be estimated as less than 4% of that required for individual coin verification with the parameters assumed above.

Customer. At the withdrawal stage, the customer performs two additional operations to obtain a batch of coins. This involves the creation of the B_i value, and the creation of its corresponding hash value. If we ignore the hash operations, the processing increases proportionally by the number of coins in the batch. For a batch size of n, this will include $2(n-1)$ additional modular exponentiations. Such processing, however, is often precomputed, and its impact may be eliminated during the withdrawal stage.

Once again, if we compare this to withdrawing n basic coins, the batch scheme is more efficient. The original scheme requires all operations to be performed for each coin, while the batch scheme only requires the calculation of the multiple B values. This translates to a saving of around 8 modular exponentations for every additional coin after the first that is withdrawn in the batch.

During payment the customer forwards the coin and responds to the challenge in the same manner as the original scheme. When spending multiple coins, although the same processing is required to compute the responses, there will actually be a communications savings as the coin is only sent once. In terms of storage, once a coin is spent the size of the batch does not decrease, as all elements of the batch need to be kept for subsequent payments to merchants. It is not until the last coin of the batch is spent that the coin may be discarded.

Merchant. When the merchant accepts a coin he must recompute the hash of B_i and insert this into its correct position to generate c'. All other steps required to verify the coin are computationally identical to the original scheme for a single batch coin. When spending multiple coins the merchant computes an additional small modular exponentiation for each B_i under the security parameter

w_i. Under the original scheme the merchant is required to perform the complete merchant payment protocol for each coin spent so the new scheme attracts n fewer $sign(A, B_1, \ldots, B_n)$ verification operations and n fewer representation checks. This equates to $6(n-1) - 1$ fewer modular exponentiations. (Note that the additional $B_i^{w_i}$'s contribute to the existing multi-exponentiation operation.)

Similar to the customer, the merchant must also provide storage space for the larger size of a batch coin. Again, this could be optimized by storing coins with an existing parent batch when received. To deposit a coin, the merchant merely forwards this to the bank, incurring only the communications penalty due to the increased coin size (when forwarding a single batch coin).

References

1. Mihir Bellare, Juan A. Garay, and Tal Rabin. Fast Batch Verification for Modular Exponentiation and Digital Signatures. In *Advances in Cryptology - Proceedings of EUROCRYPT '98*, volume 1403 of *Lecture Notes in Computer Science*. Springer-Verlag, 1998.

2. Jean-Paul Boly, Antoon Bosselaers, Ronald Cramer, Rolf Michelsen, Stig Mjolsnes, Frank Muller, Torben Pedersen, Birgit Pfitzmann, Peter de Rooij, Berry Schoenmakers, Matthias Schunter, Luc Vallee, and Michael Waidner. The ESPRIT Project CAFE - High Security Digital Payment Systems. In *Computer Security - ESORICS '94*, pages 217–230. Springer-Verlag, 1994.

3. Stefan Brands. Untraceable Off-line Cash in Wallets with Observers. In *Advances in Cryptology - Proceedings of CRYPTO '93*, volume 773 of *Lecture Notes in Computer Science*, pages 302–318. Springer-Verlag, 1993.

4. Jan Camenisch, Ueli Maurer, and Markus Stadler. Digital Payment Systems with Passive Anonymity-Revoking Trustees. In *Proceedings of ESORICS '96*, volume 1146 of *Lecture Notes in Computer Science*, pages 33–34. Springer-Verlag, 1996.

5. Agnes Chan, Yair Frankel, and Yiannis Tsiounis. Easy Come - Easy Go Divisible Cash. In *Advances in Cryptology - Proceedings of EUROCRYPT '98*, volume 1403 of *Lecture Notes in Computer Science*, pages 561–575. Springer-Verlag, May 1998.

6. David Chaum. Blind Signatures for Untraceable Payments. In *Advances in Cryptology - Proceedings of CRYPTO '82*, pages 199–203. Plenum Press, 1983.

7. David Chaum, Amos Fiat, and Moni Naor. Untraceable Electronic Cash. In *Advances in Cryptology - Proceedings of CRYPTO '88*, Lecture Notes in Computer Science, pages 319–327. Springer-Verlag, 1990.

8. Aymeric de Solanges and Jacques Traore. An Efficient Fair Off-line Electronic Cash System with Extensions to Checks and Wallets with Observers. In *Fincancial Cryptography '98*, Lecture Notes in Computer Science. Springer-Verlag, Feb 1998.

9. Tony Eng and Tatsuaki Okamoto. Single-Term Divisible Electronic Coins. In *Advances in Cryptology - Proceedings of EUROCRYPT '94*, number 950 in Lecture Notes in Computer Science, pages 306–319. Springer-Verlag, 1994.

10. Niels Ferguson. Extensions of Single Term Coins. In *Advances in Cryptology - Proceedings of CRYPTO '93*, volume 773 of *Lecture Notes in Computer Science*, pages 292–301. Springer-Verlag, 1993.

11. Niels Ferguson. Single Term Off-Line Coins. In *Advances in Cryptology - Proceedings of EUROCRYPT '93*, pages 318–328. Springer-Verlag, 1994.

12. Amos Fiat. Batch RSA. In *Advances in Cryptology - Proceedings of CRYPTO '89*, volume 435 of *Lecture Notes in Computer Science*, pages 175–185. Springer-Verlag, 1990.
13. Yair Frankel, Yiannis Tsiounis, and Moti Yung. Indirect Discourse Proofs: Achieving Efficient Fair Off-Line E-Cash. In *Advances in Cryptology - Proceedings of ASIACRYPT '96*, pages 286–300. Springer-Verlag, 1996.
14. Matthew Franklin and Moti Yung. Secure and Efficient Off-Line Digital Money. In *Proceedings of ICALP '93*, number 700 in Lecture Notes in Computer Science, pages 265–276. Springer-Verlag, 1993.
15. L. Harn. Batch Verifying Multiple RSA Digital Signatures. *Electronic Letters*, 34(12):1219–1220, June 1998.
16. Barry Hayes. Anonymous One-Time Signatures and Flexible Untraceable Electronic Cash. In *Advances in Cryptology - AUSCRYPT '90*, pages 294–305. Springer-Verlag, 1990.
17. Markus Jakobsson and Moti Yung. Revokable and Versatile Electronic Money. In *Third ACM Conference on Computer and Communications Security*, pages 76–87. ACM Press, 1996.
18. Khanh Quoc Nguyen, Yi Mu, and Vijay Varadharajan. One-Response Off-line Digital Coins. In *The Workshop Records of SAC '97*, Aug 1997.
19. Tatsuaki Okamoto. An Efficient Divisible Electronic Cash Scheme. In *Advances in Cryptology - Proceedings of CRYPTO '95*, pages 438–451. Springer-Verlag, 1995.
20. Tatsuaki Okamoto and Kazuo Ohta. Universal Electronic Cash. In *Advances in Cryptology - Proceedings of CRYPTO '91*, pages 324–337. Springer-Verlag, 1992.
21. D. Pointcheval and J. Stern. Security Proofs for Signature Schemes. In U. Maurer, editor, *Advances in Cryptology Proceedings of EUROCRYPT '96*, Lecture Notes in Computer Science, pages 387–398, Zaragoza, Spain, May 1996. Springer-Verlag.
22. Claus-Peter Schnorr. Efficient Signature Generation for Smart Cards. In *Advances in Cryptology - Proceedings of CRYPTO '89*, pages 239–252. Springer-Verlag, 1990.
23. Sung-Ming Yen and Chi-Sung Laih. Improved Digital Signature Suitable for Batch Verification. In *IEEE Transactions on Computers*, volume 44, pages 957–959, Jul 1995.

A Batch Schnorr Signature Scheme

Batch cryptography, originally proposed by Fiat [12], combines n messages into one batch for cryptographic transformation. The advantage of this is that an efficiency is attained in certain operations; for example signing or verifying n messages at once. In Fiat's and subsequent papers [1, 15, 23], the multiplicative property of RSA, is used to prepare batches. An alternative approach to the multiplicative batch techniques is to combine messages using a suitably collision resistant hash function in a way that enables a single public key operation to be performed for the whole batch.

We introduce a technique, using the Schnorr signature scheme [22], that enables n messages to be combined into one batch for signing. The basic approach is applicable to other signature schemes that employ hash functions, such as RSA. The batch signature and the individual messages may be forwarded to n different parties for individual verification. The scheme is shown to be as secure as the existing signature scheme, with an appropriate choice of hash function.

The Schnorr signature scheme [22] works in the integers modulo p, for a large prime p. An element g is selected which has order q, where q is a prime dividing $p - 1$. The public and private keys are x and h, where $0 < x < q$, and $h = g^x \bmod p$. A signer is able to generate a signature (c, r) on the message m as follows.

$$a = g^\omega \bmod p \text{ where } \omega \text{ is a random element}$$
$$1 \leq \omega \leq q - 1.$$
$$c = \mathcal{H}(m\|a)$$
$$r = cx + \omega \bmod q$$

Verification of a received signature can be performed as follows.

$$a' = g^r h^c \bmod p$$
$$\text{Verify } c = \mathcal{H}(m\|a')$$

Now, by applying a batch protocol, we may sign a batch of n messages with the following steps.

1. Generate signature on a batch of n messages $m_1, m_2, \ldots, m_n$:

$$a = g^\omega \bmod p \text{ where } \omega \text{ is a random element}$$
$$1 \leq \omega \leq q - 1$$
$$B = \mathcal{H}(\mathcal{H}_0(m_1)\|\mathcal{H}_0(m_2)\|\ldots\|\mathcal{H}_0(m_n)\|a)$$
$$r = xB + \omega \bmod q$$

2. The batch signature on m_i consists of $(B, r, h_1, \ldots, h_n, i)$, where $h_j = \mathcal{H}_0(m_j)$.
3. To verify the signature $(B, r, h_1, \ldots, h_n, i)$ on message m_i the following procedure is performed.

$$\text{Calculate } a' = g^r h^B \bmod p$$
$$\text{Verify } \mathcal{H}_0(m_i) = h_i$$
$$\text{Verify } B = \mathcal{H}(h_1\|h_2\|\ldots\|h_n\|a')$$

The security of this scheme is dependent upon an appropriate choice of hash function. We now demonstrate that if a secure hash function is used then the batch signature is as secure as the basic Schnorr signature. We first establish what should be considered a successful forgery attack, since this is not quite so obvious as in the case of the signature of a single message.

We wish to show that the batch signature scheme is secure against *existential forgery*. This means that an attacker should be unable to forge the signature of any message which has not been previously signed by the owner of the private key. Furthermore, we will allow the attacker to perform an *adaptive chosen signature attack* in which the owner of the private key can be induced to sign any sequence of messages of the attacker's choice, the next message in the sequence being allowed to depend on any of the previous messages. Finally the attack is regarded as successful if the attacker is able to derive the signature of any message not previously signed.

In an adaptive chosen signature attack on the batch signature scheme we will only regard the attack as successful if the final derived signature is not in any *batch* of previously signed messages. This is the only reasonable extension of such an attack on a basic signature scheme, because it could only be expected that the signer would sign a batch of messages if these were all presented together, rather than signing a single message in a batch of messages, the rest of which were chosen some other way (for example randomly). We make this assumption clear since otherwise there we are unable to show that a forgery possible on the batch scheme leads to a forgery on the basic scheme.

Theorem 1. *If the Schnorr signature scheme is secure against existential forgery using an adaptive chosen signature attack then so is the batch signature scheme.*

Proof. The main idea is that if (B, r) is a batch signature for the set of messages $(m_1, m_2, \ldots m_n)$, then it is also a basic Schnorr signature on the single message $M = h_1 \| h_2 \| \ldots \| h_n$, where $h_j = \mathcal{H}_0(m_j)$. This enables us to show that a forgery for a basic batch scheme leads to one for the Schnorr scheme. So we first assume that there is a successful adaptive chosen signature attack on the batch signature scheme. At each step a batch signature is obtained for the chosen message set, and finally a batch signature on a new message, say $\tilde{m}$, is obtained.

This can be converted to an adaptive chosen signature attack on the Schnorr signature as follows. At each stage the the chosen message is $\mathcal{H}_0(m_1) \| \ldots \| \mathcal{H}_0(m_n)$ if $m_1, \ldots m_n$ is the chosen message for the attack on the batch signature. After obtaining all chosen signatures the attack on the batch obtains the forged signature $(B, r, h_1, \ldots, h_n, i)$, where $h_i = \mathcal{H}_0(\tilde{m})$. As shown above, this is a Schnorr signature of the message $M = h_1 \| h_2 \| \ldots \| h_n$. According to our definition of a forgery against the batch scheme $\tilde{m}$ has not appeared in any previous batch signature found during the attack. Therefore the signature on M is a successful existential attack on the Schnorr scheme unless M appeared before as the output for a different message set. In particular this must include a message $\bar{m}$ with $h_i = \mathcal{H}_0(\tilde{m}) = \mathcal{H}_0(\bar{m})$ and $\tilde{m} \neq \bar{m}$. But this contradicts the collision free property of $\mathcal{H}_0$ so our proof is complete.

Where $\mathcal{H}$ has been chosen appropriately, the basic Schnorr signature scheme has been shown to to resist adaptive chosen message attacks using the random oracle model by Pointcheval and Stern [21]. Therefore, if we accept this model for the Schnorr scheme, we can be sure that the batch signatures are secure.

Evolution of Fair Non-repudiation with TTP

Jianying Zhou, Robert Deng and Feng Bao

Kent Ridge Digital Labs
21 Heng Mui Keng Terrace
Singapore 119613
email: {jyzhou,deng,baofeng}@krdl.org.sg

Abstract. Non-repudiation turns out to be an increasingly important security service with the fast growth of electronic commerce on the Internet. Non-repudiation services protect the transacting parties against any false denial that a particular event or action has taken place, in which evidence will be generated, collected and maintained to enable dispute resolution. Meanwhile, fairness is a further desirable requirement such that neither party can gain an advantage by quitting prematurely or otherwise misbehaving during a transaction. In this paper, we survey the evolution of techniques and protocols that had been put forward to achieve fair non-repudiation with a (trusted) third party, and present a secure and efficient fair non-repudiation protocol.

Keywords: fair non-repudiation, trusted third party, secure electronic commerce

1 Introduction

Electronic transactions become a growing trend with the development of computer networks. On the other hand, dispute of transactions is a common problem that could jeopardise business. We imagine the following scenario.

A merchant A sells *electronic goods* M (e.g. softwares, videos, or digital publications) on the Internet. Suppose a customer B wants to buy M with his credit card. Typical disputes that may arise in such a transaction could be

- A claims that he has sent M to B while B denies receiving it;
- B claims that he received M (which is bogus or illegal) from A while A denies sending it.

In order to settle these disputes by a third party arbitrator, A and B need to present evidence to prove their own claims. Such evidence may be provided by non-repudiation services.

Non-repudiation services protect the transacting parties against any false denial that a particular event or action has taken place, in which evidence will be generated, collected and maintained to enable the settlement of disputes [21]. The basic non-repudiation services that address the above disputes are

- *Non-repudiation of Origin* (*NRO*) provides the recipient of a message with evidence of origin of the message which will protect against any attempt by the originator to falsely deny having sent the message.
- *Non-repudiation of Receipt* (*NRR*) provides the originator of a message with evidence of receipt of the message which will protect against any attempt by the recipient to falsely deny having received the message.

Generally speaking, non-repudiation can be achieved with basic security mechanisms such as digital signatures and notarisation. However, fairness may be a further desirable requirement. In the above transaction, the merchant A would like to get a receipt as evidence for payment claim when sending M to the customer B. On the other hand, the customer B will be reluctant to acknowledge the receipt before obtaining M. Fair non-repudiation was considered in the Draft International Standard ISO/IEC 13888 "Information technology - Security techniques - Non-repudiation". However, the mechanisms in the current version of this document [14–16] do not support fair non-repudiation and only have limited application [21].

A fair non-repudiation protocol should not give the originator of a message an advantage over the recipient, or vice versa. This paper investigates the evolution of techniques and protocols that had been put forward to achieve fair non-repudiation, and presents a secure and efficient fair non-repudiation protocol. The following general notation is used throughout the paper.

- X, Y: concatenation of two messages X and Y.
- $H(X)$: a one-way hash function of message X.
- $eK(X)$ and $dK(X)$: encryption and decryption of message X with key K.
- $sS_A(X)$: principal A's digital signature on message X with the private signature key S_A. The algorithm is assumed to be a 'signature with appendix', and the message is not recoverable from the signature.
- $A \rightarrow B : X$: principal A dispatches message X addressed to principal B.
- $A \leftrightarrow B : X$: principal A fetches message X from principal B using *"ftp get"* operation [18] or by some analogous means (e.g. using a Web browser).

2   Approaches for Fair Non-repudiation

The origin of a message will usually be verified by a digital signature appended by the originator. To obtain evidence of receipt, the originator requires the recipient to reply with some sort of acknowledgement. There are two possible reasons for such an acknowledgment not to arrive [20]:

- *The communication channel is unreliable.* Thus, a message may have been sent but failed to reach the recipient.
- *A communicating party does not play fair.* Thus, a dishonest party may abandon execution intentionally without following the rules of a protocol.

As a result, the recipient may repudiate receipt of a message even if it has received the message by falsely claiming the failure of the communication channel.

Definition 1. A non-repudiation protocol is *fair* if it provides the originator and the recipient with valid irrefutable evidence after completion of the protocol, without giving a party an advantage over the other party in any possible incomplete protocol runs [20].

Approaches for fair non-repudiation reported in the literature fall into two categories:

- *Gradual exchange protocols* [3,6,8,11,17] where two parties gradually disclose the expected items by many steps.
- *Third party protocols* [1–4,9,10,12,13,19,20,22] which make use of an online or off-line (trusted) third party.

The gradual exchange approach may have theoretical value but is too cumbersome for actual implementation because of the high computation and communication overheads. Moreover, fairness is based on the assumption of equal computational complexity, which makes sense only if the two parties have equal computing power, an often unrealistic and undesirable assumption [5]. Hence, recent research mainly focuses on the third party approach.

At the early stage, fair non-repudiation was achieved by the use of an *on-line* (trusted) third party TTP. As the use of TTP in fair non-repudiation protocols may cause the bottleneck problem, it is necessary to minimize the TTP's involvement when designing efficient fair non-repudiation protocols. Such an attempt has been made in [20], where the TTP acts as a *light-weighted notary* rather than a delivery authority. However, the TTP still needs to be involved in each protocol run, though this might be necessary in some applications [22].

The TTP's involvement is further reduced in [1,4,22], where transacting parties are willing to resolve communications problems between themselves and turn to the TTP only as a last recourse. However, only the risk-taking party (originator) is allowed to invoke the TTP, the responder may not know the final state of a protocol run in time. If a short time limit is imposed on a protocol run, the originator may not be quick enough to invoke the TTP for recovery thus the fairness will be destroyed.

The latest effort on fair non-repudiation was made by Asokan, Shoup and Waidner [2], which uses the TTP only in the case of exceptions and tolerates temporary failures in the communication channels to the TTP. In addition, it allows either party to unilaterally bring a protocol run to completion without losing fairness. However, some flaws and security weaknesses of their protocol have been pointed out in [23]:

- The protocol performance may degrade when transmitting large messages.

- The privacy of messages being transmitted may not be well protected.
- The non-repudiation evidence may not be publicly verifiable.

It is desirable to overcome these shortcomings while maintaining the merits of the protocol.

In this paper, we will use the protocols presented in [20,22] as examples to show the evolution of techniques for fair non-repudiation, and propose a secure and efficient fair non-repudiation protocol based on the ideas from [2,20].

3 Protocol A: Using Light-weighted TTP

A fair non-repudiation protocol using light-weighted on-line TTP was proposed in [20], which supports non-repudiation of origin and non-repudiation of receipt while neither the originator nor the recipient can gain an advantage by quitting prematurely or otherwise misbehaving during a transaction. The main idea of this protocol is to split the definition of a message M into two parts, a commitment C and a key K. The commitment is sent from the originator A to the recipient B and then the key is lodged with the trusted third party TTP. Both A and B have to retrieve the confirmed key from the TTP as part of the non-repudiation evidence required in the settlement of a dispute. The notation below is used in the protocol description.

- M: message being sent from A to B.
- K: message key defined by A.
- $C = eK(M)$: commitment (ciphertext) for message M.
- $L = H(M, K)$: a unique label linking C and K.
- f_i $(i = 1, 2, \cdots)$: flags indicating the intended purpose of a signed message.
- $EOO\_C = sS_A(f_1, B, L, C)$: evidence of origin of C.
- $EOR\_C = sS_B(f_2, A, L, C)$: evidence of receipt of C.
- $sub\_K = sS_A(f_5, B, L, K)$: evidence of submission of K.
- $con\_K = sS_{TTP}(f_6, A, B, L, K)$: evidence of confirmation of K issued by the TTP.

The protocol is as follows.

$$
\begin{aligned}
&1.\ A \rightarrow B : && f_1, B, L, C, EOO\_C \\
&2.\ B \rightarrow A : && f_2, A, L, EOR\_C \\
&3.\ A \rightarrow TTP : && f_5, B, L, K, sub\_K \\
&4.\ B \leftrightarrow TTP : && f_6, A, B, L, K, con\_K \\
&5.\ A \leftrightarrow TTP : && f_6, A, B, L, K, con\_K
\end{aligned}
$$

It is assumed that A, B, and the TTP either hold the relevant public key certificates, or are able to retrieve them from a X.509 directory service [7]. It is further assumed that the communication channels linking the TTP and each transacting party (A and B) are *resilient*.

Definition 2. A communication channel is *resilient* if a message inserted into such a channel will eventually be delivered.

We examine the protocol step by step.

1. A first sends C and EOO_C to B. There is no breach of fairness if the protocol stops at Step 1 since C is incomprehensible without K.

    B needs to verify EOO_C and save EOO_C as evidence of origin of C before proceeding to the next step.

2. B has to send EOR_C to A if B wants to get K and con_K from the TTP at Step 4. There is no breach of fairness if the protocol stops at Step 2 since EOR_C can only be used to prove receipt of C rather than receipt of M.

    A needs to verify EOR_C and save EOR_C as evidence of receipt of C before proceeding to the next step.

3. A has to send K and sub_K to the TTP if A wants to get con_K from the TTP at Step 5. B could obtain K by eavesdropping, and thereby the message M, before K is lodged with the TTP. As we assume that the communication channel between A and the TTP is resilient, A will eventually be able to send K and sub_K to the TTP in exchange for con_K.

    After receiving K and sub_K from A, the TTP will generate con_K and store the tuple (f_6, A, B, L, K, con_K) in a directory which is accessible (read only) to the public. The second component in the tuple indicates the key supplier which is authenticated by the TTP with sub_K. Intruders cannot mount a denial-of-service attack by sending bogus keys to the TTP as this will not generate entries $(f_6, A, \cdots)$ in the directory.

4. B fetches K and con_K from the TTP. B obtains M by computing $M = dK(C)$, and saves con_K as evidence to prove that K originated from A.

    As we assume that the communication channel between B and the TTP is resilient, B can therefore always retrieve K and con_K. B will lose the dispute over receipt of M even if B does not fetch K after it becomes publicly available.

5. A fetches con_K from the TTP, and saves it as evidence to prove that K is available to B.

The above analysis demonstrates that if and only if A has sent C to B and K to the TTP, will A have evidence (EOR_C, con_K) and B have evidence (EOO_C, con_K).

Label L plays an important role in the establishment of a unique link between C and K. Once L and C have been committed in EOO_C and EOR_C, it is computationally hard to find $K' \neq K$ satisfying $L = H(M, K) = H(M, K')$ while $M = dK(C) = dK'(C)$.

If A denies origin of M, B can present evidence EOO_C and con_K plus M, C, K to a third party arbitrator. The arbitrator will check

- A's signature $EOO\_C = sS_A(f_1, B, L, C)$

- TTP's signature $con\_K = sS_{TTP}(f_6, A, B, L, K)$
- $L = H(M, K)$
- $M = dK(C)$

If the first two checks are positive, the arbitrator believes that C and K originated from A. If the last two checks are also positive, the arbitrator will conclude that C and K are uniquely linked by L, and M is the message represented by C and K from A.

If B denies receipt of M, A can present evidence EOR_C and con_K plus M, C, K to the arbitrator. The arbitrator will make similar checks as above.

Unlike other fair non-repudiation protocols which use the *on-line* trusted third party as a delivery authority, the trusted third party in this protocol acts as a *light-weighted notary* which only notarises message keys by request and provides directory services accessible to the public. This has two advantages.

- The trusted third party only deals with keys, which in general will be shorter than the full messages.
- The onus is now on the originator and the recipient to retrieve the key, while a delivery authority would have to keep resending messages until the receiver acknowledges the message.

4   Protocol B: Using Off-line TTP

In Section 3, the trusted third party's work load has been significantly reduced in the protocol, where the TTP only needs to notarise message keys by request and provides directory services. Such a protocol is appropriate in applications where notarisation of keys is desirable [1], or where the participants and the communications infrastructure are so unreliable that participants prefer to rely on the TTP to facilitate transactions.

An efficient fair non-repudiation protocol was proposed in [22], which further reduced the trusted third party's active involvement when the two parties are willing to resolve communications problems between themselves and want to turn to the TTP only as a last recourse. In the normal case, the originator A and the recipient B will exchange messages and non-repudiation evidence directly. The TTP will be invoked only in the error-recovery phase initiated by A when A cannot get the expected evidence from B.

Besides the notation used in Section 3, the following additional notation is used in the protocol description.

---

[1] When disputes relate to the time of message transfer, the originator and the recipient may need evidence about the time of sending and receiving a message besides evidence of origin and receipt. The TTP can time-stamp evidence con_K to identify when the message key, and thus the message, was made available.

- $EOO\_K = sS_A(f_3, B, L, K)$: evidence of origin of K.
- $EOR\_K = sS_B(f_4, A, L, K)$: evidence of receipt of K.

The protocol in the normal case is as follows.

$$1.\ A \rightarrow B : f_1, B, L, C, EOO\_C$$
$$2.\ B \rightarrow A : f_2, A, L, EOR\_C$$
$$3.\ A \rightarrow B : f_3, B, L, K, EOO\_K$$
$$4.\ B \rightarrow A : f_4, A, L, EOR\_K$$

If A does not send message 3, the protocol ends without disputes. If A cannot get message 4 from B after sending message 3 (either because B did not receive message 3 or because B does not want to acknowledge it), A may initiate the following recovery phase, which is the same as Steps 3 to 5 of the protocol in Section 3.

$$3'.\ A \rightarrow TTP : f_5, B, L, K, sub\_K$$
$$4'.\ B \leftrightarrow TTP : f_6, A, B, L, K, con\_K$$
$$5'.\ A \leftrightarrow TTP : f_6, A, B, L, K, con\_K$$

If the protocol run is complete, the originator A will hold non-repudiation evidence EOR_C and EOR_K, and the recipient B will hold EOO_C and EOO_K. Otherwise, A needs to rectify the unfair situation by initiating the recovery phase so that non-repudiation evidence con_K will be available to both A and B.

If disputes arise, A can use (EOR_C, EOR_K) or (EOR_C, con_K) as non-repudiation evidence to prove that B received M; B can use (EOO_C, EOO_K) or (EOO_C, con_K) as non-repudiation evidence to prove that M originated from A.

This protocol will be efficient in an environment where two parties usually play fair in a protocol run. Although the recipient B is temporarily in an advantageous position after Step 3, fairness can be retained by ensuring the success of the recovery phase, which relies on the assumption that the communication channels between the TTP and the participants A, B are resilient.

In practice, however, a time limit for a protocol run may have to be set so that both parties can terminate an expired protocol run safely. Then the choice of time limit in the above protocol becomes critical because that may affect the protocol fairness. If A cannot get message 4 from B, A has to rely on a successful recovery phase to rectify the unfair situation. A needs to submit the message key to the TTP in time since the TTP will not confirm A's submission once the protocol run expires. However, as we only assume that the communication channels are not permanently broken, A may not be sure that the TTP can receive its submission in time. Therefore, A has to choose the time limit big enough. This means that B may not know the final state of a protocol run in time, which is obviously unfavourable to B [2]. If B does not receive the message key from A by the deadline, B has to retrieve it from the TTP, or abandon the protocol run with a notification from the TTP.

5 Protocol C: Autonomous with Off-line TTP

Here we present an autonomous fair non-repudiation protocol using off-line TTP, which is mainly based on the ideas from [2, 20].

Definition 3. A fair non-repudiation protocol is *autonomous* if either transacting party can unilaterally bring a transaction to completion without losing fairness.

We split the definition of a message M into two parts, a commitment C and a key K. In the normal case, the originator A sends (C, K) (plus evidence of origin) to the recipient B in exchange for evidence of receipt without any involvement of the TTP. If there is something wrong in the middle of a transaction, either A or B can unilaterally bring the transaction to completion with the help from the TTP. The TTP only needs to notarise and/or deliver the message key K by request, which is usually much shorter than the whole message M. The notation below is used in the description of our protocol.

- M: message being sent from A to B.
- K: message key defined by A.
- $C = eK(M)$: commitment (cipher text) for message M.
- $L = H(M, K)$: a unique label linking C and K.
- f_i $(i = 1, 2, \cdots)$: flags indicating the intended purpose of a signed message.
- $EOO\_C = sS_A(f_1, B, L, C)$: evidence of origin of C.
- $EOR\_C = sS_B(f_2, A, L, EOO\_C)$: evidence of receipt of C.
- $EOO\_K = sS_A(f_3, B, L, K)$: evidence of origin of K.
- $EOR\_K = sS_B(f_4, A, L, EOO\_K)$: evidence of receipt of K.
- $sub\_K = sS_A(f_5, B, L, K, TTP, EOO\_C)$: evidence of submission of K to the TTP.
- $con\_K = sS_{TTP}(f_6, A, B, L, K)$: evidence of confirmation of K issued by the TTP.
- $abort = sS_{TTP}(f_8, A, B, L)$: evidence of abortion.
- P_{TTP}: the TTP's public encryption key.

Our protocol has three sub-protocols: *exchange*, *abort*, and *resolve*. We assume that the communication channels between the TTP and each transacting party (A and B) are *resilient*. We also assume that the communication channel

---

[2] This problem does not exist in the protocol described in Section 3. An arbitrary length of time limit can be set for a protocol run as long as the message key is protected from disclosure to B when A submits it to the TTP for confirmation.

between A and B is *confidential* if the two parties want to exchange messages secretly. The *exchange* sub-protocol is as follows.

1. $A \rightarrow B : f_1, f_5, B, L, C, TTP, eP_{TTP}(K), EOO\_C, sub\_K$
   IF B gives up **THEN** quit **ELSE**
2. $B \rightarrow A : f_2, A, L, EOR\_C$
   IF A gives up **THEN** *abort* **ELSE**
3. $A \rightarrow B : f_3, B, L, K, EOO\_K$
   IF B gives up **THEN** *resolve* **ELSE**
4. $B \rightarrow A : f_4, A, L, EOR\_K$
   IF A gives up **THEN** *resolve*

The *abort* sub-protocol is as follows.

1. $A \rightarrow TTP : f_7, B, L, sS_A(f_7, B, L)$
   IF resolved **THEN**
2. $TTP \rightarrow A : f_2, f_6, A, B, L, K, con\_K, EOR\_C$
   ELSE
3. $TTP \rightarrow A : f_8, A, B, L, abort$

The *resolve* sub-protocol is as follows, where the initiator U is either A or B.

1. $U \rightarrow TTP : f_2, f_5, A, B, L, TTP, eP_{TTP}(K), sub\_K, EOO\_C, EOR\_C$
   IF aborted **THEN**
2. $TTP \rightarrow U : f_8, A, B, L, abort$
   ELSE
3. $TTP \rightarrow U : f_2, f_6, A, B, L, K, con\_K, EOR\_C$

If the *exchange* sub-protocol is executed successfully, B will receive C and K and thus $M = dK(C)$ together with evidence of origin (EOO_C, EOO_K). Meanwhile, A will receive evidence of receipt (EOR_C, EOR_K).

B can simply quit the transaction without losing fairness before sending EOR_C to A. Otherwise, B has to run the *resolve* sub-protocol to force a successful termination. Similarly, A can run the *abort* sub-protocol to quit the transaction without losing fairness before sending K and EOO_K to B. Otherwise, A has to run the *resolve* sub-protocol to force a successful termination.

The *resolve* sub-protocol can be initiated either by A or by B. When the TTP receives such a request, the TTP will first check the status of a transaction identified by (A, B, L) uniquely. If the transaction has been aborted by A, the TTP will return the *abort* token. If the transaction has already been resolved, the TTP will deliver the tuple ($f_2, f_6, A, B, L, K, con\_K, EOR\_C$) to the current initiator of the *resolve* sub-protocol. Otherwise, the TTP will

- check that EOR_C is consistent with sub_K in terms of L and EOO_C,
- generate evidence con_K,
- deliver the tuple ($f_2, f_6, A, B, L, K, con\_K, EOR\_C$) to the current initiator,
- set the status of the transaction *resolved*.

The third component in the tuple indicates the key supplier which is authenticated by the TTP with sub_K. Evidence con_K can be used to prove that

- a transaction identified by (A, B, L) has been resolved successfully,
- the message key K originated from A, and
- the message key is available from the TTP by request.

The time limit on maintaining the status of a transaction (*resolved* or *aborted*) by the TTP will be defined in the non-repudiation policy, which can be reasonably long enough (mainly depending on the TTP's storage capability) so that both transacting parties are deemed to be able to consult the TTP within such a time limit to force a successful termination of a transaction when it is necessary.

If disputes arise, A can use evidence (EOR_C, EOR_K) or (EOR_C, con_K) to prove that B received the message M, B can use evidence (EOO_C, EOO_K) or (EOO_C, con_K) to prove that A sent the message M.

In comparison with the protocol in [2], our protocol has the following merits.

- The TTP's overhead will not increase when transmitting a large message M.
- The content of the message M need not be disclosed to any outsiders including the TTP.
- The evidence is publicly verifiable without any restrictions on the types of signature and encryption algorithms.

Therefore, our protocol is more secure and efficient both at the stage of exchange and at the stage of dispute resolution.

6 Conclusion

Fair non-repudiation protocols can be constructed in two ways, by gradual exchange of the expected items, or by invoking the services of a (trusted) third party. The major defects of the first approach are

- high computation and communication overheads, and
- strong assumption on transacting partys' equal computing power for fairness.

Hence, recent research mainly focuses on the second approach. As the trusted third party may become a system bottleneck, a critical issue is how to minimize the trusted third party's involvement in fair non-repudiation protocols.

There are three major advances on the research along this direction. Early efforts were to make use of a light-weighted on-line trusted third party (e.g. a fair non-repudiation protocol in [20]). Later on, an off-line trusted third party was employed in fair non-repudiation protocols (e.g. in [1, 4, 22]) but fairness may be destroyed when a time limit is imposed on a protocol run. The most recent advance is to allow either transacting party to unilaterally bring a protocol run to completion without losing fairness with the assistance of an off-line trusted third party [2]. This paper presented a more secure and efficient fair non-repudiation protocol based on the ideas from [2, 20]. An open problem is how to achieve fair non-repudiation without relying on the assumption of *resilient* communication channels between an off-line trusted third party and each transacting party.

Acknowledgements

We thank the anonymous referees for valuable comments on the draft of this paper.

References

1. N. Asokan, M. Schunter and M. Waidner. *Optimistic protocols for fair exchange.* Proceedings of 4th ACM Conference on Computer and Communications Security, pages 7–17, Zurich, Switzerland, April 1997.
2. N. Asokan, V. Shoup and M. Waidner. *Asynchronous protocols for optimistic fair exchange.* Proceedings of 1998 IEEE Symposium on Security and Privacy, pages 86–99, Oakland, California, May 1998.
3. A. Bahreman and J. D. Tygar. *Certified electronic mail.* Proceedings of the Internet Society Symposium on Network and Distributed System Security, pages 3–19, San Diego, California, February 1994.
4. F. Bao, R. H. Deng and W. Mao. *Efficient and practical fair exchange protocols with off-line TTP.* Proceedings of 1998 IEEE Symposium on Security and Privacy, pages 77–85, Oakland, California, May 1998.
5. M. Ben-Or, O. Goldreich, S. Micali and R. Rivest. *A fair protocol for signing contracts.* IEEE Transactions on Information Theory, IT-36(1):40–46, January 1990.
6. E. F. Brickell, D. Chaum, I. B. Damgard and J. van de Graaf. *Gradual and verifiable release of a secret.* Lecture Notes in Computer Science 293, Advances in Cryptology: Proceedings of Crypto'87, pages 156–166, Santa Barbara, California, August 1987.
7. CCITT. *Recommendation X.509: The directory – Authentication framework.* November 1988.
8. R. Cleve. *Controlled gradual disclosure schemes for random bits and their applications.* Lecture Notes in Computer Science 435, Advances in Cryptology: Proceedings of Crypto'89, pages 573–588, Santa Barbara, California, August 1989.
9. T. Coffey and P. Saidha. *Non-repudiation with mandatory proof of receipt.* Computer Communication Review, 26(1):6–17, January 1996.
10. B. Cox, J. D. Tygar and M. Sirbu. *NetBill security and transaction protocol.* Proceedings of the First USENIX Workshop on Electronic Commerce, pages 77–88, July 1995.
11. I. B. Damgard. *Practical and provably secure release of a secret and exchange of signatures.* Lecture Notes in Computer Science 765, Advances in Cryptology: Proceedings of Eurocrypt'93, pages 200–217, Lofthus, Norway, May 1993.
12. R. H. Deng, L. Gong, A. A. Lazar and W. Wang. *Practical protocols for certified electronic mail.* Journal of Network and Systems Management, 4(3):279–297, 1996.

13. M. Franklin and M. Reiter. *Fair exchange with a semi-trusted third party*. Proceedings of 4th ACM Conference on Computer and Communications Security, pages 1–6, Zurich, Switzerland, April 1997.

14. ISO/IEC 13888-1. *Information technology - Security techniques - Non-repudiation - Part 1: General*. ISO/IEC, 1997.

15. ISO/IEC 13888-2. *Information technology - Security techniques - Non-repudiation - Part 2: Mechanisms using symmetric techniques*. ISO/IEC, 1998.

16. ISO/IEC 13888-3. *Information technology - Security techniques - Non-repudiation - Part 3: Mechanisms using asymmetric techniques*. ISO/IEC, 1997.

17. T. Okamoto and K. Ohta. *How to simultaneously exchange secrets by general assumptions*. Proceedings of 2nd ACM Conference on Computer and Communications Security, pages 184–192, Fairfax, Virginia, November 1994.

18. J. B. Postel and J. K. Reynolds. *File transfer protocol*. RFC 959, October 1985.

19. N. Zhang and Q. Shi. *Achieving non-repudiation of receipt*. The Computer Journal, 39(10):844–853, 1996.

20. J. Zhou and D. Gollmann. *A fair non-repudiation protocol*. Proceedings of 1996 IEEE Symposium on Security and Privacy, pages 55–61, Oakland, California, May 1996.

21. J. Zhou. *Non-repudiation*. PhD Thesis, University of London, December 1996.

22. J. Zhou and D. Gollmann. *An efficient non-repudiation protocol*. Proceedings of 10th IEEE Computer Security Foundations Workshop, pages 126–132, Rockport, Massachusetts, June 1997.

23. J. Zhou, R. H. Deng and F. Bao. *Some remarks on a fair exchange protocol*. (manuscript)

Authorization in Object Oriented Databases

Yun Bai and Vijay Varadharajan

School of Computing and Information Technology
University of Western Sydney, Australia
Email: {ybai, vijay}@st.nepean.uws.edu.au

Abstract. Formal specification on authorization in object oriented databases is becoming increasingly significant. However most of the work in this field suffers a lack of formal logic semantics to characterize different types of inheritance properties of authorization policies among complex data objects. In this paper, we propose a logic formalization specify object oriented databases together with authorization policies. Our formalization has a high level language structure to specify object oriented databases and allows various types of authorizations to be associated with.

Key words: object oriented databases, inheritance, security, authorization policy, formal specification

1 Introduction

Authorization specification in object oriented databases is being increasingly investigated recently by many researchers [3, 4, 6, 7]. However, most of the work suffers from a lack of formal logic semantics to characterize different types of inheritance properties of authorization policies among complex data objects. Furthermore, it is also difficult to formally reason about authorizations associated with different objects in databases.

In this paper, we address this issue from a formal logic point of view. We propose a logical language that has a clear and declarative semantics to specify the structural features of object oriented databases and authorizations associated with complex data objects in databases. A direct advantage of this approach is that we can formally specify and reason about authorizations on data objects without loosing inheritance and abstraction features of object oriented databases. We first propose a logical language for specifying object oriented databases. This language has a high level syntax and its semantics shares some features of Kifer *elt.*'s F-logic [5]. We then extend this language based on some features of our previous formal language for authorization specification [1] to include authorization into object oriented databases.

The paper is organized as follows. In section 2, we propose a formal language $\mathcal{L}$ to specify object oriented databases. In section 3, we extend $\mathcal{L}$ to language $\mathcal{L}^a$ by combining authorization specification associated with data objects into a database. In section 4, we investigate properties of reasoning about authorizations in object oriented databases. Finally section 5 concludes the paper.

2   Object Oriented Databases Specification

The *vocabulary* of language $\mathcal{L}$ which is used to specify object oriented database consists of:

1. A finite set of *object variables* $\mathcal{OV} = \{o, o_1, o_2, \cdots\}$ and a finite set of *object constants* $\mathcal{OC} = \{O, O_1, O_2, \cdots\}$. We will simply name $\mathcal{O} = \mathcal{OV} \cup \mathcal{OC}$ as *object set*.
2. A finite set $\mathcal{F}$ of function symbols as *object constructors* or *methods* where each $f \in \mathcal{F}$ takes objects as arguments and maps to an object or a set of objects.
3. Auxiliary symbols $\Rightarrow$ and $\mapsto$.

An *object proposition* is an expression of the form

$$O \textbf{ has method } f_1(\cdots) \Rightarrow \Pi_1,$$
$$\cdots,$$
$$f_m(\cdots) \Rightarrow \Pi_m,$$
$$f_{m+1}(\cdots) \mapsto \Pi_{m+1},$$
$$\cdots,$$
$$f_n(\cdots) \mapsto \Pi_n. \tag{1}$$

In (1) O is an object from $\mathcal{O}$ and $f_1, \cdots, f_m, \cdots, f_n$ are function symbols (as object constructors). Each function symbol f takes objects as arguments and maps to some Π that is an object or a set of objects. For example, the following is an object description of a staff:

$$staff \textbf{ has method } name \Rightarrow String,$$
$$dept(Staff) \Rightarrow String,$$
$$firstdegree \mapsto 'Bachelor',$$

where $name \Rightarrow String$ represents that the type of name is a string, and method $dept$ takes type $Staff$ as a parameter and returns a type of string to indicate the dept the staff belongs to. $firstdegree \mapsto 'Bachelor'$ simply expresses that every staff should hold a Bachelor degree(a constant). An object proposition is called *ground* if there is no object variable occurrence in it.

An *isa proposition* of $\mathcal{L}$ is an expression of one of the following two forms:

$$O \textbf{ isa member of } C, \tag{2}$$
$$O \textbf{ isa subclass of } C, \tag{3}$$

where O and C are objects from $\mathcal{O}$, i.e., O and C may be object constants or variables. Clearly, isa propositions (2) and (3) explicitly represent the hierarchy relation between two objects. An isa proposition without containing any object variables is called *ground isa proposition*.

We call an object or isa proposition a *data proposition*. A data proposition is called *ground data proposition* if there is no object variable occurrence in it. We usually use notation ϕ to denote a data proposition. We assume that any variable occurrence in a data proposition is universally quantified.

A *constraint proposition* is an expression of the form

$$\phi \text{ if } \phi_1, \cdots, \phi_k, \tag{4}$$

while $\phi, \phi_1, \cdots, \phi_k$ are data propositions. A constraint proposition represents some relationship among different data objects. With this kind of proposition, we can represent some useful deductive rules of the domain in our database. A *database proposition* is an object proposition, isa proposition, or constraint proposition.

We can now formally define our object oriented database as follows.

Definition 1. *An* object oriented database Σ *is a triplet* (Γ, Δ, Ω), *where* Γ *is a finite set of ground object propositions,* Δ *is a finite set of ground isa propositions, and* Ω *is a finite set of constraint propositions.*

Now, we generally explain the semantics of language $\mathcal{L}$. Refer to [2] for the detailed semantics.

A *structure* of $\mathcal{L}$ is a tuple $I = (U, \mathcal{F}_I, \subseteq_U, \in_U, \Rightarrow_I, \mapsto_I)$, where U represents all possible *actual* objects in the domain. $\mathcal{F}_I$ is a set of functions. The objective of ordering $\subseteq_U$ is to represent the semantics of isa subclass proposition in $\mathcal{L}$. The semantics of isa membership proposition in $\mathcal{L}$ is provided by $\in_U$ in I in a similar way.

The semantics of $\Rightarrow$, however, is not quite straightforward. As we mentioned earlier, a method of the form $f(\cdots) \Rightarrow \Pi$ actually defines the function type of f. That is, f takes objects that represent types of actual objects and returns an object (or a set of objects) that indicates the type (or types) of resulting actual object (or objects). Suppose that f is a i-ary function. Then the semantics of $\Rightarrow$ is provided by mapping $\Rightarrow_I^{(i)}$ which maps the resulting object represented by $f(\cdots)$ to a $(i + 1)$-ary function $h_i : U^{i+1} \to \mathcal{P} \uparrow (U)$, where the first ith arguments in U^{i+1} are objects that correspond to the i arguments taken by f, and the $(i+1)$-th argument in U^{i+1} is the object that corresponds to the object associated with function $f(\cdots)$ in the proposition (we also call the *host object* of f). In $f(\cdots) \Rightarrow \Pi$, Π denotes the type/types of resulting object/objects for which we use a subset of U to represent all the possible actual objects that have type/types indicated by Π.

It is important to note that we require the subset of U to be *upward-closed* with respect to ordering $\subseteq_U$. A subset V of U is upward-closed if for $v \in V$ and $v \subseteq_U v'$, then $v' \in V$. The purpose of this requirement is that if V is viewed as a set of classes, upward closure ensures that for each class $v \in V$, V also contains all the superclasses of v, which will guarantee the proper inheritance property of types.

A similar explanation for $\mapsto_I$ can be given for the semantics of $\mapsto$. We now show that $\Rightarrow_I$ actually provides the type of the corresponding $\mapsto_I$.

To simplify our formalization, we will use *Herbrand universe* in any structures of $\mathcal{L}$. That is, the Herbrand universe U_H is formed from the set of all object constants in $\mathcal{OC}$ and the objects built by function symbols on these object constants.

Now we can formally define the model of a database Σ as follows:

Definition 2. *A structure* M *of* $\mathcal{L}$ *is a* model *of a database* $\Sigma = (\Gamma, \Delta, \Omega)$ *if*

1. *For each proposition* ψ *in* $\Gamma \cup \Delta \cup \Omega$, $M \models^1 \psi$.
2. *For each object proposition* ϕ, *if* $M \models \phi$, *then* $M \models \phi'$ *where* ϕ' *is obtained from* ϕ *by omitting some methods of* ϕ.
3. *For any isa proposition* O **isa member of** C *and object propositions* C **has method** $f(\cdots) \Rightarrow \Pi$ *and* C **has method** $f(\cdots) \mapsto \Pi$, *(1)* $M \models O$ **isa member of** C *and* $M \models C$ **has method** $f(\cdots) \Rightarrow \Pi$ *imply* $M \models O$ **has method** $f(\cdots) \Rightarrow \Pi$;
   (2) $M \models O$ **isa member of** C *and* $M \models C$ **has method** $f(\cdots) \mapsto \Pi$ *imply* $M \models O$ **has method** $f(\cdots) \mapsto \Pi$.
4. *for any isa proposition* O **isa subclass of** C *and object proposition* C **has method** $f(\cdots) \mapsto \Pi$, $M \models O$ **isa subclass of** C *and* $M \models C$ **has method** $f(\cdots) \mapsto \Pi$ *imply* $M \models O$ **has method** $f(\cdots) \mapsto \Pi$.

Condition 1 in the above definition is the basic requirement for a model. Condition 2 allows us to partially represent an object with only those methods that are of interest in a given context. Condition 3 is a restriction to guarantee necessary inheritance of membership, whereas Condition 4 is needed for the purpose of subclass value inheritance.

Let Σ be a database and ϕ be a database proposition. If for every model M of Σ, $M \models \phi$, we also call that ϕ *is entailed* by Σ, denoted as $\Sigma \models \phi$.

Example 1. Consider a simplified domain of staff in a department. The structure of such domain is illustrated in Figure 1.

In Figure 1, line arrows indicate subclass relations while dotted line arrows indicate membership relations in the database.

Using our language $\mathcal{L}$, our database $\Sigma = (\Gamma, \Delta, \Omega)$ is specified as follows: (1) the set of ground object propositions Γ consists of:

$$Staff \text{ has method } name \Rightarrow String,$$
$$id \Rightarrow Integer, \quad (5)$$
$$GenStaff \text{ has method } typeofwork(Staff) \Rightarrow String, \quad (6)$$
$$AcadStaff \text{ has method } research(staff) \Rightarrow \{String, \cdots, String\} \quad (7)$$
$$Alice \text{ has method } name \mapsto \text{'Alice'},$$
$$id \mapsto 111,$$
$$typeofwork(Alice) \mapsto \text{'Secretary'}, \quad (8)$$
$$Bob \text{ has method } name \mapsto \text{'Bob'},$$

---

[1] Refer to [2] for the formal definition of $\models$.

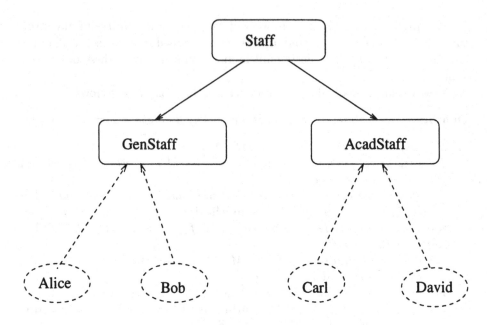

Fig. 1. A staff database.

$$id \mapsto 222,$$
$$typeof work(Bob) \mapsto \text{'}techsupport\text{'}, \quad (9)$$
$$Carl \text{ has method } name \mapsto \text{'}Carl\text{'},$$
$$id \mapsto 333,$$
$$research(Carl) \mapsto \text{'}security\text{'}, \quad (10)$$
$$David \text{ has method } name \mapsto \text{'}David\text{'},$$
$$id \mapsto 444,$$
$$research(David) \mapsto \text{'}database\text{'}, \quad (11)$$

(2) the set of ground isa propositions Δ consists of:

$$Alice \text{ isa member of } GenStaff, \quad (12)$$
$$Bob \text{ isa member of } GenStaff, \quad (13)$$
$$Carl \text{ isa member of } AcadStaff, \quad (14)$$
$$David \text{ isa member of } AcadStaff, \quad (15)$$
$$GenStaff \text{ isa subclass of } Staff, \quad (16)$$
$$AcadStaff \text{ isa subclass of } Staff, \quad (17)$$

and (3) Ω consists of two constraint propositions:

$$y \text{ isa member of } AcadStaff$$

$$\textbf{if } y \textbf{ has method } research(y) \mapsto z, \tag{18}$$

$$y \textbf{ isa member of } Staff$$

$$\textbf{if } y \textbf{ isa member of } AcadStaff, \tag{19}$$

where y and z are object variables, and notation $\{..., z, ...\}$ means that set $\{..., z, ...\}$ includes element z which is of interest.

In database Σ, we assume that objects $Integer$ and $String$ are *primitive* object constants and do not require explicit descriptions. It also presents necessary inheritance properties among different objects.

Finally, in Σ, Γ and Δ represent *explicit* data object descriptions and hierarchical relations among these objects, while Ω describes constraints of the domain which characterize some *implicit* data objects and their properties. By using these rules in Ω and facts in $\Gamma \cup \Delta$, we actually can derive new data objects with some clear properties.

3 Authorization Specification

In this section, we extend language $\mathcal{L}$ to $\mathcal{L}^a$ to specify authorization in object-oriented databases. First let us consider the following requirements in the specification of access policies in object oriented databases.

1. If a subject (user) has an access right to a complete object (class), then this should imply that this subject has the same access right to *every* method of the object (class). There may be some exceptions.
2. If a subject has an access right to a class, there may be a need that this subject should be generally allowed to access all of its subclasses. Again, some exceptions should be taken into account. For example, a general research officer can access all the research records of the class Staff except that of the class Professor. A similar requirement is also needed for memberships.
3. *causal* or *conditional* authorization policies is also needed.

The *vocabulary* of $\mathcal{L}^a$ includes the vocabulary of $\mathcal{L}$ together with the following additions:

1. A finite set of *subject variables* $\mathcal{SV} = \{s, s_1, s_2, \cdots\}$ and a finite set of *subject constants* $\mathcal{SC} - \{S, S_1, S_2, \cdots\}$. We denote $\mathcal{S} = \mathcal{SV} \cup \mathcal{SC}$.
2. A finite set of *access-rights variables* $\mathcal{AV} = \{r, r_1, r_2, \cdots\}$ and a finite set of *access-right constants* $\mathcal{AC} = \{R, R_1, R_2, \cdots\}$. We denote $\mathcal{A} = \mathcal{AV} \cup \mathcal{AC}$.
3. A ternary predicate symbol *holds* taking arguments subject, access-right, and object/method respectively.
4. Logic connectives $\wedge$ and $\neg$.

In language $\mathcal{L}^a$, a fact that a subject S has access right R for object O is represented using a ground atom $holds(S, R, O)$. A fact that S has access right R for object O's method $f(\cdots) \rightsquigarrow \Pi$ is represented by ground atom $holds(S, R, O|f)$. We use $\rightsquigarrow$ for symbol $\Rightarrow$ or $\mapsto$.

In general, we define an *access fact* to be an atomic formula $holds(s,r,o)$ (or $holds(s,r,o|f)$) or its negation. A ground access fact is an access fact without any variable occurrence. We view $\neg\neg F$ as F. An *access fact expression* in $\mathcal{L}^a$ is defined as follows: (i) each access fact is an access fact expression; (ii) if ψ is an access fact expression and ϕ is an isa or object proposition, then $\psi \wedge \phi$ is an access fact expression; (iii) if ψ and ϕ are access fact expressions, then $\psi \wedge \phi$ is an access fact expression. A ground fact expression is a fact expression with no variable occurrence in it. An access fact expression is *pure* if it does not have an isa proposition occurrence in it.

Based on the above definition, the following are access fact expressions: $holds(S,R,O) \wedge O$ **isa subclass of** C, $\neg holds(S,R,o) \wedge o$ **isa member of** C, where o is an object variable.

Now we are ready to define propositions in language $\mathcal{L}^a$. Firstly, $\mathcal{L}^a$ has the same types of database propositions as $\mathcal{L}$, i.e. object proposition, isa proposition and constraint proposition. It also includes the following additional type of *access proposition*:

$$\psi \text{ implies } \phi \text{ with absence } \gamma, \tag{20}$$

where ψ is an access fact expression, and ϕ and γ are pure access fact expressions. Note that ψ, ϕ and γ may contain variables. In this case, as before, (20) will be treated as a set of access propositions obtained by replacing ψ, ϕ and γ with their ground instances respectively.

As an example, consider the following access proposition

$$holds(S, Access, Staff|id) \wedge Alice \text{ isa member of } Staff$$
$$\text{implies } holds(S, Access, Alice|id)$$
$$\text{with absence } \neg holds(S, Access, Alice|id),$$

Intuitively, this expression says that if subject S can access staff's id record and Alice is a member of staff, then S can also access Alice's id record if the fact that S cannot access Alice's id record does not currently hold.

It is clear that our access propositions (20) provides flexibility to express different types of authorization policies on objects. However, to ensure the proper inheritance of access policies on different objects, some specific types of access policies are particularly important for all databases. The set of these kinds of authorization policies is referred to as the *generic authorization scheme* for databases. Consider

$$holds(s,r,o) \text{ implies } holds(s,r,o|f)$$
$$\text{with absence } \neg holds(s,r,o|f). \tag{21}$$

where $o|f$ indicates a method associated with object o. Intuitively, (21) says that if s has access right r on object o, then s also has access right r on each of its methods under the assumption that $\neg holds(s,r,o|f)$ is not present.

We also have the following two generic access propositions:

$$holds(s, r, c) \wedge o \text{ isa subclass of } c$$
$$\text{implies } holds(s, r, o)$$
$$\text{with absence } \neg holds(s, r, o), \qquad (22)$$

and

$$holds(s, r, c|f) \wedge o \text{ isa subclass of } c$$
$$\text{implies } holds(s, r, o|f)$$
$$\text{with absence } \neg holds(s, r, o|f). \qquad (23)$$

(22) and (23) guarantee the proper inheritance of access policies on subclasses.

Finally, the following two propositions ensure the membership inheritance of access policies.

$$holds(s, r, c) \wedge o \text{ isa member of } c$$
$$\text{implies } holds(s, r, o)$$
$$\text{with absence } \neg holds(s, r, o), \qquad (24)$$

and

$$holds(s, r, c|f) \wedge o \text{ isa member of } c$$
$$\text{implies } holds(s, r, o|f)$$
$$\text{with absence } \neg holds(s, r, o|f). \qquad (25)$$

Now we can formally define our database with associated authorizations as follows. We will refer to this kind of database as *extended object oriented database*.

Definition 3. *An extended object oriented database in $\mathcal{L}^a$ is a pair $\Lambda = (\Sigma, \Xi)$, where $\Sigma = (\Gamma, \Delta, \Omega)$ is the database as defined in Definition 1, and $\Xi = GA \cup A$ is an authorization description on Σ where GA is a collection of generic authorization propositions (21) - (25), and A is a finite set of user-defined access propositions.*

The definition of the model of the extended object oriented database is similar to the definition of the model of the object oriented database except that the access propositions have been taken into account. Refer to [2] for formal and detailed definitions and explanation.

Taking default access proposition into account, it turns out that the models of an extended object oriented database may not be unique. This is shown by the following example.

Example 2. Given an extended database $\Lambda = (\Sigma, \Xi)$, where Σ is the staff database defined in Example 1, and $\Xi = GA \cup A$, where A is a collection of the following access propositions:

$$holds(S, Own, Bob), \qquad (26)$$

$$holds(S, Own, o) \textbf{ implies } holds(S, Update, o)$$
$$\textbf{with absence } \neg holds(S, Update, o), \qquad (27)$$
$$holds(S, Own, o) \textbf{ implies } \neg holds(S, Update, o)$$
$$\textbf{with absence } holds(S, Update, o). \qquad (28)$$

(26) simply says that the user S owns object Bob in the database. (27) expresses that if S owns an object o, then S will be able to update this object under the absence of the fact that S cannot update o, whereas (28) states that if S owns an object o, then S will not be able to update this object under the absence of the fact that S can update o.

Clearly, (27) and (28) override each other. It follows that Λ has two different models I_1^Λ and I_2^Λ such that

$$I_1^\Lambda \models_\lambda holds(S, Update, Bob) \text{ and}$$
$$I_2^\Lambda \models_\lambda \neg holds(S, Update, Bob).$$

4 Reasoning about Authorizations

In this section, we investigate some properties on the inheritance of authorizations on objects in database. Due to space limit, we cannot provide comprehensive definitions, explanation and examples in here. We just give some theorems to conclude the properties on the inheritance of authorizations.

An extended database may have more than one model. In this case, every model actually represents one possible interpretation for the database with associated authorizations. However, a class of extended databases having unique models presents some interesting inheritance properties of authorizations with respect to subclass and membership relationships among objects in databases. An extended database is *well-specified* if it has a unique model.

Theorem 1. *(Subclass Authorization Inheritance) Let Λ be a well-specified extended database and S, R, C and O are arbitrary subject constant, access right constant and object constants respectively. Then the following results hold.*

(i) *If $\Lambda \models_\lambda holds(S, R, C) \wedge O$ isa subclass of C and $\Lambda \not\models_\lambda \neg holds(S, R, O)$, then $\Lambda \models_\lambda holds(S, R, O)$.*

(ii) *If $\Lambda \models_\lambda holds(S, R, C|f) \wedge O$ isa subclass of C and $\Lambda \not\models_\lambda \neg holds(S, R, O|f)$, then $\Lambda \models_\lambda holds(S, R, O|f)$.*

Theorem 2. *(Membership Authorization Inheritance) Let Λ be a well-specified complex database, and S, R, C and O are arbitrary subject constant, access right constant and object constants respectively. Then the following results hold.*

(i) If $\Lambda \models_\lambda holds(S, R, C) \wedge O$ **isa member of** C *and* $\Lambda \not\models_\lambda \neg holds(S, R, O)$,
  then $\Lambda \models_\lambda holds(S, R, O)$.
(ii) If $\Lambda \models_\lambda holds(S, R, C|f) \wedge O$ **isa member of** C *and* $\Lambda \not\models_\lambda \neg holds(S, R, O|f)$,
  then $\Lambda \models_\lambda holds(S, R, O|f)$.

The above two theorems directly follow from generic authorization scheme (21) - (25). The following two theorems, on the other hand, represent that these subclass and membership authorization inheritance can be overridden such that the consistency of authorizations can be maintained.

Theorem 3. *(Overriding of Subclass Authorization Inheritance) Let Λ be a well-specified complex database, and S, R, C and O are arbitrary subject constant, access right constant and object constants respectively. Then the following results hold.*

(i) If $\Lambda \models_\lambda holds(S, R, C) \wedge O$ **isa subclass of** C *and* $\Lambda \not\models_\lambda holds(S, R, O)$,
  then $\Lambda \models_\lambda \neg holds(S, R, O)$.
(ii) If $\Lambda \models_\lambda holds(S, R, C|f) \wedge O$ **isa subclass of** C *and* $\Lambda \not\models_\lambda holds(S, R, O|f)$,
  then $\Lambda \models_\lambda \neg holds(S, R, O|f)$.

Theorem 4. *(Overriding of Membership Authorization Inheritance) Let Λ be a well-specified complex database, and S, R, C and O are arbitrary subject constant, access right constant and object constants respectively. Then the following results hold.*

(i) If $\Lambda \models_\lambda holds(S, R, C) \wedge O$ **isa member of** C *and* $\Lambda \not\models_\lambda holds(S, R, O)$,
  then $\Lambda \models_\lambda \neg holds(S, R, O)$.
(ii) If $\Lambda \models_\lambda holds(S, R, C|f) \wedge O$ **isa member of** C *and* $\Lambda \not\models_\lambda holds(S, R, O|f)$,
  then $\Lambda \models_\lambda \neg holds(S, R, O|f)$.

For example, in a well-specified complex database Λ, $\Lambda \models_\lambda holds(Anne, Update, Staff|record)$ and $GenStaff$ and $AcadStaff$ are subclasses of $Staff$. If neither $\neg holds(Anne, Update, GenStaff|record)$ nor $\neg holds(Anne, Update, AcadStaff|record)$ are entailed by Λ, from Theorem 1, we can get that $holds(Anne, Update, GenStaff|record)$ and $holds(Anne, Update, AcadStaff|record)$.

5 Conclusions

In this paper, we have proposed a logical formalization for specifying authorizations in object oriented databases. Our work consisted of two steps: the first step involved a formal language $\mathcal{L}$ to formalize object oriented databases. We provided a high level language to specify an object oriented database and defined a precise semantics for it. Our semantics of $\mathcal{L}$ shares some features of Kifer *elt.*'s F-logic for specifying object oriented databases. But our database specification is more succinct and intuitive, and hence it has been possible to extend this by combining it with authorization structures. The second step was to extend $\mathcal{L}$ to language $\mathcal{L}^a$ by representing different types of authorizations in the database.

It has been shown that the types of authorizations in our formalism are quite flexible and can be used to reason about complex authorizations compared with other approaches.

Acknowledgement

This research is supported in part by the Australian Government Research Grant ARC A49803524.

References

1. Y. Bai and V. Varadharajan, A logic for state transformations in authorization policies. In *the Proceedings of the 10th IEEE Computer Security Foundations Workshop*, pp 173-182, Massachusetts, June, 1997.
2. Y. Bai and V. Varadharajan, A Logical Formalization for Specifying Authorizations in Object Oriented Databases. Manuscript, Nov. 1998.
3. E.B. Fernandez, R.B. France, D. Wei, A formal specification of an authorization model for object-oriented databases. In *Database Security, IX: Status and Prospects*, pp. 95-109. Elsevier Science Publishers B. V., 1995.
4. E. Gudes, H. Song, E.B. Fernandez, Evaluation of negative, predicate, and instance-based authorization in object-oriented databases. In *Database Security, IV: Status and Prospects*, pp 85-98. S. Jajodia and C.E. Landwehr (Editors). Elsevier Science Publishers B. V., 1991.
5. M. Kifer, G. Lausen, J. Wu, Logical foundations of object-oriented and frame-based languages. *Journal of ACM*, Vol. 42, No. 4 (July), pp. 741-843, 1995.
6. T.F. Lunt, Discretionary Security for Object-Oriented Database Systems, Technical Report 7543, Computer Science Laboratory, SRI International, 1990.
7. J.K. Millen, T.F. Lunt, Security for Object-Oriented Database Systems, *Proceedings of IEEE Symposium on Research in Security and Privacy*, pp 260–272, 1992.

An Analysis of Access Control Models

Gregory Saunders[1], Michael Hitchens[1], and Vijay Varadharajan[2]

[1] Basser Department of Computer Science, University of Sydney, Australia
{gsaunder,michaelh}@cs.usyd.edu.au
[2] School of Computing & Information Technology, University of Western Sydney
(Nepean), Australia
vijay@cit.nepean.uws.edu.au

Abstract. Access control in real systems is implemented using one or
more abstractions based on the access control matrix (ACM). The most
common abstractions are access control lists (ACLs) and capabilities.
In this paper, we consider an extended Harrison-Ruzzo-Ullman (HRU)
model to make some formal observations about capability systems versus
access control list based systems. This analysis makes the characteristics
of these types of access control mechanisms more explicit and is intended
to provide a better understanding of their use. A combined model providing the flexibility of capabilities with the simplicity of the ACL and
its relation to other models proposed earlier (e.g.[10, 6]) are discussed.

1 Introduction

Security is an important consideration for computer systems due to the quantity
and sensitivity of information stored in them. Defining who has access, and to
what extent, to this information is an important security function, variously
known as authorisation or access control. The basic model of access control is
the access control matrix (ACM) [11] and current access control implementations
are predominantly based on models directly drawn from the ACM model. The
essential information contained in an ACM is:

- The identity of subjects (e.g. users, etc.).
- The identity of objects (e.g. files, etc.).
- The access rights each subject has for each object.

It is unwieldy to implement the ACM model directly due to the potential number
of entries in the matrix. Also, most subjects will have no access to most objects so
that many of the entries in the matrix will be empty. The well-known drawbacks
of the ACM model (including, but not limited to, implementation efficiency)
mean that it is not directly used in practice. Access control in actual systems is
implemented by employing one or more abstractions based (more or less directly)
on the ACM. These include:

- Access control lists (ACLs).
- Capabilities [4].

- Roles [5, 14].
- Lattice based access control [13].

The ACM model is discussed in formal terms in Sect. 2. Discussion of the more popular models will be based upon the formalisations of the ACM model.

Of the abstractions listed above, ACLs and capabilities are currently the most common forms of access control (with implementations of ACLs being far more common than those of capabilities). ACLs and capabilities are very directly based upon the ACM. While other mechanisms, such as roles and lattice based access control, are related to the ACM, it is a less direct relationship. In some sense ACLs and capabilities represent the rows and columns of the ACM.

One of the primary reasons for the popularity of ACLs over capabilities is that many early implementations of capabilities had efficiency problems [7], although more recent ones, such as that for Grasshopper [2], have addressed several of these problems. Perhaps more significantly, there are certain situations where capabilities demonstrate drawbacks when compared with ACLs. These are discussed in Sect. 4. That there are problems with capabilities should come as no surprise. While ACLs explicitly hold all the information held in the ACM (subject identity, object identity, access rights), "pure" capabilities do not explicitly hold subject identity. This information is implicitly held, it being represented by whichever subjects can access the capability. This is less than entirely satisfactory, as it can be difficult to track exactly which users have access to an object. However, nowadays several ticket based access control schemes, such as DCE [15] and Sesame [9] include subject identity as part of the ticket structure.

Conversely capabilities can have certain advantages, in terms of flexibility, over ACLs. For example, with capabilities it is straightforward to give a particular user different types of access to an object. The user can simply be provided with multiple capabilities for the object, each capability specifying a different type of access. Providing multiple types of access can be useful for such purposes as sandboxing and delegation. Consider, for instance, access control in an object oriented system where access to an object is specified in terms of the methods that can be accessed in the object interface. Here we may give a user access to the object's total interface whereas different processes used by the same user may be given access to only subsets of the interface. Such a facility tends to be more difficult to achieve with ACLs. With ACLs a user is typically granted a single level of access to an object, regardless of how many ways they have of reaching that object. Problems with ACLs are noted in Sect. 3.

In this paper, we consider an extended Harrison-Ruzzo-Ullman (HRU) model to make some formal observations about capability systems vs. access control list based systems. This analysis makes the characteristics of these types of access control mechanisms more explicit and is intended to provide a better understanding of their use. Based upon the models and analysis presented we consider a combined model for access control implementations. It attempts to preserve the simplicity of ACLs and capabilities when compared to other methods of access control in actual use. This is essentially due to it preserving the more direct relationship that ACLs and capabilities have with the ACM when compared to other approaches. The modified model can be used as the basis of implementations of either ACLs or capabilities. This should result in systems which combine the current advantages of both ACLs and capabilities, while offering no less security than currently provided by such systems. We also discuss how this combined model compares with other such models proposed earlier (e.g. [10,6]).

2 A Basis for Formal Models of Access Control

HRU suggested a definition of a *protection system* based on an access matrix [8], following Lampson [11]. It is commonly suggested that the columns of this matrix, viewed in isolation, form access lists and the rows form capability lists (such as those described in [3]). HRU's model was primarily intended to make theoretical arguments about complexity issues in the analysis of rights propagation in authorization systems. Our objective is to make some formal observations about capability vs. ACL systems, hence for the purposes of our discussion, we require a base model which is an extension of HRU that is capable of describing systems without an access matrix. We therefore suggest the following definition:
A protection system consists of

1. A finite set of generic rights R.[1]
2. A set of objects O.
3. A set of subjects S such that $S \subseteq O$.
4. A set of data available in the environment E of the system. The environment is controlled by the system (i.e. it is secure).

The present state of the protection system is defined by the values of O, S and E. Changes in the state are modeled by

5. A set C of commands of the form

    command $\alpha(X_1, X_2, \ldots, X_k)$
      if r_1 **in** (X_{s1}, X_{o1}) **and**
        $\ldots$
        r_m **in** (X_{sm}, X_{om})
      then
        op_1
        $\ldots$
        op_n
    end

Here α is a name and $X_1 \ldots X_k$ are formal parameters each of which refer to either a subject or object. Let (X_s, X_o) be defined as the rights subject X_s holds for object X_o [8, page 463], which will be represented differently in each model we discuss. We allow the use of more complex conditions than the simple $[r$ **in** $(X_s, X_o)]$ to more accurately represent the behaviour of some models. Each op_i is one of the *primitive operations* in Tab. 1. Formal definitions of the effects of each operation can be found in [8].

---

[1] For example, the set R for the Unix filesystem would be *read, write, execute*

Table 1. The *primitive operations* available to the commands in C

enter r into (X_s, X_o)	delete r from (X_s, X_o)
create object X_o	destroy object X_o
create subject X_s	destroy subject X_s

6. A logical function f which is true iff an operation should be permitted.

The function formally represents the manner in which the model is used to determine if an operation should be permitted. It will typically involve two variables that depend on the access control model under consideration. The first, *op*, represents the desired operation. We are concerned not with the effect of the operation but with the rights it requires, and we do not wish to rule out the possibility that an operation may require multiple rights, thus we will treat *op* as a subset of R. The second argument somehow represents the object on which the operation is to be performed. Note that both the arguments are supplied by the *subject*, any information f requires from the *system* must be available in E.

A model of access control must specify E, C and f and may specify some or all of R. An implementation of such a model must fully specify R, O and S in addition to E, C and f. Using this basis we may define the ACM model as

M1. R contains the generic right *own*.[2] Note that R is *not* fully defined here.

M2. E contains

    s the identity of the subject on whose behalf the system is running ($s \in S$)

    P a matrix with a row for each subject and column for each object. $P[s, o]$ is a (possibly empty) subset of R containing the rights subject s holds for object o.

M3. The set of commands C is shown in Tab. 2.[3]

The commands for creating or destroying subjects are similar to $CREATE$ and $DESTROY$ for objects in Tab. 2.

M4. The function $f(s, op, o) := op \subseteq P[s, o]$.

We implicitly assume that the system is more trustworthy than the subject, hence the information like subject identity in the function comes from the system controlled environment E.

The ACM model is never implemented practically, since for any real system the matrix would be too large and sparse to maintain efficiently. Apart from these problems of implementation efficiency, the ACM has a number of other problems. Note from (M2) above, the definition of P, that there is only one set

---

[2] The *own* right controls access to commands. Space does not permit discussion of other methods of achieving this.

[3] Note that there are separate $CONFER$ and $REMOVE$ commands for each $r \in R$, since the formal parameters to each command can only identify an object or subject.

Table 2. The set C of commands for the access control matrix model

command $CREATE(obj)$
  create object obj
  enter own into $P[s, obj]$
end

command $DESTROY(obj)$
  if own in $P[s, obj]$ then
    destroy object obj
end

command $CONFER_r(friend, obj)$
  if own in $P[s, obj]$ then
    enter r into $P[friend, obj]$
end

command $REMOVE_r(enemy, obj)$
  if own in $P[s, obj]$ then
    delete r from $P[enemy, obj]$
end

command $CHOWN(new, obj)$
  if own in $P[s, obj]$ then
    delete own from $P[s, obj]$
    enter own into $P[new, obj]$
end

of rights for each $[s, o]$ pair. In this model we cannot provide multiple levels of access to an object for a particular subject. It could be argued that multiple subjects could correspond to a single real world user. This idea has some merit but there is nothing in the above model which relates members of the set S to each other. The ACM model could be extended in this direction, treating each subject as a protection domain with real world users corresponding to a number of protection domains. However, this has some problems in terms of flexibility as each subject would have a relatively fixed set of access rights. Nevertheless, there has been work which relates multiple members of S to a single user within the HRU context. Finally, the ACM is difficult to incorporate into the type systems of programming languages, due to its size. The advantages of being able to directly manipulate access control information in a programming language can be seen in various database and capability systems.

3 The Access Control List Model

Informally, ACLs can be described as a system where the access control information for an object is stored with the object. This avoids the need to maintain a large, sparse matrix. Having no central point holding all access control information improves efficiency. Most implementations of ACLs do not store an entry for each user with the object, or even for every user that actually has some level of access to the object, but will use some mechanism, for example groups, to limit the amount of information to be stored.

ACLs tend to either be inflexible, as in the short, three entry lists used by Unix which restrict the access control policies that can be implemented, or hard to manage, as in the large and dynamic lists used by Windows NT4. These problems arise from the necessity of holding all access rights combinations for a particular object in a single structure. ACLs inherit the limitation of only one set of rights per subject-object pair from the ACM. The discussion of this issue in Sect. 2 also applies here. Also, it would be difficult for such a model to be integrated into programming language type systems. While such an undertaking is not impossible, observation demonstrates that it is rarely, if ever, carried out. This is possibly due to the ACLs being (at least conceptually) stored in the filesystem with the object protected, rather than in the data area of a process. If ACLs were part of the type system of a language, as a first class data type, then manipulating objects and associated protection policies within code become straightforward operations. Such operations could be subjected to safeguards applied to other operations within a language, such as type-checking (by the compiler and at runtime, as appropriate).

3.1 Groups

Before we can give a complete formalisation of the ACL model, it is necessary to provide a formalisation of the concept of groups. Some access control systems, for example Unix, include the concept of groups of subjects to which access rights may be granted. We may formalise the concept as follows:

G1. There exist subsets of S called groups. Let the set of these groups be G.

G2. In many systems there is a world group $W \in G$ consisting of all subjects.

G3. For every subject $s \in S$ let $\gamma_s \subseteq G$ denote the set $\{g \mid g \in G \land s \in g\}$. Thus γ_s is the set of all groups in which s is a member. As the world group consists of all subjects, every subject is a member of at least that group, if no others, and therefore γ_s is not empty for any subject.

G4. To the matrix P defined in (M2) we add a row for each group. This means that P has a row for each $s \in S$ and each $g \in G$.

3.2 A Complete Model for Access Control Lists

Given a definition of groups we may now give a complete model for access control lists. In this model the list associated with each object may contain an entry for each subject and for each group which exists in the system. An operation is allowed if the required right is present in the list either in the subject's entry or in the entry for any of the groups of which the subject is a member. A different interpretation of groups presumes that the rights of a subject's groups are considered iff the rights of the subject are not specified. This second interpretation is used in the Unix filesystem.

L1. R is as in (M1).

L2. E contains
  s as in (M2).
  W as described in (G2).

γ_s as described in (G3).

l_o the set $\{s \mapsto \rho \mid s \in S \land \rho = P[s,o]\} \cup \{g \mapsto \rho \mid g \in G \land \rho = P[s,o]\}$ for each $o \in O$.

L3. C contains the commands in Tab. 2, but with $l_{obj}[s]$ substituted for $P[s,obj]$.

L4. $f(op,o) := (op \subseteq l_o[s]) \lor \exists g[(g \in \gamma_s) \land (op \subseteq l_o[g])]$.

Groups give added flexibility as, for example, altering access to a particular object for a group requires updating a single entry, rather than the entry for each user. They also allow the amount of information held in each list to be reduced. However, the problems identified in Sect. 2 have still not been fully addressed. While different levels of access to a particular object can apparently be provided to a single subject (by using different group entries), in the above model the subject has rights which are the union of all entries (primarily due to the 'or' in (L4)). The list has dynamic length and a complicated structure, making it difficult to use with a programming language.

4 Capabilities

Capabilities were first proposed by Dennis and Van Horn [3]. Since then there have been a number of attempts to implement and/or refine them [1, 2, 12, 10, 6, 16]. A capability (in its basic form) consists of a reference to and a set of rights for an object. The essential aspect of capabilities is that each object, rights pair is considered a separate entity. With ACLs each subject, rights pair is considered an integral part of the list. There is nothing inherent in the concept of storing access control information with the object to which it applies that prohibits the treatment of each subject, rights pair as a separate entity. However, this is not done for existing models and implementations, as can be gathered from Sect. 3. Any subject possessing or able to reference a capability may use it to access the object identified within it, subject to the rights stored in the capability. The major advantages of capabilities when compared to ACLs are:

- It is easier to provide a user with multiple levels of access to an object.
- They integrate more easily into the type systems of programming languages.
- Naming and protection mechanisms can be unified.

These advantages derive directly from the treatment of each object, rights pair as a separate entity. As the structure of a capability is much simpler than an ACL (even the limited form provided by Unix), they are more readily adaptable to the needs of programming languages. Even with some capability implementations which have a more complicated structure for capabilities, the conceptual storage of capabilities with the subject makes it more appealing to store them in the data areas of the subject's processes. As a capability contains a reference to the object protected, the capability can be directly used to reference the object. This unifies the naming and protection mechanisms.

4.1 A Basic Capability Model

We may formulate a basic capability model in the following manner

BC1. There exist pairs (o, ρ) in the system called capabilities. Let o be an object reference and ρ a set of rights. Possession of a capability permits access to the object to which it refers.

BC2. R contains the rights $\{destroy, write, read, derive, confer, renew\}$. Note that R is *not* fully defined here.

The rights in R define the permissions which the holder of a capability has to the object to which the capability refers *and to the capability itself*. The *destroy* right allows destruction of the object to which the capability refers, *write* allows writing and *read* allows a capability to be read from the object. The *derive* right allows a new capability to be derived from this one, *confer* permits the capability to be given to another and *renew* permits the holder of the capability to revoke all capabilities to the object. Another way of achieving the same result would be to replace some or all of the rights in R with a single right *own*.

BC3. E contains

  e the identity of the current unit of execution (e.g. process, thread, locus etc.). This 'unit of execution' forms a kind of restricted subject, hence $e \in S \subseteq O$. A user may have many such 'restricted subjects'.

  pd the Protection Domain in which we are currently executing ($pd \in O$). This is not the equivalent of subject identity since many subjects may have access to a single protection domain and a single subject may have access to many protection domains.

  Cl_e the set of capabilities possessed by $e \in S \subseteq O$. There are a number of ways this list may be implemented.

BC4. C contains the commands in Tab. 3.[4] The capabilities which may be presented to the commands in Tab. 3 are those in Cl_e and Cl_{pd}.

Note that not all commands in Tab. 3 are available in all capability systems.
The *DESTROY* command has the effect of rendering all capabilities to the destroyed object invalid. The *RENEW* command renders all capabilities to the renewed object, except $(o, \rho)'$, invalid. The *ACQUIRE* command reads a capability from an object into the capability list of the current subject.

BC5. The function $f(op, (o, \rho)) := (op \subseteq \rho) \wedge ((o, \rho) \in Cl_e \cup Cl_{pd})$

Hence the result of f is dependent on both the capabilities in Cl_e and system changes to Cl_{pd}.
The most serious flaw with pure capabilities derives from a readily observable property of (BC5). Unlike the equivalent function for ACLs, the access control function for capabilities does not explicitly employ the identity of the subject.

---

[4] Note that the formal parameters to the commands in Tab. 3 are capabilities, which are valid object (and subject) identifiers.

Table 3. The set C of commands for a basic capability system

command $CREATE((o, \rho))$
   create object o
   enter (o, ρ) into Cl_e
end

command $DESTROY((o, \rho))$
   if $f(destroy, (o, \rho))$ then
      destroy object o
end

command $RENEW((o, \rho))$
   if $f(renew, (o, \rho))$ then
      enter (o, ρ) into Cl_e
end

command $ACQUIRE((o_1, \rho_1), (o_2, \rho_2))$
   if $f(read, (o_1, \rho_1))$ and
      (o_2, ρ_2) in Cl_{o1}
   then
      enter (o_2, ρ_2) into Cl_e
end

command $DERIVE((o, \rho_1), (o, \rho_2))$
   if $f(derive, (o, \rho_1))$ and
      $\rho_2 \subseteq \rho_1$
   then
      enter (o, ρ_2) into Cl_e
end

command $CONFER((o_1, \rho_1), (o_1, \rho_2), (o_2, \rho_3))$
   if $f(confer, (o_1, \rho_1))$ and
      $f(write, (o_2, \rho_3))$ and
      $\rho_2 \subseteq \rho_1$
   then
      enter (o_1, ρ_2) into Cl_{o2}
end

This information is implicitly derived from the identity of the subject attempting access. It is assumed that if the subject can reference the capability then they are entitled to the access it embodies. This may not be the intention of the entity entrusted with formulating the security policy for the object. A well known problem with capabilities (in their basic form) is that there is no elegant way of tracking the propagation of capabilities or revoking them once they have been propagated. However, there are various proposals for handling revocation, such as the capability hierarchies proposed by Anderson [1].

4.2 Revocation with Capability Hierarchies

A capability model with capability hierarchies can be formalised as follows:

CH1. To the environment E in (BC2) we add
   Ch_o The hierarchy of capabilities for each object $o \in O$. Let $Ch_o[(o, \rho)]$
     denote the subhierarchy consisting of (o, ρ) and its children.
CH2. to the $CREATE$ command in Tab. 3 add the line enter (o, R) into Ch_o
CH3. to the $DESTROY$ command add destroy Ch_o
CH4. to $RENEW$ add destroy Ch_o; enter $(o, \rho)'$ into Ch_o
CH5. to $DERIVE$ add enter (o, ρ_2) into Ch_o
CH6. add the command

command $REVOKE((o, \rho))$
    if *revoke* in ρ then
        destroy $Ch_o[(o, \rho)]$
end

CH7. The function

$$f(op, (o, \rho)) := (op \subseteq \rho) \wedge ((o, \rho) \in Cl_e \cup Cl_{pd}) \wedge ((o, \rho) \in Ch_o)$$

While the capability hierarchy allows inspection of existing capabilities and their selective revocation, it provides no means for determining which subjects have access to a given capability. In this sense, revocation must work in an essentially 'blind' fashion. Any attempt to deny a particular subject access to an object is difficult at best, as it cannot be determined in any straightforward manner which capabilities the subject can reference. Capability implementations with a hierarchy essentially have all the problems of the basic capability model.

5   Discussion

To this point we have identified problems with each model discussed. The matrix model was difficult to implement due to its size and sparsity. It is difficult to provide multiple types of access for a single user, though this can be achieved by associating multiple subjects with each user. Further it is difficult, due to its size, to incorporate it into the type systems of programming languages.

Access control lists go some way to remedying these problems, by providing a more efficient implementation, and incorporating concepts such as groups to limit the amount of data to be stored. Nevertheless, ACLs are difficult to incorporate into the type systems of programming languages.

Capabilities also provide a more efficient means of implementing the ACM. Further their relatively simple structure enables them to be incorporated into the type systems of programming languages. However, the lack of consideration of subject identity in pure capability systems makes selective revocation difficult and the task of computing which subjects can access a given object intractable. Even when combined with Anderson's hierarchies it is difficult to track which subjects can access a given object and revocation must be done in a 'blind' fashion, without a full appreciation of which subject's access has been revoked.

It appears that the problems in the capability model are avoided by ACLs due to their consideration of subject identity. Conversely by attaching capabilities to the units of execution (rather than directly to subjects) the capability model is able to grant differing levels of access to different subjects—something not achieved in the generally employed ACL systems. In the following section we discuss a model which employs subject identity and allows multiple types of access to an object for a given user while avoiding the problems identified above.

Others have observed the advantages of combining ACLs with capabilities, such as Karger and Gong [10, 6]. Karger's SCAP system essentially makes capabilities the cached results of ACL lookups. Whilst this overcomes the security

Table 4. The $ADDSBJ$ and $DELSBJ$ commands for capabilities with users

command $ADDSBJ((o, \rho_1, \sigma_1),$	command $DELUSER((o, \rho_1, \sigma_1),$
$(o, \rho_2, \sigma_2), friend)$	$(o, \rho_2, \sigma_2), enemy)$
if $f(adduser, (o, \rho_1, \sigma_1))$ and	if $f(deluser, (o, \rho_1, \sigma_1))$ and
(o, ρ_2, σ_2) in $Ch_o[(o, \rho_1, \sigma_1)]$	(o, ρ_2, σ_2) in $Ch_o[(o, \rho_1, \sigma_1)]$
then	then
enter $friend$ into σ_2	delete $enemy$ from σ_2
end	end

problems with capabilities, it does so at the expense of their superior flexibility. Gong envisions an exception list attached to each object, listing those subjects whose capabilities for that object have been revoked, but such a system also sacrifices the flexibility of capabilities. Both authors appeal to the inability of capabilities to provide a means of tracing which users have access to a given object as justification for combining them with ACLs, but neither identifies the fundamental defect in the capability model which is the cause of this problem.

6 A Combined Model

In order to employ subject identity in the capability model, we take the hierarchical model of Sect. 4.2 and make each capability a triple consisting of object identity, rights and a set of subjects allowed to use the capability. Then

S1. To R we add $\{addsbj, delsbj\}$.
S2. To E we add s as in (M2).
S3. To C we add the commands in Tab. 4.
S4. $CREATE$ enters $(o, R, \{s\})$ into both Cl_{pd} and Ch_o
S5. $DERIVE$ enters $(o, \rho_2, \{s\})$ into both Cl_{pd} and Ch_o
S6. $CONFER$ enters s into the user set for the (o_1, ρ_2) capability.
S7. The function

$$f(op, (o, \rho, \sigma)) := (op \subseteq \rho) \wedge ((o, \rho, \sigma) \in Cl_e \cup Cl_{pd}) \wedge ((o, \rho, \sigma) \in Ch_o) \wedge (s \in \sigma)$$

This solution provides a convenient method of tracking which subjects have access to a given object, by searching the subject sets of the capability hierarchy of that object. Furthermore, revocation of an individual subject's rights can be achieved by removing them from the subjects set of the relevant capability. Finally, sets have already been incorporated into the type systems of programming languages, and thus should not pose a problem in incorporating capabilities into those type systems.

It is also possible to extend the flexibility of an ACL system by incorporating a modified form of the 'restricted subject' and 'protection domain' concepts introduced in Sect. 4.1 into an ACL system. By creating a number of restricted subjects for each normal subject then allowing an ACL to contain entries for the restricted subjects, a normal subject can cause a unit of execution to run on behalf of one of the restricted subjects, thereby giving the normal subject multiple types of access to a single object. In this case, the concepts of 'restricted subject' and 'protection domain' have been combined. Whilst this addition provides some of the flexibility of the capability model to ACLs, it does not make the incorporation of ACLs into the type systems of programming languages any easier. Indeed, it is this difficulty which prevents us from transferring the 'restricted subject' and 'protection domain' concepts directly. This would require entries in some ACLs for units of execution, which are created and destroyed too quickly for this to be practical. The ability of units of execution to contain embedded capabilities effectively reduces this problem in capability systems.

Acknowledgements

The authors wish to thank the anonymous referees for their helpful comments.

References

1. M. Anderson, R. D. Pose, and C. S. Wallace. A password-capability system. *The Computer Journal*, 29(1):1–8, February 1986.
2. A. Dearle, R. di Bona, J. Farrow, F. Henskens, D. Hulse, A. Lindström, S. Norris, J. Rosenberg, and R. Vaughan. Protection in the grasshopper operating system. In *Proceedings of the 6th International Workshop on Persistent Object Systems*, pages 54–72, September 1994.
3. J. B. Dennis and E. C. Van Horn. Programming semantics for multiprogrammed computations. *Communications of the ACM*, 9(3):143–155, March 1966.
4. R. S. Fabry. Capability-based addressing. *Communications of the ACM*, 17(7):403–412, July 1974.
5. D. Ferraiolo and R. Kuhn. Role-based access controls. In *15th NIST-NCSC National Computer Security Conference*, pages 554–563. October 1992.
6. L. Gong. A secure identity-based capability system. In *IEEE Symposium on Security and Privacy*, pages 56–63. IEEE Computer Science Press, Oakland, CA, May 1989.
7. P. M. Hansen, M. A. Linton, R. N. Mayo, M. Murphy, and D. A. Patterson. A performance evaluation of the intel iapx 432. *Computer Architecture News*, 10(4), June 1982.
8. M. A. Harrison, W. L. Ruzzo, and J. D. Ullman. Protection in operating systems. *Communications of the ACM*, 19(8):461–471, August 1976.
9. P. Kaijser, T. Parker, and D. Pinkas. SESAME: The solution to security for open distributed systems. *Computer Communications*, 17(7):501–518, July 1994.
10. P. A. Karger. Improving security and performance for capability systems. Technical Report 149, University of Cambridge Computer Laboratory, Cambridge, England, October 1988. Dissertation submitted for the degree of Doctor of Philosophy.
11. B. W. Lampson. Protection. *Operating Systems Review*, 8(1):18–24, January 1974.
12. G. J. Myers and B. R. S. Buckingham. A hardware implementation of capability based addressing. *ACM Operating Systems Review*, 14(4):13–25, October 1980.
13. R. S. Sandhu. Lattice-based access control models. *IEEE Computer*, 26(11):9–19, November 1993.

14. R. S. Sandhu, E. J. Coyne, H. L. Feinstein, and C. E. Youman. Role-based access control models. *IEEE Computer*, 29(2):38–47, February 1996.

15. J. Shirley, W. Hu, and D. Magid. *Guide to Writing DCE Applications : DCE Security Model*. O'Reilly & Associates, Inc., 1994.

16. A. S. Tanenbaum, S. J. Mullender, and R. van Renesse. Using sparse capabilities in a distributed operating system. In *Proceedings of the 6th International Conference on Distributed Computing Systems*, pages 558–563. IEEE, May 1986.

Efficient Identity Based Parameter Selection for Elliptic Curve Cryptosystems

Arjen K. Lenstra

Citibank, N.A., 4 Sylvan Way, Parsippany, NJ 07054, U.S.A.
arjen.lenstra@citicorp.com

Abstract. A method is proposed that allows each individual party to an elliptic curve cryptosystem to quickly determine its own unique pair of finite field and Weierstraß equation, in such a way that the resulting pair provides adequate security. Although the choice of Weierstraß equations allowed by this proposal is limited, the number of possible finite fields is unlimited. The proposed method allows each participant to select its elliptic curve cryptosystem parameters in such a way that the security is not affected by attacks on any other participant, unless unanticipated progress is made affecting the security for a particular Weierstraß equation irrespective of the underlying finite field. Thus the proposal provides more security than elliptic curve cryptosystems where all participants share the same Weierstraß equation and finite field. It also offers much faster and less complicated parameter initialization than elliptic curve cryptosystems where each participant randomly selects its own unique Weierstraß equation and thus has to solve the cumbersome point counting problem.

1 Introduction

Elliptic curve cryptosystems come in many different flavors. However, they all have the following in common: a point of high prime order in the group of points of an elliptic curve over a finite field. In this paper, let F_p denote the finite field (of cardinality p for a prime power p), let E be an equation defining the elliptic curve over F_p, let $E(F_p)$ be the group of points of that elliptic curve over F_p, and let Q be the point of high prime order q in $E(F_p)$. In some elliptic curve cryptosystems all participants share the elliptic curve data (F_p,E,Q,q), in others each participant selects its own curve data. In this paper these systems are referred to as shared and non-shared systems, respectively.

In either case, given shared or non-shared curve data, each participant selects its own private key and computes the corresponding public key in the following manner: party A selects a random positive integer $m_A < q$ and computes the point $G_A = m_A \bullet Q$ in $E(F_p)$ (with $\bullet$ denoting scalar multiplication in $E(F_p)$). In a shared curve system the public key of party A consists of G_A, with (F_p,E,Q,q) implicitly defined as system wide constants and presumably determined beforehand by a central authority. In a non-shared system A's public key consists of (F_p,E,Q,q,G_A), with (F_p,E,Q,q) unique to party A, and therefore more appropriately referred to as $(F_{p(A)},E_A,Q_A,q_A)$. In both systems A's private key consists of the integer m_A.

Shared and non-shared systems have their own advantages and disadvantages. An advantage of shared systems is that the part of A's public key data that is unique to A consists of just G_A instead of the five-tuple $(F_{p(A)}, E_A, Q_A, q_A, G_A)$, which facilitates key certification and communication set-up. Another advantage of the shared approach is that, since the computation involved in determining the curve data (F_p, E, Q, q) has been carried out beforehand by a central authority, none of the parties has to perform complicated or lengthy computations to generate their private and public keys: selecting a random integer and performing a scalar multiplication in $E(F_p)$ suffices. Key generation in a non-shared system may be quite involved: if party A picks finite fields and curve equations at random, highly non-trivial counting techniques have to be employed to check if an appropriate point of high prime order exists. These are probably the reasons why most elliptic curve cryptosystem proposals these days are shared systems.

Non-shared systems may, however, be preferable if security and not efficiency is the top-priority. In a shared system, it is conceivable that an attack on one participant's public key affects some other participant's security as well, in particular if an index calculus type attack against elliptic curve cryptosystems would be found. In such attacks individual problems often become relatively easy once an initial database has been built. With the current state of the art of methods to solve the discrete logarithm problem in groups of elliptic curves, however, data generated to attack a particular non-shared public key have no effect at all on the security of any other non-shared public key. This is the case even if only the underlying finite fields are different but the curve equation remains the same.

In this paper a non-shared system is proposed for which the public key data is relatively short and can easily be constructed by each participant, and such that an attack on one participant does not affect the security of any other participant. Thus the proposal combines the advantages of the more traditional shared and non-shared systems, without having any of their disadvantages. The Weierstraß models used in this proposal are not new. At least one of them even goes back to Gauss. Also, their application to elliptic curve cryptosystems has been proposed before, e.g. [3: page 158]. What is new, however, is the way each party uses its identity to select an appropriate elliptic curve (i.e., a Weierstraß model and a finite field F_p) and a suitable point of high order, and how other users reconstruct that party's public key data based on the same identity and a small number of additional bits.

The paper is organized as follows. In Section 2 the theoretical background is reviewed, in Section 3 the new non-shared elliptic curve key generation method is presented, and in Section 4 a more detailed comparison with shared and other non-shared systems is provided.

2 Background

The theoretical background on elliptic curves reviewed in this section can be verified by anyone with adequate background in elliptic curves (cf. [5]), or using any standard textbook, e.g. [6].

Table 1 lists eight Weierstraß models $Y^2 = X^3 + uX + v$ for elliptic curves. If $p \equiv 3$ mod 4 is a prime that satisfies the conditions in one of the rows of Table 1, then the Weierstraß model $Y^2 = X^3 + uX + v$ in that row defines a non-supersingular elliptic curve $E_{u,v} = E$ over F_p. In this paper only prime fields F_p are considered. The discriminant Δ of the endomorphism ring and the cardinality $|E(F_p)|$ of the group of points $E(F_p)$ of E over F_p are also listed in Table 1, where $j(m,n) = 1$ if m is a square modulo n and $j(m,n) = -1$ if m is not a square modulo n. The last column of Table 1 lists a fixed divisor of $|E(F_p)|$ (i.e., in some cases the group order is not prime). Note that the rows for $d = 7$, 11, 19, 43, 67, and 163 share the same fourth, fifth and sixth columns, with exceptions for $d = 11$ and $d = 7$ for the fifth and sixth column, respectively.

For example, if $d = 7$ and p is a prime that is 3 mod 4 for which there are non-negative integers a, b such that $a^2 + 7b^2 = 4p$ and $a \neq 1$, then $Y^2 = X^3 - 35X - 98$ defines a non-supersingular elliptic curve $E_{-35,-98} = E$ over F_p, and the cardinality of the group of points $E(F_p)$ is $p+1-j(2a,7)a$. Furthermore, $p+1-j(2a,7)a$ is divisible by 8.

Table 1. Weierstraß models.

$\Delta = -d$, with d	$Y^2 = X^3 + uX + v$, with u	v	conditions on p, d, and a, b $\in Z_{\geq 0}$	group cardinality	fixed divisor
3	0	16	$a^2+3b^2 = 4p$, $p \equiv 1$ mod 3, $a \equiv 1$ mod 3, $b \equiv 0$ mod 3	$p+1+a$	9
8	−270	−1512	$a^2+2b^2 = p$, $a \equiv 1$ mod 4 if $p \equiv 3$ mod 16, $a \equiv 3$ mod 4 if $p \equiv 11$ mod 16	$p+1-2a$	2
7	−35	−98	$a^2+db^2 = 4p$, $a \neq 1$	$d \neq 11$: $p+1-j(2a,d)a$, $d = 11$: $p+1+j(2a,11)a$	$d \neq 7$: 1 $d = 7$: 8
11	−9504	−365904			
19	−608	5776			
43	−13760	621264			
67	−117920	15585808			
163	−34790720	78984748304			

The same Weierstraß model used over two different finite fields gives rise to two different and, from a security point of view, independent groups. With the current algorithms, ability to solve discrete logarithms in one of those groups does not make it easier to compute discrete logarithms in the other group.

3 Non-shared elliptic curve key generation

Table 1 can be used for elliptic curve key generation in the following manner (for $d = 3$ this is implied by [3: page 158]): generate a random prime $p \equiv 3$ mod 4 of a specified size, try and solve the equation for a, b, d, and p for all d's in Table 1, if successful for some d then check if the group cardinality for the corresponding curve satisfies the obvious security requirements, and repeat with another prime p until a good curve has been found. This straightforward approach has the advantage that primes can be chosen having advantageous computational properties. But since it requires a relatively complicated computation (namely the attempt to solve for a given p the equation $a^2 + tb^2 = 4p$ for various t's) the following even simpler approach is used here: pick a random integer a of appropriate size, and search for a non-negative integer b until the conditions in at least one row of Table 1 are satisfied for a prime p that is 3 modulo 4, and such that the group cardinality satisfies the security requirements.

The resulting elliptic curve key generation method makes use of the following function to check if a candidate a,b pair is satisfactory for a certain d.

(3.1) Check conditions on d, a, b, and x.

This function not only checks that d, a, and b lead to a 'good' curve according to Table 1, but also checks that a point of high prime order can easily be computed on the curve as a function of the additional input parameter x. Curves that are otherwise 'good' are rejected if the prescribed x does not lead, in some standard way that is described below, to a point of high prime order (cf. Remark (3.6)).

Input: Positive integers d, a, b, x, where d is one of the values in the first column of Table 1.

Output: Either 'Failure', or d, p, q, and Q, where p and q are two primes, and Q is a point of order q in the group of the curve corresponding to d over F_p (i.e., all public key data required, except for the point G).

1. Check if the conditions in the row referred to by d and the fourth column of Table 1 are satisfied for d, a, b, and if the resulting number p is a prime that is 3 mod 4. If not, then output 'Failure' and terminate.

2. Compute the group cardinality according to the fifth column (and appropriate row), and check if it can be written as q*f for a prime q and a positive integer f ≤ 32 (the fixed divisor from the sixth column will be a factor of f). If not, then output 'Failure' and terminate. (The bound of 32 on f is arbitrarily chosen and may be replaced by any value that is convenient and that still offers acceptable security.)

3. Check that there is no integer m with $m(\ln(m*\ln(p)))^2 \le 0.02(\ln(p))^2$ for which q divides $p^m - 1$. If such an integer m exists, then output 'Failure' and terminate. (Existence of a small m for which q divides $p^m - 1$ implies that the group of points of the corresponding curve over F_p is susceptible to a subexponential-time attack based on the Weil or Tate pairing. It is well known that such curves should be avoided for cryptographic applications. The bound on m follows trivially from the heuristic runtime estimate of the Number Field Sieve based subexponential-time discrete logarithm algorithm.)

4. Compute $y = (x^3 + ux + v)^{(p+1)/4}$ modulo p, with u and v corresponding to d according to the second and third columns of Table 1, check if $y^2 = x^3 + ux + v$ modulo p (i.e., if the y thus computed is indeed the squareroot modulo p of $x^3 + ux + v$) and if so put P = (x mod p, y). If $y^2 \ne x^3 + ux + v$ modulo p, i.e., if no point with x-coordinate equal to x modulo p is on the curve indicated by d, then output 'Failure' and terminate. (The condition that $p \equiv 3$ mod 4 is required for the efficient modular squareroot computation in this step.)

5. Compute $Q = f \bullet P$ in $E_{u,v}(F_p)$ with u and v as in the previous step, and check that Q is not equal to the identity element in $E_{u,v}(F_p)$. If Q is equal to the identity element, then output 'Failure' and terminate. (Due to the way Q is constructed it has order either 1 or q; a point Q of order 1 is worthless. If d = 3 then f may be replaced by f/3 because the order 9 subgroup is not cyclic.)

6. Check that $q \bullet Q$ is the identity element in $E_{u,v}(F_p)$. If not, then output 'Failure' and terminate. (This failure indicates an inconsistency, either due to an implementation error or, when called from (3.3), to an intentional attempt to reconstruct a 'wrong' key.)

7. Output d, p, q, and Q.

For the key generation it is assumed that each participant to the system has a unique ID: a bitstring that uniquely identifies a participant and that is recognized by all other participants. Commonly such IDs are exchanged whenever two participants set up a communication channel, either as part of the respective certificates or in plain-text. Furthermore, it is assumed that all participants to the system share three hash functions $R_1(B,s)$, $R_2(B,s)$, $R_3(B,s)$, each mapping a positive integer B and a bitstring s of arbitrary length to a positive integer of B bits. These hash functions do not have to satisfy any fancy cryptographic requirements and neither do they have to be particularly efficient – anything that is convenient and that takes all bits of s into account will do.

(3.2) Non-shared identity based elliptic curve key generation.
Input: The identifying information ID of the participant generating the key and a security parameter $B \in Z_{>0}$.
Output: A public key (F_p,E,Q,q,G_{ID}) suitable for use in elliptic curve cryptosystems, the corresponding private key m_{ID}, and additional data from which F_p, Q, and q can easily be reconstructed given E or d: a bitstring s of length 32 and an 8-bit integer b_1.

This protocol should be performed by the party uniquely identified by ID (though steps 1 through 5 may in principle be carried out by any party).

1. Pick a random bitstring s of length 32 and compute $a = R_1(B,ID\|s)$, $b_0 = R_2(B,ID\|s)$, and $x = R_3(2*B,ID\|s)$, where $ID\|s$ denotes the concatenation of ID and s.

2. Let i = 0.

3. For the eight different d's given in Table 1 do the following:
   - Check the conditions on d, a, $b = b_0+i$, and x as described in (3.1). If (3.1) outputs d, p, q, and Q, then let $b_1 = i$ and jump ahead to step 6.

4. Otherwise, if (3.1) outputs Failure for all 8 different d's, then replace i by i+1 and jump back to step 3 if i < 256.

5. Return to step 1 (because all 8*256 calls to (3.1) resulted in 'Failure' a new s is needed).

6. Let d, p, q, and Q be as output by (3.1) and let E be the curve indicated by d according to Table 1. Pick a random positive integer $m_{ID} < q$ and compute $G_{ID} = m_{ID}\bullet Q$ in $E(F_p)$.

7. Output (F_p, E, Q, q, G_{ID}) as public key, m_{ID} as private key, and the key reconstruction data s and b_1.

Because a and b are B-bit integers the resulting p and q have approximately 2B and at least 2B−5 bits, respectively, where the '−5' corresponds to the bound 32 on f in step 2 of (3.1). Thus, the security of the resulting key is believed to be at least B−2.5 bits.

An important aspect of (3.2) is that the (F_p, Q, q) part of a party's public key can be reconstructed very easily given the party's ID, E (or d), and the s and b_1 resulting from the construction of (F_p, E, Q, q). Since E and d can be encoded using 3 bits, any other party only needs 3 + 32 + 8 bits plus the ID and value for B to reconstruct F_p, Q, and q. The details are as follows.

(3.3) Public key reconstruction.
Input: Identifying information ID, security parameter B, 32-bit string s, 8-bit integer b_1, and 3 bits indicating E and d.
Output: Either 'Failure' or (F_p, Q, q).
1. Compute $a = R_1(B, ID\|s)$, $b = R_2(B, ID\|s) + b_1$, and $x = R_3(2*B, ID\|s)$.
2. Check conditions on d, a, b, and x as described in (3.1). If (3.1) returns 'Failure', then output 'Failure' and terminate.
3. Otherwise, output (F_p, Q, q) with p, q, and Q as output by (3.1).

(3.4) Cheap public key reconstruction. If the public key reconstruction (3.3) is performed on data retrieved from a certificate, then the check of the conditions on d, a, b, and x in step 2 of (3.3) can be sped-up considerably, under the assumption that the certification authority performed the full check as described in (3.1). For instance, the two primality checks on p and q can be omitted (where q can be found after trial division up to at most 32), and also the check that Q has indeed order q can be omitted. This implies that reconstruction of the (F_p, Q, q)-part of a public key from certified data can be performed at the cost of essentially a single (p+1)/4-th powering in F_p. The time required for this exponentiation is very small compared to the time required for the 'standard' operation in elliptic curve cryptosystems, namely full scalar multiplication in the group of the elliptic curve.

Lengths of s and b_1. The lengths of s and b_1 should in principle depend on B. In (3.2) the lengths are arbitrarily chosen in such a way that the choices work satisfactorily for any reasonable value of B. Smaller s and b_1 imply that fewer bits have to be exchanged and/or certified for public key exchange. Larger s and b_1 mean that for a given ID and B more different curves may be selected. The values 32 and 8 lead to more different curves than any particular ID will ever want to generate for any reasonable fixed value of B and do not cause noticeable communication overhead.

(3.5) Performance. If for an integer d as in Table 1 and a randomly picked pair a, b the conditions on a are satisfied, then the probability that a, b, and d lead to a prime p as specified in the fourth column of Table 1 is approximately the same that a randomly picked number of the same size as p is prime. Thus, it may be expected that step 1 of (3.1) (as called by step 3 of (3.2)) is successful for some d after O(B) attempts. The probability of success of step 2 of (3.1) is of the same order of magnitude, but with a much better constant because cofactors up to 32 are allowed. So, $O(B^2)$ attempts may be expected before step 2 of (3.1) is successful. Steps 3, 5, and 6 of (3.1) have a negligible probability of failure, and Step 4 of (3.1) fails with probability approximately 0.5. It follows that the runtime of (3.2) is dominated by the $O(B^2)$ probabilistic compositeness tests on approximately 2B-bit numbers, in steps 1 and 2 of (3.1). In practice (3.2) runs quite fast. For instance, for B = 90 public keys are on average produced in less than ten seconds on a 133MHz Pentium.

Key reconstruction (3.3) is dominated by the two probabilistic compositeness tests on approximately 2B-bit numbers in steps 1 and 2 of (3.1), the (p+1)/4-th powering in step 4 of (3.1), and the check that q • Q is the identity element in step 6 of (3.1). In practice it takes a fraction of a second. The runtime required by the 'cheap' key reconstruction (3.4) is dominated the (p+1)/4-th powering in step 4 of (3.1), and thus almost negligible in practice.

(3.6) Remark. In (3.1) a curve that would otherwise be good (i.e., a curve for which step 4 of (3.1) is reached) is rejected if a point with x-coordinate equal to x mod p is not on the curve (step 4 of (3.1)), or if such a point is on the curve but does not lead to a point of order q (as in step 5 of (3.1)). Here x is chosen in (3.2) as $R_3(2*B,ID\|s)$ so it can easily be reconstructed. If speed of the public key generation process is important, then (3.1) can trivially be modified so that it looks for the smallest non-negative j such that (x+j) mod p instead of x mod p satisfies the requirements in steps 4 and 5 of (3.1). Obviously, the resulting j would have to be included in the key reconstruction data s and b_i, thereby increasing the number of bits required for key reconstruction. A two or three bit j may speed up the key generation process by a factor two (cf. (3.5)), without affecting the length of the key reconstruction data in a substantial way.

Implementation. Elliptic curve arithmetic can be implemented in many different ways (cf. [1, 4]). The most efficient choice depends on hardware characteristics of the device to be used and is outside the scope of this paper. Assuming that elliptic curve arithmetic is available, implementation of the key generation and reconstruction method proposed in this paper is entirely straightforward based on the descriptions in (3.1), (3.2), (3.3), and (3.4).

4 Comparison

As explained in Section 1, in a shared elliptic curve cryptosystem the part of A's public key data that is unique to A consists of a single point G_A on the curve. If an L-bit finite field is used, then G_A can trivially be encoded in 2L bits: L bits for the x-coordinate and L bits for the y-coordinate. It is common practice, however, not to encode the full y-coordinate, but to let the recipient of the public key perform a modular squareroot computation to derive the y-coordinate from the x-coordinate. As argued above this squareroot computation is negligible compared to the ensuing cryptographic operations (in particular if p ≡ 3 mod 4). Since one additional bit is needed to indicate which of the two squareroots should be used, G_A can be encoded in

L + 1 bits. It follows that the amount of data to be exchanged or certified is L + 1 + |ID| bits, where |ID| denotes the length of the identifying information ID.

In a non-shared elliptic curve cryptosystem party A's public key data consists of the five-tuple $(F_{p(A)}, E_A, Q_A, q_A, G_A)$. Encoding of these data requires L bits for p(A), in general 2L bits for a randomly selected Weierstraß model to specify E_A, L + 1 bits each for Q_A and G_A (at the cost of two modular squareroot computations), and approximately L/2 bits to encode the difference between p(A) and the group order, plus the cofactor of q_A in the group order. The total number of bits to encode $(F_{p(A)}, E_A, Q_A, q_A, G_A)$ is equal to 5.5L+2. The amount of data to be exchanged or certified is 5.5L + 2 + |ID| bits.

In the non-shared system from Section 3 the (F_p, Q, q)-part of the public key data can be reconstructed, at the cost of one modular squareroot, from ID, B, and an additional 3 + 32 + 8 = 43 bits, as shown in Section 3. Since B may be assumed to be a system wide parameter (of value approximately equal to L/2), the total amount of data to be exchanged or certified is L + 44 + |ID| bits. Compared to the shared system, 43 more bits have to be carried along, and one additional modular squareroot has to be performed during key reconstruction. An additional 43 bits and single modular squareroot are a small price to pay for the additional security obtained.

Compared to the traditional non-shared system, during key exchange or certification 4.5L − 42 bits are saved by the method from Section 3, and the same number of modular squareroots is required. Furthermore, public key generation according to the new method is straightforward, whereas traditional non-shared systems require curve point counting software. The latter can be done using either complex multiplication (CM) techniques (thereby restricting the range of curves that can be used) or using the Schoof-Elkies-Atkin (SEA) algorithm (for truly random curves). Both the CM-based and the SEA-based methods are considerably more complicated than the approach from Section 3. Intuitively, the security of the SEA approach ranks highest, followed by CM, followed by the new method (cf. [2]), but as explicitly stated by the same authoritative source, there is no evidence whatsoever that this intuition is correct. Thus, given the current state of the art, the security offered by the newly proposed non-shared system and either type of traditional non-shared system (CM or SEA) seems to be the same.

Acknowledgments. Acknowledgments are due to Rene Schoof for providing the rows for d > 3 of Table 1 and for helpful discussions.

References

1. Cohen, H., Miyaji, A., Ono, T.: Efficient elliptic curve exponentiation using mixed coordinates. In: Ohta, K., Pei, D. (eds.): Advances in Cryptology – Asiacrypt'98. Lecture Notes in Computer Science, Vol. 1514. Springer-Verlag, Berlin Heidelberg New York, (1998) 51-65
2. Frey, G.: Remarks made during lecture at ECC'98, Waterloo, 1998

3. Koblitz, N.: Constructing elliptic curve cryptosystems in characteristic 2. In: Menezes, A.J., Vanstone, S.A. (eds.): Advances in Cryptology – Crypto'90. Lecture Notes in Computer Science, Vol. 537. Springer-Verlag, Berlin Heidelberg New York, (1991) 156-167
4. Montgomery, P.L.: Speeding the Pollard and elliptic curve methods of factorization. Math. Comp. 48 (1987) 243-264
5. Schoof, R.: Private communication, 1997
6. Silverman, J.H.: The Arithmetic of Elliptic Curves, Graduate Texts in Mathematics, Vol. 106. Springer-Verlag, Berlin Heidelberg New York, (1986)

Characterization of Optimal Authentication Codes with Arbitration *

Dingyi Pei[1], Yuqiang Li[2], Yejing Wang[3], Rei Safavi-Naini[4]

[1] Graduate School at Beijing of USTC, China /dypei@sun.ihep.ac.cn
[2] Guangzhou Normal University, China /{gztcdpei,gztcimis}@scut.edu.c n
[3,4] University of Wollongong, Australia /{yw17,rei}@uow.edu.au

Abstract. Abstract. In this paper we study authentication codes with arbitration (A^2-codes). An A^2-code is called optimal if its cheating probabilities achieve their information-theoretic lower bounds, and has minimum number of keys. We give characterization of optimal A^2-codes in terms of combinatorial designs. This means that construction of optimal A^2-codes is reduced to the construction of the corresponding combinatorial structures.

1 Introduction

In a traditional authentication code (A-code) there are three participants: a *transmitter, a receiver* and an *opponent*. Transmitter and receiver trust each other. The opponent attempts to *impersonate* transmitter or *substitute* a message sent to the receiver. Simmons [7] extended this model by considering possible attacks from transmitter and receiver. He introduced a fourth participant, called *arbiter*, who is trusted and arbitrates if transmitter or receiver cheats. This is called *authentication code with arbiter or* A^2-code. The model and constructions of A^2-code was further studied by Johansson [3], Desmedt at al [1] and Obana et al [5].

The following three types of spoofing attacks are considered.

Attack O_r by the opponent: after observing a sequence of r distinct messages $m_1, m_2, \cdots, m_r$, the opponent sends a message m, $m \neq m_i, 1 \leq i \leq r$ to the receiver and succeeds if the receiver accepts the message as authentic and the message represents a distinct source state from those represented by m_i, $1 \leq i \leq r$.

Attack R_r by the receiver: after receiving a sequence of r distinct messages $m_1, m_2, \cdots, m_r$, the receiver claims to have received a message m and succeeds if the message m could have been generated by the transmitter and represents a distinct source state from those represented by m_i, $1 \leq i \leq r$.

Attack T by the transmitter: the transmitter sends a message to the receiver and then denies having sent it. The transmitter succeeds if this message is accepted by the receiver as authentic and if it is not of the messages that the transmitter could have generated using his encoding rule.

---

* Authors 1, 2 are supported by the Grant No. 19531020 of NNSF of China and the grant E47 of NSF of Guangdong. Authors 3,4 are partially supported by Australian Research Council Grant Number A49703076.

Let $\mathcal{S}$ denote the set of all source states and $\mathcal{M}$ denote the set of all possible messages. An encoding rule of the transmitter is an one-to-one mapping from $\mathcal{S}$ to $\mathcal{M}$. Let $\mathcal{E}_T$ denote the set of all encoding rules of the transmitter. A decoding rule f of the receiver is a mapping form $\mathcal{M}$ onto $\mathcal{S}\cup\{\text{reject}\}$. For each source state $s \in \mathcal{S}$, the subset $\mathcal{M}(f,s) \subset \mathcal{M}$ denotes the set of messages that corresponds to s under the mapping f. The sets $\mathcal{M}(f,s)$, $s \in \mathcal{S}$, are disjoint for different source states. Let $\mathcal{E}_R$ denote the set of all decoding rules of the receiver.

Before transmission, the receiver selects a decoding rule $f \in \mathcal{E}_R$ and secretly gives it to the arbiter. The arbiter selects one message from $\mathcal{M}(f,s)$ for each source state $s \in \mathcal{S}$ forming an encoding rule e and secretly gives it to the transmitter. In this case we say that the encoding rule e is valid under the decoding rule f. The source state s which the transmitter wants to send is encoded by the message $m = e(s)$, then it is transmitted over the channel. The receiver checks whether a received message is valid (i.e. it is in some set $\mathcal{M}(f,s)$) and recovers the source state. When disputes between the transmitter and the receiver occur, the arbiter checks whether the message under dispute is valid for the encoding rule used by the transmitter. If and only if it is valid, the arbiter accepts that it is sent by the transmitter.

Let P_{O_r} denote the probability of success for the attack O_r, P_{R_r} denote the probability of success of the attack R_r and P_T denote the probability of success of the attack T. It was proved ([3] and [9]) that

$$P_{O_r} \geq 2^{H(E_R|M^{r+1}) - H(E_R|M^r)} \tag{1}$$

$$P_{R_r} \geq 2^{H(E_T|E_R, M^{r+1}) - H(E_T|E_R, M^r)} \tag{2}$$

$$P_T \geq 2^{H(E_R|M', E_T) - H(E_R|E_T)} \tag{3}$$

Here M^r is the random variable for the first r messages sent by the transmitter, E_T the random variable for the encoding rules of the transmitter, E_R the random variable for the decoding rules of the receiver, and M' the random variable for messages that are not valid under the given encoding rules. We use $H(Z|Y)$ to denote the conditional entropy.

It is easy to deduce from the above three inequalities that

$$|\mathcal{E}_R| \geq (P_{O_0} \cdots P_{O_{t-1}} P_T)^{-1}, \tag{4}$$

$$|\mathcal{E}_T| \geq (P_{R_0} \cdots P_{R_{t-1}} P_{O_0} \cdots P_{O_{t-1}})^{-1}, \tag{5}$$

for any positive integer t, $\leq |\mathcal{S}|$.

An A^2-code is called *optimal of order t* if (1) and (2) hold for r, $0 \leq r \leq t-1$, and (3),(4) and (5) also hold with equality.

The main aim of this paper is to find the necessary and sufficient conditions for optimal A^2-codes (see §2). In other words, we will give a characterization of optimal A^2-codes in terms of combinatorial designs (SPB t-designs and RSPB t-designs, see Definition 2 and 3). A similar problem is considered in [6] and [10]. We follow a similar approach for A^2-codes in this paper.

Obana and Kurosawa[5] considered optimal Cartesian A^2-codes with $t=2$. They proved that the optimum A^2-code is equivalent to an affine resolvable + BIBD design. The result of this paper holds for general optimal A^2-codes. The combinatorial characterization of optimal Cartesian A^2-codes for any t in terms of resolvable block designs with some additional properties can be also deduced from this general result (see §5).

2 Main Result

Definition 1 *Let* v, b, k, λ, t *be positive integers. A* t-$(v, b, k; \lambda, 0)$ *design is a pair* $(\mathcal{M}, \mathcal{E})$ *where* $\mathcal{M}$ *is a set of* v *points and* $\mathcal{E}$ *is a set of* b $k-$*subsets, called blocks, of* $\mathcal{M}$ *such that any* t-*subset of* $\mathcal{M}$ *either occurs in exactly* λ *blocks or does not occur in any block.*

We call a $t - (v, b, k; \lambda, 0)$ design a *partially balanced t-design* (PB t-design).

Definition 2 *A PB* $t-design$ $t - (v, b, k; \lambda, 0)$ *is called strong, SPB t-design, if for any* r, $1 \le r \le t$, *it is also a* $r - (v, b, k; \lambda_r, 0)$ *design . We denote it by* $t - (v, b, k; \lambda_1, \cdots, \lambda_t, 0)$.

Definition 3 *Let* v, b, k, c, λ, t *be positive integers. A PB t-design* $(\mathcal{M}, \mathcal{E})$ *is called restricted (RPB t-design) if* $|\mathcal{M}|=v, \mathcal{E} = \{\mathcal{E}_1, \cdots, \mathcal{E}_b\}$, *each block* $\mathcal{E}_i$ *is divided into* k *parts, each part has* c *points of* $\mathcal{M}$. *Any t-subset of* $\mathcal{M}$ *either occurs in exactly* λ *blocks in such a way that each point of the t-subset occurs in one part, or does not exist such blocks at all.*

We denote a RPB t-design by $t - (v, b, k, c; \lambda, 0)$. Similarly we can define RSPB t-design $t - (v, b, k, c; \lambda_1, \cdots, \lambda_t, 0)$.

Let $\mathcal{S}^r$ denote the random variable associated with the first r source states adopted by the transmitter. Let

$$p(\mathcal{S}^r = (s_1, s_2, \cdots, s_r)) > 0 \tag{6}$$

iff $s_i \ne s_j$, $1 \le i < j \le r$.

For a given decoding rule $f \in \mathcal{E}_\mathcal{R}$, the set

$$M(f) = \bigcup_{s \in \mathcal{S}} \mathcal{M}(f, s)$$

is the set of all valid messages for f. For a given $m^r = (m_1, \cdots, m_r) \in \mathcal{M}^r$, define the set

$$\mathcal{E}_R(m^r) = \{f \in \mathcal{E}_R | m_i \in M(f), f(m_i) \ne f(m_j), 1 \le i < j \le r\}.$$

Let

$$\mathcal{M}_R^r = \{m^r \in \mathcal{M}^r | \mathcal{E}_R(m^r) \ne \emptyset\}.$$

For a given encoding rule $e \in \mathcal{E}_T$, let

$$\mathcal{M}(e) = \{e(s) | s \in S\}$$

be the set of all valid messages for e. An encoding rule e is valid under a decoding rule f iff $e(s) \in M(f, s)$ for any $s \in S$.

Suppose the encoding rule e is valid under the decoding rule f, define

$$\mathcal{M}'(e) = \mathcal{M} \backslash \mathcal{M}(e),$$

$$\mathcal{M}'_f(e) = \mathcal{M}(f) \backslash \mathcal{M}(e).$$

For a given $f \in \mathcal{E}_R$, let

$$\mathcal{E}_T(f) = \{e \in \mathcal{E}_T | e \text{ is valid under } f\}$$

For a given $e \in \mathcal{E}_T$, let

$$\mathcal{E}_R(e) = \{f \in \mathcal{E}_R | e \text{ is valid under } f\}$$

We assume that $p(E_R = f) > 0$ for any $f \in \mathcal{E}_R$ and $p(E_T = e | E_R = f) > 0$ for any $e \in \mathcal{E}_T(f)$. In the following, for simplicity, we write $p(f)$ instead of $p(E_R = f)$, $p(e|f)$ instead of $p(E_T = e | E_R = f)$ and so on in the following. It follows that $p(e) > 0$ for any $e \in \mathcal{E}_T$ and $p(f|e) > 0$ for any $f \in \mathcal{E}_R(e)$.

For any message $m \in M$ we assume that there exists at least one decoding rule f such that $m \in M(f)$, otherwise the message m can be deleted from $\mathcal{M}$. Given a decoding rule f, for any message $m \in \mathcal{M}(f)$, we assume that there exists at least one encoding rule $e \in \mathcal{E}_T(f)$ such that $m \in \mathcal{M}(e)$, otherwise the message m can be deleted from $\mathcal{M}(f)$.

Our main result is the following theorem.

Theorem 1 *The necessary and sufficient condition for an A^2-code $(S, M, \mathcal{E}_T, \mathcal{E}_R)$ being optimal is as follows.*

(i) The encoding rules in $\mathcal{E}_T$ are equally probable and the decoding rules in $\mathcal{E}_R$ are also equally probable. It can be deduced that $\mathcal{E}_T(f)$ and $\mathcal{E}_R(e)$ also have uniform probability distribution.

(ii) For any given $m^r \in M_R^r$, the probability $p(S^r = f(m^r))$ is constant for all $f \in \mathcal{E}_R(m^r)$.

(iii) For any given $e \in \mathcal{E}_T$ the pair

$$(\mathcal{M}'(e), \{\mathcal{M}'_f(e) | f \in \mathcal{E}_R(e)\})$$

is a 1-$(v - k, P_T^{-1}, k(c - 1); 1, 0)$ design where $v = |M|$, $k = |S|$, c is a positive integer. In fact, $c = |\mathcal{M}(f, s)|$ for all $f \in \mathcal{E}_R, s \in S$.

(iv) For any given $f \in \mathcal{E}_R$, the pair

$$(\mathcal{M}(f), \{\mathcal{M}(e) | e \in \mathcal{E}_T(f)\})$$

is a SPB t-$(kc, (P_{R_0} P_{R_1} \cdots P_{R_{t-1}})^{-1}, k; \lambda_1, \cdots, \lambda_t, 0)$ design where $\lambda_t = 1, \lambda_r = (P_{R_r} \cdots P_{R_{t-1}})^{-1}, 1 \le r \le t - 1$.

(v) The pair

$$(\mathcal{M}, \{\mathcal{M}(f)|f \in \mathcal{E}_R\})$$

is a RSPB t-$(v, (P_{O_0} \cdots P_{O_{t-1}} P_T)^{-1}, k, c; \mu_1, \cdots, \mu_t, 0)$ design where

$$\mu_t = P_T^{-1}, \mu_r = (P_{O_r} \cdots P_{O_{t-1}} P_T)^{-1}, 1 \le r \le t - 1.$$

3 Lower Bounds

Assume that one decoding rule and one valid encoding rule are chosen.

Let $P(m|m^r)$ denote the probability of the event that the message m is accepted by the receiver given that the first r messages $m^r = (m_1, m_2, \cdots, m_r)$ have been accepted, where $m_1, \cdots, m_r, m$ represent different source states. We have

$$P(m|m^r) = \sum_{f \in \mathcal{E}_R(m^r * m)} p(f|m^r).$$

Let $P(m|f, m^r)$ denote the probability of the event that the message m could have been generated by the transmitter given the decoding rule f and the first r messages $m^r = (m_1, \cdots, m_r)$ where $m_1, \cdots, m_r, m$ represent different source states. We have

$$P(m|f, m^r) = \sum_{e \in \mathcal{E}_T(f, m^r * m)} p(e|f).$$

where

$$\mathcal{E}_T(f, m^r) = \{e|e \in \mathcal{E}_T(f), m_i \in \mathcal{M}(e), 1 \le i \le r\}.$$

Let $P(m'|e)$ denote the probability of the event that the message $m' \notin \mathcal{M}(e)$ is accepted by the receiver given the encoding rule e. We have

$$P(m'|e) = \sum_{f \in \mathcal{E}_R(e, m')} p(f|e).$$

where

$$\mathcal{E}_R(e, m') = \{f|f \in \mathcal{E}_R(e), m' \in \mathcal{M}_f(e)\}.$$

Now we give the definitions for P_{O_r}, P_{R_r} and P_T as follows.

$$P_{O_r} = \sum_{m^r \in \mathcal{M}^r} p(m^r) \max_{m \in \mathcal{M}} P(m|m^r),$$

$$P_{R_r} = \max_{f \in \mathcal{E}_R} \sum_{m^r \in \mathcal{M}^r} p(m^r|f) \max_{m \in \mathcal{M}} P(m|f, m^r)),$$

$$P_T = \max_{e \in \mathcal{E}_T} \max_{m' \notin \mathcal{M}'(e)} P(m'|e),$$

The following three propositions on the information-theoretic lower bounds of P_{O_r}, P_{R_r} and P_T respectively can be proved in a way similar to that of Theorem 1 in [5].

Proposition 1 *The inequality*

$$P_{O_r} \geq 2^{H(E_R|M^{r+1})-H(E_R|M^r)} \tag{7}$$

holds for any integer $r \geq 0$. The equality holds iff for any $m^r \in \mathcal{M}^r$, and $m \in \mathcal{M}$ with $\mathcal{E}_R(m^r * m) \neq \emptyset$ the ratio

$$\frac{p(f|m^r)}{p(f|m^r * m)}$$

is independent of m^r, m and $f \in \mathcal{E}_R(m^r * m)$. When this equality holds, the probability P_{O_r} equals to $P(m|m^r)$ and also to the above ratio.

Proposition 2 *The inequality*

$$P_{R_r} \geq 2^{H(E_T|E_R,M^{r+1})-H(E_T|E_R,M^r)} \tag{8}$$

holds for any integer $r \geq 0$. The equality holds iff for any $m^r \in \mathcal{M}^r$, $m \in \mathcal{M}$ and $f \in \mathcal{E}_R(m^r * m)$ with $\mathcal{E}_T(f, m^r * m) \neq \emptyset$ the ratio

$$\frac{p(e|f, m^r)}{p(e|f, m^r * m)}$$

is independent of m^r, m, $f \in \mathcal{E}_R(m^r * m)$ and $e \in \mathcal{E}_T(f, m^r * m)$. When this equality holds, the probability P_{R_r} equals to $P(m|f, m^r)$ and also to the above ratio.

Proposition 3 *The inequality*

$$P_T \geq 2^{H(E_R|E_T,M')-H(E_R|E_T)} \tag{9}$$

holds. The equality in it holds iff for any $e \in \mathcal{E}_T, m' \in \mathcal{M}'(e)$ with $\mathcal{E}_R(e, m') \neq \emptyset$ the ratio

$$\frac{p(f|e)}{p(f|e, m')}$$

is independent of e, m' and $f \in \mathcal{E}_R(e, m')$. When this equality holds, the probability P_T equals $P(m'|e)$ and also the above ratio.

The following two propositions give the lower bounds on $|\mathcal{E}_R|$ and $|\mathcal{E}_T|$ respectively.

Proposition 4 *The number of decoding rules of the receiver is lower bounded by,*

$$|\mathcal{E}_R| \geq (P_{O_0} P_{O_1} \cdots P_{O_{t-1}} P_T)^{-1} \tag{10}$$

Suppose that P_T and P_{O_r}, $0 \le r \le t-1$ achieve their lower bounds in (7) and (9). Then the equality in (10) holds iff

$$H(E_R|E_T, M') = 0, \quad H(E_R|M^t) = H(E_R|E_T)$$

and E_R has a uniform probability distribution.

Proposition 5 *The number of encoding rules of the transmitter has the lower bound*

$$|\mathcal{E}_T| \ge (P_{O_0} P_{O_1} \cdots P_{O_{t-1}} P_{R_0} \cdots P_{R_{t-1}})^{-1} \tag{11}$$

Suppose P_{O_r}, P_{R_r}, $0 \le r \le t-1$ achieve their lower bounds in (7) and (8). Then $|\mathcal{E}_t|$ achieves its lower bound in (11) iff

$$H(E_T|E_R, M^t) = 0, \quad H(E_R|M^t) = H(E_R|E_T)$$

and E_T has a uniform distribution.

Remark *Since*

$$\begin{aligned} H(E_T|E_R, M^t) &= H(E_R, E_T|M^t) - H(E_R|M^t) \\ &= H(E_T|M^T) + H(E_R|E_T) - H(E_R|M^t) \end{aligned}$$

The condition that $H(E_T|E_R, M^t)=0$ and $H(E_R|M^t) = H(E_R|E_T)$ is equivalent to that of $H(E_T|M^t)=0$.

4 Combinatorial Structure of Optimal A^2-codes

The following corollaries will provide a bridge between the information-theoretic lower bounds of P_{O_r}, P_{R_r} and P_T and the combinatorial structure of optimal A^2-codes.

Corollary 1 *Suppose that E_R has a uniform probability distribution and*

$$P_{O_r} = 2^{H(E_R|M^{r+1})-H(E_R|M^r)}, 0 \le r \le t-1 \tag{12}$$

Then for any $m^r \in \mathcal{M}^r$, $m \in \mathcal{M}$ with $\mathcal{E}_R(m^r * m) \ne \emptyset$, we have

$$P_{O_r} = |\mathcal{E}_R(m^r * m)|/|\mathcal{E}_R(m^r)|.$$

Corollary 2 *Suppose that $E_T(f)$ has a uniform probability distribution and*

$$P_{R_r} = 2^{H(E_T|E_R, M^{r+1})-H(E_T|E_R, M^r)}, 0 \le r \le t-1 \tag{13}$$

Then for any $m^r \in \mathcal{M}^r, m \in \mathcal{M}, f \in \mathcal{E}_R(m^r * m)$ with $\mathcal{E}_T(f, m^r * m) \ne \emptyset$,

$$P_{R_r} = |\mathcal{E}_T(f, m^r * m)|/|\mathcal{E}_T(f, m^r)|.$$

Corollary 3 *Suppose that $E_R(e)$ has a uniform probability distribution and*

$$P_T = 2^{H(E_R|E_T,M')-H(E_R|E_T)},$$

Then for any $e \in \mathcal{E}_T$, $m' \in \mathcal{M}'(e)$ *with* $\mathcal{E}_R(e,m') \neq \emptyset$,

$$P_T = |\mathcal{E}_R(e,m')|/|\mathcal{E}_R(e)|.$$

The optimal A^2-codes have a requirement for the probability distributions of S^r.

Corollary 4 *Suppose (12) and (13) hold. Then for any* $m^r \in \mathcal{M}_R^r$, *the probability* $p(f(m^r))$ *does not depend on* $f \in \mathcal{E}_R(m^r)$ $(0 \leq r \leq t-1)$.

Corollary 5 *If* $P_{R_0} = 2^{H(E_T|E_R,M)-H(E_T|E_R)}$ *then* $|\mathcal{M}(f,s)| = c$ *is a constant for any* $f \in \mathcal{E}_R$ *and* $s \in \mathcal{S}$. *Furthermore* $c = P_{R_0}^{-1}$.

Now based on the above discussion it is not difficult to prove Theorem 1. The proof will be given in the final version of this paper.

5 Optimal Cartesian A^2-codes

An A^2-code is Cartesian (without secrecy) if one can always know the source state from the message sent by the transmitter. In a Cartesian A^2-code for any $m \in \mathcal{M}$ there is a unique $s \in \mathcal{S}$ such that $m \in \mathcal{M}(f,s)$ for all $f \in \mathcal{E}_R(m)$. Let

$$\mathcal{M}(s) = \{m \in \mathcal{M} | m \in \mathcal{M}(f,s) \text{ for } f \in \mathcal{E}_R(m)\}$$

It is clear that

$$\mathcal{M} = \bigcup_{s \in \mathcal{S}} \mathcal{M}(s).$$

Lemma 1. For an optimal Cartesian A^2-code, the value $|\mathcal{M}(s)|$ is a constant for any $s \in \mathcal{S}$.

Lemma 2. Let $\mathcal{S}, \mathcal{M}, \mathcal{E}_R, \mathcal{E}_T$ be an optimal Cartesian A^2-code of order t. For any $e \in \mathcal{E}_T$ and $m^t = (m_1, m_2, \cdots, m_t) \in \mathcal{M}(e)^t$, we have

$$\mathcal{E}_R(e) = \mathcal{E}_R(m^t).$$

Let (V, B) be a block design where V is a set of n points and B is a family of blocks. Each block contains the same number of points of V.

Definition 4[5] *A block design* (V, B) *is called* α-*resolvable if the block set* B *can be partitioned into classes* $C_1, C_2, \cdots, C_k$ *with the property that in each class every point of* V *occurs in exactly* α *blocks.*

We are interested in α-resolvable design with the following properties:

There exists a positive integer $t < k$ such that

P1 A collection of i, $1 \leq i \leq t$ blocks from different classes either intersect in u_i points or does not intersect at all.

P2 Denoted by T the set of all t-tuples $(B_{i_1}, \cdots, B_{i_t})$ where blocks $B_{i_1}, \cdots, B_{i_t}$ are from different classes $C_{i_1}, \cdots, C_{i_t}$ with $B_{i_1} \cap \cdots \cap B_{i_t} \neq \emptyset$ and for any u, $u \leq k, u \neq i_1, \cdots, i_t$ there exists a unique $B_u \in C_u$ such that $B_{i_1} \cap \cdots \cap B_{i_t} \subseteq B_u$. Furthermore for any $j (1 \leq j \leq t)$ blocks $B_{i_1}, \cdots, B_{i_j}$ from different classes $C_{i_1}, \cdots, C_{i_j}$ with $f \in \bigcap_{r=1}^{j} B_{i_j}$, let

$$T_f(B_{i_1}, \cdots, B_{i_j}) = \{(B_{i_{j+1}}, \cdots, B_{i_t}) | (B_{i_1}, \cdots, B_{i_t}) \in T, f \in \bigcap_{r=1}^{t} B_{i_r}\}.$$

The value $|T_f(B_{i_1}, \cdots, B_{i_j})|$ is either λ_j or zero, where λ_j is a constant. Let

$$T(f) = \{(B_{i_1}, \cdots, B_{i_t}) \in T | f \in \bigcap_{r=1}^{t} B_{i_r}\}.$$

Then $g = |T(f)|$ is also a constant.

P3. Let $(B_{i_1}, \cdots, B_{i_t}) \in T$. For any block $B_r \in B$, if $B_r \neq B_{i_j}, 1 \leq j \leq e$, and $B_r \neq B_u, u \neq i_1, \cdots, i_t$ (where B_u is defined in **P2**), then $|B_r \cap B_{i_1} \cap \cdots \cap B_{i_t}| = 0$ or 1.

A combinatorial characterization of Cartesian optimal A^2-codes in terms of α-resolvable block design with properties **P1, P2** and **P3** can be deduced from Theorem 1. Let $(\mathcal{S}, \mathcal{M}, \mathcal{E}_R, \mathcal{E}_T)$ be an optimal Cartesian A^2-code. Let $B = \{\mathcal{E}_R(m) | m \in \mathcal{M}\}$. It can be shown by Theorem 1 that $(\mathcal{E}_R, B)$ is a c-resolvable block design with properties **P1,P2** and **P3** where $c = |\mathcal{M}(f, s)|$. The block set B is partitioned into classes $C_1, C_2, \cdots, C_k$ where $C_i = \{\mathcal{E}_R(m) | m \in \mathcal{M}(s_i), s \in \mathcal{S}\}$. The properties P1, P2 and P3 correspond to the items (v), (iv) and (iii) of Theorem 1 respectively. We have the following theorem.

Theorem 2 *Suppose there exists a c-resolvable design (V, B) in which B is partitioned into classes $C_1, \cdots, C_k$ with properties **P1, P2** and **P3** and such that all classes have the same number of blocks. Then there exist an optimal Cartesian A^2-code with uniform probability distribution on $\mathcal{E}_T$ and $\mathcal{E}_R$. The code has the following parameters:*

1. *The number of source states is k.*
2. *The number of messages is $|B|$.*
3. $|\mathcal{E}_R| = |V|, |\mathcal{E}_T| = g/\mu_t, |\mathcal{E}_R \circ \mathcal{E}_T| = |V|g$
4. $P_{O_r} = \mu_{r+1}/\mu_r, P_{R_r} = \lambda_{r+1}/\lambda_r, P_T = 1/\mu_t, 0 \leq r \leq t - 1.$

*Conversely, if there exists a Cartesian optimal A^2-code then there exists a c-resolvable block design with properties **P1, P2** and **P3**.*

6 Conclusion

Optimal A^2-codes which have the minimum cheating probabilities and the minimum size for the key spaces, are the most interesting class of A^2-codes. In this paper we have given a characterization of these codes in terms of the combinatorial designs. Thus construction of optimal A^2-codes is reduced to the construction of the combinatorial designs with the properties given in Theorem 1. All the known optimal A^2-codes are Cartesian ([8],[2],[9],[4]). Construction of non-Cartesian optimal A^2 -codes is an open problem.

References

1. Y.Desmedt and M.Yung, Arbitrated Unconditionally Secure Authentication Can Be Unconditionally Protected against Arbiter's attacks, Advances in Cryptology-CRYPTO'90, 177-188(1991).
2. T.Johansson, On the construction of perfect authentication codes that permit arbitration, Advances in Cryptology-Crypto'93, Lecture Notes in Computer Science 773, Springer-Verlag, 1994, 343-354.
3. T.Johansson, Lower bounds on the probability of deception in authentication with arbitration,IEEE Trans. Inform. Theory, Vol.40, No.5, 1994, 1573-1585.
4. Y.Li, A note on authentication codes with arbitration, Chinese Quarterly Journal of Mathematics, Vol.12, No.4, 1998, 103-106.
5. S.Obana and K.Kurosawa, A^2-code=affine resolvable + BIBD, First international Conference, ICICS'97, Lecture Notes in Computer Science 1334, Springer-Verlag, 1997, 130-143.
6. D. Pei, Information-theoretic bounds for authentication codes and block designs, J.Cryptology, Vol.8(1995), 177-188.
7. G. J. Simmons, Message authentication with arbitration of transmitter/receiver disputes, Advances in Cryptology-Eurocrypt'87, LNCS 304, Springer-Verlag, 1988, 151-165.
8. G. J. Simmons, A Cartesian product construction for unconditionally secure authentication codes that permit arbitration, J.Cryptology, Vol.2(1990), 77-104.
9. Y. Wang, Information-theoretic lower bounds for authentication codes with arbitration. Advances in Cryptology-Chinacrypt'98, Science Press, 1998, 99-104.
10. R. Safavi-Naini, L. Tombak, Combinatorial characterization of A-codes with r-fold security. Advances in Cryptology- Asiacrypt'94, LNCS 917, Springer-Verlag, 1995, pp 211-223.

Appendix: Example

Now we look at the combinatorial structure of the Cartesian optimal A^2-code with order $t = 2$ constructed by T.Johansson[3]. We check that it satisfies the conditions given in Theorem 1.

Let F_q be the finite field with q elements. Fix a line L_0 in the projective space $PG(3, F_q)$ of dimension 3. The points on L_0 are regarded as source states. The receiver's decoding rule f is a point not on L_0. The transmitter's encoding rule is a line e not intersecting L_0. An encoding rule e is valid under a decoding rule f iff the point f is on the line e. A source state s is encoded by an encoding e into the message $e(s) = \langle e, s \rangle$ which is the unique plane passing through e and s. The receiver accepts a message iff the decoding rule f is contained in the received plane.

Now consider the combinatorial structure of this A^2-code. There are $q + 1$ points on L_0, thus $|\mathcal{S}| = q + 1$. The messages are all planes intersecting the line L_0 in one point. This is the same as all planes not containing the fixed line L_0. The total number of planes is $q^3 + q^2 + q + 1$ and the number of planes containing the line L_0 is $q+1$. Thus $|\mathcal{M}| = q^3 + q^2$. The receiver's decoding rules are all points not on L_0. The total number of points is $q^3 + q^2 + q + 1$, thus $|\mathcal{E}_R| = q^3 + q^2$.

For a given decoding rule f, the encoding rules which are valid under f are all lines passing through the point f but not intersecting L_0. The total number of lines passing through f is $q^2 + q + 1$, among them $q + 1$ lines intersect L_0. Thus $|\mathcal{E}_T(f)| = q^2$. The decoding rules under which a given encoding rules e is valid are all points on the line e , thus $|\mathcal{E}_R(e)| = q + 1$.

Given a decoding rule f and a source state s, there are q planes passing through f and s but not containing L_0. Thus $c = |\mathcal{M}(f, s)| = q$ and $|\mathcal{M}(f)| = q(q + 1)$.

Consider an encoding rule $e \in \mathcal{E}_T$. Any message $m \in \mathcal{M}'(e)$ is a plane intersecting e at a unique point f . It means that m is contained in a unique $\mathcal{M}'_f(e)$. Thus $(\mathcal{M}'(e), \{\mathcal{M}'_f(e) | f \in \mathcal{E}_R(e)\})$ is a $1 - (q^3 + q^2 - q - 1, q + 1, q^2 - 1; 1)$ design.

Consider a decoding rule $f \in \mathcal{E}_R$. Any message $m \in \mathcal{M}(f)$ is a plane containing f and intersecting L_0 at a unique point. There are q lines passing through f but not intersecting L_0 in the plane. This means that there are q encoding rules $e \in \mathcal{E}_T(f)$ such that $m \in \mathcal{M}(e)$. Any two messages $m_1 \in \mathcal{M}(f, s_1)$ and $m_2 \in \mathcal{M}(f, s_2)$ with $s_1 \neq s_2$ are two planes passing through f and intersecting L_0 at different points s_1 and s_2 respectively. These two planes have a unique common line passing through f and not intersecting L_0. Thus m_1 and m_2 are contained in a unique $\mathcal{M}(e)$, $e \in \mathcal{E}_T(f)$. Two messages $m_1, m_2 \in \mathcal{M}(f, s)$ are two planes passing through f and s. The common line of them is the line connecting f and s. Hence m_1 and m_2 could not be contained in one $\mathcal{M}(e)(e \in \mathcal{E}_T(f))$. Thus $(\mathcal{M}(f), \{\mathcal{M}(e) | e \in \mathcal{E}_T(f)\})$ is a SPB 2-$(q(q + 1), q^2, q + 1; q, 1, 0)$ design.

Any message m is a plane containing $q^2 + q$ points not on L_0. Hence $m \in \mathcal{M}(f)$ for $q^2 + q$ decoding rules f. Any two messages m_1 and m_2, if they are two planes intersecting L_0 at two different points s_1 and s_2, then there are $q + 1$ decoding rules f such that $m_1 \in \mathcal{M}(f, s_1)$ and $m_2 \in \mathcal{M}(f, s_2)$; if they are two planes intersecting L_0 at the same point, then there are no decoding rules f such that $m_1 \in \mathcal{M}(f, s_1)$ and $m_2 \in \mathcal{M}(f, s_2)$ with different s_1 and s_2. Thus $(\mathcal{M}, \{\mathcal{M}(f) | f \in \mathcal{E}_R\})$ is a RSPB 2-$(q^3 + q^2, q^3 + q^2, q^2 + 1; q^2 + q, q + 1, 0)$ design.

The conditions (iii), (iv) and (v) of Theorem 1 are satisfied by this A^2-code. If conditions (i) and (ii) are also satisfied, then this A^2-code is optimal. Using Theorem 1 we can find that

$P_{O_0} = \frac{q^2 + q}{q^3 + q^2} = \frac{1}{q}, P_{O_1} = \frac{q + 1}{q^2 + 1} = \frac{1}{q}, P_{R_0} = \frac{q}{q^2} = \frac{1}{q}, P_{R_1} = \frac{1}{q}, P_T = \frac{1}{q + 1}$,

$|\mathcal{E}_R| = q^3 + q^2 = (P_{O_0} P_{O_1} P_T)^{-1}, |\mathcal{E}_R| = q^4 = (P_{O_0} P_{O_1} P_{R_0} P_{R_1})^{-1}$,

as shown in [3].

A Functional Cryptosystem Using a Group Action

Akihiro Yamamura

Telecommunications Advancement Organization of Japan,
1-1-32 Shin'urashima, Kanagawa-ku,
Yokohama, 221-0031 Japan
e-mail: yamamura@yokohama.tao.go.jp

Abstract. The main purpose of this paper is to examine applications of group theoretical concepts to cryptography. We construct a backward deterministic system employing the action of the modular group on the upper half plane and the amalgamated free product structure of the group. We invent a geometrical algorithm that finds the normal form of an element of the modular group effectively. This algorithm makes our backward deterministic system tractable. Using the backward deterministic system, we invent a public-key cryptosystem in terms of a functional cryptosystem.

Keywords: public-key cryptosystem, functional cryptosystem, backward deterministic system, modular group, amalgamated free product

1 Introduction

Many public-key cryptosystems rely on the difficulty of solving a few specific problems such as finding the prime factorization of a composite number and the discrete logarithm problem. While the existing systems depending on the hardness of these problems are considered secure, there is still deep concern about the security of these systems. We must not deny the possibility that a genius eventually discovers a fast algorithm to solve those problems in the near future. In fact Shor [13] invented a fast algorithm for prime factorization and the discrete logarithm problem based on quantum computing although practical realization of such a computational device has many difficulties at the present moment. We also note that Adleman [1] reported that a DNA computer solves a 7 vertex and 14 edge instance of the Hamiltonian path problem. Therefore we should avoid the situation that all the cryptosystems in hand depend on a few principles. Our intention is to provide backup cryptosystems for the currently working cryptosystems depending on difficulties of solving a few specific problems. We propose a public-key cryptosystem as a first step toward inventing a scheme of cryptography using new technologies from mathematics other than number theory. We employ the modular group and import several ideas from combinatorial group theory. The encryption and decryption of our cryptosystem are based on the uniqueness of a certain expression of an element of the modular group and its action on the upper half plane.

First, we briefly review a functional cryptosystem which is the basic scheme of ours. We give the definitions of a backward deterministic system and a morphism between two backward deterministic systems. Then we demonstrate how to construct a backward deterministic system using a group action on a certain space.

Secondly, we recall basic results on combinatorial group theory. An amalgamated free product of groups is introduced and explained. We also recall several fundamental results on the modular group. The modular group is the group of 2×2 matrices over rational integers with determinant one. It is known that the modular group is an amalgamated free product of finite cyclic groups. We give a geometrical algorithm that finds the normal form of a matrix in the modular group using the action of the modular group on the upper half plane. The algorithm is very efficient because of its geometrical nature.

Thirdly, we provide a public-key cryptosystem in terms of a backward deterministic systems using the action of the modular group on the upper half plane. A similar cryptosystem using the modular group was introduced in [14]. Our approach is different from them in that ours is based on a functional cryptosystem and also our decryption algorithm is faster. We explain the public key, the private key, the encryption and decryption methods. We discuss issues on the proposed system.

2 Functional cryptosystems

The concept of a functional cryptosystem was introduced to build a public-key cryptosystem using grammar theoretical concepts (see [4], [5], [9], [10] and [11]). In this section we review several concepts and terminologies. Let $\mathcal{X}$ be a set and f_i a function of $\mathcal{X}$ into $\mathcal{X}$ for each $i \in I$ where I is a finite set. We suppose that there is an element $x \in \mathcal{X}$ such that if we have

$$f_{i_1} \circ f_{i_2} \circ \ldots \circ f_{i_n}(x) = f_{j_1} \circ f_{j_2} \circ \ldots \circ f_{j_m}(x)$$

where $i_1, i_2, \ldots, i_n, j_1, j_2, \ldots, j_m \in I$, then $n = m$ and $i_k = j_k$ for every $k = 1, 2, \ldots, n$. The triple $(\{f_i \ (i \in I)\}, \ x, \ \mathcal{X})$ is called a *backward deterministic system*. Now let $(\{f_i \ (i \in I)\}, \ x, \ \mathcal{X})$ and $(\{g_i \ (i \in I)\}, \ y, \ \mathcal{Y})$ be backward deterministic systems. The *morphism* ϕ of $(\{f_i \ (i \in I)\}, \ x, \ \mathcal{X})$ to $(\{g_i \ (i \in I)\}, \ y, \ \mathcal{Y})$ is a mapping $\phi : \mathcal{X} \to \mathcal{Y}$ satisfying $\phi(x) = y$ and also $\phi \circ f_i = g_i \circ \phi$ for each $i \in I$. Assume that $p = f_{i_1} \circ f_{i_2} \circ \ldots \circ f_{i_n}(x)$. Let $q = \phi(p)$. Then we have

$$q = \phi(p) = \phi(f_{i_1} \circ f_{i_2} \circ f_{i_3} \circ \ldots \circ f_{i_n}(x))$$

$$= g_{i_1}(\phi(f_{i_2} \circ f_{i_3} \circ \ldots \circ f_{i_n}(x)))$$

$$= g_{i_1} \circ g_{i_2}(\phi(f_{i_3}(\ldots f_{i_n}(x)) \ldots))$$

...

$$= g_{i_1} \circ g_{i_2} \circ \ldots \circ g_{i_n}(\phi(x))$$

$$= g_{i_1} \circ g_{i_2} \circ \ldots \circ g_{i_n}(y).$$

Note that the morphism ϕ preserves information on the sequence $i_1 i_2 \ldots i_n$. We employ backward deterministic systems to construct a public-key cryptosystem. The most significant point in making up a public-key cryptosystem is to supply a trapdoor. In the case of a functional cryptosystem, the idea is to find two backward deterministic systems with distinct complexities and an effectively computable morphism between them. We require that one of the backward deterministic systems $(\{f_i \ (i \in I)\}, \ x, \ \mathcal{X})$ is harder than the other in the following sense: Let $p = f_{i_1} \circ f_{i_2} \circ \ldots \circ f_{i_n}(x)$. If we are given the point p on $\mathcal{X}$, we have no efficient way to find how we apply f_i's on x to get the point p. We remark that there is a unique way to obtain p by applying f_i's on x, since $(\{f_i \ (i \in I)\}, \ x, \ \mathcal{X})$ is backward deterministic. On the other hand, the other backward deterministic system $(\{g_i \ (i \in I)\}, \ y, \ \mathcal{Y})$ is feasible, that is, if we have $q = g_{i_1} \circ g_{i_2} \circ \ldots \circ g_{i_n}(y)$, there is an efficient algorithm that finds how to apply g_i's on y to get q, that is, the algorithm that finds the sequence $g_{i_1}, g_{i_2}, \ldots, g_{i_n}$. A morphism ϕ of $(\{f_i \ (i \in I)\}, \ x, \ \mathcal{X})$ into $(\{g_i \ (i \in I)\}, \ y, \ \mathcal{Y})$ is a part of the trapdoor of the cryptosystem. We publicize the backward deterministic system $(\{f_i \ (i \in I)\}, \ x, \ \mathcal{X})$ and keep $(\{g_i \ (i \in I)\}, \ y, \ \mathcal{Y})$ and ϕ secret. A message sender encrypts a message $i_1 i_2 \ldots i_n$ where $i_1, i_2, \ldots, i_n \in I$ into the composition $f_{i_1} \circ f_{i_2} \circ \ldots \circ f_{i_n}$ of the mappings, computes the point $p = f_{i_1} \circ f_{i_2} \circ \ldots \circ f_{i_n}(x)$ on $\mathcal{X}$ and then sends p to a legal receiver. The legal receiver operates the trapdoor ϕ to the encrypted text p and get $q = \phi(p)$. Since ϕ is a morphism of the backward deterministic systems, we have $q = g_{i_1} \circ g_{i_2} \circ \ldots \circ g_{i_n}(y)$. Then the legal receiver can obtain the sequence of the mappings $g_{i_1} \circ g_{i_2} \circ \ldots \circ g_{i_n}$ using the efficient algorithm for $(\{g_i \ (i \in I)\}, \ y, \ \mathcal{Y})$. Hence, the original message $i_1 i_2 \ldots i_n$ can be obtained by the legal receiver. On the other hand, an eavesdropper may be able to get a message p and $(\{f_i \ (i \in I)\}, \ x, \ \mathcal{X})$ is public information. However, the eavesdropper cannot obtain the sequence of mappings $f_{i_1} \circ f_{i_2} \circ \ldots \circ f_{i_n}$ from the information p and the backward deterministic system $(\{f_i \ (i \in I)\}, \ x, \ \mathcal{X})$, since the system $(\{f_i \ (i \in I)\}, \ x, \ \mathcal{X})$ is intractable. Therefore, the cryptosystem is secure in principle. If we can find a pair of backward deterministic systems and a morphism satisfying the computational complexity requirements, we can employ them to build a public-key cryptosystem. This type of a cryptosystem is called a *functional cryptosystem*.

We now propose a functional cryptosystem using a group action on a certain object in mathematics. Let G be a group, $\mathcal{X}$ a non-empty set (or some other mathematical object). We say that G *acts* on $\mathcal{X}$ if there is a mapping ρ of $G \times \mathcal{X}$ into $\mathcal{X}$ (we usually denote the image $\rho(g, x)$ of (g, x) under ρ by gx) satisfying the followings:

(i) For $a, b \in G$ and $x \in \mathcal{X}$, we have $(ab)x = a(bx)$.

(ii) For $x \in \mathcal{X}$, we have $1x = x$ where 1 is the identity element of G.

Suppose that a group G acts on a set $\mathcal{X}$. Then each element g of G can be regarded as a one-to-one function of $\mathcal{X}$ onto $\mathcal{X}$ under the rule $x \to gx$ for $x \in \mathcal{X}$. Now we consider a homomorphism ϕ of a group G acting on a set $\mathcal{X}$ to a group H acting on a set $\mathcal{Y}$. Assume that a mapping f of $\mathcal{X}$ into $\mathcal{Y}$ satisfies

$$f(gx) = \phi(g)f(x)$$

for each $g \in G$ and $x \in \mathcal{X}$. Let $g_i \in G$ for each $i \in I$ where I is a finite set. Let $x \in \mathcal{X}$. Suppose that $(\{\phi(g_i) \, (i \in I)\}, f(x), \mathcal{Y})$ is a backward deterministic system. Then clearly $(\{g_i \, (i \in I)\}, x, \mathcal{X})$ is also a backward deterministic system. The mapping f is a morphism between two systems. We offer a concrete example of such a functional cryptosystem using the modular group in Section 5.

3   The modular group

The group of 2×2 matrices over rational integers with determinant 1 is called the *modular group* and denoted by $\mathrm{SL}(2, Z)$, that is,

$$\mathrm{SL}(2, Z) = \left\{ \begin{pmatrix} a & b \\ c & d \end{pmatrix} \mid a, b, c, d \in Z \; ad - bc = 1 \right\}.$$

Let A and B be the matrices in $\mathrm{SL}(2, Z)$ given by

$$A = \begin{pmatrix} 1 & -1 \\ 1 & 0 \end{pmatrix}, \qquad B = \begin{pmatrix} 0 & -1 \\ 1 & 0 \end{pmatrix}.$$

It is easy to see that $A^6 = B^4 = 1$ and $A^3 = B^2$. Furthermore, it is known that A and B generate $\mathrm{SL}(2, Z)$. As a matter of fact, $\mathrm{SL}(2, Z)$ has the presentation

$$Gp(A, B \mid A^6 = B^4 = 1, \; A^3 = B^2).$$

This simply implies that $\mathrm{SL}(2, Z)$ is the free product of the cyclic group $< A >$ of order 6 and the cyclic group $< B >$ of order 4 amalgamating the cyclic group $H = \; < A^3 > \; = \; < B^2 > \; = \; \{I, -I\}$ of order 2 (see [2], [8] and [12] for details). Therefore, every element of $\mathrm{SL}(2, Z)$ is uniquely written as a normal form. We choose $\{I, A, A^2\}$ as the set of coset representatives of H in $< A >$. We choose $\{I, B\}$ as the set of coset representatives of H in $< B >$. Then every element in $\mathrm{SL}(2, Z)$ is uniquely written as $s_1 s_2 \ldots s_n$ where s_n is in H and each $s_k \; (k = 1, 2, \ldots, n-1)$ is A, A^2 or B such that if s_k is in $\{A, A^2\}$, then s_{k+1} is in $\{B\}$ and vice versa. We note that $s_n = \pm I$ since $s_n \in H = \{I, -I\}$. For example, ABA^2, BAB, $BABA^2BABA^2B \; A^2BA^2$ are in the normal form. In general, every element can be uniquely written as a normal form with respect to generators A_1, B_1 of the modular group subject to the relations $A_1^6 = B_1^4 = 1$, $A_1^3 = B_1^2$. Such generators can be obtained as conjugations of A and B by a matrix in the modular group.

Algorithm 1

For an element M in the modular group, there is a linear time algorithm to find the normal form for M. In fact, there is an algorithm to find the normal form for an element of an amalgamated free product of groups. The detail of Algorithm 1 is given in Appendix.

We now review the action of the modular group on the upper half plane of the Gaussian plane. We denote the *upper half plane* by $\mathcal{H}$, that is,

$$\mathcal{H} = \{z \in C \mid Im(z) > 0\}$$

where C is the field of all complex numbers and $Im(z)$ is the imaginary part of the complex number z. Let M be a matrix in $\mathrm{SL}(2, Z)$. A *fractional linear (Möbius) transformation* f_M determined by the matrix M is given as follows. For $z \in C$,

$$f_M(z) = \frac{az + b}{cz + d}$$

where $M = \begin{pmatrix} a & b \\ c & d \end{pmatrix}$. It is easy to see that for $z \in \mathcal{H}$, we have $f_M(z) \in \mathcal{H}$. A group action of $\mathrm{SL}(2, Z)$ on $\mathcal{H}$ is naturally induced as follows:
For M in $\mathrm{SL}(2, Z)$ and $z \in \mathcal{H}$ $Mz = f_M(z)$. Obviously $\mathrm{SL}(2, Z)$ acts on $\mathcal{H}$ in terms of fractional linear transformation. The equivalence relation on $\mathcal{H}$ is induced by the group action as follows: For $z_1, z_2 \in C$, $z_1 \sim z_2$ if there is $M \in \mathrm{SL}(2, Z)$ such that $Mz_1 = z_2$. We refer the interested reader to [6] and [12] for the details of the action of the modular group on the upper half plane $\mathcal{H}$. We now give a geometrical algorithm that finds the normal form (up to $\pm I$) for a given matrix $M \in \mathrm{SL}(2, Z)$ with respect to the matrices A and B. We define regions $\mathbf{O}$, $\mathbf{P}$, $\mathbf{Q}$ and $\mathbf{R}$ as follows:

$$\mathbf{O} = \{z \in C \mid |Re(z)| \leq 1/2,\ 1 \leq |z|\},$$

$$\mathbf{P} = \{z \in C \mid Re(z) \geq 1/2,\ 1 \leq |z|\},$$

$$\mathbf{Q} = \{z \in C \mid 1 \geq |z|,\ 1 \geq |z - 1|\},$$

$$\mathbf{R} = \{z \in C \mid 1 \geq |z|,\ 1 \leq |z - 1|\} \cup \{z \in C \mid Re(z) \leq -1/2\}.$$

We note that $\mathbf{O}$ is the *fundamental domain* (see [6] or [12] for more details of the fundamental domain). We now describe the algorithm that for a given point $z \in \mathcal{H}$ which is equivalent to $y \in \mathbf{O}$ finds the matrix N such that $Nz = y$ and its normal form using geometry on the upper half plane.

Algorithm 2

INPUT: A point $z \in \mathcal{H}$ which is equivalent to the point y in the interior of $\mathbf{O}$.
OUTPUT: The matrix N such that $Nz = y$ and its normal form with respect to A and B.

Step 0) Let z be the given point. Let L be the empty list ( ).
Step 1) If z is in $\mathbf{O}$, then return L and the algorithm ends.
Otherwise go to Step 2).
Step 2) If z is in $\mathbf{P}$, then set $z \Leftarrow A^{-1}z$ and push A into L from the right hand side, that is,

$$L \Leftarrow (X_1, X_2, \ldots, X_n, A)$$

if $L = (X_1, X_2, \ldots, X_n)$ where X_i is A, A^2 or B.
If z is in $\mathbf{Q}$, then set $z \Leftarrow A^{-2}z$ and push A^2 into L from the right hand side, that is,

$$L \Leftarrow (X_1, X_2, \ldots, X_n, A^2)$$

if $L = (X_1, X_2, \ldots, X_n)$.
If z is in $\mathbf{R}$, then set $z \Leftarrow B^{-1}z$ and push B into L from the right hand side, that is,

$$L \Leftarrow (X_1, X_2, \ldots, X_n, B)$$

if $L = (X_1, X_2, \ldots, X_n)$.
Then go to Step 1).

Proposition 1. *The algorithm above stops within $2n + 1$ steps if the length of the normal form for N is n. Moreover, if $L = (X_1, X_2, \ldots, X_n)$ where X_k is A, A^2 or B, then the normal form for N with respect to A and B is $X_1 X_2 \ldots X_n$ up to $\pm I$.*

Proof. We note that A and B generate $SL(2, Z)$ and that $\mathbf{O}$ is a fundamental domain of $\mathcal{H}$. It follows that every point p on the upper half plane can be written as $p = Mq$ where q is in $\mathbf{O}$ and $M \in SL(2, Z)$. Furthermore, it is easy to verify that

$$A\mathbf{O} \subset \mathbf{P}, \quad A\mathbf{R} \subset \mathbf{P}, \quad A\mathbf{P} \subset \mathbf{Q}, \quad A\mathbf{Q} \subset \mathbf{R} \cup \mathbf{O}$$

and

$$B\mathbf{O} \subset \mathbf{R}, \quad B\mathbf{P} \subset \mathbf{R}, \quad B\mathbf{Q} \subset \mathbf{R}, \quad B\mathbf{R} \subset \mathbf{O} \cup \mathbf{P} \cup \mathbf{Q}.$$

Suppose that N is in $SL(2, Z)$ and that its normal form is $X_1 X_2 \ldots X_n$ where X_k is A, A^2 or B for each $k = 1, 2, \ldots, n$ up to $\pm I$. Take an arbitrary point y from $\mathbf{O}$. We can obtain information of the first letter of the normal form by the position of the point Ny on the upper half plane. If X_1 is A, then Ny must lie in $\mathbf{P}$. If X_2 is A^2, then Ny must lie in $\mathbf{Q}$. If X_1 is B, then Ny must lie in $\mathbf{R}$. For instance, if $X_1 X_2 = AB$, then Ny must be in $\mathbf{P}$ and we obtain $X_1 = A$ and $X_2 = B$. Similarly we can deduce in other cases. We should note that the algorithm ends exactly in n steps if the length of the normal form is n.

To find the matrix N and its normal form with respect to A and B, one can employ the standard reduction algorithm (Algorithm 7.4.2. in [2]) and Algorithm 1 in the following way. By the standard reduction algorithm we can find the matrix N as a product of the matrices T, T^{-1} and S where

$$T = \begin{pmatrix} 1 & 1 \\ 0 & 1 \end{pmatrix}, \quad S = \begin{pmatrix} 0 & -1 \\ 1 & 0 \end{pmatrix}.$$

Since we are looking for the normal form with respect to A and B, first we must rewrite T, T^{-1} and S by the words on A and B. We replace T, T^{-1} and S by AB^3, BA^5 and B, respectively. We note that $T = AB^3$ and $S = B$ hold in the modular group. Hence, we can write the matrix N as a product of the matrices A and B. Then we get the normal form of N by using Algorithm 1. We remark that we do not know a bound of the running time of the standard reduction algorithm whereas Algorithm 2 ends at most $2n + 1$ steps. The running time for rewriting and performing Algorithm 1 costs extra running time compared to Algorithm 2. Hence, Algorithm 2 is fasted than using the standard reduction algorithm and Algorithm 1 as long as we are looking for the normal form with respect to A and B.

We remark that since we can find the normal form for a matrix $M \in \mathrm{SL}(2, Z)$ with respect to the matrices A and B within liner time using Algorithm 2, we can also find the normal form for M with respect to the other generators A_1 and B_1 of $\mathrm{SL}(2, Z)$ satisfying the relations $A_1^6 = 1 = B_1^4$ and $A_1^3 = B_1^2$ by using Algorithm 1 and Algorithm 2 consecutively within linear time.

4   A functional cryptosystem using the modular group

Let us define two backward deterministic systems using the action of $\mathrm{SL}(2, Z)$ on the upper half plane and apply the scheme of functional cryptosystems in Section 2. Let A_1 and B_1 be generators of $\mathrm{SL}(2, Z)$ subject to $A_1^6 = B_1^4 = 1$ and $A_1^3 = B_1^2$. We have seen that there are infinitely many choices for A_1 and B_1. We choose a word V_1, V_2 on letters A_1 and B_1 such that V_1 and V_2 generate a free subsemigroup of $\mathrm{SL}(2, Z)$, that is, if for two words $X_1, X_2 \in \{V_1, V_2\}^+$, we have $X_1 = X_2$ in $\mathrm{SL}(2, Z)$, then $X_1 = X_2$ as words on $\{V_1, V_2\}$. The following words V_1 and V_2 violate the condition above. We set $V_1 = A_1 B_1$ and $V_2 = A_1 B_1 A_1 B_1$. Then we have $X_1 = V_1 V_2$ and $X_2 = V_2 V_1$, and hence, $X_1 = X_2$ holds in the modular group although $X_1 \neq X_2$ as words on $\{V_1, V_2\}$. Furthermore, we require that every concatenation of V_1 and V_2 is in the normal form with respect to A_1 and B_1, that V_1 is not an initial segment of V_2 and that V_2 is not an initial segment of V_1. For example, the matrices $(B_1 A_1)^i$ and $(B_1 A_1^2)^j$ form a free subsemigroup of $\mathrm{SL}(2, Z)$ for all positive integers i and j and satisfy our requirements. It is easy to find such a pair of matrices in general using the combinatorics on words. We choose a matrix M arbitrarily from $\mathrm{GL}(2, R)$ and set

$$W_1 = M^{-1} V_1 M, \qquad\qquad W_2 = M^{-1} V_2 M.$$

Recall that $\mathrm{GL}(2, R)$ is the group of all 2×2 invertible matrices on the real number field R. We note that W_1 and W_2 are $\mathrm{SL}(2, R)$ since for each $i = 1, 2$ we have

$$det(W_i) = det(M^{-1} V_i M) = det(M^{-1}) det(V_i) det(M)$$

$$= \frac{1}{det(M)} det(V_i) det(M) = det(V_i) = 1.$$

We should note that $SL(2, R)$ acts on the upper half plane $\mathcal{H}$ in the same way as $SL(2, Z)$ acts on $\mathcal{H}$ in terms of fractional linear transformations. Let $\mathcal{X} = M^{-1}\mathcal{H} = \{M^{-1}q \mid q \in \mathcal{H}\}$. Let p be a point on $\mathcal{X}$ such that the point Mp is in the interior of the fundamental domain $\mathbf{O}$. Therefore $SL(2, Z)$ acts faithfully on Mp up to $\pm I$, that is, if $LMp = NMp$ for $L, N \in SL(2, Z)$ then we have $L = \pm N$. Let $f_M : \mathcal{X} \to \mathcal{H}$ be the fractional linear mapping defined by

$$f_M(q) = Mq.$$

Let $G = M^{-1}SL(2, Z)M$. The homomorphism $\phi : G \to SL(2, Z)$ is given by

$$\phi(N) = MNM^{-1}.$$

Then it is easy to see that $f_M(Nx) = \phi(N)f_M(x)$ for each $N \in G$ and $x \in \mathcal{X}$. We can easily verify that $(\{W_1, W_2\}, p, \mathcal{X})$ and $(\{V_1, V_2\}, f_M(p), \mathcal{H})$ are backward deterministic using the uniqueness of normal forms of a matrix in the modular group. Obviously f_M is a morphism between them. We follow the scheme described in Section 2 to build a functional cryptosystem using these backward deterministic systems.

Public-key: The backward deterministic system $(\{W_1, W_2\}, p, \mathcal{X})$.

Private-key: The backward deterministic system $(\{V_1, V_2\}, f_M(p), \mathcal{H})$.

We suppose that the plaintext to be sent is the sequence $i_1 i_2 \ldots i_n$ where $i_k \in \{1, 2\}$ for $k = 1, 2, \ldots, n$.

Encryption method:
Compute the matrix $W_{i_1} W_{i_2} \ldots W_{i_n}$ and call this matrix E. We note that

$$E = M^{-1}V_{i_1}MM^{-1}V_{i_2}M \ldots M^{-1}V_{i_n}M = M^{-1}V_{i_1}V_{i_2} \ldots V_{i_n}M.$$

Then, let E act the point p on $\mathcal{X}$ by the fractional linear mapping determined by the matrix E. Compute the point $f_E(p) = Ep$ and call it q, that is, $q = Ep$. Since G acts on $\mathcal{X}$, the point q is on $\mathcal{X}$. Now the point q is sent to a legal receiver. Therefore q is the encrypted message for the original message $i_1 i_2 \ldots i_n$.

Decryption method:
Employing Algorithm 2, the legal receiver finds the normal form $X_1 X_2 \ldots X_l$ where X_k is A or A^2 or B for $k = 1, 2, \ldots l$ such that $Mq = X_1 X_2 \ldots X_l(Mp)$. We denote the matrix $X_1 X_2 \ldots X_l$ by N. Hence, $Mq = N(Mp)$. Since $SL(2, Z)$ is generated by A_1 and B_1 (by our choice of A_1 and B_1), both A and B are written as products of matrices A_1 and B_1. We suppose that $A = Z_1(A_1, B_1)$ and $B = Z_2(A_1, B_1)$ where $Z_1(A_1, B_1)$ and $Z_2(A_1, B_1)$ are words on A_1 and B_1. By substituting $Z_1(A_1, B_1)$ for A and $Z_2(A_1, B_1)$ for B, respectively, the legal receiver gets

$$N = Z_{j_1}(A_1, B_1)Z_{j_2}(A_1, B_1) \ldots Z_{j_l}(A_1, B_1)$$

where j_k is 1 if X_k is A and j_k is 2 if X_k is B. Employing Algorithm 1, the legal receiver obtains the normal form of N with respect to A_1 and B_1. By the uniqueness of expression of the normal form and our requirements on V_1 and V_2, the legal receiver obtains the sequence $V_{i_1} V_{i_2} \ldots V_{i_n}$, and hence, the original plaintext $i_1 i_2 \ldots i_n$.

Small example:

We see how we encrypt and decrypt a small message. Let $V_1 = BA = \begin{pmatrix} -1 & 0 \\ 1 & 11 \end{pmatrix}$, $V_2 = BA^2 = \begin{pmatrix} -1 & 1 \\ 0 & -1 \end{pmatrix}$ and $M = \begin{pmatrix} 2 & 1 \\ 1 & 1 \end{pmatrix}$. Then $W_1 = M^{-1}V_1 M = \begin{pmatrix} -3 & -1 \\ 4 & 1 \end{pmatrix}$ and $W_2 = M^{-1}V_2 M = \begin{pmatrix} 0 & 1 \\ -1 & -2 \end{pmatrix}$. Assume that $p = \frac{i-3}{4}$ and that the plaintext is 121. Then $f_M(p) = 2i \in \mathcal{O}$ and 121 is encrypted as the point

$$q = W_1 W_2 W_1 p = \frac{4i - 350}{320}.$$

The legal receiver decrypts it by computing $Mq = \frac{380-8i}{30-4i}$, and then, feeding Mq to Algorithm 2. Then the normal form $BABA^2 BA$ is obtained. Since $V_1 = BA$ and $V_2 = BA^2$ generate the free subsemigroup of the modular group, the plaintext 121 is retrieved.

Comparison with the previous work:

In [14] to construct a public key cryptosystem the amalgamated free product structure of the modular group and the uniqueness of the normal form are used as in the present paper. The plaintext is a bit sequence $i_1 i_2 \ldots i_n$ and encrypted as the matrix $E(x) = W_2(x)W_1^{i_1}(x)W_2(x)W_1^{i_2}(x) \ldots W_2(x)W_1^{i_n}(x)W_2(x)$ where $W_1(x)$ and $W_2(x)$ are 2×2 matrices over the polynomial ring over the complex numbers. Decryption is done by operating the homomorphism given by the substituting the secret key a for x in $E(x)$ followed by the conjugation by a matrix M that is secret. Then $ME(a)M^{-1}$ is the decrypted message and we can find its normal form using Algorithm 1 and the standard reduction algorithm. Then it must be in the form $V_2 V_1^{i_1} V_2 V_1^{i_2} \ldots V_2 V_1^{i_n} V_2$, and hence, the legal receiver can retrieve the plaintext $i_1 i_2 \ldots i_n$. In this cryptosystem, encrypted message is a 2×2 matrix over the polynomial ring whereas the one in the present paper is a point on the upper half plane. The scheme in the present paper is based on the scheme of the functional cryptosystem, whereas the one in [14] is not. The author believes that basing on the scheme of the functional cryptosystem makes our system more or less clearer than the one in [14].

5 Several issues

We briefly discuss several issues on the proposed cryptosystem in this section. Since the encryption and decryption depend on the free semigroup structures of subsemigroups of corresponding groups and the conjugation by the elements of $GL(2, R)$ preserves the freeness of subsemigroups, to break the system an eavesdropper may want to find a matrix N in $GL(2, R)$ such that NW_1N^{-1}, NW_2N^{-1} are in $SL(2, Z)$. If the eavesdropper can find such a matrix N, he may be able to use Algorithm 1 and Algorithm 2 to break the cryptosystem. To find such a matrix N it is necessary to solve a system of matrix equations

$$NW_1N^{-1} = U, \qquad NW_2N^{-1} = V$$

where U, V, N are unknown such that $U, V \in SL(2, Z)$ and $N \in GL(2, R)$. This system consists of 11 equations of 12 variables over the field of real numbers. We note that if N is found then U, V are automatically derived. There are infinitely many solutions for this system of equations in principle because the number of the variables is larger than the number of the equations. We know a solution, that is, the matrices M, V_1 and V_2 form one of the solutions. There is no known algorithm to solve the system of equations of this type as far as the author knows. Numerical analysis method may be able to work to solve the system of equation, however, it gives just an approximation of the solution N. Hence, we do not know whether or not numerical analysis method really works. Moreover, we can possibly avoid such an attack by restrict the field of real numbers to a finite extension field of the field of rational numbers. It is possible to realize the field operation of a splitting field of an irreducible polynomial over the field of rational numbers on computers. We should also note that N is not necessarily equal to M and that if N is distinct from M, the eavesdropper still has a problem to decrypt the message because N does not necessarily yield free generators of a free subsemigroup of $SL(2, Z)$ satisfying our requirements. For, even if matrices U_1 and U_2, words on generators A_2 and B_2 of $SL(2, Z)$ subject to the relations $A_2^6 = 1 = B_2^4$ and $A_2^3 = B_2^2$, form a set of free generators of a free subsemigroup, a concatenation of them is not necessarily in the normal form with respect to A_2 and B_2, and hence, there is still a trouble to retrieve the plain text.

Another possible attack is to find the matrix E and decompose it directly to the product of W_1 and W_2. There might be a smart way to find and decompose the matrix E. Of course, if the matrix E is found, then the eavesdropper can decompose E by guessing the decomposition and then checking whether or not it gives the correct answer. However, this is a non-deterministic polynomial time algorithm and so takes exponential time. Hence, it is slow for the breaking the system. Therefore, the backward deterministic system $(W_1, W_2, p, \mathcal{X})$ is considered intractable. On the other hand, the backward deterministic system $(V_1, V_2, f_M(p), \mathcal{H})$ is tractable because we can employ geometry of the upper half plane. In mathematics, geometry often provides a fast algorithm as Algorithm 2. The first backward system is associated to the space $\mathcal{X}$ which is intractable, on the other hand, the second system is associated to the upper half plane that we have good understanding. The difference between the two systems lies in geometry.

Another issues on the cryptosystem is the practicality. The proposed cryptosystem is fairly experimental, and hence, the practicality has not been investigated so far. Several issues to be considered are expansion of messages, key sizes and rounding errors among others. Expansion of messages happens in the proposed cryptosystem. To avoid this we may want to find an alternative group action and the backward system such that expansion does not happen.

References

1. L.M.Adleman, Molecular computation of solutions to combinatorial problems, Science, 266 November 11 (1994) 1021–1024
2. D.E.Cohen, *Combinatorial Group Theory: A Topological Approach*, (Cambridge University Press, Cambridge) (1989)
3. H.Cohen, *A Course in Computational Algebraic Number Theory*, Springer, New York, (1996)
4. J.Kari, A cryptoanalytic observation concerning systems based on language theory, Discr. Appl. Math. 21 (1988) 265-268
5. J.Kari, Observations concerning a public-key cryptosystem based on iterated morphisms, Theor. Compt. Sci. 66 (1989) 45-53
6. N.Koblitz, *Introduction to Elliptic Curves and Modular Forms*, Springer, New York (1991)
7. R.C.Lyndon and P.E.Schupp, *Combinatorial Group Theory*, Springer, New York, (1976)
8. J.J.Rotman, *An Introduction to Theory of Groups*, Springer, New York (1995)
9. A.Salomaa, A public-key cryptosystem based on language theory, Computers and Security, 7 (1988) 83-87
10. A.Salomaa, *Public-Key Cryptography*, Springer, Berlin, (1990)
11. A.Salomaa and S.Yu, On a public-key cryptosystem based on iterated morphisms and substitutions, Theor. Compt. Sci. 48 (1986) 283-296
12. J-P.Serre, *A Course in Arithmetic*, Springer, New York (1973)
13. P.Shor, Polynomial-time algorithms for prime factorization and discrete logarithms on a quantum computer, SIAM J. Comp. 26 (1997) 1484-1509
14. A.Yamamura, Public-key cryptosystems using the modular group, International Workshop on Practice and Theory in Public Key Cryptography, LNCS vol 1431, (1998) 203-216
15. G.Zémor, Hash functions and Cayley graphs, Designs, Codes and Cryptography 4 (1994) 381-394

Appendix:

INPUT: A decomposition $u_1 u_2 \ldots u_n$ of an element g in $G_1 *_{H_1 = H_2} G_2$ as a product of alternate sequence of elements from G_1 and G_2
OUTPUT: The normal form $s_1 s_2 \ldots s_n$ of g.

Step 0) We note that $u_1 \in G_1$ or G_2. We now assume that $u_1 \in G_1$. Then we have $u_1 = s_1 v_1$ where s_1 is a representative of H in G_1 and $v_1 \in H$. We rewrite g as

$$g = s_1 v_1 u_2 u_3 \ldots u_n.$$

We note that $s_1 \in G_1$ and $u_2 \in G_2$. In the case that $u_1 \in G_2$, we do the similar process.

Step 1) We suppose that we have

$$g = s_1 s_2 \ldots s_m v_m u_t u_{t+1} \ldots u_n$$

where $v_m \in H$ and s_i is a representative of G_1 or G_2 for $i = 1, 2, \ldots m$ such that if $s_i \in G_1$ then $s_{i+1} \in G_2$ or vice versa and also if $s_m \in G_1$ then $u_t \in G_2$ or vice versa. If there is no u_j in the sequence, we have a sequence of the form

$$g = s_1 s_2 \ldots s_m v_m$$

where v_m is in H. Set $s_{m+1} \Leftarrow v_m$. Then we return the normal form

$$g = s_1 s_2 \ldots s_m s_{m+1}$$

and the algorithm terminates.

Now we assume that s_m is a representative of G_1. Then u_t is in G_2 and we can write $v_m u_t = s_{m+1} v_{m+1}$ where s_{m+1} is a representative of G_2 and $v_{m+1} \in H$.

Step 2)

If $s_{m+1} \notin H$, then we have

$$g = s_1 s_2 \ldots s_m s_{m+1} v_{m+1} u_{t+1} \ldots u_n.$$

We should note that $s_{m+1} \in G_2$ and $u_{t+1} \in G_2$. Then go to Step 1).

If $s_{m+1} \in H$, then we have $s_m s_{m+1} v_{m+1} u_{t+1} \in G_1$ since $s_m, u_{t+1} \in G_1$ and $s_{m+1}, v_{m+1} \in H \subset G_1$. Then we have

$$s_m s_{m+1} v_{m+1} u_{t+1} = s'_m v'_m$$

where s'_m is a representative of G_1 and $v'_m \in H$. Then set $s_m \Leftarrow s'_m$ and $v_m \Leftarrow v'_m$. Then we have

$$g = s_1 s_2 \ldots s_m v_m u_{t+2} \ldots u_n.$$

We should note that $s_m \in G_1$ and $u_{t+2} \in G_2$ if it exists (as $u_t \in G_2$).

In the case that s_m is a representative of G_2 and u_t is in G_1, we do the dual procedure. Then go to Step 1).

At each stage of Step 2), the number of u_k's is reduced. Hence, the algorithm ends within at most $2n + 1$ steps if the length of the input is n. Therefore, Algorithm 1 takes only linear time.

Author Index

Springer
and the
environment

At Springer we firmly believe that an
international science publisher has a
special obligation to the environment,
and our corporate policies consistently
reflect this conviction.
We also expect our business partners –
paper mills, printers, packaging
manufacturers, etc. – to commit
themselves to using materials and
production processes that do not harm
the environment. The paper in this
book is made from low- or no-chlorine
pulp and is acid free, in conformance
with international standards for paper
permanency.

Springer

Lecture Notes in Computer Science

For information about Vols. 1–1492
please contact your bookseller or Springer-Verlag